THE VAN LEER JERUSALEM FOUNDATION SERIES

INTELLECTUALS AND TRADITION
Editors: S.N. Eisenstadt and S.R. Graubard

SCIENCE AND VALUES: Patterns of Tradition and Change
Editors: A. Thackray and E. Mendelsohn

INTERACTION BETWEEN SCIENCE AND PHILOSOPHY
Editor: Y. Elkana

SOCIETY AND POLITICAL STRUCTURE IN THE ARAB WORLD
Editor: Menahem Milson

SOCIALISM AND TRADITION
Editors: S.N. Eisenstadt and Yael Azmon

PHILOSOPHICAL ANTHROPOLOGY
by J. Agassi, *Boston University and Tel Aviv University*

FRAGMENTATION AND WHOLENESS
by D. Bohm, *London University*

SOCIETY AND POLITICAL STRUCTURE IN THE ARAB WORLD

Edited by

Menahem Milson

HUMANITIES PRESS, NEW YORK

Library of Congress card number: 73-86068
ISBN 391-00258-9

Published in the United States of America
by Humanities Press, Inc., 450 Park Avenue South,
New York, N.Y. 10016

Printed in U.S.A. by
NOBLE OFFSET PRINTERS, INC.
New York, N.Y. 10003

CONTENTS

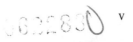

EDITOR'S PREFACE

The "Arab world" is a comparatively modern geopolitical term which became current when Arab nationalism evolved as the dominant form of collective identity in the Arabic-speaking lands. For the non-Arab the term "Arab world" conveniently covers a very large and complex area with some twenty states, but for the Arab it implies much more – connotations of national greatness and hopes for future progress and power. These expectations hinge in one way or another on the concept of Arab unity.

The modern era has witnessed two very important developments – the collapse of the old imperial order, that of the Ottoman Empire, under which the lands of the Middle East were more or less effectively united; and a decline in the unifying power of the traditional Islamic world-view which buttressed that imperial system.

However, whereas the old unifying world-view was replaced by another unifying ideology – that of Arabism – the collapse of the former political order led to the rise of separate states, the development and progress of which depend to a large extent on the success of each of them in developing a political community and recruiting its members to solve the particular problems of each country. Whereas in the pre-modern system there was a kind of compatability between the political structure and the world-view (the political order and the ideological system sustaining each other), there is considerable tension, and sometimes even contrast, between the prevalent pan-Arab ideology and the new political order of separate states with their different and often conflicting interests.

Students of the Arab world are faced with the double task of examining both the realm of ideas and symbols common to all Arab countries and of studying individual areas and countries. It seems, however, that of these two areas of study that of the common intellectual tradition of the Arab world usually receives more attention than the variety of political forms and socio-economic conditions in individual Arab countries. It is this variety to which the present volume is dedicated, and it constitutes an attempt to approach the study of the Arab world through an examination of six individual societies. Limitations of time and space prevented us from including additional studies on other countries. The countries covered in this volume were not chosen as a sample representative of all Arab countries, since there can hardly be such a thing. The six were selected for their own significance and interest. Some of these countries – Egypt and Syria – are regarded as most important in Arab cultural and political tradition itself, since they are the heartlands of the Arab world. Of the six societies studied only five are sovereign states. The Palestinian Arab national movement, subject of one paper, has not achieved a state of its own. The other two studies examine topics which are not exclusively limited to one Arab country, but which in a way concern the Arab world as a whole. However, even in these cases, the approach involves examination of concrete social and political circumstances rather than attention to phenomena on the abstract generalized level. These two studies are dedicated to the Bedouin – or as the author prefers to call them, the nomads – and to military coups d'etat in Arab countries.

Gabriel Baer in his study of modern Egyptian society emphasizes the basic differences between Egypt and the other countries of the Middle East, especially in regard to the power of the central government and its effective control of the country. Describing the characteristic traits of Egyptian society, Baer notes that it is remarkably homogeneous, which sets it apart from other Middle Eastern countries, such as Syria or Iraq. The author observes that the administrative efficiency of the central government helped to bring about a quicker disintegration of traditional social units in Egypt than in other Middle Eastern countries. On the other hand, he notes that the overwhelming weight of the state apparatus was one of the causes which prevented the emergence of genuine new social agencies with integrating functions appropriate to modern circumstances – for example, effective municipal organizations. Professor Baer notes that the new revolutionary regime has been very successful in taking control of the central government and of the country, as it were, at one stroke while effectively preventing any serious forms of organized opposition. This may be partly due to the overwhelming preponderance of the center over the periphery.

The revolution of 1952 brought to the center of power in Egypt a group which is Egyptian and is seen as such by itself and by the people. By contrast, the Egyptian identity of the former royal house and large parts of the ruling elite was rather dubious. This certainly adds to the affinity between the political center and the periphery. The traditional traits of Egyptian society and the preponderance of the center over the periphery as analyzed by Professor Baer, combined with the basic homogeneity of Egyptian society, all seem to support the position of an incumbent government. Paradoxically enough, it is these very qualities which seem to make it difficult for a government to mobilize nationwide *active* support for the execution of new policies, since such mobilization would require the emergence of intermediate social organizations and secondary centers in the big cities as well as in the rural areas. Since the old regime did not wish to mobilize the masses, it required no more than acquiescence and achieved the necessary legitimation via the intermediary links of the religious hierarchy, especially its lower echelons. Professor Baer notes that in contrast with the old regime, the new regime has not been very successful in establishing such intermediary links, and there is a wide gap between the intellectuals, bureaucrats and army officers on the one hand, and the urban and rural lower classes on the other. The recurrent attempts by the Egyptian government to establish organizations whose principal aim is to recruit the Egyptian masses for active participation in its socio-economic policies is clear proof that Egyptian leaders are well aware of this very basic problem on the road to modernization.

By contrast with Egypt, Syria has a very heterogeneous population. Many religious and ethnic groups differ significantly from the Sunni Arab majority. Topography further complicates control over the mountainous regions, where a number of turbulent minority groups, such as the Druse and ʻAlawis, are centered. When the period of modernization from the 1830s to our time is surveyed, one of the most interesting developments is the shift in power between the various communities in Syria. As noted by Moshe Maʻoz, this period – from the Ottoman reforms *(tanẓīmāt)* until the early years of Syrian independence – was marked by the dominance of the ruling elite, some 100 Sunni families, while the group now in power consists of ʻAlawi officers, members of a traditionally despised heterodox minority. Understandably these officers do not exercise their power in the name of their sectarian community, but emphasize a common Syrian identity, yet their ʻAlawi origin is well recognized. This situation once again poses a striking difference between Syria and Egypt, where there is no communal distinction between the ruling elite and the people. The Syrian military elite must thus seek to cover all signs of communal particularism and emphasize Syrian identity, together with allegiance to a generally revered Arabism. The social philosophy of the ruling elite has produced periodic attempts toward secularization, which seem to raise opposition, sometimes quite violent, when the applied measures are too blatant. It is of course more than likely that under the banner of religious opposition all sorts of other grievances and resentments find vent.

Ma'oz points out that in the last decade, social and economic reforms have greatly contributed to progress for large masses of peasants. He concludes that in the course of the last generation a strong governmental center was established in Syria for the first time in centuries, a center which for the time being has succeeded in overcoming the centrifugal and autonomous tendencies of various ethno-religious groups. It is yet to be seen how stable and permanent the present equilibrium can be.

Yehoshua Porath examines in his article the social aspects of the emergence of the Palestinian Arab national movement. In his analysis of the history of Palestine in the 19th century, Porath observes that the period of the Ottoman reforms *(tanẓīmāt)* strengthened the position of the urban notables at the expense of rural sheikhs, a phenomenon observed also by Ma'oz in Syria. This fact is of crucial importance to the whole history of the Arab national movement in Palestine, in which city leadership became dominant. Within this urban elite the position of Jerusalem and of its leading families is central. Porath's study of the Palestinian Arab national movement in the 1920s and 1930s is a micro-analysis of the role of social factors and local politics in the emergence of the national movement.

The study indicates how family and local rivalries as well as suspicion between Christian and Muslim have often hampered the effectiveness of the movement. Another factor seen to have weakened the movement is the gap between the city leadership and the countryside. Although on the whole the villagers accepted city leadership, the contacts between these two social groups seems to have been very tenuous. The urban political elite seems to have worked most of the time without realizing the immense potential of recruiting massive support among the fellaheen. The outbreak of the Arab revolt in 1936 showed the great potential of the rural class, but by that time the divided urban elite was not able to effectively direct that potential.

The partition of Palestine and the 1948 war radically changed the structure of Arab society in Palestine. Some of these changes are very briefly noted by Porath at the end of his study, where he concludes that among the West Bank Arabs, and to a lesser degree among Arabs of Israeli nationality, leadership remained in the hands of the important families with a tradition of leadership as notables and the prestige of propertyholders. Among the refugees traditional prestige vanished with property, and the place of the former notables was taken by younger men with modern education and a readiness for political struggle.

Uriel Dann notes that Jordan is no self-evident entity like Egypt. Nevertheless, having existed for two generations, first as an Emirate and later as a Kingdom, Jordan has evolved a certain socio-political pattern whose main contours are clear. Dann emphasizes that the dedication and loyalty of the ruling group, with the King at its head, to the present "Image of Jordan" is the fundamental factor in sustaining the state. Dann briefly subdivides the Jordanian population into various sectors with distinct political features, namely, Transjordanians proper and Palestinians of various groups. He then focuses on the rather limited elements in the population which he considers politically significant. Here the analysis is based on the distinction made between establishment and anti-establishment elements. Dann defines establishment in a special sense (narrower than the common usage), namely, the high level decision-makers, high level decision-enforcers, and political manipulators.

It is with this sense of the term in mind that one should read the very informative analytical lists which Dann offers. His careful and detailed analysis of people in positions of power in the Hashemite Kingdom clearly shows that a very specific and small group holds power and perpetuates the Jordanian state according to its image as they perceive it. The group consists of Transjordanians, primarily the King's relatives, and the Bedouin sheikhs and officers attached by personal loyalty to him. The top military and police offices are held by members of these groups, and the interdependence of the regime and the Bedouin tribes of Transjordan becomes strikingly clear. The mainstay of Bedouin existence is the pay they receive for their military service, and this fact is obviously well recognized by them. Their ability to continue their way of life depends on this source of livelihood, whereas the regime, dependent on their military services, must keep them satisfied in order to retain their loyalty, which is essential for maintaining the existence of the Jordanian state.

L. Carl Brown emphasizes the fact that contemporary Tunisia presents a picture of relative stability and uniformity of national purpose, unlike most other Arab countries. Continuity of leadership has been personified by Bourguiba for well over a generation. Moreover, states Brown, Tunisia has a group leadership with organizational roots extending back to the 1920s, a leadership which evolved and was shaped in the dialectics of everyday social and political confrontation. Brown surveys the Tunisian path to modernization during the past century and a half and discusses it in terms of modernization theories. He notes that Aḥmad Bey of Tunisia played a role comparable to that of Muḥammad 'Alī in Egypt, and of Sultan Maḥmūd in the Ottoman Empire. Aḥmad Bey started the processes of modernization primarily with the motive of being able to face the ascendancy of Europe; in the process, he managed to give Tunisia a decisive push along the road to modernization. His most important contribution appears to be the development of a small and dynamic minority committed to the cause of change and Westernization.

Brown attaches great significance to the fact that the Neo-Destour party has since the 1930s called attention to the plight of the powerless and the poor. The party was committed as much to modenize the country as to fight against foreign domination. Thus its attention was not exclusively devoted to an anti-colonial struggle, but was drawn to the fight against underdevelopment. It seems essential to grasp this quality of the political elite in Tunisia, with its double dedication, in order to understand the Tunisian way in politics, which is rather different from that of other Arab countries. Brown tends to believe that the Tunisian leadership has been successful in consolidating a genuine new world-view, capable of sustaining a modern political structure and national community. He maintains that Tunisia offers a classic example of gradual development without spasmodic and violent leaps, and he ventures to learn a lesson from the Tunisian case – applicable to other developing countries – namely, that power does not always grow out of the barrel of a gun.

The study of the Sudan in this volume is concerned only with the Islamic, Arabic-speaking part of that country, i.e., North Sudan, the dominant area. The very bitter and bloody conflict between the Arab north and the non-Arab south is beyond our scope. Gabriel Warburg centers his study on the two chief social forces in North Sudan – the tribes and popular Islam. He observes very interesting lines of development in these two traditional social forces. Tribal society has maintained many of its traditional features and much of its influence over members. The tribes persisted as socio-economic units due to their remoteness from the centers of government, poor communications, and a lack of economic incentives; hence, the slow pace of urbanization. Warburg notes, however, that the tribes declined as a political force, especially during the period of the Anglo-Egyptian Condominium. The decline was caused by the fact that the heads of the tribes agreed to act as the docile administrative agents for the central government, and thus lost their independent position. Conversely, the popular Islamic movements gained in political influence. Even among the tribes themselves, the power of popular Islamic leadership and especially that of the *Anṣār* was at times greater than that of the tribal heads, insofar as political representation in the state was concerned. Warburg emphasizes that this expansion in the sphere of influence of popular Islam from the realm of religion to that of politics was recognized both by the government and by the population. He notes that when the tribe lost its political power it sought the protection of the religious order to which it belonged. The tribal population had no need for modern political parties centered in the towns and headed by university graduates. The tribe as a socio-economic unit and popular Islam as a focus of religious and political loyalty fulfilled the needs of most Sudanese.

We learn that all the competing political forces group themselves round the two movements of popular Islam, the Khatmiyya and the *Anṣār.* It is interesting to observe that the new intelligentsia could not establish a power center of its own and take control of the affairs of the state. The only non-traditional force capable of doing that was the army. Warburg points out that the military revolt of 1958 was carried out with the tacit agreement of the religious leadership. We observe that this religious leadership can use its influence to give support or act as an opposition. This leadership is, however, unable of itself to assume control and hence it is bound to decline as a political force when it confronts the modern organization of a military regime.

Military regimes and military coups d'etat have been among the most outstanding political phenomena in the Arab countries during the last generation. Eliezer Be'eri tallies no fewer than twenty-six coups d'etat from September 1961 until December 1970, a period which he terms "the '60s" for the purpose of the present article. The military coups d'etat in the Arab countries are termed in Arabic *thawra,* i.e., revolution; their declared purpose invariably is to achieve national goals and to further social progress. It seems, however, that the record of military regimes established after such revolutions in achieving socio-economic progress and stability is not noticeably better than that of the so-called reactionary or conservative regimes in the Middle East. Nevertheless, the army, once in power, is able to hold its own against other political factors; and even if, as in the Sudan, a military regime was replaced by a civilian government, the change was temporary, and the civilian regime was ended by another military coup.

It seems to the editor that in order to understand this phenomenon we must also take into consideration certain cultural attitudes to power and government deeply rooted in Islamic tradition, which tend to discourage resistance to the incumbent government, no matter how it assumed power. The very possession of coercive power becomes, as it were, a source of political legitimation.

One can hardly expect to have a volume dedicated to Arab society without reference to the Bedouin. After all, the Bedouin are regarded by themselves, as well as by other Arabs and non-Arabs, as the most Arab of Arabs. Bedouin tribes are to be found in all Arab countries and considerable parts of the population are descendants of Bedouin. Even though they may have been sedentary for some generations still they retain some of the attitudes which are the legacy of their tribal ancestors. Furthermore, the desert-born ethos of the Bedouin is deeply rooted in the common cultural heritage of the Arab world. Much has been written about Bedouin social ideals and about the tribal organization as a political and military unit founded on genealogical affiliation. Emanuel Marx sets out in his study to complement and correct this picture of the Bedouin by analyzing the ecological factors affecting the life of the nomads and their tribal organization.

Marx notes that there is considerable ecological variety in Bedouin territory. Some regions have fertile soil and an abundant supply of water, and if these resources were exploited more intensively they could adequately support a densely settled population. Other regions may have fertile soil but suffer from a shortage of water and consequently can support only a very small settled population. Therefore part of the population is forced to wander in small groups over the area in order to draw water when and where it is available. When the reserve is exhausted in one place, the camp moves to another location, in a fairly regular annual cycle. The Bedouin herds sometimes exploit land that is not fit for cultivation and which without this exploitation would remain unused. However, notes Marx, the Bedouin prefer to pasture their herds on good, rain-soaked land. Indeed, every tribe must have access to such land in order to be able to maintain its herds during the dry season. Periods of political turmoil, when settlements are destroyed and agricultural land is released for pasture, are therefore convenient for the Bedouin. On the other hand, the Bedouin tribe is not self-sufficient; the Bedouin must have in their vicinity a settled population in order to be able to sell their animals and to purchase foodstuffs and other products. However, when land becomes scarce and thus an expensive economic factor, the breeding of animals in the nomadic way loses its economic advantage.

Marx stresses that the Bedouin tribe is a territorial unit. The size of the territory required by the tribe for its pasture and the outside political forces brought to play on the tribe are the factors which determine the number of its members. The author notes that a network of personal relationships (marriage, clientship) spreads over the whole tribal territory, thus promoting cooperation and interdependence between members of the tribe. These relationships are viewed by the author as channels of communication between the parties involved through which they coordinate their activities and carry on and settle their disputes. Two factors, which often appear in concert, bring about the decline of the Bedouin: a strong central government and a growing population.

It is not, perhaps, out of place to remark here that the ecological explanation presented by Marx is not intended to cover up the significance of other factors shaping the Bedouin way of life and the tribal grouping. One cannot overlook the external factor of boundaries which governments enforce. This is a comparatively modern factor which influences the Bedouin tribe and its ecology, since it interferes with free pasture and disturbs or alters the tribal cycle of migration. Still more important, one should recall that tribal genealogy – like sanctified symbols elsewhere – assumes a significance of its own and interacts in a very complex and dynamic way with other more material factors.

The articles collected in this volume were originally presented in a series of colloquia on Society and Political Structure in the Arab World held in the Van Leer Jerusalem Foundation from November 1970 to June 1971. I am deeply grateful to Dr. Yehuda Elkana, the director of the Foundation, for originally encouraging me to organize these colloquia and later to assemble and edit the papers for presentation in book form. This volume owes much to Professor S.N. Eisenstadt, whose advice was a great help to me in defining the subject and scope of the colloquia. I cannot conclude without recording my personal thanks to Mr. D. Ben-Yaakov for his help with the English style of the manuscript and to Miss Jeanne Kuebler who saw the book through the publication process with professional competence and dedication.

Menahem Milson

Jerusalem
July 1973

NOTE ON TRANSLITERATION

Arabic terms and personal names are rendered according to a system of transliteration commonly used by Arabists. The transliterated form as a rule reflects the spelling in Literary Arabic with occasional exceptions: names of Bedouin tribes in Emanuel Marx's article are transcribed according to their dialectal pronunciation; some of the Sudanese and North African names are given in their commonly used spelling reflecting local dialectal forms. Well-known place names are given in their most common English form. We have not used a diacritical signs in the names of sects or communities which usually appear in English dictionaries nor in place names.

BASIC FACTORS AFFECTING SOCIAL STRUCTURE, TENSIONS, AND CHANGE IN MODERN EGYPTIAN SOCIETY

GABRIEL BAER

In his famous *Philosophy of the Revolution,* Jamāl ʻAbd al-Nāṣir drew three circles within which Egypt must move and act: the Arabs, Africa, and Islam. This scheme is correct, at least as regards the many common characteristics of Egyptian and other Islamic and African societies. Furthermore, to a great extent, Egyptian society forms part of Arab society. In recent years, numerous attempts have been made to analyze the structure and processes of Islamic, African, and especially Arab society, and I shall not try to repeat or summarize the analyses of the scholars who ventured into this field. I rather propose to investigate the basic differences between Egypt and other countries of the Middle East and then try to find out the influence these differences had on the structure, tensions, and change of Egyptian society as compared with these other countries.

It would seem that the main fundamental difference between Egyptian society and that of other countries in the Middle East is the overwhelming preponderance of the center in Egypt, as against a greater diffusiveness of power and social functions in other Middle Eastern countries. Since ancient times, the principal basis of Egypt's economy was agriculture, which, because of lack of rainfall, depended on a more or less elaborate regular system of irrigation. Only a powerful and continuous central authority could ensure the establishment and maintenance of such a system.[1] Moreover, the Nile and the flatness of the country enabled every government in Egypt to reach the most remote parts of the state with comparative ease, while elsewhere in the area, mountains, swamps, and other natural obstacles hampered communications and made efficient state control extremely difficult. Consequently, in Egypt, through the ages, more consistently than anywhere else in the Middle East, the state was the exclusive owner of, or had decisive control over, all the land, effectively controlled taxation and all forms of economic activity, was the exclusive builder and owner of almost all means of communication, recruited a central army and prevented the emergence of local forces, and also administered the country and dispensed justice through a centrally appointed bureaucracy.[2] This state bureaucracy was equally omnipotent in the countryside and in the towns and thus prevented the emergence of autonomous institutions in the towns – in contrast with a number of other countries in the Middle East.[3] Consequently, the system which came nearest to European feudalism in the Middle East, namely, the grant of agricultural estates to the army in return for a pledge of military service, lasted for a shorter time in Egypt than in other parts of the Middle East. It was introduced into Egypt at least one century after Niẓām al-Mulk (last quarter of the eleventh century C.E.) had established it elsewhere and was abolished as a result of the Ottoman conquest of Egypt at least three centuries before it was finally liquidated in the other parts of the Ottoman Empire. Similarly, among the Middle Eastern military regimes of our generation, the Egyptian is the most stable, and its effectiveness in implementing total control over the economic and social resources of the country and of eliminating any focus of local power (and potential opposition) was correspondingly greater.

What was the effect of this difference on the structure and changes of Egyptian society in our age of modernization? The disintegration of the traditional units in Arab society since the end of the eighteenth century has often been analyzed.[4] It has been pointed out that Western influence accelerated the dissolution of communal and organizational ties, and that the integrating function of the former traditional agencies was not fully assumed by new ones appropriate to the new conditions. The result was an increasing tendency to rootlessness.[5] It would seem to us that the characteristic features of Egyptian society have had the effect of making this process much faster and more thorough in Egypt than in other countries of the Middle East.

On the one hand, the administrative efficiency of the central state power caused a faster and more radical disintegration of traditional social units than elsewhere in the Middle East. The settlement and detribalization of Egypt's Bedouins preceded the parallel process in the Fertile Crescent by more than half a century, and as a result tribal units have almost completely ceased to exist in Egyptian society, whereas they continue to play social and political roles in all other Arab countries except Lebanon. The obvious reason for this difference was the ability of the central government in Egypt to effectively implement policies of land registration and Bedouin settlement. Two developments brought about the detribalization and settlement of the

Bedouins: firstly, the earlier and more complete economic transformation of Egypt – consisting in the transition from subsistence agriculture to cash-crops – which served as an incentive for Bedouins to acquire land and become farmers; and, secondly, the much faster development of modern transport, which affected one of the most important branches of Bedouin economy (camel breeding). Similar reasons brought about the complete dissolution of the village community in Egypt – but not in all other countries of the Middle East. The most important attribute of the village community, common tenure and periodical redistribution of village lands, is still extant in some parts of the Fertile Crescent (and was the rule in this region until a generation ago). But in Egypt the development of private landownership in the 1850s put an end to this custom. The guarantee of security by a strong central government during the nineteenth century eliminated the necessity to separate the various city quarters by gates and put an end to feuds between the inhabitants, especially the youth, of different quarters. Thus, town quarters in Egypt ceased to be a focus of solidarity among their inhabitants. This cannot be said about many towns in the Fertile Crescent: the social importance of the town quarter in Damascus, for instance, seems to have been much more persistent.[6] Similarly, the professional guilds of craftsmen, merchants, and people engaged in transport and services still existed in Damascus at least as late as the 1920s, while in Egypt they had already disappeared by the time of the First World War. Again, one of the reasons was the fact that the Damascus guilds were much more autonomous and less dependent on the government or connected with its administrative machinery.

On the other hand, the overwhelming weight of the state apparatus was certainly one of the main reasons which prevented the emergence of genuine new agencies with integrating functions. It has been pointed out repeatedly that there is no cooperative spirit among the Egyptian village youth – as in villages of other countries – and no organizations or associations exist on a village basis. All writers and sociologists who studied Egyptian villages found no traces of communal or organized life. "The Egyptian village is not a community in the social sense, not an organism, but a mass."[7] Apparently, the attempt at establishing cooperatives in recent years has not changed the situation. From the beginning, the members of these new cooperatives were allowed no initiative, and all the power was in the hands of administrators employed by the state or the Cooperative Central Commission. In the towns, the town quarters and guilds have not been replaced by professional organizations or trade unions capable of fulfilling the social functions of the old units – again because of management by the state bureaucracy. Even in the "liberal age" of modern Egyptian history, the trade unions were headed by a member of the royal family, Prince 'Abbās Ḥalīm, for about two decades. After the Free Officers' coup, government control increased. The dissolved trade unions were recognized by the state in the form of a single union for each craft or profession, their leaders were selected, or appointed, by the government, and the whole organization was put under the control of army officers. Thus, "between the insecurities of industrial life and direction of trade unions by the state, the urban working class has been unable to find the spontaneous organizational ties it needs for protection and self-respect."[8]

Similar conclusions must be drawn with regard to the establishment of municipalities. While in many spheres of socio-economic and socio-political legislation Egypt preceded other parts of the Ottoman Empire, in municipal legislation it lagged far behind. Attempts to implement Ottoman municipal codes were made in Turkey and the Arab provinces – but not in Egypt. One of the main explanations for this is the traditional predominance of central government in Egypt.[9] Even according to recent legislation, the chairmen of town councils are appointed by the president of the Republic, many members are nominated by the governor or represent ministries, and even the elected members must come from those occupying high positions in the single party established by the state. The municipal council may be dissolved by the president of the Republic. Thus, after having accelerated the dissolution of traditional integrating agents, such as the tribe, the village community, the town quarter, or the guild, the central power impedes the evolution of new voluntary bodies capable of fulfilling social functions – both in the countryside and in the towns.

The lack of municipal organization is closely connected with the absence of an independent urban bourgeoisie. It has been pointed out that the Arab countries began to industrialize very late for the following reasons: the narrowness of the market, low agricultural productivity, the unfavorable social structure, the scarcity of iron and coal, the dearness of fuel, the poor transport systems, the paucity of investment capital, the absence of industrial credit, and the lack of technicians, skilled workmen, and entrepreneurs. Moreover, the nature of the relationship between the Arab countries and the West further impeded industrial development and the emergence of a bourgeoisie, since the financial, fiscal, and educational policies of Western powers towards the Arab countries was detrimental to such a development.[10]

The specific structure of Egyptian society has further obstructed the emergence of an independent bourgeoisie. In the course of the nineteenth century, the higher bureaucracy developed into large landowners, mainly by receiving land grants from the rulers. On the other hand, village notables and former Bedouin *shaykhs* who had become large landowners were appointed to government service and moved to the towns. Sometimes these landowner-officials also entered other economic spheres, especially as contractors for the government. At the same time, rich merchants began to acquire large estates – both because agricultural development made land investment profitable, and because landownership had become the most important criterion of social status. Many of them, or members of their families, also served as government officials.[11] As a result of this interpenetration, no urban bourgeoisie emerged in Egypt. There was no social class of Egyptians whose principal interest concentrated in the towns and in the promotion of urban economy, except, perhaps, for some foreign minorities – Greeks, Italians, Jews – who were unable to play an active role in Egyptian society and politics because they did not belong to the main body. By the middle of the twentieth century, a compact elite of large landowners had concentrated in Cairo. They dominated the urban economy and ruled the country through their close connection with the royal family, their control of the parties and parliaments, and their positions in the administration. In this structure there was no place for an independent urban middle class.

If this was the situation in the "democratic" and "liberal" age, the military regime has certainly not been more favorable to the development of an urban middle class. Apparently, the officers who seized power in 1952 originally had the idea to create such a class: one of the declared objects of land reform was to divert capital from land acquisition to industrial investment. However, capital first went into building and the acquisition of urban real estate, and, when the Egyptian government tried to stem this tendency by imposing limits on private building, landowners began to hoard gold and use their capital for speculation. The result was the drastic nationalization laws of 1961 – which reflected the complete disappointment of the ruling officer group with the prospect of building an Egyptian bourgeoisie through private enterprise and large industry, thus modernizing Egypt's economy and society.

The new policy consistently led to eliminating the independence of all economic and social units and has been described as follows: "With increasing government control over the economy, and with the increasingly large government share in all new investments, the older, more traditionally oriented interest groups are rapidly becoming like the newer, more bureaucratically oriented groups. It is a matter of highest concern to the government that the leadership of the various interest groups should be cooperative with the various ministries and with the leadership of the Socialist Union. Insofar as the ministers themselves are not elected presidents of the various interest associations, individuals designated by ministers from the bureaucracy itself or the military are elected."[12]

It has been pointed out that leadership in all areas of Middle Eastern life, in general, is increasingly being seized by a class clustered around a core of salaried civilian and military politicians, organizers, administrators, and experts. This class has been called "the salaried new middle class," and it has been claimed that it assumes a far more important role than the property-owning middle class. "Neither in capital, organization, nor skills do the merchants and middlemen control anything comparable to that power which can be mastered by the machinery of the state and hence utilized by the new salaried class. . . . By controlling the state . . . this new salaried class has the capabilities to lead the quest for the status, power, and prosperity of middle-class existence by ushering in the machine age."[13] The overwhelming preponderance of the center in Egypt, which is, in our view, the decisive characteristic of Egyptian society as compared with other societies in the Middle East, makes it necessary to reexamine the validity of, and revise, the above-quoted analysis with regard to Egypt. One cannot say with regard to Egypt that "the salaried middle class" assumed a far more important role than the property-owning middle class because, as we have seen, the latter had never enjoyed an independent existence in Egypt at all, and the joint elite of landowners, capitalists, and higher bureaucracy that ruled Egypt before the military revolution has been completely liquidated. With due reservation concerning the use of the terms "bourgeoisie" and "aristocracy," the following seems to be a correct analysis of what has happened: "The contemporary history of Egypt is marked by the rise of the petty bourgeoisie; certain groups deriving from this class have become the ruling class since the military coup of 1952 and have gradually been transformed into a bourgeoisie of a new type, a state bourgeoisie, which has replaced the old ruling class, the bourgeois aristocracy."[14] Secondly, but not less important, the term "middle class" implies that one deals with a class that occupies an intermediate position between other classes situated partly above and partly below it. This can no longer be said about the Egyptian ruling class of officer politicians and their bureaucracy and technocracy. Their social origin was in families of officials and officers, liberal professions, merchants and contractors, village notables, etc., i.e., groups which in other societies would be defined as "middle class." However, there can be no doubt that they have become not only the ruling class but even the "upper class" of Egyptian society.[15] The fact that there exists no "middle class" of importance in Egypt, no significant intermediate social layer – today even less than before the revolution – constitutes a principal characteristic of Egyptian society with far-reaching consequences regarding cohesion and change.

So far, we have examined the significance of the preponderance of the center in Egyptian society for the structure of, and changes in, the socio-economic units of this society. We now propose to investigate the influence of this characteristic trait on changes in the social functions of kinship and religion in Egyptian society. *A priori,* one would assume that a powerful central authority rigorously dedicated to making nationalism the faith of all Egyptians would have the effect of reducing the importance of kinship and religion as social ties determining the loyalties of the citizen. However, reality has been much more complicated. Evidence is contradictory, but the net conclusion to be drawn from the total amount of information available is that the family seems to have retained its vitality as a social unit. The least to be said with certainty is that the social functions of the Egyptian family have not disappeared faster, or to a larger extent, than in other parts of the Middle East. In the villages, the family is the basic social unit around which individual life is centered, but the extended family seems to be stronger and more effective as an economic unit among families owning larger tracts of land than among landless peasants or owners of very small plots.[16] Even in towns family ties are still quite strong, although the older kind of family loyalty is deteriorating. "Trade unions, social security, and factory legislation, for example, mean that the state is beginning to do what the working-class family may be still willing but is increasingly unable to do in a way that satisfies modern demands. As the state performs more of these functions, including that of education and regulation of marriage, the traditional family will perform them to a decreasing extent."[17] But this is the case all over the Arab world today and not the result of specific conditions in Egypt. A modern industrial society in which family ties are replaced by the individual contractual relationships has not yet been established.

A similar conclusion would be valid with regard to the social function of religion in Egyptian society. In this case the evidence is unanimous and unequivocal. In the 1930s, one anthropologist found that in the village he studied, "the family is the social unit; over it the only meaningful unit is the community of believers, the Muslims; all differences of origin, nation and race disappear in this unit." Another scholar came to the same conclusion at mid-century: "The villagers refer to themselves as well as to other Moslems by the term 'nation of the Moslems'. . . . For the villagers, the world is classified into believers and non-believers, on the basis of the Moslem faith, and they are hardly aware of concepts like race or class."[18] Although some changes may be perceived in the towns, religion has not yet abandoned its place as the predominant principle forming group consciousness. Thus, a study carried out in Alexandria in the mid-1950s showed that the greatest degree of individual participation was still in the traditional formal groups based on religion and kinship and in unorganized or informal ones, such as the "café group."[19] It is, perhaps, significant that (according to another study dating from about the same time) almost two thirds of Egyptian workers interviewed preferred Koran readings to all other broadcasts.[20] One of the ideologists of revolutionary Egypt has recently summed up the situation as follows: "We continue to this day to believe that religion rules the souls, especially of the popular classes."[21] The centralistic state of Egypt did not bring about any change in this respect, neither before, nor after, the military revolt. The centralistic character of the Egyptian body politic has only widened the gap between administrative and economic change, on the one hand, and cultural and educational change, on the other. Egypt made exceptionally great progress in transport, but is remarkably in arrears with literacy.[22] Thus, the administrative and socio-economic units of society were affected by the developments of the last 150 years, but not the social function of religion. Moreover, since Islam does not discriminate between state and religion, Egyptian nationalism (and nationalism in most Islamic countries, for that matter), has never been secular, but always blended with a smaller or larger dose of religion. Even the authoritarian "socialistic" military regime has declared that "our people believe . . . in a firm spiritual bond which ties it to the Islamic world."[23] One of the theorists of this regime advanced the need to "recognize that Islam has laid down for us the highest ideal and aim for all times."[24] Moreover, the regime promotes Islamic education in Egyptian schools by providing premises for prayers, religious books for school libraries, and by organizing competitions among pupils on religious subjects. During the month of Ramaḍān, teachers are instructed to deal in class with the victories of Islam.[25]

The fact that kinship and religion have not lost their social function in Egypt has brought about the failure of one of the most important efforts of the military regime in the field of social change – the campaign for the propagation of family planning. Such campaigns have been launched since the revolution a few times, but, in all cases, the program petered out after an initial impetus. Every time birth control centers were set up, whose purpose it was to guide the populace in family planning, the government invariably had to admit, after a few months, that there was very poor response to its initiative.

The attitude of official Islam towards birth control is ambiguous. Koran and tradition can be cited for opposite views – which enabled Egyptian religious leaders to declare both their opposition to, and their support of, birth control. Since the establishment of the military regime and its dedication to the program of family planning, declarations of the latter kind were predominant. This, however, did not prevent Egyptians belonging to the lower strata of society from expressing their belief, time and again, that "religion" was against birth control. Whatever the texts may say, this belief has decisive social significance. When the present writer had the opportunity of talking to many Egyptians of the lower classes after the 1956 war, most of them mentioned "religion" as one of the reasons why birth control was out of the question for them.

The preservation of ties of kinship has had a similar effect. The most widespread explanation of Egyptians of the lower strata of society for their opposition to birth control is that the more children a family has, the better they will be able to support their parents. Furthermore, large families are favored among this group because they strengthen the social position of the family vis à vis other families in the village or the town quarter. In view of the prevalence of these attitudes, the birth rate has not yet decreased – except among a very small layer of educated town dwellers.

This has had a disastrous effect on the socio-economic structure of Egypt and on its prospects in the future. For while the social functions of kinship and religion remained intact, and, therefore, the birth rate did not fall, the preponderance of the central power facilitated the fast progress of measures taken to reduce the death rate. The success of these measures was dependent on the attitudes of the population to a small extent only; in the main, their results were directly proportional to the progress of medicine and to the efficiency of the central administration. Thus, the Egyptian government was able to reduce the death rate and the rate of infant mortality tremendously by building hospitals, by forcing the population to submit itself to inoculations and injections, by the widespread use of insecticides, and, recently, by the use of antibiotics. The result was an enormous rise in the natural rate of increase of the population which is still going on. Thus, in the short period between 1960 and 1965, there was only a very small decrease in the birth rate from forty-three to forty-one per mille, while the death rate was reduced from nineteen to fourteen per mille, thus causing a rise in the rate of population growth from 2.4 to 2.7% per annum.[26]

The gap between the persistence of traditional attitudes among the people and the growth of central administrative efficiency thus defeats the social policies of the military regime. This found its most drastic expression in land reform. One of the original aims of land reform was "the establishment of a new class of small landowners."[27] However, after the implementation of land reform and the distribution of vast estates among the peasants, the rate of increase in the number of small landowners was still much lower than the rate of growth of the population. As a result, landowners today form a smaller percentage of the rural population than in 1952 – before the reform – and landless fellahs, a larger one. Thus, the average yearly increase in the number of owners of less than five feddans was 1.2% during the decade preceding the reform; 0.9% during the years 1952–61; and 1.1% yearly between 1961 and 1964 (the total number of landowners grew by 1.2% per annum before and after the reform). Since population growth has surpassed 2.5% per annum and even approaches 3%, the percentage of landless peasants must have grown.[28] This conclusion probably remains true even if we deduct the migration into towns. The landless peasants, who form a large proportion of Egypt's population, constitute the most backward group of this population; as long as this proportion grows, the prospects of changing the social structure of Egypt and the attitudes of the population are gloomy.

Although the centralistic power structure in Egypt had no decisive influence on the social function of religion among the broad masses of the Egyptian population, it brought about changes in the position of the *'ulamā'* (religious scholars) and their importance in Egyptian society. In the integrated society of the eighteenth century, the *'ulamā'* had fulfilled the function of an intellectual elite, deeply loyal to the basic values and institutions of their society; they taught submission to established authority and enjoyed general respect as the representatives and defenders of the Islamic community. This function formed the basis of the *'ulamā'* class as an institution and of the power which its members were able to wield.[29] As a result of the disintegration of political power in Egypt at the end of the eighteenth and the beginning of the nineteenth century, the *'ulamā'* were able to acquire dominant positions in the economic and political field and thus become a most powerful group. However, this golden age of the *'ulamā'* lasted no longer than it took Muḥammad 'Alī to consolidate his rule and reestablish the grip of the central government.[30] From then onward, their influence and importance declined; evidence for this is found in various eyewitness accounts of social life in Egypt during the nineteenth century. There was, perhaps, a certain revival of their power between the two World Wars, especially of the Cairo establishment centered around al-Azhar, as a result of the rivalry between the king and the Wafd and the creation of political parties. As in former times, the *'ulamā'* profited by the splitting of central power into different, and even antagonistic, foci. The military revolt put an end to this interval, and, since the middle of the century, the central religious establishment has been increasingly subjected to the absolute domination of Egypt's political rulers.

While the social importance of religion among Egypt's population has not declined faster than in other parts of the Middle East, the establishment of the *'ulamā'* has been hit much harder. Egypt is the only country in the Middle East (except Turkey) which has abolished the religious *Sharī'a* courts, and even matters of personal status are now being dealt with by civil courts (although most religious judges have been transferred to civil courts, and personal status is being judged by them according to religious law). By abolishing the family *waqf* in 1952 and nationalizing *waqf khayrī* (public endowment) in 1957,[31] the military regime undermined the economic basis of the influence wielded by the religious establishment. No other country in the Middle East achieved such radical results. Moreover, after the minister of *waqf* affairs had been, for many years, a *shaykh* and former member of the Muslim Brotherhood, the ministry was put into the hands of an army officer, and today the minister of religious affairs is a person without a background in the religious establishment. In addition, the state increasingly interferes with the functioning of religious institutions: it dictates sermons to the preachers in the mosques and has acquired a decisive say in the educational policy of the religious al-Azhar University, which is being assimilated more and more to the other state universities (there are no private universities in Egypt). Finally, the officers' regime liquidated another organized body based on religion, the Muslim Brotherhood, at least as an open legal association. Although there was some rivalry between the

Brotherhood and part of the *'ulamā'*, many of the latter certainly derived support from this organization, which propagated Islam as the basis on which Egyptian society should be built.

The old intellectual elite of the *'ulamā'* constituted an important integrating agent of Muslim society. Together with the decline of the *'ulamā'* a new secular intellectual elite emerged; however, for various reasons, this new elite was unable to fill the gap in Egyptian society which the decline of the *'ulamā'* had left.

The modern secular intellectual usually does not entreat the Egyptian people to submit to established authority. True, most of those who received secondary or higher education sooner or later became government officials or technical experts, and thus constitute part of the ruling bureaucracy and technocracy or are just tools of the regime. But these are not members of a class whose functions can be compared with those of the *'ulamā'* in former times. The group that is actually comparable is what is sometimes called the intelligentsia, i.e., those with a modern education, who live for, and by, political and social ideas or, in other words, the politically conscious unofficial section of the modern intellectual elite.[32] Apparently, the more centralized and authoritarian the system of government is, the greater the probability that it would not find a common language with the intelligentsia. Modern intellectuals consider it their privilege to express and propagate their own ideas, whatever they are – which is, in most cases, incompatible with the ideological uniformity of a centralized authoritarian regime. Moreover, while in Syria the present regime has been established by a political party with an ideology – the Ba'th – in Egypt, ideology was gradually developed by the military group years after it had seized power, and the attempts to establish a party from above have failed so far. The regime has often blamed the intellectuals for this – which is one of the many indications of the fact that the latter have not found their place in the society established by the revolution.

In 1961 this problem aroused a long public controversy, which was discussed in *al-Ahrām* under the heading *"Azmat al-muthaqqafīn"* (the crisis of the intellectuals). The controversy began with a series of articles by Luṭfī al-Khōlī, in which he made the accusation against the intellectuals that, after the revolution of 1919, most of them of middle-class origin "abandoned the tasks of their positive historical role" and became ministers and high officials. He blamed them for lack of originality, for locking themselves up in an ivory tower, and for having no interest in the problems of their country.[33] Later Muḥammad Ḥasanayn Haykal joined the discussion, stating that the intellectuals had no clear picture of what was going on, either because of their class connections, which removed them from the real demands of the popular struggle, or because of their aloofness from this struggle. They should not have just cooperated (*an yataʿāwanū)* with the revolution; they should have interacted *(an yatafāʿalū)* with it; they should have adopted its case, given it a national theory, and moulded its revolutionary faith.[34] Dr. Majdī Wahba, a professor of English literature at Cairo University and himself a representative of this modern Egyptian intelligentsia, explained the nonparticipation of the intellectuals in the army's action of 1952, their feeling of frustration and withdrawal into self – "the intellectuals' return to their cultural barracks" – by "the uniqueness . . . of Egypt's development relative to that of the other newly independent countries, a fact that created dissension between the different sectors of Egyptian society and therefore among the different intellectual groups, whereas in Black Africa, for example, the intellectuals constituted 'the vanguard of the new apparatus of the state'; the economic poverty of the Egyptian intellectuals, lower middle-class in origin, a fact that 'compels them to appear as propagandists for the government's rule instead of being its critics'." And he concluded: "the intellectual feels that Gamal Abdel Nasser is basically right. But at the same time he feels the need to formulate a certain amount of criticism by the very fact of his nature. This internal contradiction in the very heart of the Arab intellectual's personality tears him apart inside and makes him an unproductive being."[35] Since these words were written, late in 1961, the estrangement of the Egyptian intellectuals from Egypt's rulers has become more severe; there have been student riots against the regime – a remarkable development in authoritarian Egypt – and many who were able to leave Egypt did so.

On the other hand, the modern secular intellectuals certainly are unable to represent the Egyptian masses and to be recognized by them as their representatives. In the first place, the two groups have different belief systems, and it will certainly take some generations to bridge the gap between them. The belief system of the broad layers of the Egyptian people is a combination of folk culture and religious beliefs and rituals, the former predominant in the villages and the latter in the towns. As against this, the modern intellectuals have, for about a century, attempted to evolve an ideology adapted to modern conditions of life instead of the traditional belief system of Islam.[36] These attempts have been marked by ups and downs, and the results were unsatisfactory, to say the least. But the various attempts have a secular attitude as a common point of departure. If Islam figured in the new ideologies, it did so for political opportunistic reasons, rather than as a result of deep conviction. The following report about a Syrian judge is certainly relevant for the situation in Egypt as well. The judge found it almost impossible to administer Western legal codes among people used to the rule of custom or of the Koran. He said he was unhappy "because I am educated among ignorant people. They can't understand me and I can't do according to their mentality . . . By myself I can't do anything because it is a huge task to educate a whole nation."[37] Although the *'ulamā'* were educated, they had established perfect communication with the ignorant and illiterate masses of the Egyptian people since they shared a common belief system. Among the contemporary groupings, only the Muslim Brotherhood enjoyed mass support, for the same reason. The groups established by the modern intellectuals which were based on secular nationalism or communism never succeeded in establishing strongholds among the popular layers of Egyptian society, neither in the villages nor in the towns.

An additional reason for the lack of communication between the modern intellectual, or even the modern bureaucrat, and the lower classes is the fact that they, in contrast to the *'ulamā'*, did not have a connecting link at their disposal for communication with these classes, namely, the religious functionaries in every village and mosque: the *imāms, khaṭībs,* and *wā'iẓes.* After the central religious establishment had been completely subjected to the domination of a military authoritarian state, the *'ulamā'* could no longer use this link in order to communicate the ideas and orders of the new regime, nor were the secular intellectuals and bureaucrats able to establish contact with the local religious functionaries. The latter lived too close to the people to change their traditional attitudes. Thus, while the al-Azhar *shaykhs* and the *muftīs* of Cairo announced their support of the government's campaign for family planning and declared that Islam did not oppose birth control, the local religious functionaries preached the opposite. At the end of 1965, for instance, they were attacked in the press because in their sermons they propagated procreation and preached against birth control. Physicians and administrators of family-planning units complained of the hostility of the religious preachers, in spite of the explicit sanction given to birth control by the Shaykh al-Azhar. One of these preachers, when ordered to propagate birth control in his sermons, offered passive resistance by fastening the following written announcement to the *minbar* (pulpit) of his mosque: "We received an order from the Department of Mosques in the Waqf Ministry that it is necessary to infuse into the consciousness of the masses the advantages of family planning, and that some of the heads of the schools of law have authorized this from the point of view of religious law."[38]

We find, thus, a wide gap between the urban elite, the intellectuals, the bureaucrats, the technocrats, and the army officers, on the one hand, and the urban and rural lower classes, on the other. This gap, together with the disintegration of traditional units of society and the nonemergence of modern replacements – as analyzed above – could be the principal reasons for one of the major problems of Egyptian society today from the point of view of social change: the lack of individual involvement in public affairs.

True, the typical relationship of the individual to the state in many countries of the Middle East has for centuries been avoidance, or hostility, on the part of those outside the ruling group. There have been no agencies to inculcate a civic spirit in these countries. So long as Middle Eastern governments did not disturb the Muslim's relationship to his God and his religious community, he was content to let the government have its own way.[39] However, this tendency was obviously stronger in countries like Egypt in which the central power was more effective, and where, therefore, no intermediate agencies developed which could have stimulated participation of the individual in public affairs. This lack of participation by the people was one of the major disappointments of the revolutionary regime in Egypt, as witnessed by 'Abd al-Nāṣir himself:

Before July 23rd, I had imagined that the whole nation was ready and prepared, waiting for nothing but a vanguard to lead the charge against the battlements, whereupon it would fall in behind in serried ranks, ready for the sacred advance towards the great objective. And I had imagined that our role was to be the role of a commando vanguard. I thought that this role would never take more than a few hours. Then immediately would come the sacred advance behind us of the serried ranks and the thunder of marching feet as the ordered advance proceeded towards the great objective. I heard all this in my imagination, but by sheer faith it seemed real and not the figment of imagination. Then suddenly came reality after July 23rd. The vanguard performed its task and charged the battlements of tyranny. It threw out the tyrant and then paused, waiting for the serried ranks to come up in their sacred advance toward the great objective. For a long time it waited. Crowds did eventually come, and they came in endless droves – but how different is the reality from the dream! The masses that came were disunited, divided groups of stragglers. The sacred advance toward the great objective was stalled, and the picture that emerged on that day looked dark and ominous; it boded danger. At this moment I felt, with sorrow and bitterness, that the task of the vanguard, far from being completed, had only just begun.

And elsewhere in the same booklet:

Many people . . . stood to one side as mere spectators, observing our revolution, as though they had nothing to do with it. They only waited for the result of a struggle between two opposing forces, neither of which concerned them. Sometimes I resent this. Sometimes I demand of myself and my comrades: why don't they come out of their hiding places to speak up and to act? This is only to be accounted for, in my opinion, by the sediments of the Mamluk rule. The Mamluk amirs had fought each other, and their horsemen had met in fierce battles on the streets, while the people would stampede to their houses, locking themselves in, and thus avoiding a struggle which was not their concern.[40]

The problem is, of course, that the same attitude persisted a century and a half after the liquidation of the Mamluks, at a time when the government was dealing with matters which, according to the ideas of the modern elite to which 'Abd al-Nāsir belonged, should be the concern of the people. For instance, villagers never appreciated the benefits of government-sponsored economic institutions before the revolution, such as banks for agricultural credit, because it involved becoming implicated with government procedures, and they considered it safest to keep away from governmental institutions.[41] The same attitude persisted after the revolution. The following is evidence by a supporter of the new regime with strong connections in the countryside:

In the past rural society isolated itself from the ruling power because it felt that this power always opposed it. Rural society was therefore compelled to adopt a system of unwritten laws originating from its reality in order to solve its problems independently from the ruling power. . .

. . . This hidden system of laws still governs the countryside at present, thirteen years after the revolution whose leader emerged from the ranks of the people . . .

Although the revolution has recently made great efforts, through local government, to bridge the deep abyss separating the countryside from the ruling power . . . it will need much more efforts before it reaches its goal.[42]

But not only illiterate fellahs refrain from having anything to do with the government. Studies of the urban population led to similar conclusions: members of the urban population also conceived of the state as separated from the private world and think that the two should not be mixed up. According to their attitude, the needs of the state are the affairs of the state alone. Moreover, even the educated classes are reluctant to participate in public affairs and generally abstain completely from doing so. "Political support for the regime, while not deficient, is generally passive. The absence of opportunities for effective participation renders the government a relatively distant, cold object however much its leaders may appear psychologically familiar and warm."[43]

There can be no doubt that, in so far as the centralized, authoritative socio-political structure of Egypt destroyed traditional integrating links between the different parts of the socio-political framework and prevented the emergence of new ones, it aggravated this lack of participation. Therefore, the recurring attempts of the military regime to establish an organization whose principal aim was the recruitment of Egypt's population for participation in the economic, social, and political activities of the new elite have, so far, failed completely. The first of the three attempts, the Liberation Rally *(Hay'at al-taḥrīr),* failed in its main purpose of organizing active support for the regime. This failure has been explained by the fact that the leaders trusted the enthusiasm of the masses and refrained from building a reliable core – a cadre. The Rally also failed to stir the masses to take a hand in the reform of Egypt's society. The Rally's ambitious projects, based as they were on mass volunteering, never got to the stage of implementation. At the end, the Rally's functions were taken over, one by one, by the government, and the movement had in fact ceased to exist long before its official dissolution in January 1958.[44]

The second organization, the National Union *(al-Ittiḥād al-qawmī)* was established in 1957, and its life was even shorter than that of its predecessor. In its structure, election of committees on the lower levels was combined with nomination and screening from above. It was hoped that in this way mass support for the social and national aims of the government would be recruited and a cadre of leaders would be established on the intermediate level. However, this attempt was also a complete failure. Two years after the establishment of the National Union, *Rūz al-Yūsuf* wrote: "When the National Union members submitted their candidacies . . . they had given no thought to their tasks; all they wanted was to be regarded as government officials, and after they had been elected, they still looked to the government for instructions." The correspondent of *The Economist* commented about the National Union that "little gets done, and even less is understood by the people concerned. Thus the villages, called upon to vote, voted for the same families who have always been dominant, and the web breaks off long before it reaches the centre." More than a year later, *Rūz al-Yūsuf* again wrote that some communities were completely inactive while others included five members of the same family. And at the end of 1961, 'Abd al-Nāṣir admitted that the National Union had been "turned into a mere organizational facade, unmoved by the force of the masses and their genuine demands." This time he blamed the infiltration of reaction into the National Union for having brought about the failure.[45]

In mid-1962 the National Charter provided for the establishment of the third organization, the Socialist Arab Union *(al-Ittiḥād al-ishtirākī al-'arabī).* It differed from its predecessor in the provision that basic units were to be formed now also in the factories, workshops, companies, ministries, cooperatives, and professional syndicates, and that half the seats on its elected bodies at all levels must be occupied by farmers and workers. Theoretically, the most important innovation was the distinction between active and associate members because this was intended to establish, at long last, the desired cadre of politically involved intermediate party workers who would, in the end, achieve the involvement of wider circles of the population in public affairs. In fact, however, the distinction has never been made. In February 1966 Ḥasanayn Haykal wrote in *al-Ahrām:* "The structure of the single party in Egypt is sound in theory; in practice it is bad . . . principally because of the bureaucracy, the lack of revolutionary cadres, and the lack of coordination in action."[46] In the program included in his discourse of 30 March 1968, 'Abd al-Nāṣir again declared that the Socialist Union had not in fact been built from the basis to the top by elections, and he announced the reorganization of the union. However, the essential problems have not yet been solved, namely, the formation of sufficient cadres in order to bring about the participation of the citizen in public affairs and to control the executive apparatus of the state.[47]

So far, we have dealt with the popular lack of participation in public affairs and lack of cooperation with the government. But at least as significant from the point of view of social tensions and changes is the lack of cooperation among individuals in Egyptian society. It has been pointed out that one of the typical aspects of Middle Eastern society, in general, is the inability of people to associate for cooperative action. Whenever a social need is felt, the first impulse is to turn to the central government for help.[48] Solidarity among villagers appears only on occasion, in the face of some external threat; it does not persist and does not assume organized form. Village elders may sign and collectively present a petition concerning some village affair or other, but fellahs seldom take organized action for the sake of a common cause. About the Egyptian village, in particular, it has been said that there is no cooperative spirit among the village youth, as in villages of other countries, and even more striking is the absence of organizations and associations on a village basis.[49] Moreover, Arab life has been described as being filled with interpersonal rivalry. "Poverty and frustration . . . are so pervasive that there is a great deal of what we may call 'free floating hostility.' . . . Conflict is so much on the verge of breaking out that interpersonal relations seem to be largely directed at avoiding or covering up the slightest tendency toward the expression of difference."[50] Again, 'Abd al-Nāṣir described this trait of Egyptian society very eloquently:

> We were not yet ready. So we set about seeking the views of leaders of opinion and the experience of those who were experienced. Unfortunately, we were not able to obtain very much. Every man we met had no purpose except to kill someone else. Every idea we listened to was nothing but an attempt to destroy some other idea. If we had gone along with everything we heard, we would have killed off all the people and torn down every idea, and there would have been nothing left for us to do but sit down among the corpses and ruins, bewailing our evil fortune and cursing our wretched fate.
>
> We were deluged with petitions and complaints by the thousands and hundreds of thousands, and had these complaints and petitions dealt with cases demanding justice or grievances calling for redress, this motive would have been understandable and logical. But most of the cases referred to us were no more or less than demands for revenge, as though the revolution had taken place in order to become a weapon in the hand of hatred and vindictiveness.
>
> If anyone had asked me in those days what I wanted most, I would have answered promptly: To hear an Egyptian speak fairly about another Egyptian. To sense that an Egyptian has opened his heart to pardon, forgiveness and love for his Egyptian brethren. To find an Egyptian who does not devote his time to tearing down the views of another Egyptian.
>
> In addition to all this, there was a confirmed individual egotism. The word 'I' was on every tongue . . .[51]

Sociological studies have time and again confirmed this characteristic feature of Egyptian society. A comparative study of attitudes among college students of ten countries showed the Egyptians to be especially suspicious. In listing three influential events in their lives, Egyptians mentioned, more often than any others, disagreeable experiences that engendered distrust of people. The reply to another question showed Egyptians leading all other respondents in the proportion agreeing with the statement that the "world is a hazardous place, in which men are basically evil and dangerous."[52] Similarly, a study of Egyptian prisoners of war has shown that conflicts among soldiers constituted a serious problem of discipline. They gave the impression that there did not exist among them anything equivalent to what one would call *camaraderie.*[53]

The lack of individual cooperation in the Middle East, in general, has been explained by the collapse of Islamic civilization following the

Crusades and Mongol invasions. Such cooperation, so it is claimed, became impossible under the arbitrary and extortionate governments which oppressed the poverty-stricken region.[54] This could be at least part of the explanation, although further investigation may yield more detailed results. In any case, it seems that lack of cooperation prevailed in Egypt more than in other parts of the Middle East. For instance, in our studies of the history of the guilds in the Middle East, we found that, while in Egypt funds for mutual help did not exist in any of the guilds except that of the shoemakers, a provident fund and other arrangements for mutual help were an important aspect in the activities of Turkish guilds.[55] It is highly probable that in this case, too, the preponderance of the central power was responsible for the difference. One author claimed that for fifty centuries, governments in Egypt encouraged the formlessness of peasant society – which has been helped by the absence of coordination between homogenous elements – since this greatly strengthened central authority.[56] In fact, the impact of central power probably was not intentional, but rather indirect. By eliminating all intermediate or local groups and units, it never left as much scope for voluntary action of citizens involving cooperation among themselves as in countries with a less centralist and authoritative structure. Thus, the only framework for solidarity which remained was kinship.

To sum up: it has been our proposition in this paper that the principal trait of Egyptian society, compared with other societies in the area, is the overwhelming preponderance of central power. We have found that this characteristic feature of Egyptian society accelerated the destruction of traditional socio-economic units and impeded the emergence of new ones; it undermined the position of the religious establishment and contributed to the failure of a new intellectual elite to fulfill the function of an integrating agent formerly fulfilled by the *'ulamā'*; and it aggravated the tendency towards polarization inherent in Egyptian society. Excessive central power has been unfavorable for the development of an independent urban middle class and of intermediate independent economic and social units, and it has furthered, albeit indirectly, the absolute and relative growth of a class of landless peasants and jobless urban *lumpen-proletariat.* As a result, most individuals in Egyptian society are only slightly involved in public affairs, keep aloof from anything connected with the government, and refrain from participating in the political process. Moreover, one finds little cooperation among individuals and much hostility and distrust.

Are there indeed no other basic features of Egyptian society which may also be at least an indirect result of the centralistic power structure of Egyptian society and which could have an opposite effect, i.e., a tendency towards integration? It would seem to us that the main fundamental characteristic favorable to the eventual development of greater integration is the religious and ethnical homogeneity of Egypt's population. Non-Egyptians never constituted more than two percent of the population, and in recent years this element has been almost completely eliminated. There are different estimates of the percentage of Copts, but it is highly improbable that at any time in the twentieth century their proportion exceeded ten percent of the population. Islamization, especially in recent years, further reduced this percentage. Moreover, although there is some concentration of Copts in certain towns and specific districts of Upper Egypt, their social structure and customs are very similar to those of the Muslims. The majority of Copts are peasants, there are no great differences between the levels of education of Copts and Muslims, and even less in other social conditions. Many customs are common to both communities: circumcision, marriage and funeral customs, laws of inheritance, and visits to the same saints' tombs.[57]

Another phenomenon operating in the same direction is probably connected with the homogeneity of the population and the relatively high development of communications between the different parts of the country. More than in other countries of the Middle East, the dialect of the capital, Cairo, spread all over the country and developed into a regional or standard dialect spoken by some people in other places as well. Moreover, dialect differentiation (i.e., the splintering of the language into many dialects) is much stronger in the Fertile Crescent than in Egypt – at least if one takes into account the area concerned.[58] In addition, until a few generations ago, the ruling class spoke Turkish, and later partly French, while today the ruling elite speaks Arabic, i.e., the same language as the rest of the population. However, neither religious and ethnical homogeneity nor linguistic affinity are sufficient bases to mitigate the disintegrating effects of the overwhelming preponderance of the center on social structure and its detrimental effect on social change.

It has often been claimed that developing countries need a centralistic power structure and an authoritarian regime to bring about social change. There can be no doubt that the fact that Egypt has had such a structure and regime involved certain advantages. One obvious advantage was the resulting stability of government. This stability enabled revolutionary Egypt to carry out certain parts of her program of social change – which Syria and Iraq failed to implement under much more favorable circumstances, because of the frequent changes of regime. Egypt was much more successful in eliminating local opposition to social reforms and remnants of the old social order than countries of the Middle East with a less centralistic power structure. Moreover, it was much easier for Egypt, than for those countries, to plan the development of national resources with a view to furthering social change: Egypt could launch a program of industrialization and considerably expand the network of communications – two basic prerequisites for social change. An authoritarian regime, whose leaders are dedicated to modernization, has much better facilities to use the educational network and the mass media for transmitting ideas to the population and urging it to take part in implementing the regime's plans.

In fact, Egypt has so far succeeded in utilizing only part of these advantages. The military regime has been much more successful in expropriating large estates and overcoming opposition by the old elite, than in using its centralistic power for carrying out development plans and influencing the basic attitudes of Egypt's population toward social change. Moreover, as we have seen, the preponderance of the central power also impeded social change in many ways. By aggravating the tendency towards polarization in the structure of Egyptian society, it has broadened the gap between the elite and the intellectuals, on the one hand, and the masses, on the other, and eliminated intermediate links capable of transmitting change initiated by the elite. Thus, the present regime has been unable, for more than fifteen years, to create political cadres whose task it would be to inculcate the new social and political ideas in the masses and urge them to take part in the changes of society conceived by the modern elite. The predominance of the central power has prevented the emergence of independent interest groups capable of initiating change. It has created a gap between administrative and economic change, on the one hand, and cultural and educational change, on the other, and thus brought about a disequilibrium detrimental to smoothly developing change – as we have seen with regard to family planning and land reform.

To conclude, it is extremely doubtful whether the preponderance of the central power has in fact been advantageous to genuine social change. Consequently, it would seem that from this point of view Egypt's specific power structure has negative, rather than positive, effects.

NOTES

1 Cf. W.F. Edgerton, "The Question of Feudal Institutions in Ancient Egypt," in *Feudalism in History,* ed. Rushton Coulborn (Princeton, 1956), p. 122.

2 Cf. Coulborn, p. 255: "... Its [the Old Kingdom's] disintegration was not followed anywhere in Egypt by feudal developments and a ghost empire; instead there followed after a relatively short period of disintegraton a new empire, that of the Eleventh and Twelfth Dynasties... But there were regions nearby Egypt in which there may have been feudalization and certainly there were nomads and perhaps other barbarians. These are Palestine, Syria, Libya, and Upper Nubia." Egypt is a classical example of what has been called "hydraulic society." See Karl Wittfogel, *Oriental Despotism: A Comparative Study of Total Power* (New Haven, 1957), *passim* (and bibliography cited there). However, Wittfogel is not clear at all about other Middle Eastern societies; thus, he says on p. 167 that Ottoman Turkey was a hydraulic society, but on pp. 170–1 he shows that in fact the opposite was the case.

3 Cf. Claude Cahen, "Zur Geschichte der städtischen Gesellschaft im islamischen Orient des Mittelalters," *Saeculum* 9 (1958): 59–76; id., *Mouvements populaires et autonomisme urbain dans l'Asie musulmane du Moyen Age* (Leiden, 1959).

4 See, e.g., Charles Issawi, "The Arab World's Heavy Legacy," *Foreign Affairs,* April 1965, pp. 501–12.

5 Cf. Morroe Berger, *The Arab World Today* (New York, 1962), pp. 101–2.

6 Cf. Jacques Berque, *Les Arabes d'hier à demain* (Paris, 1960), pp. 18; 225–6. We are quoting from the French original because the English translation has distorted the meaning by translating *quartiers* as "districts."

7 Henri Ayrout, S.J., *The Egyptian Peasant* (Boston, 1963), p. 113.

8 Berger, p. 104.

9 See Gabriel Baer, *Studies in the Social History of Modern Egypt* (Chicago, 1969), pp. 190–209.

10 Cf. Issawi, pp. 506–7.

11 For detailed treatment of this development, see Gabriel Baer, *A History of Landownership in Modern Egypt* (London, 1962), pp. 45–60; 136–46.

12 Leonard Binder, "Egypt: The Integrative Revolution," in *Political Culture and Political Development,* ed. L.W. Pye and S. Verba (Princeton, 1965), p. 430.

13 Manfred Halpern, *The Politics of Social Change in the Middle East and North Africa* (Princeton, 1963), pp. 52–4.

14 Hassan Riad, *l'Egypte nassérienne* (Paris, 1964), p.8.

15 Cf. Eliezer Beeri, "Social Origin and Family Background of the Egyptian Army Officer Class," *Asian and African Studies* 2 (1966): 1–40.

16 Hamed Ammar, *Growing up in an Egyptian Village* (London, 1954), pp. 42–4.

17 Berger, p. 142.

18 H.A. Winkler, *Bauern zwischen Wasser und Wüste* (Stuttgart, 1934), p. 137; Ammar, pp. 72–3.

19 Berger, p. 103.
20 D.L. Lerner, *The Passing of Traditional Society – Modernizing the Middle East* (Glencoe, Ill., 1958), p. 234.
21 Muḥammad Muṣṭafā ʿAṭā, *Naḥw waʿy jadīd* (Cairo, n.d.), p. 98.
22 For detailed analysis of this problem, see Charles Issawi, "Asymmetrical Development and Transport in Egypt, 1800–1914," in *Beginnings of Modernization in the Middle East,* ed. W.R. Polk and R.L. Chambers (Chicago, 1968), pp. 383–400.
23 U.A.R. Information Service, *Mashrūʿ al-mīthāq 21 Māyō 1962* (The Charter) (Cairo, n.d.), p. 123.
24 ʿIṣmat Sayf al-Dawla, *Usus al-ishtirākiyya al-ʿarabiyya* (Cairo, 1965), p. 372, as quoted by Hamid Enayat, "Islam and Socialism in Egypt," *Middle Eastern Studies,* 4, no. 2 (Jan. 1968), p. 152.
25 See, e.g., *al-Ahrām,* 18 August 1964; *Akhbār,* 7 November 1969, as quoted in *Hamizrah Hehadash* 15 (1965): 144; and 20 (1970):192.
26 Data supplied to Egyptian Press by General Jamāl ʿAskar, director of the Central Institute of Statistics, *al-Ahrām* and *al-Jumhūriyya,* 13 July 1966.
27 Sayyid Marʿī, *al-Islāh, al-zirāʿī fī miṣr* (Cairo, 1957), pp. 33; 227–8; 233.
28 For detailed data and analysis, see Gabriel Baer, "New Data on Egypt's Land Reform," *New Outlook* 10, no. 3 (March–April 1967): 26–9.
29 See H.A.R. Gibb and Harold Bowen, *Islamic Society and the West,* vol. 1, pt. 2 (London, 1957), pp. 70 ff.
30 Cf. Baer, *History of Landownership in Modern Egypt,* pp. 60–3.
31 Cf. Baer, *Studies,* pp. 88–92. There was a distinction between two types of *waqfs* (religious endowments): *waqf ahlī* or *dhurrī* (family *waqf*), the income of which was allocated to the family of the man who made the endowment, and *waqf khayrī,* whose income was designated for public purposes.
32 H. Seton-Watson, "The Role of the Intelligentsia," *Survey,* August 1962, pp. 24–5.
33 Lutfī al-Khōlī, "Al-quwā al-mutaṣāriʿa fī thaqāfatinā al-muʿāṣira," *al-Ahrām,* 15 March 1961; id., "Azmat ibdāʿ . . . wa- ʿumq naẓra . . . wa-minhāj" ibid., 16 March 1961.
34 *Al-Ahrām,* 2 June 1961; 16 June 1961.
35 Quoted in Anouar Abdel-Malek, *Egypt: Military Society* (New York, 1968), pp. 194–5.
36 See Nadav Safran, *Egypt in Search of Political Community* (Cambridge, Mass., 1961).
37 Lerner, p. 277.
38 *Al-Jumhūriyya,* 16 November 1965; and *al-Ahrām,* 26 March 1966, as quoted in A. Karni, "Changing Attitudes to Birth Control in the Middle East," *Hamizrah Hehadash* 17 (1967): 239.
39 Berger, pp. 294–5.
40 Jamāl ʿAbd al-Nāṣir, *Falsafat al-thawra* (Cairo, n.d.), pp. 20–1; 44. Our translation is based on the published English translation, *Egypt's Liberation* (Washington 1955), pp. 32–4; 63–4. Corrections were made by collating it with the original.

41 Ammar, p. 81.
42 Muḥammad ʻAbd Rabb al-Nabī, "Problems of the Socialist Union in the Countryside," *al-Talīʻa,* May 1965, pp. 77–8.
43 Binder, p. 402.
44 Shimon Shamir, "The Five Years of Egypt's 'Liberation Rally'," *Hamizrah Hehadash* 8 (1957): 261–78.
45 *Middle East Record,* 1960, pp. 478–89; 1961, pp. 587–90; 627-31; and the following sources as quoted in *MER: Rūz al-Yūsuf,* 19 October 1959; *The Economist,* 12 March 1960; *Rūz al-Yūsuf,* 29 May 1961; *al-Ahrām,* 17 October 1961.
46 *Al-Ahrām,* 11 February 1966. Cf. R. Costi, "La réorganization de l'Union Socialiste Arabe en R.A.U.," *Cahiers de l'Orient Contemporain,* no. 73 (December 1968): 8–12.
47 Costi. See also reports about the Congress of the A.S.U. in July 1969 in the Egyptian Press which confirm this conclusion.
48 Charles Issawi, "Economic and Social Foundations of Democracy in the Middle East," in *The Middle East in Transition,* ed. W.Z. Laqueur (London, 1958), pp. 46–7.
49 Winkler, ibid.
50 Berger, p. 161.
51 ʻAbd al-Nāṣir, pp. 22–3. Our translation is based on *Egypt's Liberation,* pp. 34–6.
52 James M. Gillespie and Gordon W. Allport, *Youth's Outlook on the Future* (New York, 1955), p. 23, as quoted in Berger, p. 163.
53 Personal information. The study has not yet been published.
54 Issawi, "Economic and Social Foundations of Democracy in the Middle East," p. 47.
55 Gabriel Baer, *Egyptian Guilds in Modern Times* (Jerusalem, 1964), pp. 114–6; id., "The Administrative, Economic and Social Functions of Turkish Guilds," *International Journal of Middle East Studies* 1, no. 1 (January 1970): 44–6.
56 Ayrout, p. 113.
57 Cf. Gabriel Baer, *Population and Society in the Arab East* (London and New York, 1964), pp. 97–8.
58 The author is grateful to Professor Haim Blanc of the Department of Arabic Language and Literature at the Hebrew University for this information.

SOCIETY AND STATE IN MODERN SYRIA

MOSHE MA'OZ

INTRODUCTORY REMARKS

In 1946, when Syria became an independent republic, it was in many respects a state without being a nation-state, a political unit without a political community and without a society united by a system of common values. The population was largely heterogeneous and split by conflicts and rivalries among religious communities, classes, and ethnic groups; indeed, even among inhabitants of different regions. Many of these communities and ethnic groups tended to live in isolation from others, did not recognize an exclusive central authority, and lacked any strong feeling of identification with a Syrian national entity.

Even today, twenty-five years after gaining independence and some fifty years after becoming a separate political unit, Syria still lacks a crystallized political society like that of some other Arab states, despite all efforts and achievements in this direction in the last two generations.

The reasons for this situation are historical-political, socio-economic, cultural and psychological, geographical and topographical – interwoven and mutually influenced. The aim of this essay is to discuss some of these factors – within the framework of a review covering the socio-political changes in Syria during recent times – and to examine the imprint of those changes on the population and their influence on the development of a Syrian political community.

THE HISTORICAL BACKGROUND

From the end of the Umayyad Kingdom up to the beginning of the twentieth century, Syria has virtually never been a separate political-administrative unit with a strong central-local government. It was part of vast empires with distant centers and was ruled for many generations in a rather loose way, subdivided into a number of provinces. In the provincial capitals and in other regions of the country, mainly in the mountainous and desert fringes, centers of rule and authority existed, separated from each other and largely autonomous in respect to the imperial center.

This phenomenon, especially conspicuous in the long Ottoman period, determined the socio-political characteristics of modern Syria. The Ottoman government, which attributed secondary importance to the Syrian *eyalets* (provinces) – as compared with Anatolia and the Balkans – confined its objectives to the following spheres: preserving the supreme authority of the sultan and defending the highways to Egypt; collection of taxes and increased exploitation of local resources; securing the annual *hajj* (pilgrimage) caravan to Mecca.

To realize these objectives, the Ottoman government applied limited manpower, small garrisons, and moderate funds – which merely sufficed to sustain a weak rule with limited order and security, mainly in the centers of the Syrian provinces.

The resulting void was filled by the heads of the various groups in the region, not always without the agreement or consent of the Ottoman government. Rural and tribal *shaykhs*, feudal overlords, chiefs of big clans, communal and religious notables, and powerful patricians ruled in various parts of the country, sometimes providing a degree of security which the imperial government could not maintain.[1] These leaders did not merely base their status on the old social structure which had prevailed in the areas from early times, but also on an ancient concept of rule recognized by the Ottomans. Accordingly, the central government avoided any direct involvement in the social life of the local population, and allowed them to exist in autonomous fashion, according to the traditional framework of the extended family, the tribe, the quarter, the religious community, and the like.

Apart from social influence, some of the local leaders also commanded substantial military and economic power, due to their rule over armed peasants or urban semimilitary organizations, and also because of the nature of Ottoman feudal rule which granted them the privilege of tax collection and jurisdiction in the rural regions.

In this way, small socio-political centers crystallized, which were granted, or were able to achieve, varying degrees of autonomy within the Syrian *eyalets*.

One type of center were the *millets* of the Christian and Jewish communities, to which the state granted limited socio-religious autonomy, jurisdiction in marital affairs, education, and the collection of certain taxes. However, Christians and Jews were politically inferior: barred from carrying arms and deprived, by and large, of the possibility of reaching senior positions in the administration.

Apart from the *millets,* centers of considerable political and social autonomy arose in Syria among the peoples of the mountainous and desert fringes. These were the powerful Bedouin tribes, such as the 'Anaza, the Shammar, the Banū Ṣakhr, and the 'Adwān, which roamed the edges of the Syrian and Transjordanian desert; as well as the Muslim heterodox sects and linguistic minority groups in the outlying mountains of Syria; the Nuṣayris (or 'Alawis) of Jabal Ansariyya in the Latakia region; the Druze of Jabal Druze in the Houran (and certainly in Southern Lebanon); the Mutawalli Shiites in the Anti-Lebanon region (but mainly in Jabal 'Āmil, Southern Lebanon); the Ismailis in the Salamia mountains near Ḥama; and the Kurds and Turkomans in the passes of the Taurus range. Those groups exploited their geographical or topographical advantages and relied on their social or tribal structure in fostering a semi-independent status, sometimes even challenging or threatening the regional Ottoman regime. Furthermore, because of the communal and religious solidarity – developed as a traditional defense against zealous Muslim orthodoxy – political particularism (with resulting seclusion) was especially powerful among the heterodox Muslim communities. These sects, together with linguistic minorities and the non-Muslim protected *millets,* contributed to the growth of two additional phenomena in Syrian life: ethnic heterogeneity and sharp contrasts among the various groups.

This heterogeneity manifests itself in the great number of minority groups, differing from the Arabic-speaking Muslim majority (about sixty percent) in religion or language.[2] Between this majority and the minorities, rivalries caused mainly by religious zeal existed for hundreds of years. The most conspicuous contrasts were those between Sunni Muslims (even non-Arabs) and the various Muslim heterodox communities, as well as among the various Christian sects. In addition, all Muslims were rivals of the Christians, and both Muslims and Christians were set against the Jews.

Contrasts and tensions were also prominent among ecological groups: nomads and fellahs, townsmen and villagers, and within those groups themselves – between the Rwala (Ruwāla) and Wuld 'Alī tribes; or the villages of the Qays and Yaman factions. There were also the frictions between different classes or big urban families; and the traditional political and economic rivalry between Damascus and Aleppo.

In summary, the Syrian socio-political life was characterized by the lack of a strong central government, a multitude of regional power centers, political administrative splits, social seclusion, and communal, religious, regional, and social contrasts. All this took root during the four hundred years of Ottoman rule to such an extent that it was liable to persistently delay any political and social change which could have influenced the development of a modern society and political community in Syria.

THE FAILURE OF MODERNIZATION

The modernization movement which began in Syria in the 1830s was intended to bring about a far-reaching change of the traditional socio-political system, while emphasizing the following trends: the abolition of local regional power centers and formation of a strong central government; upsetting traditional social frameworks and establishing equal status for the various communities; as well as fostering the attachment of the entire population to one center.

Although the era of modernization brought about some changes in the governmental-political relations of Syria, the above aims were not achieved until the middle of the twentieth century. Moreover, modernization enhanced intercommunal contrasts and class polarization, introduced new tensions in the populations, and thus delayed the process of turning Syria into an orderly political society.

The causes for the failure of modernization in Syria were twofold: on the one hand, the resistance of the population and its leadership to changes designed to upset the traditional system; and, on the other hand, the defects of the modernizing process itself; that is, the modernizing movement in Syria – as opposed to Egypt – was not uniform and systematic and did not originate from within. It was introduced (and forced) by governments outside Syria: from Cairo (by Muḥammad 'Alī), from Istanbul (by the Ottomans), and later from Paris (by the French). Syria was administered by the various regimes with different methods and varying efficiency and, to a certain extent, with different trends. In addition to the influence of various governments, modernization was also influenced by other foci of change with their own tendencies, sometimes opposed to those of the government. These foci were, on the one hand, the great European

Powers and various Western institutions active in politics, society, the economy, and in education; and, on the other hand, the Arabic literary renaissance and the Arab national movement, which left their imprint on culture, thought, and ideology. It is thus evident that the process of modernization from its beginning to the middle of the twentieth century, rather than assisting, actually obstructed the development of a crystallized society and a political community in Syria.

Changes in Power Relations

The main aims of the two movements of modernization in nineteenth century Syria, Egyptian and Ottoman, were undoubtedly identical: destruction of local centrifugal forces and the establishment of one strong center; breaking the politico-military and socio-economic power of the rural, tribal, and urban leadership; and substituting direct subordination to the central government for the subordination of every individual to the head of his social group. The principal means of achieving those goals were also similar: disarming the various groups; conscription of young men; abolition of the feudal method of tax collection, and in particular the *iltizām* (the lease of taxes), and replacing it with direct taxation; the removal of local rulers and their replacement by officials of the central government.

The reform regime of Ibrāhīm Pasha – the first stage of modernization in Syria – accomplished great achievements in every one of the above-mentioned fields during the approximately nine years of rule (1831–1840). Assisted by considerable armed forces, comparatively efficient administration, and brutal compulsion, Ibrāhīm Pasha succeeded in weakening the autonomous and semi-independent groups in the mountainous, rural, and urban regions; and, despite widespread uprisings, he established a strong central authority for the first time in Syria's modern history. The period of his rule was, however, too short to effect far-reaching changes in political relations and in the social structure.

Ibrāhīm Pasha's main contribution to modernization in Syria consisted of opening the way for changes – by shaking the ancient order and establishing new frames. Yet, numerous pitfalls remained. For example, many groups which had experienced his drastic regime strengthened their resistance to the reforming trends of the central authority. The Ottoman governors who returned to Syria after the Egyptian occupation were bound to carry on what Ibrāhīm had initiated if they wished to profit from the achievements of the previous regime.

The Ottoman administration was, however, incapable of following the style of the Egyptian regime, mainly because it lacked the efficient tools of government previously enjoyed by Ibrāhīm. The Ottoman governors were lacking in authority as well as being insufficiently provided with financial means. Some of them, and the majority of the junior officials, were corrupt, inefficient, and unwilling to carry out reforms. The army, though effective, was too small to carry out all its assignments or to implement effective sanctions required to impose reforms.

A further series of difficulties encountered by the Ottoman reform movement (as compared to the Egyptian) originated in the hesitations and doubts which afflicted the liberal reform circles of the central government, and the conflicts and struggles between them and the conservative enemies of reform. Due to these and other causes, i.e., pressures exerted by the Great Powers, and because of the inefficient organs of government, the Ottoman regime in Syria was compelled to compromise on modernization. They thus forfeited the achievements of the previous Egyptian regime and permitted a strengthening of the centrifugal forces which had been weakened by Ibrāhīm. These forces became a major obstacle to reform during the greater part of the nineteenth century.

For example, the Ottoman regime did not exploit the advantage achieved by Ibrāhīm Pasha in his power relations with local elements, manifested by total disarmament and large-scale conscription. The Turks did not merely refrain from continuing this trend upon their return to Syria, but even distributed large quantities of arms among the population, especially in the mountain districts and among the Bedouin, intending to win their cooperation for removing the Egyptian army from the country. These arms were evidently not returned to the government, but ultimately directed against it when it later attempted to impose direct rule in the mountain and desert areas. Ibrāhīm Pasha had anticipated this, as he ironically remarked to an Ottoman general after 1840: "You with the assistance of the English have expelled me. You have again put arms into the hands of the mountaineers; it cost me nine years and ninety thousand men to disarm them. You will yet invite me back to govern them."[3]

Furthermore, the reestablished Ottoman regime did not hasten to impose general conscription – because of its relative weakness and fear of popular resistance and of loss of prestige. In 1850, when the regime initiated large-scale mobilization, it faced numerous revolts which seriously hampered the execution of this scheme. The number of recruits actually reaching the Ottoman army in that year, and during several later decades, was relatively small (about ten percent of those subject to conscription) compared to the Egyptian period, and hardly contributed to weakening the local leaders. The Ottoman reform regime also failed to diminish the socio-economic power of these leaders by refraining from imposing direct taxation, as implemented by the Egyptians, instead of the semi-feudal system. Following several abortive attempts to impose direct taxes, the Ottomans returned to leasing taxes *(iltizām)* in the rural regions and refrained from interfering with other forms of feudal tax collection. For example, out of five hundred villages in the Aleppo district in 1845, 380 were leased as *iltizām,* sixty as *malikana* (tax farming for life), fifty belonged to the *waqf* (religious foundation), and ten to the *sipahis* (feudal cavalry).[4]

These semifeudal practices hampered direct subordination of the peasantry to the central government and endowed the local notables and *shaykhs* with financial resources and power over vast rural regions. As a result of these defects in the Ottoman reform movement, the various territorial centers of Syria regained power and returned to an autonomous or semi-independent way of life, while the central government lost in authority and prestige. The local centers distinguished for renewed power and militancy were the Muslim heterodox communities, 'Alawis, Mutawallis, and in particular the Druze, and the great Bedouin tribes of the 'Anaza and Shammar and the Wuld 'Alī. The Bedouin tribes, who had been driven into the desert and harassed by the armies of Ibrāhīm Pasha, once again controlled extensive rural areas, interurban roads, and the international caravan routes. They continued to exploit the defenseless peasants, greatly damaged agriculture and commerce, and disrupted traffic and public security. The mountain dwellers also quickly regained strength after the heavy blows which they had suffered during the Egyptian period; they refused submission to the Ottoman regime and even endangered their neighboring regions. This mainly applied to the Druze of the Houran and the Leja. Enjoying territorial concentration, topographical advantage, communal solidarity, and social cohesion, they evinced an obstreperous rebelliousness towards the central government and gravely damaged its authority and prestige. The 1879 report by Midḥat Pasha provides just one evidence for this: "These people have completely lost all respect for the government to which they no longer furnish any troops or taxes."[5] Moreover, the Druze of the Jabal (who occasionally received military support from their brethren in Lebanon and political support from the British consuls) more than once cut the supply of wheat from the Houran to Damascus and caused serious disruption of security in extensive regions along the Damascus–Beirut and the Damascus–Tiberias routes.

The Turks applied various methods to control these separatist elements – mostly short-range measures with a negative influence on the future power relationships in the region. Whereas the military punitive expeditions against the Bedouin or the mountaineers were sporadic and could not destroy the autonomy of the mountain and desert regions, the placatory gestures of the regime towards regional leaders – the bestowing of titles or appointments as commanders of special cavalry units – further enhanced their usurped authority and insolence. Moreover, the old method of "divide and rule," by which the Turks had instigated tribes, families, and communities against each other, caused great mutual bloodshed, and also revived the social and communal conflicts among the population of Syria.

Only during the latter half of the nineteenth and mainly towards the turn of the twentieth century did the central government apply a systematic policy, with bigger forces and modern means, against the various centrifugal trends. A string of fortresses was built on the border of the Syrian desert, new roads were pushed into mountainous regions, railroads laid between the local centers, and telegraph lines established between Istanbul and the Syrian cities. By these means, and by the continuous use of large military units, the government succeeded in harassing the desert tribes and encouraging their settlement, while penetrating the mountainous center and establishing an Ottoman presence, at first, in Jabal Ansariyya and in the Mutawalli concentration of Anti-Lebanon, and, later, in Jabal Druze also. Towards the end of their rule in Syria, the Ottoman government succeeded – by execution, arrests, deportation, and disarming, as well as by taxation and conscription – in largely destroying the political and military power of the territorial elements, subduing them for the first time in centuries to a direct central government.

Historical factors once again upset the process of centralization in Syria, initiated by Ibrāhīm Pasha, later renewed by the Turks, and continued intensively under Fayṣal's short rule in Damascus. The French occupied Syria in July 1920 and turned back the clock.

True, they did not permit a military-political recovery of power by territorial elements and crushed the 'Alawi uprisings of 1919 and 1920 and the big Druze rebellion in 1925–26. Nevertheless, in principle, the French fostered the socio-political autonomy of the Druze, the 'Alawis, and, to a certain extent, even of the Bedouin. In the early 1920s, 'Alawi and Druze "states" were established and granted complete autonomy in the administration of their internal affairs and complete independence from Syrian local government, which lasted during almost the entire period of the French Mandate. The Bedouin tribes concentrated in the Jazira region received extensive autonomic authority during this period. The traditional social structures of those territorial elements, which remained entirely untouched in the period of Ottoman modernization, existed almost unchanged in the mandate period: the communal and tribal organization and the patriarchal and feudal way of life of the heterodox and Bedouin communities – all this sustained and strengthened the socio-political seclusion and separation of the regional centers outside the big cities.

The Crystallization of the Urban Oligarchy and the Increasing Polarization among the Social Strata

Parallel to the developments in the mountain and the Jazira regions, processes crucial to the developing system of socio-political relations occurred in the larger Syrian cities and in their rural surroundings. The most important process was the crystallization in the power of the traditional urban leadership, mainly in Damascus and Aleppo, to the extent of creating centers of self-government and socio-political influence. This was accompanied by an economic strengthening of the urban leadership and the impoverishment of the lower classes among the rural and urban population – developments which continued virtually undisturbed during most of the modern period and were actually supported by most of the Turkish governors and the French mandatory authorities.

The Egyptian regime, which initiated modernization in Syria during the 1830s successfully and for the first time, shook the political-military and socio-economic power of the traditional urban leadership: the heads of the great families, the *'ulamā'* (religious scholars), and other notables and feudal lords. Conscription and disarmament damaged the military strength of the armed groups and their chiefs, such as the local Janissaries and the *ashrāf* (people tracing their genealogy to the Prophet Muḥammad) organizations. The secularization of the legal system and the diminution in the authority of the *Sharī'a* (Islamic Law) courts weakened the status of the Muslim religious authorities. The abolition of the *iltizām* in the rural areas, and its replacement by direct government tax collection, greatly reduced the incomes of the notables. Furthermore, the limited role of the traditional urban elite in the new advisory council (*majlis shūrā*) greatly damaged their public prestige. The Egyptian regime apparently tried to replace this elite with a new urban leadership consisting of middle-class representatives, merchants and artisans, both Muslims and non-Muslims. In every town, such representatives were nominated as members of the new councils, assisting the governor with advice in matters of administration, commerce, and law. But the authority of the council members was, nevertheless, meager, and their social or communal origins could not have given them the requisite status or identification in the eyes of the populace during the short-lived Egyptian rule. Complete failure of this initial experiment was inevitable.

The new Ottoman regime also tried, upon its return to Syria, to fill the regional councils with representatives of the middle classes and the non-Muslim communities. But these were quickly removed or neutralized by the heads of the veteran elite, the *a'yān* (notables) and *'ulamā'*, who took over the advisory council in the course of recouping their power. True, the urban elite was not allowed to rebuild its military power, which had been an important source of political strength throughout the long period of the "pashas' rule" – during which armed and violent struggle for power occurred in the city, and the pashas' armies were strong enough only to take one side in the struggle, and not always the winning one. Under the new Ottoman regime, power relations changed radically and the army attained decisive domination over the urban militias. For one thing, these private armed groups were now greatly weakened by conscription and disarmament which continued under the Ottomans; secondly, the new Ottoman army of enlisted men was more reliable, better trained, and strong enough to assert its power in the cities. Armed power and violence, the previous pillars of the urban notables, were neutralized. They now had to gain their power from appointments in the administration, public status, and economic ability; and the new Ottoman regime offered such possibilities in abundance. The public administration, which expanded in the era of modernization, absorbed a number of educated notables and placed them in the provincial and municipal offices and in the judicature. The administration of religious institutions – the *Sharī'a* courts, the *waqf* (religious endowment), the mosques, and religious education – were again left in the hands of the Muslim notables. Moreover, the Ottoman government in the Syrian provinces, which did not possess sufficient authority, needed the indigenous elite for the introduction of unpopular reforms, especially conscription and the personal tax (*farda*). The representatives of this elite, the *a'yān* and *'ulamā'*, were thus allowed to take over the councils established in order to assist the implementation of reforms;

through the councils they received extensive powers in the administration, the fiscal and economic structure, in the judicature, and in the supervision of law and order.[6]

By controlling the councils and other public institutions, the urban notables managed to rebuild and strengthen their status and even to enrich themselves – largely at the expense of the people, whom they excluded from political activity – while widening the socio-economic gap between the masses and the upper class. For example, members of the council did not merely succeed in evading taxation and conscription, but they even usurped the tax farms (*iltizām*) in the neighboring rural areas, collecting sums greatly exceeding the official rates from the peasants. Some of the tax farming notables even forced the peasants to hand over their wheat for a low price, and then sold it at a higher price in the cities. If the peasant refused to obey, the tax farmer (*multazim*) could impose fines, punishments, or even refuse them the seeds needed for sowing in the next season. Because of these exactions, many peasants ended in poverty – which was further aggravated by the fact that Bedouin tribes imposed a protection fee and/or stole their crops; government officials and irregular soldiers collecting taxes took food and fodder for free and sometimes drafted the peasants and their cattle for public works. Some peasants chose to migrate to safer places; many had to borrow money in order to pay their taxes or buy new seeds. Loans carrying a high rate of interest – sometimes up to fifty percent per annum – involved them in heavy debts, sometimes to the brink of bankruptcy. At this stage, the peasants were forced to sell their land rights to a moneylender or a tax farmer (who was often the moneylender himself or his representative) or to one or another of the urban notables.

The Ottoman Land Law of 1858 was indeed intended to stop this process and to secure the rights of the small landowners by registering their lands. In practice, however, this law effected exactly the opposite: many peasants, fearing that this registration might mean paying further taxes or might entail conscription, agreed, or even preferred, to register their land in the name of a local *shaykh* or urban notable. As a result, many peasants became poor tenants or farm workers, while much land property was concentrated in the hands of a small number of urban elite families, who in this way increased their income.

Socio-economic polarization among the classes was not limited to the rural regions, but included the cities. The notables invested income from their farms in commerce, real estate, and enterprises, as well as moneylending. In the course of the nineteenth century, their economic power was thus consolidated to an unprecedented degree and acted as a significant support of their political status. The middle class, on the other hand, was severely hit by a market overflowing with imported European merchandise of high quality and low prices (partly as a result of the low tax custom duties imposed due to the capitulation agreements). Muslim merchants and small traders did not benefit from this flowering commerce with Europe, for it was mainly handled by Christian and Jewish merchants (and Muslims of the upper class). Groups of merchants and artisans could not defend their interests via their guilds, which were also stagnant and disintegrating.

Furthermore, many of these occupational groups, as well as the masses of the employed and the urban proletariat, suffered from conscription and the system of taxation. The drafting of young men for long periods reduced the number of earners in a family and caused impoverishment – since only a few could pay the exemption fee from army service (*badal*). The method of taxation was unjust and not progressive: the main municipal tax was collected on a personal basis and only after many years and popular pressure was it turned into a property tax *(vergi)*. But even then the notables succeeded in evading the payment of their share, either assisted by relatives – members of the *majlis* who conducted the assessment of property for taxation – or by bribing officials. The main burden, thus, fell on the other classes, aggravated existing poverty, and, possibly, contributed to the process of socio-economic polarization between these classes and the elite a further factor – a confidence gap.

The gap between the wealthy elite and the middle and lower classes, both urban and rural, persisted during the mandatory period without serious attempts on the part of the French to reduce it by initiating reforms.

In the cities, for instance, the process of decay in the traditional handicrafts and home industries continued. It was caused by the competition of imported goods or those made in the modern local factories, gradually established in the main by the upper class, as well as by local Christian and French investors. The rate of pay in industry also declined because of competition from Armenian immigrants who arrived by the thousands; working conditions were deplorable and social legislation rudimentary. There was unemployment among the middle class – who abandoned their traditional occupations and looked for jobs in the civil service – and among the unskilled proletariat, continuously reinforced by a host of peasants escaping the grim conditions in their villages.

Indeed, the French Mandate did almost nothing to improve the conditions of the peasantry, which constituted some seventy percent of the population. The French apparently intended to improve conditions and aid the farmers: modern land registration was carried out, the *mushā'* (joint ownership) lands were divided and registered, government land was put up for sale on convenient terms, and even an agricultural credit bank was founded. These reforms, however, hardly helped the small peasant, who could not afford to buy the offered state lands or were unable to fulfill the terms of a credit contract. Only the big landowners and wealthy farmers found a way to buy these lands and utilize the credits to increase the area under cultivation and its profitability.

The rich urban landowners did not confine themselves to agriculture and continued to invest their money in commerce and in the modern industries which developed in Syria towards the end of the mandate – mainly food and textiles. As during the Ottoman period, they invested part of their profits in secondary and university education for their sons and relatives in Syria and abroad. Those later occupied positions in the mandatory Syrian administration, while their parents continued to possess great political and economic power, just as they used to in the Ottoman past.

In summary, the Syrian ruling elite – some one hundred Sunni Muslim families, owners of vast properties and financial assets – continuously controlled the institutions of self-rule in their towns and represented the oligarchy of their cities in the other political institutions established in their country for more than a hundred years prior to Syria's independence. These notables packed the municipal and legal councils, which were established by the Ottoman reform regime in the regional centers during the nineteenth century. They also occupied the majority of seats in the municipal and legislative councils, parliaments, and governments in Syria during the French Mandate. This urban oligarchy utilized their political and public status to increase their assets, and encouraged, to a certain extent, the process of impoverishment of the lower strata, mainly the peasants. They carefully maintained the socio-economic gap by using their powers throughout the greater part of the nineteenth and in the first half of the twentieth century.

Intercommunal Contrasts

Intercommunal and intersectarian polarization was a further process which developed among the Syrian population in the nineteenth century era of modernization and did not cease even in the mandatory period. At the beginning of the 1870s, the wife of the British consul in Damascus described intercommunal relations as follows: "They hate one another. The Sunnites excommunicate the Shiahs and both hate the Druzes; all detest the Ansariyyehs; the Maronites do not love anybody but themselves and are duly abhorred by all; the Greek Orthodox abominate the Greek Catholics and the Latins; all despise the Jews."[7]

The Sunnis continued to hate, loathe, and/or despise both the various heterodox sects and the different non-Muslim communities. Nevertheless, Sunni circles did not hesitate to mobilize heterodox sects to carry out pogroms against the Christian communities. The 'Alawis, Mutawallis, and Druze needed no Sunni encouragement to harm the Christians among them. In some places, mainly the mountains, the Christians fought back: the Armenians in the Taurus, Christians of the Latakia and Anti-Lebanon regions (and, of course, the Maronites of Lebanon). Elsewhere, especially in the cities, grave disputes split the various Christian sects, particularly the Greek Orthodox, Greek Catholics, and Latins. None of these communities ever missed a chance to join the Muslims – Sunni or not – in persecuting the Jews, and often initiated such action themselves. The Jews, for their part, took every opportunity to take revenge on their Christian enemies and sympathized with the Muslims when they attacked Christians.

The axis of intercommunal conflict was naturally the Sunni majority; its relations with the other communities and sects was determined, not only by religious–sectarian motives, but also by other factors, economic, social, and political. These varied from place to place and were largely influenced by the historical developments.

Sunni Muslims and Heterodox Muslims

Relations between the Sunni majority and the heterodox communities were traditionally founded on the religious–sectarian contrast. The Sunnis regarded the Shiites, 'Alawis, Druze, and Ismailis as heretics and agnostics, avoided social contact with them, and strove to subdue, or even annihilate, them. The military power and topographical advantage of these mountain communities greatly hampered these Sunni aims. Of all heterodox communities, the 'Alawis were most exposed to the pressure of their Sunni neighbors because of their comparative weakness. They formed a narrow majority (sixty percent) among the people of the Jabal Ansariyya and were subdivided into various clans and factions, ruled with a heavy hand by their tribal and religious leaders. In addition, they were oppressed by

Sunni feudal overlords, owners of most of the region's lands, and detested and shunned by their Sunni and Christian neighbors for their peculiar manners and rituals, and for their social and cultural backwardness. As a result of all this, the 'Alawis were in constant bloody conflict with the region's other communities, the Sunnis in particular. These communities often exploited the splits and rivalries among the 'Alawis and, with governmental assistance, inflicted heavy losses in men and property on them.

The Druze were an absolute majority in their Jabal, Jabal Druze. They were ruled by a few heads of clans (the region's landowners) and displayed unity and solidarity against exterior threats. Thus, not only did they not suffer from persecution by their Sunni neighbors, but they also actually caused great damage to the latter, particularly in the villages of the Houran. The Druze successfully fought the Bedouin tribes in the Houran, as well as the Kurdish and Circassian cavalry used by the government to police the region. (The latter, being Sunni Muslims, hated the heterodox communities greatly.)

The violent animosity between the Sunni and the heterodox sects did not abate during the modernization period and in certain ways even became exacerbated. The Turks continued to foster intercommunal conflicts and to incite armed Sunni villagers, Bedouin nomads, and urban Kurdish mercenaries against the Mutawallis, 'Alawis, and Druze. Sunni notables did not hesitate to exploit their high position and great authority to harm other communities and to infringe upon their rights. It is true that during the nineteenth century some intercommunal solidarity developed in reaction to Egyptian and Turkish conscription and oppression. But these were sporadic manifestations and did not truly moderate the deep-seated communal hatreds.

The French mandatory regime, like its Ottoman predecessor, did nothing to ease these ancient tensions; indeed, it tried to maintain intersectarian polarization and took certain steps to enhance it: e.g., separating the Jabal Druze and the Jabal Ansariyya from Sunni Syria and granting political autonomy to these regions; jurisdiction in personal matters; the separate administraton of the Druze and 'Alawi *waqf* from the Sunni *waqf;* furthermore, establishing special Druze and 'Alawi educational systems, differing from the other parts of Syria and revealing a French imprint; and, finally, concentrating soldiers of minority communities in special units used to crush Sunni demonstrations and uprisings. Such measures undoubtedly strengthened isolationist tendencies among the Druze and 'Alawis and encouraged their self-confidence. On the other hand, they enraged the Sunni majority and deepened its hatred and suspicion of the minorities.

Muslims and Christians

Relations between the Sunni Muslims (and the heterodox) and the Christian communities during the period under survey bore a more markedly polarized character than that between the Sunnis and the other Muslim sects.

Traditionally, the attitude of Muslims towards non-Muslims – Christians and Jews – has been one of contempt and scorn towards these protected communities. These inferior subjects paid a poll tax, wore special clothes, did not carry arms, and were subjected to other social and political limitations. Muslims occasionally humiliated their Jewish and Christian neighbors, maltreated and inflicted physical injuries on them, exposed them to blackmail, and forcibly converted their children. By the beginning of the nineteenth century, and in particular during the period of modernization, Muslim feelings of scorn and contempt for the Christians turned into a deep and burning hatred; the relations between Muslims and Jews hardly changed. In various places in Syria, a great number of violent outbreaks and pogroms against Christians occurred during most of the nineteenth and the first part of the twentieth century. The outstanding incidents were in Aleppo (1850), Damascus (1860), and in the Armenian regions of Northern Syria (1909). In Damascus, for example, Muslim masses, incited by the *'ulamā'* and reinforced by Druze rioters, attacked the Christian quarter, killed and wounded thousands of men, women, and children, while looting, burning, and destroying churches and houses. They did not attack Jews.

This radical change of the Muslim attitude to the Christians in the nineteenth century was initiated by a number of factors, mainly connected with the reforms forced upon the Syrian population by the Egyptians and Turks. These regimes, each in its own way, granted freedom of worship and equal rights in state institutions to non-Muslim subjects – for the first time in the history of the Muslim world.

The entire Muslim population rebelled against such rules of equality, which appeared gravely injurious to Muslim religion, tradition, and the foundations of the Islamic state. Many Muslims, led by the *'ulamā'*, were shocked at the sight of Christians publicly performing religious rites; they opposed equal rights for non-Muslims in the law courts and in local government and were concerned by the abolition of the poll tax as well as by the possibility of conscripting non-Muslims. Muslim religious-political resistance was further enhanced by socio-economic motives: the Muslim middle class of merchants, artisans, and officials felt seriously deprived at the sight of non-Muslim merchants controlling most of the foreign trade, and by the increasing control of Christian (and Jewish) officials over government offices – in particular, those concerned with fiscal matters. Many Muslim peasants resented the high interest rates they had to pay to non-Muslim money lenders, and the urban masses looked enviously upon the new houses, churches, and monasteries rising in the Christian quarters.

The anti-Christian motives of the urban elite, *'ulamā'* and notables, were mainly of a political-religious nature and largely shaped the scope and character of communal conflict. The Muslim notables feared that the equal status granted to Christians would not only damage the Islamic character of the country, but would also endanger their own positions in government institutions and in the political community of the Ottoman state. Assuming that the new rights accorded to the Christians meant not only equality, but even constituted an advantage over the Muslims, the *'ulamā'* and other local groups feared that the relatively large Christian element, better educated and commanding economic means, would increasingly control the country, assisted by the European powers.

The tendency of Syria's Muslims to identify local Christians with the European powers and consider them a "fifth column" was initiated by Napoleon's invasion of the Holy Land in 1799. It was further enhanced during the Greek uprising in the 1820s and turned into deep suspicion and increasing fear in the course of the nineteenth century – in view of the Russian victories over the Turks, and the aid which Russia and other European states extended to Balkan nations in their revolts against the Ottoman regime.

The Western Powers, Britain and France, though allies of the Ottoman Empire, were not cleared of suspicion, and the local Muslim population was convinced that they were hostile to the Turkish authority in Syria and "in union with the Christians they wished to overset it."[8] The Muslim fear of the European-Christian plot against their country originated in the perception of the cultural, religious, economic, political, and diplomatic relations between European states and organizations and the Christian communities.

Churches and foreign missionary organizations had close ties with, and greatly assisted, the various Christian sects. European commercial companies appointed local Christians as their agents or representatives, and the Western Powers, through their consuls in the region, gave protection to, and interfered on behalf of, the various Christian communities. Indeed, they even used their military power to protect the Syrian Christians: British and French war ships patrolled Syria's coast at times of intercommunal tension, and a French expeditionary force landed in Lebanon during the civil riots of 1860. Worse than that, British and French forces conquered Ottoman territories without provocation: the French occupied Algeria (1830), Tunisia (1881), and Morocco (1907); the British, Cyprus (1878) and Egypt (1882). These operations substantiated Muslim fears of European aggression, assisted by local Christians.

Syria's Christians themselves, by openly relying on the foreign consuls and by their alienation from the Ottoman regime and their Muslim neighbors, greatly nourished these suspicions. The local Christians undoubtedly preferred European to Turkish rule, even after being granted equal rights. Experience had taught them not to trust the intentions of the Ottoman reforms, and they did not believe that they would be allowed to live on equal terms with their Muslim neighbors.

From all this, it can be seen that not only did the Muslims refuse to accept the Christians as equal partners in a new Ottoman society, but the Christians themselves were reluctant to be integrated, though willing to enjoy equal rights. They preferred to be isolated in their communities and quarters and to rely on the protection of the Great Powers. On the other hand, they hastened to use their new rights – such as tolling of church bells, holding of processions, etc. – without taking into consideration the feelings of conservative Muslims, who had not seen such phenomena for ages. Such conduct on the part of the Christians was hardly compatible with that of a minority aware of its limitations and sincerely wishing to reach an understanding with the majority, but rather that of a group which overestimates its importance. This Christian behavior constituted, in fact, an element of provocation, which actually sparked most of the outbreaks of violence and Muslim-Christian hatred in the nineteenth century.

Violence obviously deepened the abyss between Christians and Muslims to an unprecedented degree in the history of Ottoman Syria. A considerable part of the Christians, concluding that it was no longer possible to live in Muslim Syria, emigrated to safer places in the Middle East – such as Egypt and the Sudan – or to places outside that region – England, America, or Australia. This emigration, encouraged by economic prospects abroad, comprised some 330,000 people between 1860 and 1914.[9]

Most of the Christians remaining in Syria continued to isolate themselves from their Muslim neighbors and relied on the Great Powers, Russia, France, and Britain, until the decline of the Ottoman regime.

During the mandate period, this tendency was greatly encouraged by the French, especially among the Catholic communities – a traditional French protectorate – and also among other non-Arab Christians, e.g., Armenians and Assyrians (though weak among the Greek Orthodox and other Christians who were Arab in origin). The communal religious autonomy of the Christian sects, based on the Ottoman *millet,* continued, and even expanded, under the mandate, including religious freedom, jurisdiction in matters of personal status and inheritance, as well as administration of the *waqf* and communal education. These autonomous rights were officially recognized by the Syrian constitution of 1930, which also provided the heads of the Christian communities with an official status and granted the communities representation in official institutions. In fact, Christians enjoyed preferential status in public administration, both through French encouragement and thanks to their high educational level. Apart from the higher educational level through foreign and communal schools, the Christians also benefited from a period of economic flourishing – not without help from the French. All of this contributed to the fostering of communal separatism, while further widening the socio-economic and cultural-political gap between Christians and Muslims in Syria.

TRIALS AND OBSTACLES ON THE WAY TO A POLITICAL COMMUNITY

As we have seen, the socio-political development which Syria underwent in the modern era enhanced intercommunal conflict, widened the gaps between classes, and fostered separatism and isolation of various social groups in semi-independent autonomous centers. These grave developments, which started even before the nineteenth century, constituted an obvious obstacle to the crystallization of the Syrian population as a political community. In addition, modern Syria lacked other important conditions essential to a political society, mainly, a central authority, ideological consensus, and a territorial identity.

For hundreds of years, up to the middle of the twentieth century, Syria lacked any exclusive central authority, which could have served as a focus of identity and loyalty for the mass of the inhabitants and could have imposed its discipline on the majority of the population. It is certainly true that, for generations, the Ottoman sultans consituted a center of religious-political allegiance for the majority of Syria's population, the Sunni Muslims. This center, however, was geographically distant and became a mere abstraction for lack of governmental authority and the inability to maintain internal security. Nearer and more concrete was the family, tribe, or village, which provided security and held their basic loyalty, though, on the other hand, weakening political – if not religious – identification with the sultan. Members of the non-Sunni communities and sects apparently felt no loyalty whatever, whether political or religious, to the Ottoman regime. The only social group which identified itself with the sultan and the empire, in both aspects, were members of the religious and administrative establishment in Syria, being fully integrated in the Ottoman Muslim community.

Ideas of Ottoman–Syrian Patriotism

The aim of the Ottoman modernization movement in the years 1839–1876 (the *Tanẓīmāt*) was to expand the sphere of popular identification with the state, including the members of non-Muslim communities. The *Tanẓīmāt* leaders and the Young Ottomans thought it best to establish a framework for a new political community; the basis of its identity was to be Ottoman supra-communal and not Muslim, and all the sultan's subjects were to participate, without difference of religion. In order to achieve this end, the reform movement strove to foster the sultan's authority in the districts, improve the general standard of living, and grant equal status to the non-Muslims. However, as the political authority of the Sultan gained strength in the Syrian provinces, his spiritual authority declined among the Muslim population because of this secular policy. Turkish linguistic and cultural values could obviously not have any attraction for the Syrian population, the majority of which was Arab. Furthermore, the territorial limits of the Ottoman Empire were too extensive to ensure the identification of population groups living in a traditional way.

The elements of Arabic language and culture and of Syrian territorial identity – which the idea of Ottoman community lacked – were the very basis of a small cultural-ideological circle which originated in Syria in the middle of the nineteenth century. Professing Syrian supra-communal patriotism, this circle was founded by a handful of Beirut Christian intellectuals, mainly Orthodox and Protestant, following the 1860 massacres in Lebanon and Damascus. In contrast with most native Christians, who preferred to continue their insular approach toward the Muslims and rely on foreign aid or emigrate, these few intellectuals looked for a joint life with their neighbors of other communities. They believed that the communal and religious loyalties splitting the population could be replaced by a Syrian secular patriotism based on a common homeland, language, and culture. Christian intellectuals, such as Butrus al-Bustānī, Fāris al-Shidyāq, Khalīl al-Khūrī, Marūn al-Naqqāsh, and others, themselves contributed to the revival of Arabic language and culture. They established an Arabic literary society and theater, wrote articles, and conducted research in the Arabic language. By means of these tools of expression, these intellectuals – Butrus al-Bustānī in particular – initially advanced the concepts of "homeland" (*waṭan*), "love of homeland" (*ḥubb al-waṭan*), and "land *(bilād*) of Syria." They preached the initiation of "a new era for Syria within the limits of the Ottoman Empire."[10] The concept "Syria" was apparently borrowed from Christian or European sources, or possibly from the definitions used by the Byzantines and the Crusaders centuries before. Their notions of secularism and patriotism obviously originated in contemporary European national movements.

The patriotic, cultural Syrian circle and the Ottoman reform movement had some common aspects. Both movements, drawing their ideas from the West, postulated the establishment of a new political community founded on the principles of separating religion from state and of equality for all citizens loyal to the common homeland, the Ottoman Empire. The fact that the Syrian patriotic circle emphasized identification with the Syrian province and the Arabic language caused no conflict between the two movements during the 1860s and 1870s. On the contrary, personal contacts between adherents of the two trends were established, and the Syrian cultural movement even received support from the Ottoman regime. Butrus al-Bustānī and Fāris al-Shidyāq received literary awards from the sultan, and personalities such as Khalīl al-Khūrī and Marūn al-Naqqāsh were appointed officials in the Ottoman administration.

The reforms which the Ottomans implemented in Syria for the realization of their political plans could, directly or indirectly, have assisted the advance of Syrian patriotism. At the beginning of the 1860s, modern government secondary schools (*rüshdiye*) were opened in the Syrian towns, the purpose of which was to encourage patriotic values and "to lessen the mutual ill feelings . . . between the two sects."[11] Other means of communication were also developed in Syria in that period: roads were built, telegraph lines laid, printing presses established, and newspapers published. Other developments concerning the governmental administrative domain had some potential tendencies toward Syrian territorial identity and unity, with Damascus as a center.

For instance, while still under Egyptian rule, geographical Syria (*bilād* [or *barr*] al-Shām) was united as one territorial administrative unit and centrally governed from Damascus, which also was the residence of the central *majlis* (advisory council), supervising the local councils in all Syrian towns. Even under the renewed Ottoman regime, Damascus was, for long periods, the residence of the *sar'askar,* or the *mushīr* – the commander in chief of the Arabistan army, responsible for law and order in the whole of Syria.

Damascus enjoyed priority over the rest of the Syrian district towns in other respects also. It was a prominent Islamic center, the assembly place for annual pilgrimages to Mecca, the location of the Umayyad mosque and famous *madrasas* (Muslim colleges) and the residence of the most notable *'ulamā'*.

Moreover, beginning in the middle of the 1860s, the jurisdiction of the Damascus vilayet was greatly enlarged, and its name changed to the "Vilayet of Syria." Gifted Ottoman rulers, such as Rashīd Pasha and Midḥat Pasha, greatly improved government, internal security, education, and the general infrastructure of the vilayet, seeking to implant a sense of good citizenship in the inhabitants.[12] A special council, subordinated by the governor, was founded in 1867 with representatives of the districts in the vilayet, in order to advise on, and discuss matters of, development. In 1876, four notables were chosen to represent the Syrian Vilayet in the Ottoman parliament at Istanbul.

Simultaneously, the activity of the Syrian patriotic-cultural circle increased and received a political undertone. In 1875 a few young Christians among Bustānī's followers established a small secret society, whose aims were to secure autonomy for Syria in a union with Lebanon and recognition of Arabic as the official language.

These demands appeared in leaflets distributed by the members of the society in various Syrian towns during the rule of Midḥat Pasha (1878–81), including such catch phrases as "sons of Syria," "Syrian devotion," "Arab pride," and "degenerate Turks." According to the reference quoted, the secret society included Druze and Muslims, as well as Christians, had connections with Midḥat Pasha, and their common aim was the independence of Syria based on Egypt's model.[13] At this stage, however, the Ottoman authorities intervened by arresting and deporting two members of the society. Shortly after this, Midḥat Pasha was also deported, and the cooperation between the Ottoman reform movement and the Syrian patriotic circle ceased.

Examining this historical episode, it should be emphasized that, despite all that was said and done by these movements in the course of several decades (beginning in the 1840s, and in particular in the 1860s and 1870s), Syrian territorial patriotism and the feeling of Ottoman identification did not affect the majority of the Syrian population, but was limited to small circles for many more years to come. An experienced traveler and observer visiting Syria at the end of the 1850s described the situation as follows: "Patriotism is unknown .... There is not a man in the country whether Turk or Arab, Mohammedan or Christian who would give a para (penny) to save the Empire from ruin. The patriotism of the Syrian is confined to the four walls of his own house; anything beyond them does not concern him."[14] Even at the beginning of the twentieth century, no change in Syrian patriotism was evident. According to contemporary testimony, that of a Christian Syrian intellectual and senior government official, "the patriotic bond [*irtibāt waṭanī*] is weak and concerns only a few members of the upper class."[15]

Indeed, identification for most of the people, Muslims and Christians, was still concentrated in the family, village or town, and community, in accordance with the traditional social structure, unchanged during the nineteenth century.

Religious zeal and intercommunal enmity were still strong among the majority of the population, regardless of community or religion, due to the deep-rooted sectarian outlook and the general cultural and educational insularism. Traditional Muslim education in the *kuttāb* (traditional school for elementary religious education) and *madrasa* – which included most of the Muslim students – was on a low level and provided Muslim values only. The Christian communal schools, on the other hand, provided the community's youth with a narrowly sectarian Christian education. The new educational systems established after 1860 could not, or were not intended to, teach Syrian patriotism and religious tolerance. The governmental education system remained limited, absorbed mainly Muslim pupils, and had an Ottoman or (in the time of 'Abd al-Hamīd) Ottoman–Muslim orientation. Similarly, the missionary educational system scarcely included Muslim pupils, and fostered an attachment to European cultural values.

Even the extension of the Syrian Vilayet and the increased administrative status of Damascus did not bring the inhabitants of the other Syrian districts any nearer to an identification with the Syrian Vilayet, or to forbearance for their ancient rival, Damascus.

Aleppo, the traditional rival of Damascus, also extended its jurisdiction northwards – including a substantial non-Arab and non-Muslim population – and consistently developed a strong orientation towards Mosul, Baghdad, Adana, and Istanbul, rather than towards Damascus and Beirut. From 1840 this last town itself rapidly became an important commercial and administrative center – the capital of a major vilayet, the residence of European diplomats, and a strong competitor of Damascus for regional seniority. In Lebanon a Maronite Lebanese political community crystallized at that time – under foreign patronage and in isolation from the other Syrian provinces.

Even in central and southern Palestine – in the Jerusalem, Nablus, Hebron, and Gaza districts – signs of a Palestinian, Muslim-Christian identity were developing towards the end of the nineteenth century, which were stronger than any phenomena in the Vilayet of Damascus, with its heterogeneous population. For one thing, the rivalries between Muslims and Christians in Damascus itself were fiercer than in the Jerusalem area. The reasons for these differences must be sought in the fact that Damascus was a city with a larger Muslim majority and a more conservative atmosphere, and in the memories of the 1860 massacre in Damascus, which were still fresh and caused continuous intercommunal tension. Secondly, in Damascus, the Christians were prosperous whereas many Muslims suffered poverty, while in Jerusalem, both Muslims and Christians flourished. Finally, the local Jewish element influenced Muslim–Christian relations differently in the two regions. In Palestine, the Jewish Zionist settlement was an alien political element, strange and threatening, which evoked a feeling of unity and identity with the country (greatly influenced by the Zionist example) on the part of both Christians and Muslims. In Damascus, the Jews were only a small religious minority – the extent of whose integration served to underline Christian estrangement. The Jews even sided with the hostile attitude of the Muslims towards the Christians and at times even tried to nourish it.

During the period under review, there were, as already mentioned, some instances of cooperation and solidarity among the different communities in Syria, Muslim, Christian and Druze, through common resistance to conscription or other oppressive aspects of the Ottoman regime. These were, however, sporadic occurrences, which did not supersede past attitudes and could not change the deeply-rooted prejudices of vast strata in the various communities. According to a report by a British consul in the region, in 1907, "No symptom is noticeable which would tend to support the belief that any cohesion exists between the different classes of people . . . religious differences are still as powerful as ever to effect a cleavage among neighbours and fellow-citizens."[16]

An Ideological Split among the Muslim Elite

At this point it must be stated that in the second half of the nineteenth century, there occurred a process of political change in Syria, not only, as we have seen, among Christian intellectuals, but also among the local Muslim leadership. Among these people, an absolute ideological-political consensus no longer existed toward the end of the nineteenth century.

The entire political and religious Muslim elite obviously rejected the idea of a secular Syrian patriotism and considered it dangerous. Simultaneously, however, the feeling of identification with the sultan and the empire weakened among part of this elite, precisely because of the idea of a secular Ottoman patriotism initiated by the *Tanẓīmāt* leadership.

The secular reform policy of the Sultan 'Abd al-Majīd (1839–61) provoked doubts among traditional Muslim circles in Syria, regarding the right of the sultan (whom they labeled *"al-khā'in,"* the betrayer of Islam) to lead the Muslim world. In these circles, reform appears to have fanned the latent feelings of difference between Arab and Turk and reemphasized the special position of the Arabs in Islam. In some places in Syria, during the sixth and seventh decades of the nineteenth century, hopes of "separation from the Ottoman Empire and the formation of a new Arabian state under the sovereignty of the Shereef of Mecca"[17] were expressed – as was also the aim of independence for *"al-bilād al-Shāmiyya"* (the land of Syria) under the Amir 'Abd al-Qādir, a Damascus notable of Algerian origin.[18]

Later, under the tyrannical rule of Sultan 'Abd al-Ḥamīd, Muslim intellectual leaders of Syrian origin, such as 'Abd al-Raḥmān al-Kawākibī and Rashīd Riḍā, pleaded for the return of the caliphate to the Arabs. However, these expressions of Arab consciousness were weak and sporadic during the entire second half of the nineteenth century and became a major trend only at the beginning of the twentieth century – as a reaction to the secular nationalism of the Young Turks.

The majority of the religious and administrative establishment, the *'ulamā'*, members of the councils and senior officialdom, still regarded themselves as part of the Ottoman Muslim political community and remained loyal to the regime up to its last day. To the extent that political-religious identification with the sultan became weakened during the period of the reformer 'Abd al-Majīd, it recovered under the conservative Sultan 'Abd al-Ḥamīd II, who was a zealous Muslim.

'Abd al-Ḥamīd II interrupted the attempts of the *Tanẓīmāt* leaders and heads of the Young Ottomans to establish a supra-communal Ottoman political community, reemphasized the Muslim nature of the state, and adopted a rigid pan-Islamic policy. Accordingly, 'Abd al-Ḥamīd acted to strengthen the loyalty of the Muslim population and, in particular, its leadership in Syria. *'Ulamā'* and notables of Syrian towns, such as Yūsuf al-Nabhānī and Ḥusayn al-Jisr, won his benevolence, while others were nominated to be his close aides. These were Shaykh Abū al-Hudā, advisor to 'Abd al-Ḥamīd, and Aḥmad 'Izzat Pasha, secretary to the Sultan – both sworn personal rivals of al-Kawākibī and Riḍā, the supporters of an Arab caliphate and among the forefathers of the Arab national movement.

Thus, by the eve of World War I, two political trends competed among the Muslim Syrian elite: Arabism, the manifestations of which were the secret societies, al-Fatāt in particular; and the stronger stream of Ottomanism, which was especially popular with circles close to the government and public administration.

The common characteristics of these two movements were defined in Ernest Dawn's interesting article as follows: "The conflict between Arab nationalists and Ottomanists in pre-1914 Syria was a conflict between rival members of the Arab elite. At the center of each camp were members of the highest stratum of Syrian society, who constituted a majority of the members of each faction . . . . The conflict essentially, then, was of the type that was traditional in Near Eastern society. The new element was the ideological definition of the conflict."[19]

Further common qualities were strong Islamic feelings, on the one hand, and a lack of defined Syrian patriotism on the other. These feelings were particularly strong among members of the establishment, who considered themselves Ottomans and Muslims, residents of Aleppo, Damascus, or Beirut, and not Arab Syrians. For example, the nine representatives elected in 1876 to the Ottoman parliament on behalf of the Syrian Vilayet did not act as one group, whether Syrian, Arab, or whatever, and did not raise any matters concerning Syria in parliament.[20]

Members of the Arab nationalist societies, many of whom were Syrians (mainly Muslims with a Christian minority) considered themselves, above all, Arabs (and Muslims) and demanded autonomy for all Arab countries. Nevertheless, while raising these demands, these Arab nationalists thought of *al-Bilād al-shāmiyya* as a center of the Arab sphere and of Damascus *(al-Shām)* – past capital of an Arab empire – as the future capital of an Arab state.[21]

Progress and Retardation during the Interwar Period

Only after World War I did the feeling of a separate Syrian entity gradually influence members of the Arab national movement in Syria. This was mainly due to the establishment of a separate political-territorial framework in Syria by the Great Powers.

The first and foremost achievement in the formation of this entity was reached during Amir Fayṣal's rule in Syria (1918–1920) with the establishment of independent Syrian Arab government institutions and local political parties. The names given to those bodies indicate the crystallization of a Syrian identity. The governments of Fayṣal were, in chronological order: "The Arab Military Government of Syria," "The Arab–Syrian Government," and the "Kingdom of Syria." The institution which was to serve as a kind of national assembly was called "The National Congress" and also the "Syrian Congress," whereas the parties represented in that institution called themselves "The Independent Pan-Arab Party" (connected with al-Fatāt) and the "United Syrian Party."[22] Fayṣal also acted to attach the minorities to the new Syrian state under the motto: "Religion to God, the homeland to all." He appointed leaders of the Muslim and heterodox communities to the regional administration and allocated seats in the Syrian congress and government to Christians: Yūsuf al-Ḥakīm and Fāris al-Khūrī served as ministers in various governments. Simultaneously, Fayṣal acted toward the Arabization of state institutions and the educational system and founded an academy for the Arabic language in Damascus.

With the abolition of Fayṣal's Syrian Arab Kingdom, an important element for the creation of a political community in Syria was lost, but feelings of Syrian identity did not slacken. On the contrary, they gained considerable support among members of the national movement during the French Mandate. This process was assisted by the formation of a separate political framework with local government institutions – cabinet, parliament, etc., established by the French – and by the concentration of the national movements' struggle on obtaining independence for Syria being partly at the expense of pan-Arab unity.

The National Bloc (*al-Kutla al-waṭaniyya*), which led the struggle against the French, included personalities and groups of varied political background and from different parts of the country: the Istiqlāl headed by Shukrī al-Quwatlī and based on the anti-Turkish al-Fatāt, together with circles of the People's party of 'Abd al-Rahmān al-Shahbandar who, in the past, had cooperated with the Turks. These personalities, as well as Jamīl Mardam – all from Damascus – united with individuals like Ibrāhīm Hanānū and Sa'dallah al-Jābirī of Aleppo, and Hāshim al-Atāsī from Homs. Among the *Kutla* leaders, mainly Sunni Muslims, Orthodox and Protestant Christians were prominent, such as, the brothers Fāris and Fayiz al-Khūrī who held ministerial offices in various Syrian governments, or Edmond Humsi and Edmond Rabbat who joined the national Syrian delegation in the 1936 negotiations with France. The national movement even established close contacts with Druze leaders, such as Sultan al-Aṭrash, and çooperated with him during the 1925 uprising against the French, and also later.

The joint struggle of these personalities and groups against the mandatory rule undoubtedly contributed to the reinforcement of Syrian national consciousness among various circles of the population and among the Muslim and Christian urban intelligentsia in particular. This consciousness, however, was not as crystallized and extensive as in Egypt, or even Lebanon or Iraq, and could not have constituted a sufficient basis for a Syrian political community.

As opposed to developments in Egypt, Iraq, and even in Lebanon, the mandatory regime in Syria greatly damaged the process of establishing a political community. The French interrupted the first Syrian steps towards independence and unity when they put an end to Fayṣal's regime, reduced the areas of the historical Syrian vilayets by annexing vast areas in the Tripoli, Biqā', and Sidon districts in 1920, and by surrendering the Sanjaq of Alexandretta to Turkey in 1938. The mandatory government also weakened the political centrality of Damascus and the territorial unity of the country by reviving, establishing, and even enlarging the interregional gaps, and strengthening the forces of marginal centrifugality. At the beginning of the 1920s, Syria was divided into four "states": Damascus, Aleppo, and the 'Alawi and Druze districts. After some years, Damascus and Aleppo were united in the "state of Syria," but the 'Alawi and Druze "states" continued to exist separately. The Jazira region was also administered separately, whereas Alexandretta enjoyed broad autonomy until annexation by Turkey. Simultaneously, the French foiled tendencies of Syrian national unity and increased inter-communal contrasts by encouraging, for example, polarization in the educational system. In 1938, for instance, only thirty-one percent of the Syrian students, mostly Muslims, attended government schools, as compared to thirty-eight percent who attended private (communal) schools, mainly Christians, and twenty percent in foreign schools, again mainly Christians. The Christian pupils, about one third of the total, received a largely communal or foreign education, compared with the "national" education of the Muslim pupils in towns and with the traditional Islamic education in the rural regions.[23]

Apart from the gap in educational level and the contrasts between various communities, polarization among the classes was also not encountered under the mandate. During the entire mandate period, there was almost no rise in the standard of living, nor change in the ways of life, for the middle and lower classes, least of all for the peasants; while at the same time, the situation of the upper classes, the rich landowners and merchants, improved.

These socio-economic contrasts were not merely due to negligence on the part of the mandatory regime, but resulted from a purposeful upper class policy, by those who controlled the reins of self-rule in Syria.

In summary, the national leadership of mandatory Syria was partly responsible for the retarded crystallization of the Syrian people towards one society and political community. The national parties, as well as the "moderates," centered around personalities and families controlling vast properties and represented narrow class interests. They were mainly interested in sustaining the status quo created during the Ottoman period and refrained from drawing up any long-range plans for progress among the rural and urban masses.

Because of similar reasons, or out of pure negligence, the National Bloc leaders, when in power, also refrained from taking radical measures to change and improve the educational system. Neither did they act to weaken religious zeal and foster intercommunal tolerance. It is indeed true that the national leadership under Fayṣal, and in the mandatory period, placed some Christian personalities in their first ranks and issued guidelines and slogans concerning freedom of conscience and belief, religious tolerance, and patriotic brotherhood; however, all this was limited to written words and did not penetrate the consciousness of the rank and file in the national movement – not to mention the masses.

For example, the liberal policy of Amīr Fayṣal toward the Christians evoked grave complaints from conservative circles among the members of the Syrian congress and beyond. Furthermore, certain clauses of the Syrian constitution (1930), composed under the direction of the *kutla* representatives, mentioned freedom of conscience and religion, as well as equal rights for all citizens (Par. 6, 15, 28), but these were not wholly implemented due to objections by senior officials and Muslim *'ulamā'*. A subcommittee of the Permanent Mandates' Commission, which investigated this matter in 1934, stated,

"The commission regretted to note that the application of the Syrian legislation prescribing equality before the law is still sometimes impeded through the absence of a spirit of tolerance on the part of the autochthonous authorities."[24] Four years later, in 1938, the law of personal status (1936), which expressed the constitutional principle of freedom of conscience and religion, was annulled under pressure from the *'ulamā'*.[25] As in the Ottoman past, the Muslim masses continued to express their objections to intercommunal equality through acts of violence against Christians. During the uprising of 1925, for example, Christians suspected of collaboration with the French were attacked in Damascus, and in Ḥoms the local Christian governor was assassinated by Muslims. In 1936 grave clashes occurred between Muslims and Christians in Aleppo, and in the Jazira such clashes were even more frequent.

Some of these clashes certainly resulted from Christian or French provocation, such as using Armenian troops against Muslim rebels and arming the Christian population of Damascus during the 1925 revolt. Nevertheless, the Syrian national leadership cannot be freed from all blame for these unstable intercommunal relations. The leadership did not use its political status and prestige to guide the masses towards values of patriotic brotherhood, but, instead, stimulated their negative emotions for the purpose of opposing the mandate. Although the national leadership fought for Syria's independence, it did not invest enough thought and action in the formation of Syria's political community, namely, by narrowing the gaps between the various population groups and by directing progress from the limited traditional loyalties towards a feeling of Syrian national identity.

As previously stated, most of the population in mandatory Syria did not identify itself as Syrian Arab. The minority communities – both Muslim and Christian, with the exception of the Christian Orthodox and Protestant intellegentsia – continued to rely on the French Mandatory regime. The rural and tribal masses, and a considerable portion of the urban lower classes, continued to live within the limits of family and regional loyalties and considered themselves Sunni Muslim Arabs – rather than Syrian Arabs.

Even among the more advanced urban members of the national movement, the feeling of a single Syrian entity was not as strong as parallel sentiments in the neighboring Arab countries. Among these circles, regional tendencies and/or the pan-Arab orientation were still strong due to the continuing tradition of the past (Damascus versus Aleppo) or the persisting belief in Arab unity (originating in Syria): the main reason obviously being the lack of a strong Syrian local center or a great national leader, who could have served as a focus of authority, unity and identification – like Zaghlūl and Naḥḥas in Egypt, or even Fayṣal and the monarchy in Baghdad.

The leadership of the Syrian National Bloc consisted of personalities with regional, rather than national, influence (Ibrāhīm Ḥanānū, who had great prestige, died in 1935, and Hāshim al-Atāsī, the other national leader, was old and without political stature). This leadership appeared as a united body as long as the struggle against the French predominated. Following the agreement of 1936, however, the Bloc and its leaders again split on personal-family and regional-local issues, while political differences served as additional causes of separation. The *kutla* leader, Jamīl Mardam, was attacked by some of his rivals for the concessions he made to the French in the 1936 agreement. One such rival was ʻAbd al-Rahmān al-Shahbandar, leader of the 1925 uprising, with pro-Hashemite tendencies; in 1937, together with Munīr al-Ajlānī and Zakī al-Khatīb, he established the Patriotic Front party (later, the Constitutional Bloc), but was harassed by the government; some of his supporters were arrested, and he was murdered in 1940.

Other national leaders, who severely criticized Jamīl Mardam and finally succeeded in removing him from the office of prime minister and from the *kutla* leadership, were Shūkrī al-Quwatlī, former head of the Istiqlāl group, and the Aleppo notable, Saʻdallah al-Jābirī. In 1943, after the resumption of *kutla* activities, al-Quwatlī became leader of the Bloc and president of Syria, whereas al-Jābirī became prime minister. In 1947 Jamīl Mardam, the deposed Damascus leader, resigned from the *kutla* and established the Republican party, and in 1948 young leaders of the Aleppo *kutla* branch rebelled and founded the People's party, with an Iraqi orientation. The remnant of the *kutla* survived under al-Quwatlī's sole leadership (al-Jābirī died in 1947), changed its name to the National party, and opened Syria to Saudi and Egyptian influence.

Syria was at last freed from the French and became an independent republic in 1946. However, though a sovereign state, it had neither a crystallized political community nor a united society. Experiments to establish a Syrian entity failed; and the socio-political development in the course of one hundred years of modernization did not abolish the religious, regional, and social contrasts among the Syrian population.

Yet once the French had gone, a new generation of young Syrian leaders were in a better position to embark upon the appallingly difficult task of achieving national unity and of bringing about socio-political change.

SOCIO–POLITICAL CHANGES SINCE INDEPENDENCE

The seeds of socio-political change which sprouted in Syria following independence had already been planted in the middle of the mandatory period. The conditions for, and the beginnings of, a new urban middle class – i.e., lawyers, clerks, students, public employees, and skilled workers – were created. The basis for a national army, in which the lower and middle classes and a considerable portion of the minority communities served, was also laid. These two social groups, which succeeded in developing beyond the control of the traditional elite, implemented changes in independent Syria via an array of organizations which they founded: modern political parties, headed by the Ba'th, and groups of young officers of lower class and of minority origins. In their own way, these elements strove – in mutual struggle and, sometimes, in cooperation – toward the establishment of a new society as well as a broad and clearly defined political community.

The new Syrian middle class emerged in the mid-1930s – due to the expanding public and governmental administration, the growth of industry, and the broadening of the educational system. The increasing need for clerical staff, lawyers, and other specialists for the mandatory and local administrations, the need for technicians and skilled workers in modern industry – all this led a rising number of urban youngsters from various strata to acquire professional, high school, or academic qualifications, or to specialize in various branches of industry.

Many of these young people were embittered by the social gap and the system of exploitation; they rebelled against their low wages, and some were dismissed in periods of unemployment. They also resented other failures of the old national leadership in various domains. Conspicuous in the sphere of national policy were the abortive agreement of 1936, the loss of Alexandretta in 1938, and the defeat by Israel in 1948. In internal politics, the inability of the political leadership to solve the problem of the Druze, 'Alawi, and Jazira minorities' separatism became evident after independence. In the parliamentary domain, intrigue, corruption, and bribery were rampant.

All this led part of the new middle class to aim at changes in the regime and strive for a more prominent place among the leadership of the state. Others sought to climb the social ladder by virtue of the education which they had acquired and to assume senior positions in government and public administration.

The Emergence of Radical Parties and Young Officers

Social and political agitation manifested themselves in the establishment of a series of new parties organized on Western patterns and proclaiming progressive political or social trends. The most prominent among them were: the Syrian Nationalist party (PPS) and the Syrian Communist party, the organization of which had begun in 1930; the League for National Action was established in 1935; the Arab Resurrection party (Ba'th) was founded in 1940 (and in 1953 merged with the Arab Socialist party). All these shared common principles: national independence, social (or socialist) and economic reform, and secularization of public life. They disagreed, however, on the question of national territorial identity: whereas the League for National Action and the Arab Resurrection party strove toward an all-Arab union, the Syrian Nationalist party and also, to a certain extent, the Communist party preferred the territorial limits of Syria.

None of these parties, however, could realize its aims in the face of conditions in the 1930s and 1940s because of their internal situation and relations among themselves. The ruling system, parliament and government, was in the hands of the national conservatives, who represented the upper class and were opposed to any change. The radical parties, too small and weak, operated separately, were sometimes harassed by the regime, and were not permitted to participate in elections.

The only force that could effect a change in the political and social system was the army officers.[26] Being partly of middle and lower-class origin, most of this group shared the political resentments of the new middle class and were disappointed by the incompetence of the civilian leadership. The Syrian officers' cadre was motivated – apart from their ambition for power – by the need to provide a strong regime and subdue the autonomous and centrifugal tendencies of the minorities and the Bedouin. Some of the officers – with social and class consciousness, or influenced by the radical parties – wanted to reduce the socio-economic gap and advance the deprived strata.

Those motives were, wholly or partly, present in the military coups of 1949 or formed the basis for the resultant regimes, mainly during the long rule of Adīb Shīshaklī (1949–1954). The latter, like Ḥusnī al-Za'īm (the first coup's leader), established a dictatorship and dissolved the parties. By legislation and force, he tried to weaken the communal structure of the minorities and reduce the power of Bedouin chiefs. Above all, for the first time in modern Syrian history, Shīshaklī initiated and executed a large-scale agricultural reform. He limited landownership[27] and increased the taxes on large estates; he requisitioned former state lands usurped by the great landlords and limited the future acquisition of such lands. In addition, state lands were allotted to peasants, and the establishment of agricultural cooperatives encouraged.

In this reform policy, the tyrant Shīshaklī, like Za'īm, was helped by Akram Hourani (Hawrānī), head of the Arab Socialist party and one of the united Ba'th leaders. The Syrian ruler was also connected with Anṭūn Sa'āda, leader of the Syrian Nationalist party (PPS), and was influenced by its ideas and organization. However, Shīshaklī did not publicly identify himself with either of these radical parties. He turned his back on them and, in 1952, established his own party, the Arab Liberation Movement. This act lost him the potential public support of a considerable part of the new middle class; and, since he was also unpopular with the veteran parties (which he outlawed) and with the territorial minorities (the Druze in particular), he remained practically without backing. In 1953 all Syrian parties endorsed a national pact against Shīshaklī. He was ousted in 1954 by a military coup: the chief mediators between the army and the parties being Akram Hourani and other Ba'th leaders.

1954: The Turning Point

The end of the Shīshaklī period marked a turning point in the socio-political development of Syria in many ways; the main effect was connected with a change of the relations of power between the upper and other classes.

The veteran oligarchy recovered their rule over parliament and government in 1954 – via the veteran Peoples' party and National party – but their political and socio-economic power was temporarily reduced by the hostile policies of Shīshaklī. But, foremost, the threat to the status of this ruling elite from the lower classes and radical forces increased. Indeed, the movement for agricultural reform, led by Shīshaklī and Hourani, though it did not achieve real and important results, greatly agitated the peasants and incited them to a vehement struggle against the landowners. Similarly, the vast economic development (in agriculture and industry) at the beginning of the fifties (mainly by private enterprise) enlarged the employed laboring and urban proletarian classes, imbuing them with class consciousness and economic aspirations. In 1954–56 large-scale, tumultuous strikes broke out in various Syrian cities for wage increases, improvement of social conditions, and recognition of the freedom of association.[28]

The deep social unrest of the urban employed and the peasants was exploited by the radical parties, and many joined their ranks. The Ba'th won greater sympathy and support than its two rivals, the Communist party and the Syrian Nationalist party (PPS). In contrast to the latter groups, the Ba'th was very active (through Akram Hourani) among the masses of peasants and among the minorities and did not limit itself to the intelligentsia and the urban employed. Unlike the Syrian nationalists and Communists, the Ba'th believed in a pan-Arab, rather than a pan-Syrian, orientation; in Arab socialism, rather than in communism. Moreover, this party was neutral and not identified with any of the Great Powers. In 1954 the Ba'th emerged as the third largest party in parliament and received sixteen out of 142 seats; the number of its delegates increased in subsequent years, and its public influence grew.

This did not satisfy the Ba'th leaders. Like the leaders of other parties, they realized that parliament and the electorate no longer served as a source of political power, and that the key to power lay in the hands of the military officers. From the beginning of the coups, the party leaders exerted tremendous efforts to gain influence among the middle-ranking and junior officers. Here too, the Ba'th outdistanced its rivals. In 1950 Akram Hourani used his position as Shīshaklī's minister of defense to establish strong contacts with the army cadre and to direct young relatives and followers to the military college at Ḥoms. Among the outstanding officers attached to Hourani and the Ba'th in the mid-fifties were: 'Adnān al-Mālikī, deputy chief of staff in 1955; Muṣṭafā Ḥamdūn, leader of the military coup which unseated Shīshaklī; and 'Abd al-Ḥamīd Sarrāj, chief of intelligence and Syria's strong man during the period of the United Arab Republic. Among the officers close to other radical parties, Ghassān Jadīd, member of the Syrian Nationalist party (and one of the leaders of the coup against Shīshaklī), must be mentioned as well as 'Afīf al-Bizrī, Communist sympathizer and chief of staff in 1957.

The national conservative parties, which in the past had not considered the army a center of power, also tried to gain influence among the senior officers; e.g., Sāmī Ḥinnāwī, leader of the coup against Za'īm, was apparently attached to the People's party and restored it to power in 1949. Similarly, Fayṣal al-Atāsī, a relative of the *kutla* leader Hāshim al-Atāsī, headed the revolt against Shīshaklī; Rasmī al-Qudsī, a relative of Nāẓim al-Qudsī of the People's party, was the candidate of the veteran leadership for the office of chief of staff after Shīshaklī's removal.

With Shīshaklī's removal in 1954, a struggle for power began within the officer corps. The first stage of the contest took place between officers sympathizing with the Syrian Nationalist party (PPS), with Ghassān Jadīd their head, and Ba'th officers, led by 'Adnān al-Mālikī. This Ba'th officer brought about Jadīd's resignation from the army in April 1955; in revenge, al-Mālikī was later murdered by a PPS member. In reaction, the Ba'thists and Communists jointly worked to remove PPS activists from inside and outside the army. Many were arrested and tried; the party was outlawed and almost ceased to function in Syria.

The next stage of the struggle involved the veteran conservative leadership and the radical officers, followers of the Ba'th and Communist parties. The first aim was to fill the position of chief of staff, held by Shawkat Shuqayr, a Druze officer taking a neutral stand. After some abortive attempts, the conservative group succeeded in dismissing this officer and nominating Tawfīq Niẓām al-Dīn, brother of a landowner with substantial holdings and minister in Ṣabrī al-'Asalī's government. The new chief of staff and his civilian supporters now tried to neutralize the radical senior officers and remove them from positions of influence. But these officers, Ba'thists, Communists, and unidentified radicals, held on to their positions.

In the same period, 1955–57, the influence of the radical officers was growing as a result of a strengthening among the civilian radical bloc. Traditional anti-Western sentiments developed in Syria and reached a peak during the signing of the Baghdad Pact; parallel feelings of sympathy for the Eastern bloc appeared and grew among the population, following the arms deal of 1955 and the technological agreement with Russia in 1957. Riding these waves of sentiment were the leaders of the radical bloc in the Syrian parliament (responsible for these agreements). They reorganized a national front consisting of the Ba'th leaders, Khālid al-'Aẓm ("the red millionaire"), the minister of defense, and Khālid Bakdāsh, the Communist leader, elected to parliament in 1954. Under their pressure, the conservative Chief of Staff Tawfīq Niẓām al-Dīn was removed in 1957, and 'Afīf al-Bizrī was nominated – a compromise among the various radical groups.

At this stage, the Ba'th leaders became concerned by the growing influence of their Communist partners in the army, assisted by 'Afīf al-Bizrī, and in civilian government, by the two Khālids, Bakdāsh and al-'Aẓm. The Ba'thists, together with leaders of the veteran national guard, feared a Communist takeover in Syria.

Syria's leaders at that time also saw themselves threatened from outside by the neighboring pro-Western countries: Turkey and Iraq – both signatories of the Baghdad Pact – and Israel. A union with

Egypt, with which Syria had cooperated for years in matters of defense and foreign affairs (and with which negotiations for a federal union had been proceeding for several months), seemed the only solution. Union with a strong and internationally prestigious Egypt could, in the view of the Syrian politicians, reduce external Western pressures and eliminate the Communist threat from within. Moreover, according to the Ba'th leaders, sponsors of the union, such a federation with Egypt would realize one of the party's main principles, Arab unity, and also enhance the socio-political revolution in the Syrian region.

The United Arab Republic Period: Shifting the Balance of Power

The union with Egypt was, indeed, a decisive step in the socio-political change of Syria since the Shīshaklī period, which brought about the decline of the traditional ruling class – the big capital owners and the leaders of veteran parties – and the emergence of radical political elements, together with new social strata.

In the period of the union with Egypt, the conservative capitalist oligarchy suffered deadly blows. The leaders of the veteran national movements were removed from power, their parties were dissolved, and their publications discontinued. Many rightist senior army officers were likewise neutralized or dismissed.

Parallel to the aboliton of their political and public power, the economic strength of the upper classes was also reduced in the wake of a series of socialist reforms: nationalization of the banks and large private enterprises; supervision of imports; a high income tax (up to ninety percent) for the rich. But, the primary method used was land reform. Accordingly, some three million dunams were confiscated from the large landowners, with each of them entitled to retain a maximum of eight hundred dunams of irrigated or three thousand dunams of unirrigated land.

This land reform also greatly injured the chiefs of the nomad tribes in the Jazira and elsewhere, in whose names vast areas belonging to the tribe were registered. Apart from this, the tribal law of March 1956 granting the chiefs autonomous rights (mainly in matters of jurisdiction) was annulled. The tribesmen were compelled to carry identity cards, became subject to conscription, and to all other laws.

Simultaneously, the economic and social status of the middle and lower classes improved. Thousands of peasant families received land; in some villages cooperatives were established and, in others, mainly in the Houran, the *mushā'* system (joint ownership) was abolished.

Medical and educational services were improved and expanded in urban and rural areas, and public works carried out. In the cities, workers benefited from improved social services and low-cost housing, and the low-income groups enjoyed a progressive tax system. The condition of the new middle class also improved in unprecedented fashion. Young intellectuals were absorbed in the expanding educational system and in the new administration. Pro-Nasserist and radical activists occupied senior positions in the government institutions of the Syrian district, replacing members of the veteran parties. Young army officers were promoted to high positions, replacing the rightist or extreme leftist officers, who were removed or pensioned. Among these young army officers, many were from the minority communities – a phenomenon which indicated the growing integration of the minorities in Syria's political life.

Integration of the Minorities in Political Life

A further socio-political change in Syria following independence, and mainly after the Shīshaklī period, concerned, indeed, the weakening of the minorities' autonomous status and sectarian tendencies and their integration in political life.

The newly independent Syria, as previously mentioned, faced difficult minority problems created in the course of generations and crystallized during the French Mandate. The territorial communities – Druze, 'Alawis, and, to a lesser extent, also the Kurds and other minorities in the Jazira – had a tradition of extensive self-government and posed a grave challenge to the new Syrian regime. These minorities, and the various Christian communities, also enjoyed communal-religious and/or educational-cultural autonomy. They tended towards communal isolationism and thus constituted an obstacle on the way to the formation of a crystallized society and a political community.

In spite of this separatism, most of the communities sent representatives to the Syrian parliament, and though granting official recognition to their separatism, this representation also accorded the minorities a share in the power of the state.

One of the first steps taken by the Syrian government after independence was to reduce or abolish communal representation in parliament, as part of the trend towards integration. Between 1947 and 1949, the parliamentary representation of the Christian communities was reduced from nineteen to fourteen delegates, the 'Alawis from seven to four, and the Druze from five to three delegates. The Jewish representation – one delegate – was abolished; and the Kurds,

Turkomans, and Circassians no longer had separate representation, but were included in the Arab Sunni majority. Under Shīshaklī, communal representation was further reduced, and in 1953 a bill completely abolishing the communal system in parliament was passed. Further legislation abolished separate jurisdictional rights in matters of personal status, which the French had granted the 'Alawis and the Druze. These communities, like the Shiites and Ismailis, were now subject to Syrian law, though the Druze were granted some separate rights, similar to those enjoyed by their brethren in Lebanon.[29] Shīshaklī also forbade the existence of communal clubs or associations, as well as regional and racial organizations – all of which were ordered to adopt Arabic names, and hold all proceedings in Arabic (which also became the exclusive language in the state schools).

In addition to the Arabization trend in public life, Shīshaklī also fostered the Islamic character of the country and its public institutions. At least half of the members on every board of directors of every association in Syria had to be Muslims; and in a draft constitution prepared under Shīshaklī's supervision in 1950 Islam was established as the state religion – in contrast to the 1930 mandatory constitution, in which Islam was merely the president's religion.

This series of orders and regulations sparked agitation among the communities and minorities. The various Christian minorities, including the Greek Orthodox, resented and vehemently protested against this infringement of their parliamentary representation and the intention to declare Islam the official religion. As a result, and following pressure by Christian and other members of parliament, the 1950 constitution – and later also the 1953 constitution – declared that Islam is the president's religion. The Armenians, on the other hand, who were also hurt by the Arabization of the educational system, partly preferred to emigrate from Syria, whereas the Kurdish tribes of Jazira (which also had suffered from Shīshaklī's anti-tribal policy) showed signs of restlessness and agitation.

These minorities, obviously the Christian communities, were, however, not strong enough to resist or endanger the central regime. Not so were certain elements among the territorial communities – the Druze and 'Alawis. Not only were they nourished on a tradition of autonomy and isolation, but they also had military power and favorable topographical conditions. Thus, they actually exploited the central government's weakness in the first years of Syrian independence to extract various privileges.

The Syrian authorities, immediately after independence, made great efforts to destroy the military and political strength of the Druze and 'Alawis and to impose the central government's authority. In the summer of 1946, for example, the government sent a large force to Jabal Ansariyya to fight an 'Alawi uprising headed by Sulaymān al-Murshid: the rebels were defeated, al-Murshid surrendered and was later sentenced to death and executed.

In 1952, another uprising followed the dismissal of 'Alawi officers and the assassination of Muḥammad Ḥasan Nāṣir, an 'Alawi colonel, commander of the Syrian air force. Groups of 'Alawis, under the command of Mujīb al-Murshid, son of Sulaymān, attacked government forces, but were quickly subdued, and Mujīb himself was shot and killed.

In contrast, the Syrian government initially feared to challenge the Druze on the battlefield and preferred to weaken the Jabal Druze leaders, the house of Aṭrash, by fostering a rival branch, the *Sha'biyya,* headed by the house of Abū 'Asalī. In spite of the government's support, the *Sha'biyya* were defeated in battle at the end of 1947, and their sole achievement was to obtain from the government two out of three seats in parliament allocated to the Druze in 1949.

The military dictatorships of Za'īm and Shīshaklī could not tolerate further opposition centers in the Jabal Druze and initiated severe countermeasures: Husnī al-Za'īm sent the army to Jabal Druze to enforce conscription and disarm and subdue the inhabitants. The Druze reacted by participating energetically in the coup against Za'īm. Shīshaklī ordered the arrest and dismissal of Druze officers for taking part in an alleged pro-Hashemite plot, as well as the arrest of some of Sultan al-Aṭrash's sons, on charges of conspiracy with foreign elements and activities against the regime. As a result, a big uprising broke out at the beginning of 1954 in Jabal Druze, but was soon crushed by the Syrian army using tanks and aircraft.

The crushing of the Druze revolt in 1954 became a turning point in the balance of power between the central government and the mountain-dwelling heterodox communities. The Damascus government, for the first time, achieved decisive military superiority over these centrifugal forces through the use of sophisticated weapons and a big and well-trained army; the seclusion and political autonomy of these elements was terminated. From then on, the heterodox communities began to take an increasing part in the political life and the struggles for power which took place in the country, both within the parties – mainly the Ba'th – and through the army. They thus became involved in a process which had begun some time before among Christian communities, mainly Orthodox and Protestant, and the Kurdish urban element, namely, the process of integration.

For example, in the 1954 elections, sixteen Christians were elected to parliament for the People's party, the National party, and as independent candidates. Christian personalities, such as Fāris al-Khūrī, Mikhā'īl Ilyān, Michel 'Aflaq, and others, held leading positions on the political scene of the 1950s as party leaders, ministers, and prime ministers. Personalities of Kurdish origin, too – such as Ḥusnī al-Za'īm, Muḥsin al-Barāzī, Sāmī Ḥinnāwī, Fawzī, Silū, and Khālid Baqdāsh – played important roles in Syrian politics of that period.

Similarly, Druze and 'Alawi personalities began to participate in the political life of Syria within the framework of the military groups and the political parties. 'Alawi officers, for instance, commanded the Syrian air force: Muḥammad Ḥasan Nāṣir in 1950, and Azīz 'Abd al-Karīm in 1952. The Druze officers, Amīn Abū 'Assāf and Fadl Allāh Abū Manṣūr, were actively involved in the coups against Za'īm, Ḥinnāwī and Shīshaklī.

Following the latter's removal, the Druze leaders, Ḥasan al-Aṭrash (of the Constitutional Bloc) and Manṣūr al-Aṭrash (of the Ba'th) were elected to the Syrian parliament; Ḥasan even served as minister of agriculture in 1954 and as secretary of state in 1955. In 1954 another member of the al-Aṭrash family, Zayd, was nominated as general inspector of police.

It must, however, be mentioned that a considerable number of these politicians and officers, especially the Druze and 'Alawis, still possessed strong communal solidarity and a close attachment to their communities. They tended to hire members of their communities as assistants and preferred to nominate such individuals for offices under their supervision: Ḥusnī al-Za'īm, for example, nominated Muḥsin al-Barāzī his closest aide, and placed garrisons under the command of Kurdish officers in the Syrian towns.[30] Some even gave preference to communal interests when they were at odds with those of the state. Druze officers rebelled against Za'īm and Shīshaklī when they tried to impose the central authority in Jabal Druze. The communities themselves, on the other hand, had strong sentiments of identification with their representatives in the army and the government; when the latter were hurt, the communities revolted. Such cases occurred in 1952 when 'Alawi officers were dismissed and Ḥasan Nāṣir assassinated; and, similarly, when Ḥasan and Zayd al-Aṭrash were accused of treason in 1957.

Other factors which still prevented complete integration of the minorities in political and social life originated in the isolated socio-communal structure of the communities, in a suspicious attitude on the part of the central authorities, and in the tense intercommunal relations. Thus, for example, offensive incidents by zealous Muslims against Christian religious institutions were common during the fifties,[31] and from time to time, administrative measures were taken by the government against Druzes, 'Alawis, and particularly against the Kurdish population in the Jazira, who showed no signs of integration.

Nevertheless, the accelerated pace of modernization and secularization in the way of life; the growth of communications media; the fragmentation of party activities; and the expansion of the state educational system – all contributed to bringing people of different communal origin, mainly the young, closer to each other and to planting the seeds of a common identity. In addition, as previously mentioned, the socio-economic changes in Syria during the 1950s shook the rigid socio-communal structure and weakened the status and influence enjoyed by heads of the communities and the big and wealthy families.

The reforms of the fifties, especially those carried out during the period of the United Arab Republic, improved the conditions of the lower classes among the minorities and may even have aroused their class consciousness – attaching them to the overall process of socio-economic change which the Syrian population experienced. Above all, the ever-increasing affiliation of the minority communities to the radical parties, especially to the Ba'th, and the growth in the number of conscripts from these communities, mainly 'Alawis and Druze, potentially increased the share and influence of young people from minority communities in the important socio-political developments, which Syria experienced in the sixties.

POLITICAL AND SOCIAL DEVELOPMENTS DURING THE 1960S

When the union with Egypt ended in September 1961, the foundations for the socio-political developments during the following decades were already laid. The balance of power between the ruling traditional stratum and the radical elements drastically shifted towards the latter. The way was paved for the emergence of the middle and lower strata and for the establishment of a new political elite, consisting of army officers and young politicians of rural origin; whereas the power base of the former elite – men of property and veteran politicians from Damascus and Aleppo – was almost irrevocably shattered.

This veteran elite indeed tried to turn back the clock at the beginning of the sixties and participated in the coup which dismantled the union with Egypt. Supported by moderate political and economic circles in the army and beyond, it returned for a while to rule over parliament, government, and the related institutions. Representatives of the capitalist-conservative group reoccupied most of the parliamentary seats: The Peoples' party, twenty-two percent; the National party, fourteen percent; Muslim Brotherhood, independent, and tribal representatives, forty-two percent. In the government headed by Ma'mūn al-Kuzbarī, the conservative bloc also commanded the majority, and it hurried to annul the nationalization of the banks and to reestablish private enterprise damaged during the time of the union. It also slowed down agrarian reform and amended the reform law of 1958 in favor of the big landowners.

However, the new Syrian regime could not go too far in reestablishing the former political, economic, and social system. The conservative bloc was not well organized or united and lacked broad public support. It particularly lacked army backing – which had brought it to power in the first place. The senior officers who controlled the army consisted of moderate rightist elements, but had to consider pressures from the radical cadres, which grew and had been strengthened during the United Arab Republic period.

Thus, some six months after the emergence of the new regime, an agreement was reached at the general officers' convention in Ḥoms (April 1962), following which a civilian moderate leftist government headed by Bashīr al-'Azma was established; it reenacted most of the reforms discontinued by the short-lived rightist regime.

However, the new civilian regime was weak and unstable and proved unable to withstand the pressures exerted upon it in matters of internal and foreign policy, particularly with regard to relations with Egypt. These pressures came from the extreme right – the bourgeoisie and the Muslim Brotherhood – as well as from the extreme left – the Communists and certain Ba'th circles; all this, apart from Nasserist pressures and Egyptian subversion.

The Ba'th Regime: Social and Economic Reforms

The initiative for the establishment of a strong, stable regime again came from the army. The radical elements among the officers united under Ziyād al-Ḥarīrī and on 8 March 1963 carried out a military coup d'état, which established the Ba'th, or neo-Ba'th, regime of Syria. Indeed, among the group of officers who carried out the coup, the Ba'thist, or pro-Ba'thist, officers constituted the most united and dynamic body. This group probably initiated the coup – encouraged by the Ba'thist coup in Iraq in February 1963 – and was supported by the efficient apparatus of the party in seizing power in the army and state. Shortly afterwards, the Ba'th officers dispensed with their principal partners: Ziyād al-Ḥarīrī went abroad and was not allowed to return, and his supporters were eliminated; the pro-Nasserist officers were also removed after an abortive counter-coup in July 1963.

The basis for the Ba'th regime in Syria was thus laid. Ba'th officers completely controlled the National Council of the Revolutionary Command – the body with the highest authority – as well as the government, in which Ba'th representatives held all key positions.

The Ba'th leaders in 1963 were not the founders and veterans who had steered Syria toward union with Egypt in 1958. In the main, they were relatively young and new party members, with a social origin different from that of the veterans and addicted to a different ideology.

The Arab Socialist Resurrection party, which was originally established at the end of 1953, consisted of members with a heterogeneous social background, ecological origin, and communal affiliation. On the other hand, its members were drawn from the new middle class, the intelligentsia, and the young bourgeoisie: most came from the big cities, especially Damascus; in part they were Sunni Muslims and, in part, Christian Orthodox, Protestant, and others. By and large they hailed from the Resurrection party of Michel 'Aflaq and Ṣalāh al-Dīn al-Bīṭār. On the other hand, the United party absorbed Sunni peasants and soldiers of the Syrian lowlands, originally members of Akram Hourani's Arab Socialist party, as well as 'Alawi, Druze, and Ismaili soldiers who had joined the party during the fifties.

Ba'th membership, drawn from people of village and provincial origin, increased during the fifties, not exclusively on account of the party's socialist leanings, but also because of efficient organization in areas outside the big cities. In spite of the growing number of Ba'th members from the lower strata, the party was mainly run by members of the new urban middle class, pioneers in the struggle against the traditional ruling elite. But the Ba'th activists among the urban intelligentsia wore out in the political struggle of 1954–58 and lost their power during the period of the union with Egypt, whereas the rural communal elements attached to the party gained strength through the central focus of power in the state – the army. Young people from the provinces and from the minorities were drawn to the army in increasing numbers, hoping to improve their social and economic status. Some of these young men were sent to officers' courses or promoted by senior Ba'th officers who were seeking to strengthen their influence by increasing the number of their followers – members of their community or party – in the officers' cadre. These new and young officers, many of them 'Alawis or Druze, quickly rose in the military hierarchy, while the veteran officers' cadre, mostly Sunni Muslims, was shattered following the military coups of 1949–54, the struggle for power in the army during 1954–58, and the big purges in the officers' cadre during the union with Egypt and in 1961–62.[32]

Struggle for Power among the New Rulers

Those young officers of provincial and minority origin were the backbone of the March 1963 coup. They established a new regime in the name of the Ba'th, since most of them were party members or sympathizers and considered themselves bound by its mission – though in many ways they deviated from the original course of the Ba'th. They used the party and its veteran leaders to legitimize their regime but did not allow any real power to the veteran leadership. In short, they sought to use the party apparatus to strengthen their hold on the public and take over the party leadership. At the end of 1964, they completely excluded the veteran leadership from the political life of Syria: Ṣalāḥ al-Bīṭār was removed, Michel 'Aflaq went into exile voluntarily, while Amīn al-Ḥāfiẓ, leader of the young officers, established himself as ruler of Syria.

But then, a fierce struggle took place in the top ranks of the new rulers. This struggle has continued up to the present, with climaxes in February 1966 and November 1970 taking place between communal groups, personalities, as well as military and civilian factions.

Thus, for example, in 1965 there was a split among the new political elite – between Amīn al-Ḥāfiẓ, the strong man, and Ṣalāḥ Jadīd, the chief of staff and former ally of al-Ḥāfiz in their joint struggle against the veteran moderate civilian leadership. Ṣalāḥ Jadīd (an 'Alawi) surrounded himself with officers of 'Alawi and Druze origin and strove to seize power. Al-Ḥafīẓ, a Sunni Muslim, forced to defend himself, relied upon his former rivals, members of the moderate civilian leadership, who were also mostly Sunni Muslims. The Jadīd faction, however, controlled the centers of power in the army, air force, armored corps, and commandos. In February 1966 they seized power and unseated their rivals by means of a coup d'état.

Following the coup, the temporary and unprecedented cooperation between 'Alawi and Druze officers was terminated. The latter, led by Salīm Ḥāṭūm, chief of the commando units, suspected that they had not received a due share of power and tried to mobilize the support of moderate elements in the army and party. The 'Alawi officers' cadre, however, led by Ṣalāḥ Jadīd and Ḥāfiẓ al-Asad, commander of the air force, enjoyed a clear numerical and tactical superiority in the army command and the party leadership. They overcame the Druze faction and removed it from key positions. Druze officers, headed by General Fahad al-Shā'ir, were dismissed, and Salīm Ḥāṭūm, who had escaped to Jordan, was executed upon his return to Syria in 1967; while Mansūr al-Aṭrash, member of the veteran leadership of the Ba'th, was detained.

Further dismissals and purges carried out among the regime's top ranks were also of a communal nature. For example, three members of the Jundī family, of Ismaili origin and controlling sensitive key positions, were discharged: 'Abd al-Karīm, chief of intelligence; Sāmī, minister of information and, later, ambassador in Paris; and Khālid, chairman of the workers' union and commander of the workers' armed militia. Following the Six Day War, a Sunni faction from Houran was also dismissed for their reservations concerning the strengthening of the 'Alawi element in the government and for criticizing the regime's failures during the war. Among the members were Muḥammad Zu'bī, minister of information, and Aḥmad al-Suwaydānī, chief of staff.

However, communal affiliation was not the only, nor even the foremost, factor in the struggle for power among the Syrian top ranks in the 1960s. Other factors of equal weight at times overcame communal loyalty, e.g., personal and factional interests, one manifestation of which was the continuous struggle for power between Ṣalāḥ Jadīd and Ḥāfiẓ al-Asad, heads of the ruling 'Alawi faction. This contest, which began behind the scenes in 1966, erupted in September 1969 and was concluded with Asad's victory in November 1970. It also emphasized a further central dimension of the conflicts among the ruling elite, which acted parallel to the personal or factional factor: namely, the continuous struggle between the military and the civilian leadership of the Ba'th.

At one stage of this struggle, the two Syrian 'Alawi leaders found themselves on opposing sides: after leaving the army, Jadīd became the party's boss, whereas al-Asad, minister of defense and commander of the air force, continued to control the army. Once again the army defeated the party in the struggle for authority.

The rivalry between the military and the civilian leadership, which started with the March 1963 coup, also had a political aspect apart from the personal or communal background. The sides frequently disagreed on foreign policy and security issues, e.g., relations with

Egypt, the Palestine problem, the struggle against Israel; or on economic and interior affairs, such as relations with leftist elements outside the Ba'th, the scope of socialist reforms, and the priority of big development enterprises.

Nevertheless, the two branches of the new Syrian elite agreed on central principles of Syria's socio-economic and national policies, sometimes joining forces to carry them out.

Socio-Economic Reforms

The central principle of the regime in socio-economic matters was expressed in the temporary constitution of 1964, in which Syria was declared a "socialist popular democratic state," for which a socialist economy was officially adopted. This policy was essentially a continuation of the socialist reforms carried out in the U.A.R. period and carried on the revolution which had started at the end of the fifties. The implications of this policy were, *inter alia,* state-owned means of production and social services, limitation of private ownership, securing proper social conditions for the workers, and encouragement of cooperatives.

In the domains of industry, commerce, services, and finance, the Ba'th regime completed state ownership and control over the main basic enterprises. Hundreds of big plants, export and import companies, banks and insurance companies, and the network of wholesale commerce were nationalized. On the other hand, medium and small plants, and companies and shops were allowed to operate privately with the framework of the regime's pragmatic tendency to refrain from total violation of private enterprise, which in the past had always been the driving force in Syrian economy. Thus, even enterprises which had been nationalized in the U.A.R. period were now returned to their original owners, compensation was paid, and measures undertaken to encourage small and medium-scale private capital investment and the establishment of joint private and state enterprises.

Public and nationalized industrial plants – which in 1965 comprised seventy-five percent of all capital invested in industry – were given a board of directors with four representatives of the workers and one for each of the following institutions: the trade unions, the Ba'th, and the government. Forty percent of each plant's profits was distributed among the workers (twenty-five percent in cash, ten percent for housing, and five percent for social services) and the rest equally divided between the plant – for its development – and the state – for the development of national industry. Consequently, working conditions and social benefits continuously improved and included compulsory vacations with full pay, social and medical insurance, etc. Simultaneously, efforts were made to increase worker output by, *inter alia,* linking wages to productivity.

The big socio-economic reforms of the Ba'th were not confined to the cities and the urban workers, but were primarily directed to the rural regions and peasant masses, who form some seventy percent of the population. Agrarian reform was obviously the major event. It enlarged and completed the reforms carried out in the U.A.R. period, designed to limit private landownership and distribute the requisitioned surplus among the peasants and tenants. The new law of agrarian reform, published in June 1963, was more extensive than that of 1958 under the U.A.R. It limited ownership of land from 150 to five hundred dunams of irrigated, or eight hundred to two thousand dunams of unirrigated, land (according to the rainfall in the regions) as against eight hundred dunams of irrigated, and three thousand dunams of unirrigated, land during the U.A.R. period. The law also limited the quota of land which could be given to a landowner's spouse and sons. On the other hand, the reform law of 1963 – similar to that of 1958 – granted every farmer eighty dunams of irrigated, or three hundred dunams of unirrigated, land in exchange for payment of one quarter of the land's value over twenty years. The payments were allocated to the regional cooperation fund (during the U.A.R. period, they went to the state treasury) in order to finance agricultural development and establish social institutions for the members of the cooperatives. The establishment of such cooperatives was, in fact, another major aim of the reform. According to the cooperatives' law, every cooperative would receive fifteen to thirty thousand dunams of irrigated, or sixty to eighty thousand dunams of unirrigated, land and would be equipped with modern machinery and tools.

Following the agricultural reform laws of 1958 and 1963, more than 12.5 million dunams of land (9.6 million dunams of unirrigated, 2.3 million dunams of uncultivated, and the remainder irrigated land) were requisitioned.[34] In the course of those years, four million dunams (mainly unirrigated land) were divided among landless peasants. Already in 1964 some one hundred thousand peasants received lands (as compared to half this number during the entire U.A.R. period). These figures increased over the years and ultimately comprised a total of 750,000 people, one quarter of Syria's farmers.

The condition of peasant tenants was also improved through legislation which protected their rights and increased their share of the crop compared to that of the landowners (the latter's share dropped from thirty-three percent of the yield in the U.A.R. period to twenty-five percent).

Finally, the number of agricultural cooperatives in Syria grew and reached 935 at the beginning of 1968; 520 in areas outside the reform.[35] These cooperatives, which were established in fourteen percent of Syria's villages by about seven hundred peasant organizations, received extensive support from the regime and the party in everything connected with improvement of cultivation, marketing, and administration.

The Ba'th Regime: A New Political Center

The radical and extensive reforms, which have already been carried out for some fifteen years, are undoubtedly leading Syria toward a socio-political revolution – for the first time in its modern history. Agrarian reforms and other measures destroyed the economic base of the traditional elite, landowners, big merchants, and the like, and reversed their social status. The political power of this class was shattered completely as a result of the parties' dissolution (with the exception of the Ba'th party) and the arrest or deportation of its veteran leadership. As a ruling class and a political elite, they have ceased to exist.

A new elite has developed, consisting of army officers and young politicians, mainly from provincial towns and villages and partly of 'Alawi origin. In addition, the emergence of vast strata of the population, peasants, laborers, employees, and intelligentsia, has been ensured. Based on these strata, a new society, directed by the new political elite and combined within the Syrian entity, is being continuously established.

The basic conditions for the creation of such a society already existed after the end of the French Mandate and Syria's political unification. However, to overcome the immense obstacles on the way to fusing a heterogeneous population into one political community, Syria needed a long rule by a strong and stable regime with a consistent policy. This, indeed, is the crux of the problem.

Since 1945/46 and up to the March 1963 coup, Syria enjoyed only two short periods of stability: the Shīshaklī regime and the U.A.R. period. During these periods important steps towards founding a new Syrian society were taken, but this process was disturbed and retarded in the intermediate, unstable periods. However, for ten consecutive years since 1963 (and for the first time since its independence), Syria has been ruled by the Ba'th (or neo-Ba'th) party which, in spite of the tussle at the top, proved itself to be stable, powerful, and, to a certain extent, consistent. From the beginning, this regime has systematically acted to enhance the crystallization of the Syrian community, while utilizing the achievements of the former regimes in various spheres.

As previously mentioned, in the sphere of governmental relations, Shīshaklī was the first Syrian ruler to succeed in breaking the centrifugal centers of power in the mountain and desert fringes, and in establishing a strong central regime at Damascus (Aleppo was also reduced to secondary significance). Nevertheless, this ruler was unable to establish a conspicuous political center which could impose complete authority over the population or gain its obedience and loyalty; all this, despite the fact that Shīshaklī ruled through a military dictatorship, dispersed the parties, and established an exclusive ruling party. The U.A.R. regime's failure was similar, as were the measures it undertook to centralize its rule. Both excited resistance among broad circles of the population and army and finally collapsed. The present regime, however, has succeeded in achieving considerable authority and control among the population – even surviving heavy defeats, such as that of June 1967. The regime undoubtedly utilizes previous achievements, in particular those of the U.A.R. period, in organizing centralized rule. The army, the intelligence services, and the police are certainly used to neutralize opposition elements. At the same time, the present Syrian regime derives power from other sources. One important source of the regime's authority and strength is its attachment to the Ba'th, from which it derives ideological nourishment for its policies, legitimization for its actions, and the apparatus to organize the supporting masses.

The Ba'th party apparatus covers the entire country, down to small and faraway villages, with many thousands of members organized in a precise and detailed hierarchy. A considerable part of the party's activists or, as they are defined, "progressive elements who believe in socialism," have been nominated to senior posts in governmental and municipal administration;[36] others received nominations and were asked to join in a "popular supervision" of the public administration because of the "importance of the administrative system at the present stage of the revolution."[37]

The Ba'th also runs the trade unions, such as the workers' and peasants' unions, and various public organizations such as the students' and womens' organizations, through which it controls and influences thousands of members and their relatives. Moreover, some of these institutions have been established especially as "frontline organizations" in order to mobilize extensive public support for the regime. Other organizations, set up by the party to assist in controlling the masses, are of a military or semimilitary nature, such as the national guard, the armed workers' militia, the armed peasants' militia, and the youth battalions. (At the beginning of 1967 these organizations were placed under the Ministry of Defense, for fear of their adopting a stand opposing the military faction.)

It is to be assumed, however, that the regime does not merely rely on the party members' discipline and on the people's obedience to the police and army, but also on a certain amount of loyalty and identification on the part of certain circles among the Syrian population.

Undoubtedly, among the masses of the employed, workers and peasants in particular, there is sympathy and loyalty to the regime which has steadily improved their conditions, increased their income, and given them social security. This is true to some extent also of the intelligentsia and the urban proletariat, which benefited economically from the regime and partly identifies itself with its social and foreign policies – whether leftists or nationalists. The regime has tried to foster the sympathies of those groups, firstly, by collaborating with progressive political elements which were not part of the Ba'th. Personalities, for instance, who were known for their attachment or sympathy for the Communist party, the Hourani faction, and certain Nasserist groups were invited to serve in various Syrian governments (although of course they had to content themselves with portfolios of lesser importance). Secondly, the Ba'th regime consistently adopted an extremist and aggressive anti-Western and anti-Israel foreign policy, in response to certain emotions felt by many Syrians and to prove its attachment to the cause of Arab nationalism. Among the most conspicuous expressions of this extremist foreign policy were, on the anti-Western front, the conflict with the Iraqi (British) Petroleum Company, the attack on the Tapline, and the fostering of relations with the USSR; and, on the Israeli front, attempts to divert the Jordan, support of Fataḥ (*al-Fatḥ*), and the later establishment of *al-Ṣā'iqa*, which inflamed the border with Israel and provided the spark which ignited the June 1967 War. The Ba'th regime even succeeded in using the June defeat to strengthen the masses' solidarity and increase its general control. In all Syrian villages, Homeland Defense committees (*lijān al-difā' 'an al-waṭan*) were established after the war: they consisted of representatives of the party, police, popular army, and other organizations, aimed at uniting and organizing the people in the "crucial struggle against imperialism and Zionism."[38]

National Education

The Ba'th regime did not content itself with taking such measures to win the people's sympathy and identification. To achieve the more important objective of crystallizing a new Syrian society, the regime used the expanding national (and party) communications network extensively: radio, television, press, and the state educational system.[39] In this sphere, the present regime profited greatly from the investments and achievements since Syria's independence.

The national education system has expanded vastly since the end of the mandate. Whereas the number of schools in Syria during the mandate doubled between 1925 and 1945 (from 366 to 658) it increased tenfold between 1945 and 1964. The total has reached 3804, i.e., 3146 schools have been added.[40] Naturally, the increase in the number of pupils was commensurate. The 1950 laws of free and compulsory education now include most of Syria's male children born after 1956.[41] Secondary education has also been expanded impressively: between 1955 and 1964, twelve thousand pupils were graduated from secondary schools, as compared with three thousand in the entire mandate period.[42]

Together with the great expansion of the educational system, there was a steep decrease in the number of foreign and private (communal) schools from forty percent to nineteen percent of all schools in 1951, following the republic's educational policy, in particular Shīshaklī's. A further decrease occurred during the 1950s and 1960s, particularly under the U.A.R.,[43] and the Ba'th. A law of September 1967 ruled that the management of private schools should be conducted by officials of the Syrian ministry of education, that all teachers not having Syrian citizenship would be dismissed, and that all accept the national curriculum in full. These regulations affected more than six hundred private schools – elementary, preparatory, and secondary – with some 150,000 pupils. Some five hundred obeyed the regulations: private communal schools of Armenians, Greek Orthodox, Protestants, and Muslims. Some 120 more schools of Catholic communities, which did not abide by the regulations, were requisitioned by the regime.[44]

The national curriculum in Syria obviously underwent decisive changes since the establishment of the republic. The heritage of the French Mandate – French language and culture – has been uprooted, and the values of Arabism – language, culture, and history – have been developed and emphasized.[45]

The network of private communal schools was forced to accept this national teaching plan during the Shīshaklī period, and again in the U.A.R. interval, though still more drastically under the Ba'th regime. For example, according to the September 1967 regulations, the private communal schools are permitted to teach, besides the official curriculum, only one foreign language four hours weekly, and the language of the religious rite, two hours weekly. The textbooks, including those dealing with religious matters, have to receive preliminary authorization from the ministry of education.

According to Syria's minister of education, Sulaymān al-Khīsh, the textbooks "must not reflect communalism in those schools which used to teach communal topics that no longer agree with the thought patterns of our generation."[46] According to the minister, the aim of the private school reform in September 1967 is, moreover, "to impose a teaching method which will guarantee conceptual coordination among the citizens in order to achieve national unity . . . as they advance step by step towards the end of the revolution and towards . . . a free, united, and socialist society."[47]

This leads us to consider the image and nature of the society and political community which the Ba'th regime has sought to establish in Syria since 1963. What is its social structure, ideological basis, and national territorial identity? In what does it differ from the image of society under previous regimes? And to what extent did the Ba'th regime succeed in realizing this historical mission?

An Arab Syrian Socialist and Secular Society?

A partial answer to the question, which type of society the Ba'th regime wishes to establish, is to be found in the above declaration of the Syrian minister of education: "a free, united, and socialist society." This definition is undoubtedly an application of the three basic principles of the Ba'th: unity, liberty, and socialism.

Indeed, according to the Ba'th party's conception, the society to be established will consist of the masses of workers, peasants, and intelligentsia. Excluding the ruling feudal and capitalistic strata, it will be free of nepotic, communal, religious, class, and regional contradictions: it will be based on a socialist regime which, unlike Western socialism or communism, is an Arab socialism deriving from Arab nationalism. It seems that the Ba'th regime adopted this concept as a whole with varying emphasis and several deviations, originating in the political reality based on the social origin of the ruling elite and influences from outside the party.[48]

Unlike the former Ba'th, which leaned upon the intelligentsia and on the new urban middle class, the neo-Ba'th prefers the working class, in particular the peasants, to which most of the regime's heads belong. Secondly, as opposed to the Ba'th, which interpreted socialism in terms of "social justice," "etatism," and "Arab nationalism," with a "petit bourgeois" character (similar to the Shīshaklī regime), the neo-Ba'th regards socialism in scientific Marxist terms of the "working-class struggle" and the "people's ownership of the means of production." The reason for such an attitude is also to be found in the social origin of the regime's leaders and in the influence of a Marxist group; their attitude is encouraged by the Soviet example and is supported by the Communists.

The Attitude to Communalism

Another difference between the veteran Ba'th and the present Ba'th regime is connected with the application of the principle of the society's liberation from communal and religious disunion. All theoretically agreed that communalism should be abolished. As mentioned above, the various Syrian regimes since the end of the mandate even acted vigorously to realize this aim, the most prominent to do so being the Shīshaklī regime. The Ba'th party, as part of the coalition, then supported this policy. However, whereas in the past the policy of abolishing communalism injured the minority communities and did not commit the Sunni Muslim majority, under the Ba'th regime of the 1960s, both the majority and minority communities were affected, while the 'Alawi community profited.

Theoretically, the 'Alawi members of the political elite seek to conceal their communal origin and merge as equals in a Syrian Arab political community. Outwardly, they appear as Syrian Arabs and not as 'Alawis: they share with the other Syrians, Sunnis, Druze, and Christians, the administration of the state, army, and party institutions. The leaders of these are mainly Sunni: the president of the state (until 1971), most members of the cabinet, the chief of staff and high ranking officers, the secretary general of the party, etc. However, the 'Alawis continue to hold the most important positions in the army and government. 'Alawi officers command the elite units: the air force, armored corps, the commandos. Similarly, the party apparatus remains at this writing under the control of Ṣalāḥ Jadīd, and key positions in the government – the defense, interior, foreign, and agriculture portfolios – were held by 'Alawi ministers.

An Attempt at De-Islamization

The principle of the abolition of communalism is attached to, and combined with, a broader conception of secularity as a necessary basis for the new society. Here, too, the Ba'th regime had an approach different from that of the veteran Ba'th party. In theory, the party professed secularity but, nonetheless, regarded Islam as a central element of national and cultural identity. It did not object, for instance, to a paragraph in the Syrian constitution of 1950 and 1953 which stated that the religion of the president should be Islam. This paragraph, missing from the constitution during the U.A.R. period, reappeared in the temporary Ba'th constitution of 1964. Only since May 1969, under the neo-Ba'th regime, was this paragraph completely omitted and a vague statement left: "Islamic jurisprudence is a main source of legislation." A further difference between the 1969 constitution and those of 1950, 1953, and 1964 is the oath taken by the president of the republic and members of the People's Council (or National Council according to the 1964 constitution and defined as the "highest governmental institution in the country"). As opposed to the version, "I swear by Allah Akbar," which appears in the 1953 and 1964 constitutions, the 1969 constitution says, "I swear by my honor and belief . . . " (52, 60).[49] (But, in 1971, Ḥāfiẓ al-Asad, Syria's new ruler, reintroduced the old version of the presidential oath).

The Ba'th regime apparently tried to relieve the "Islamic complex" which faced the veteran Ba'th party with a severe dilemma, and established the principle of secularity as the ideological basis of Syrian society. The secular tendency of the regime, which is probably the most pioneering and bold of all "progressive" Arab regimes in the area, was also expressed in internal policy. Similar to other tendencies, this was due to the communal origin of the regime's leaders and their striving to blur the sectarian-religious element which emphasizes the difference between them and the Sunni majority.

At this point it should be indicated that, in its secular conception, the Ba'th leadership is related to the Communist party and especially to the Syrian Nationalist party (PPS), by whom they seem to have been influenced at various stages of their political development.

An Emphasis on Syrian Uniqueness and Arab Heritage

The leaders of the neo-Ba'th were influenced by, and related to, these two parties more than to the veteran Ba'th members in another important political-ideological aspect: the emphasis on Syrian territorial singularity and on a Syrian Arab identity, in preference to the traditional pan-Arab tendency of the national movement and the veteran Ba'th. In theory, the new Ba'th stands for Arab unity, declaring that Syria is part of the Arab homeland, and that the Arab people of the Syrian region are part of the Arab nation. In fact, however, this regime, since its establishment, has adopted an extremely independent inter-Arab policy, sometimes opposing Egypt's leadership and even isolating Syria from the other Arab states. The new leaders of the Ba'th granted priority to the formation of Syria's socio-political regime over the achievement of the hoped-for Arab unity. They emphasized Syria's singularity as a more progressive and revolutionary state than the other Arab states. This policy is somewhat similar to Shīshaklī's tendency (which was also influenced by the Syrian Nationalist party) to foster Syria's independence, reform the regime, and stress Syria's glorious past and special place in the Arab world. But, contrary to the Sunni Muslim Shīshaklī, who tried to establish the Syrian political community on Islamic values as well, the Ba'th leaders acted to neutralize and abolish the religious element as a basis of the new society.

Instead, the heads of the regime emphasize the pure Arabism of the Syrian community even more than Shīshaklī, since Arab cultural and linguistic values compose the common strong bond for most of the Syrian population: 'Alawis, Sunnis, Druze, and Christians.

Indeed, of all the elements fundamental to the concept of the new Syrian political community, the values of Arab cultural heritage are probably the most stable, since most of the population – with the exception of the Kurds in the Jazira, the Armenians, and certain Catholic circles – are nourished by them. (The Catholics were hit, as mentioned above, by the nationalization of communal schools; the Kurds also suffered greatly by the Ba'th policy of Arabization in the northern Jazira, combined with deportations and large-scale arrests of Kurdish tribesmen.)

A further common denominator is the feeling of Syrian territorial identity, based on the habit of living side by side in the political-administrative framework of Syria existing for two generations – a framework which was fostered by the regimes of Shīshaklī during the 1950s and the Ba'th in the 1960s. This feeling was undoubtedly deepened and strengthened due to the failure of the union with Egypt and subsequently by 'Abd al-Nāṣir's death (though it is possible that it was not accepted by the various unionist circles and remnants of the veteran Ba'th).

Popular Reaction Against Secularism

In contrast, however, the notions of socialism and particularly secularism professed by the regime are more of a liability than an asset in the concept of a Syrian-Arab national community. It is known, for example, that a considerable portion of the traditional urban middle class – craftsmen, merchants, and clergymen – are hostile to the socialistic, secular nature of social and economic life. They oppose the Ba'th, though this regime considers them part of the working class and although they were organized by the regime in trade unions of craftsmen, shopkeepers, etc., and, to a certain extent, could carry on with private economic activity without interference. The ideological and social identification of those circles obviously differs extensively from the leftist-socialist and radical-secular *Weltanschauung* of the new regime and is related to the orthodox Muslim and conservative system of loyalties of the old regime. Some of them had social, economic, or political connections with the veteran political elite; many were, and still are, under the influence of the *'ulamā'* and the Muslim Brotherhood.

It seems that during the last decade both these elements, the Brotherhood and the *'ulamā'* – attached to and interwoven with each other – began to replace the leadership of the veteran national parties as leaders of the conservative and traditional groups in Syria. Parallel to the decrease in the socio-economic and political influence of the old elite, these religious, conservative elements became increasingly active as a focal point of economic and spiritual discontent among the traditional middle class.

The Muslim Brotherhood, for example (which reorganized in 1949 in the Socialist Islamic Front), together with the *'ulamā'*, registered strong opposition to the reforms of Ḥusnī Za'īm, which implied the abolition of the *waqf* and the introduction of new penal and civil codes; they also pressed for the introduction of a paragraph into the 1950 Syrian constitution which would establish Islam as the state religion. These elements were extremely active in times of critical change – such as after the fall of Shīshaklī or the disintegration of the U.A.R. – and tried to gain political influence by way of demonstrations and strikes.

As the Ba'th regime came to power and the other parties were outlawed, these conservative, religious elements, in cooperation with others, led the opposition. A few examples follow: in March and April 1964 and again in January 1965, the *imāms* in the mosques of Ḥama and other towns preached against the "godless" regime, called for the defense of "religion and freedom," and used slogans such as "Allah Akbar – either Islam or Ba'th." Subsequent to these declarations, extensive strikes and demonstrations were held in Ḥama, Aleppo and Damascus. The regime took severe countermeasures. The large mosque in Hama was shelled following some alleged firing (in April 1964) on the armed forces from it; some tens of people were killed, many *'ulamā'* arrested and court-martialed, and shops which had closed during the merchant's strike were forced to open.[50] The *'ulamā'*, however, did not surrender and in March 1966 many of them refused to participate in the festivities marking the third anniversary of the Ba'th revolution. Shaykh Ḥasan Ḥabanaka, head of the *'ulamā'* in Damascus, even declared that he would fight heretical tendencies in the regime. He was detained in July 1966, but later released.

The tension between the conservative elements and the Ba'th regime reached a climax in May 1967 following the publication of an atheistic article in the army weekly *Jaysh al-Sha'b,* on the twenty-fifth of April. The author, Ibrāhīm Khalās, declared, among other things, that the only way to the design of Arab culture and Arab society is by forming an Arab socialist man who believes that God, religions, feudalism, capitalism, imperialism, and all other values upon which the former society was based are but mummies in the museum of history.[51] In reaction to this, merchant strikes and mass demonstrations broke out in Damascus, Aleppo, and Ḥama, which lasted three days and were accompanied by severe clashes with the armed forces. The regime reacted by arresting thousands of merchants and *'ulamā'*; Shaykh Ḥabanaka was also arrested, and his property confiscated. The mass media accused him of conspiring against the regime in cooperation with Salīm Ḥāṭūm, Munīf al-Razzāz, and other members of the veteran Ba'th leadership,[52] and with receiving financial support from Saudi Arabia. According to Damascus radio (7 May 1967), the atheistic article itself was planted in the *Jaysh al-Sha'b* as part of an American-Israeli reactionary conspiracy and in cooperation with anti-revolutionary elements and "merchants of religion" in order to fight the achievements of the revolution and provoke communal rivalries.[53]

The article in *Jaysh al-Sha'b* hurt not only the feelings of conservative Muslim circles, but also of Christian clerical circles. Christian bishops of various communities protested vehemently against the secular tendency of the regime as expressed in the article; Greek Orthodox clergymen even took part in the demonstration against the regime in Ḥama, and leaders of the Catholic community in Damascus demanded the release of Shaykh Ḥabanaka and other *'ulamā'* who had been arrested.[54]

A few months later, in September 1967, the Christian communities themselves were very directly and tangibly hit by the law for the nationalization of communal education and the restriction and supervision of religious studies. Heads of the Catholic communities emphatically protested against the law and claimed that it contains "ingredients of hostility toward Christian institutions which from the beginning of Muslim history had an honorable treatment."[55] Many communal schools were shut, and about fifteen thousand Christian pupils transferred their studies to Lebanon. The Christian Orthodox, who had a tradition of cooperation with the national movement, were also displeased with the regime's policy: in November 1969, for example, violent demonstrations were held by Orthodox Christians in Ḥoms in reaction to the regime's involvement in the election of the local Greek Orthodox bishop. A number of people were killed, and hundreds arrested during the demonstrations.

Those events represent the development of a tendency unprecedented in the annals of modern Syria: the cooperation of Muslim and Christian religious circles in opposition to the secular policy of the Ba'th. A similar tendency was also discernible with Muslims and Christians of other circles: not only among the veteran political elite and leadership of the Nationalist party which were affected by the regime's reforms, but, to some degree, also among Muslims and Christians of the new middle class – intelligentsia and petit bourgeoisie – who were ejected from the centers of political activity by natives of the provinces and villages. Moreover, there is substance to the supposition that broad circles of the Syrian population – both urban and rural, Sunni and Christian, Druze and others – have been embittered and enraged over what seemed to them a takeover by the "backward" 'Alawis in the country, while removing the members of other communities from their positions. Most eminent, as regarded by these circles, was the communal gathering (*taktīl ṭā'ifī*) of 'Alawis in the army, for which initially Ṣalāḥ Jadīd was responsible.[56]

CONCLUSIONS

In conclusion, it may be said that in the course of the last generation, a strong governmental center was established in Syria for the first time in centuries – a center which succeeded in overcoming the centrifugal and autonomous tendencies of various social groups and in gaining considerable authority over the population as a whole.[57] Inter-regional fragmentations were abolished, class differences reduced, loyalty to Arab cultural and national values fostered, and the feeling of Syrian territorial identification amplified. The socio-political revolution and the drive for economic development during the last decade greatly contributed to the socio-economic progress of the broad mass of peasants and laborers and turned them into potential raw material for a united society and a nucleus for a Syrian political community.

However, the path to the crystallization of Syria into one society and political community worthy of the name is still a long one, and obstacles are numerous. The traditional social frameworks of the enlarged family, the tribe, or the religious community are still strong among a considerable part of both the rural and urban populations and hinder the consolidation of society. The contrasts between village and city have not been eliminated. The same applies to class contrasts: it seems that with the traditional urban middle class, feelings of embitterment and deprivation were observable; and most conspicuously, communal solidarity and intercommunal polarization did not vanish, but in certain respects grew stronger among Christians, Druze, and even among Sunnis. Indeed, for the first time since the mandate, feelings of communal solidarity and religious protest could be observed even among the Sunni Muslim majority in reaction to the 'Alawi takeover and to the secular policy of the regime.

A military junta with a non-Muslim attitude taking control questions the legitimacy of the central regime for many Syrians and weakens the identification of the majority with the new political elite. Values such as Arabism, Syrianism, and socialism, for which the new regime stands, are still insufficient to achieve a consensus and to serve as a general basis for a Syrian political community, as long as they are disconnected from Islam and not under its influence.+

\+ Since the writing of these lines, a turning point has been observed in the Syrian regime's attitude toward the values of Islam. Ḥāfiẓ al-Asad, the new ruler of Syria who ousted Ṣalāḥ Jadīd, a fellow member of his community, began visiting mosques and meeting with Muslim religious leaders while trying to appease Muslim Sunni conservative circles. But when at the end of February 1973 the draft of Syria's permanent constitution again omitted the "Islamic clause," violent demonstrations broke out in Ḥoms, Ḥama, and Damascus. The demonstrators, led by Muslim *'ulamā'*, fiercely protested against the non-Islamic draft constitution and against the 'Alawi domination of Syria.

FOOTNOTES

1 Albert Hourani, "The Changing Face of the Fertile Crescent in the Eighteenth Century," *A Vision of History* (Beirut, 1961), pp. 40–1.

2 About forty percent of the present population of Syria belong to religious and/or linguistic minorities. More than half of them belong to Arabic-speaking communities differing in their religious belief. Thus the Muslim heterodox sects: 'Alawis (11.5% of the Syrian population), Druze (3%), Ismaili and Mutawalli-Shiites (1.5%); the Christian communities: Greek Orthodox (4.7%), Greek Catholics and other Arabic-speaking Christians (3.1%). The rest belong to non-Arabic-speaking ethnic groups: Sunni Muslim Kurds (8.3%), Turkoman (3%), and Circassians – and the remainder are Armenians (4.2%), Syrian Christians (2%), and Nestorians.

3 F. Walpole, *The Ansayrii and the Assassins* (London, 1851), 3:127.

4 "Rural Syria in 1845," *Middle East Journal* 16 (1962): 508, report by Consul Werry, Foreign Office Archives (F.O.) 78/1389 (Aleppo, 17 February 1845).

5 Quoted from a cable to the Grand Vezir on 18 October 1879; 'Alī Ḥaydar Midḥat, *The Life of Midḥat Pasha* (London, 1903), p. 183.

6 Concerning the jurisdiction of the Ottoman *majlis* in the Syrian provinces and the process of taking control by the *a'yān* and *'ulamā'*, see Moshe Ma'oz, "Syrian Urban Politics in the Tanzimat Period," *Bulletin of the School of Oriental and African Studies* 29, pt. 2 (1966): 277–301.

7 Isabel Burton, *The Inner Life of Syria* (London, 1875), pp. 105–6.

8 F.O. 195/194, no. 25 (Beirut, 21 March 1842).

9 Charles Issawi, *The Economic History of the Middle East* (Chicago, 1966), p. 269.

10 *Nafīr Sūriyya* 25 October 1860; see also Albert Hourani, *Arabic Thought in the Liberal Age* (London, 1962), pp. 101, 274–5.

11 F.O. 78/1586, no. 1 (Damascus, 10 January 1861).

12 Cf., for example, Shimon Shamir, "The Modernization of Syria," in *Beginnings of Modernization in the Middle East,* ed. William R. Polk and Richard Chambers (Chicago, 1968), pp. 374–5.

13 A.L. Tibawi, *Modern History of Syria* (London, 1969), pp. 161–2.

14 John Murray, *A Handbook for Travellers in Syria and Palestine* (London, 1858), 1: XLVI.

15 Yūsuf al-Ḥakīm, *Sūriyya wa'l-'ahd al-'uthmānī* (Beirut, 1966), 1: 84.

16 F.O. 195/2255, no. 32 (Jerusalem, 10 August 1907).

17 F.O. 78/1389, no. 33 (Aleppo, 7 August, 1858); cf. Moshe Ma'oz, *Ottoman Reform in Syria and Palestine* (Oxford, 1968), pp. 246–7 & f.n.

18 'Ādil al-Ṣulḥ, *Suṭūr min al-Risāla* (Beirut, 1966), pp. 98–100.

19 Ernst Dawn, "The Rise of Arabism in Syria," *Middle East Journal* 16 (1962): 163.

20 Tibawi, p. 150.

21 Cf. Hourani, *Arabic Thought,* pp. 186–7.

22 Sāṭi' al-Ḥusrī, *Yawm Maysalūn* (Beirut, 1947), p. 229.

23 Albert Ḥourani, *Syria and Lebanon* (London, 1946), pp. 93–5.
24 League of Nations, Report of the Permanent Mandates Commission Twenty-seventh session (1935).
25 Albert Hourani, *Minorities in the Arab World* (London, 1947), p. 77.
26 Concerning the Syrian officers cadre and its position in politics and society, see: Eliezer Be'eri, *Ha-Qetzuna we-ha-shilton ba'olam ha'aravi* (Merhavia, 1967), pp. 48–62; 97–119.
27 In 1951, twenty-nine percent of Syrian land was held by owners of large estates; thirty-three percent was the property of medium-sized landowners; and only fifteen percent was held by small farmers. See Gabriel Baer, "Agricultural Reform in Syria and Iraq," (in Hebrew) *Hamizrah Hehadash* (*The New East*) 3 (1950/51): 30.
28 See, for example, *Hamizrah Hehadash* (*The New East*), publication of the Israeli Oriental Society, 5 (1954/59): 300; 6 (1954/55): 56; 7 (1956): 211.
29 J.N.D. Anderson, "The Syrian Law of Personal Status," *BSOAS*, 17 (1955): 34–5.
30 Patrick Seale, *The Struggle for Syria* (London, 1965), pp. 60, 62.
31 *Al-Ḥayāt*, 30 October 1956; quoted in *Hamizrah Hehadash* 7 (1956/57): 153.
32 Compare Munīf al-Razzāz, *al-Tajriba al-murra* (Beirut, 1967), p. 159.
33 For details see Ḥizb al-Ba'th al-'arabī al-ishtirākī, *al-Taḥawwul al-ishtirākī fi 'l-rīf* (1967), pp. 46–8; 60–1. For the law of the agrarian reform of 1958 see Eva Garzousi, "Land Reform in Syria," *Middle East Journal* (1963): 83–90.
34 *Hamizrah Hehadash* 17 (1967): 322. In 1964 a further quarter of a million dunams of land were confiscated; *ibid.*, 20 (1970): 74.
35 *Al-Ba'th,* 27 Feb. 1968.
36 *Al-Ba'th,* 1 March 1967.
37 From a speech by Ḥabīb Ḥaddād, member of the party's regional leadership, *al-Ba'th,* 16 Aug. 1967.
38 *Al-Ba'th,* 17 Nov. 1967.
39 The number of radio sets, for example, grew from fifty thousand in 1950 to 260,000 in 1960 and to 1,745,000 in 1965. See Rizkallah Hilan, *Culture et development en Syrie* (Paris, 1969), p. 311.
40 Ibid., p. 290.
41 Tibawi (p. 413) claims that all Syrians born after 1956 receive compulsory education. According to another source, the law on compulsory education has not been fully implemented, especially concerning girls; see Hilan, p. 291. See also statistics in F.I. Qubain, *Education and Science in the Arab World* (Baltimore, 1966), p. 15.
42 Qubain, pp. 20–2.
43 See *Hamizrah Hehadash* 6 (1959/61): 51.
44 See: *al-Jadīd,* 29 Sept. 1967; *al-Ḥayāt,* 1 Oct. 1967 and 24 Oct. 1967; *al-Ba'th,* 12 Oct. 1967; *al-Nahār,* 13 Oct. 1967.
45 Hilan, pp. 286–7.
46 *Al-Ba'th,* 2 Oct. 1967.
47. *Al-Ba'th,* 11 Sept. 1967.

48 Cf. Rivka Yadlin, "The Neo-Ba'th Ideology" (in Hebrew) in *Arab Socialism,* ed. Z. Goldberg (Beit Berl, 1970), p. 129.
49 *Al-Thawra,* 3 May 1969.
50 Compare to Eric Rouleau, "The Syrian Enigma: What is the Ba'th? " *New Left Review* 45 (Sept.–Oct. 1967): 64; Tibawi, pp. 415–7.
51 According to *al-Ḥayāt,* 5 May 1967.
52 *Al-Ba'th,* 8 May 1967; 10 May 1967.
53 *Al-Ba'th,* 12 May 1967.
54 *Al-Nahār,* 9 May 1967.
55 *Al-Nahār,* 3 December 1967.
56 Compare to Razzāz, pp. 158–9 and to Martin Seymour "The Dynamics of Power in Syria," *Middle Eastern Studies* (Jan. 1970): 39.
57 For an excellent analysis of the creation of the new center in Syria, see Avi-Dan, "Elites and Centre in Syrian Society," *Hamizrah Hehadash* 18 (1968): 205–22.

SOCIAL ASPECTS OF THE EMERGENCE OF THE PALESTINIAN ARAB NATIONAL MOVEMENT

YEHOSHUA PORATH

THE STRUCTURE OF THE ELITE

Throughout the period of Ottoman rule in Palestine, the social order of the country was largely reminiscent of that in the emirate of Mount Lebanon, though without an emir. The area extending from the Hebron hills in the south to the Jezreel Valley in the north, with the exception of the urban areas, was divided up into subdistricts (*nawāḥī,* singular *nāḥiya,*) headed by local *shaykhs.*[1] These subdistricts preserved their identity for generations and were tied to each other in alliances based on the division into Qays and Yaman. They shared a similar way of life and society. In some, at least, there existed a special legal order based on rural custom and judgment by the *shaykhs* according to a well-developed and recognized procedure.[2] At least some of these subdistrict *shaykhs* were the heads of Bedouin tribes; and it is probable that they acquired their status as subdistrict *shaykhs* in the course of their tribe's settlement in a given territory.[3] The status of the subdistrict *shaykhs* was, above all, a product of their being the tax farmers (*multazimūn*) of their areas.[4] Their function was hereditary in their families, although not always passing from father to son, and there were cases of the role's being transferred from one family of *shaykhs* to another located in a different village.[5]

The *shaykh* was required each year to obtain confirmation of his status by the Ottoman ruler, which was granted by sending the *shaykh* a cloak (*khila'*). Simultaneously with this ceremony, a decision was made as to the size of the yearly tax assessed for the subdistricts in that year.[6] The *shaykhs* had at their disposal a military force which was recruited, when necessary (usually for fighting between the Qays and Yaman camps), from the ranks of the *fellahs.*

With the restoration of Ottoman rule in Palestine in 1840, the Ottoman government began making efforts to liquidate the status and power of the *nawāḥī shaykhs*. The *khaṭṭ-i sharīf* of Gülhane decreed the abolition of tax farming (*iltizām*). Though it is true that the efforts to abolish tax farming were fruitless until the end of the nineteenth century and the start of the twentieth,[7] the nature of the *iltizām* did begin to change. When the Ottoman government first attempted to abolish the *iltizām* (1839), it soon discovered that it was powerless to introduce direct tax collection by officials. It therefore reintroduced the *iltizām* three years later,[8] although it seems that several changes took place in the procedure. In the past, the Ottoman governor had been charged with farming out the *iltizām*. In the Palestinian *nawāḥī*, this meant giving the *shaykhs* an annual confirmation of their right to collect the taxes of their *nawāḥī*. The main innovation of the renewed *iltizām* was the entrustment of tax farming and supervision of collection to the provincial *majlis al-idāra* (administrative council). "The powers of the *Majlis al-Idāra*," wrote Gad Frumkin (who worked in the last years of Ottoman rule as a jurist in the Treasury Department of the Jerusalem Provincial Administration) "included, *inter alia*, the farming out of the tithe and other taxes, which the government does not collect directly, but rather farms out *to the highest bidder*, in exchange for a predetermined sum which the tax farmer pays to the Treasury. Whatever he succeeds then in collecting from the tax-payers goes into his own pocket. He collects the tithe, in kind or in cash, *from the fellahs who have to pay it,* under the supervision of gendarmes with whom he or his emissaries go to the villages."[9]

It would seem that in the areas around Jerusalem, and probably in Samaria as well, this system led gradually to the weakening of the position of the *nawāḥī shaykhs* and to their replacement as tax farmers by urban notables. Our conclusion is that the village *shaykhs* were incapable of competing for this post with the urban notables, who were wealthier, and the *shaykhs* were thus superseded as tax farmers by urban tax farmers who collected taxes directly from the *fellahs*. It should also be remembered that it was these notables who manned the *majlis al-idāra,* forming it into an instrument for the enhancement of their own status, influence, and property. As a result, towards the end of Ottoman rule, an element was created which helped to strengthen the class of urban notables at the expense of the village *shaykhs.*[10] In addition, from 1840 on, the Ottoman authorities directed a vigorous campaign aimed at checking the *shaykhs'* military power, while their powers of jurisdiction were also taken from them.

Little by little, the *shaykhs* were incorporated into the Ottoman administration, becoming village *mukhtārs* appointed by the government. As a result of this systematic policy, the power of the village and subdistrict *shaykhs* declined, and at the end of the nineteenth century few traces were left of their administrative powers.[11]

Notwithstanding the *shaykhs'* decline from the point of view of administrative prerogatives, the social position of the *shaykhs* and the *nawāḥī* survived to no small degree as units of social affiliation. At the end of 1920, Shaykh 'Abd al-Ḥamīd Abū Ghūsh was considered to be, not only the head of his family and village, but also the leader of the twenty villages of the Banī Mālik *nāḥiya,* and the *shaykhs* of the adjacent *nawāḥī* saw themselves similarly.[12] Three years later, the villages in the Ramallah subdistrict were required to maintain additional police stations at their own expense (according to the Law for the Prevention of Crimes), in view of the high rate of robberies in the area. The local population organized to oppose this governmental step. Their spokesmen were the village *mukhtārs,* and the organization to present their protests was based on the traditional division into subdistricts.[13]

Even in the late 1920s and early 1930s, traces of this division were still to be found. In 1929, when the Palestinian Arab Executive organized a fund-raising campaign for the Arab victims of the disturbances and wanted to expand its collection of funds to the rural areas, it did so through the village *shaykhs* and, again, according to the traditional division into subdistricts.[14] Fellah participation in the al-Nabī Mūsā celebration continued, even in the 1930s, to be organized on the basis of this division, with the villagers taking part in the festivities under their particular banners.[15]

The preservation of the subdistricts gave the *shaykhs* who headed them political power and made them a factor in the struggle for leadership within the Palestinian Arab community.

The gradual decline in the authority of the village and subdistrict *shaykhs* did not leave a vacuum. They were replaced by the layer of urban notables (*a'yān*). Already in the eighteenth century, this group had consolidated its power and status in Ottoman society. The decline in the power of the central government, the disintegration of the *sipāhī* (Ottoman "feudal" cavalryman) system, the deterioration of the Janissaries, and the struggle between the Imperial Janissaries (those who continued to be considered "Servants of the Porte") and local Janissary units *(yarliyya)* – all had greatly weakened the authority of the central government and its representatives (the vali, governor, Arabic *wālī*) in the various provinces. This course of development made it possible for local power elements – local dynasties of rulers, Bedouin tribes, and the urban *a'yān* – to rise to greatness and attain crucial positions of influence, and sometimes even of control.[16]

The rise in the power of the urban *a'yān* was accelerated in the nineteenth century. With the beginning of the *Tanẓīmāt* reform process and the Ottoman restoration in Syria, the Ottoman authorities looked for ways to enhance this layer's tie with the government and to make it partner in the efforts to further the administration. They therefore set up in the various provinces councils (probably under the influence of the precedent set by Muḥammad 'Alī's rule), which functioned alongside the governor, and in which the local *a'yān* were represented, along with the major administrative officials of the province.

However, the main result of this innovation was the opposite of what the authorities had expected. The local *a'yān* managed to subvert the council (*majlis*) into their instrument. They exerted influence over the local administration by way of the council and used it to check the vali whenever he attempted to put into effect reforms likely to challenge their position. The vali's ability to oppose the wishes of this layer was thus limited. His appointment was for one year only, while the *a'yān,* as local residents, were much better versed in the province's affairs. Without their experience and knowledge, it was highly doubtful that the vali could have found his way. This policy had been adopted in order to forestall the creation of overly powerful valis, who might become a danger to the position of the central government, but it led to just what the authorities had feared: the vali's weakness necessarily became that of the central power. The central government understood this and in 1852 attempted to correct the situation by considerably enlarging the powers of the vali; but it seems that this step was taken too late, when the strength of the local elements was already excessive.[17] The power of the local *a'yān* did indeed decline slightly, but this group was nevertheless one of the important factors in the failure of the reform efforts under Aḥmad Shafīq Midḥat, vali of the vilayet of Syria (Damascus) from 1878 to 1880.[18]

The influence of this class on local administration was also reinforced by the fact that it staffed many posts in that administration. Members of this class, which provided the *'ulamā'* and the various religious functionaries, were the first to receive a relatively modern education in the new schools of the empire, and thus from this layer alone, or in the main, was it possible to recruit candidates for the new administrative apparatus of the *Tanẓīmāt* era.

The abolition of the hereditary *iltizām,* which had previously been entrusted to the subdistrict *shaykhs,* and its replacement by tax farming concessions sold to the highest bidder, contributed greatly to the strengthening of the urban *a'yān*'s status. The wealth of the *a'yān* enabled them to compete with the subdistrict *shaykhs* for the privilege of *iltizām.* But along with this economic factor, another was also at work – their status in the new Ottoman administration. The farming out of taxes was entrusted to the administrative council (*majlis al-idāra*) of the province, and there can be no doubt that the *a'yān* exploited their influence in these councils to secure *iltizāms* for themselves.[19]

This development is closely connected with the result of the faulty execution of the Ottoman Land Law of 1858. The fact that the application of the law was entrusted to the local administration, under the direction of the *majlis al-idāra,* nullified the legislators' intention. Instead of the state's rights on *mīrī* (government) land, and cultivators' rights to cultivate, being strengthened, the *a'yān* succeeded in registering large tracts of land in their names. Land, the taxes of which had been farmed out to *a'yān,* was now registered in their names. The fellahs' accumulation of heavy debts and fear of registering their rights in the government land registers only aided the urban notables.[20]

As a result of these processes, the urban *a'yān* acquired a firm position in the civil and religious administrations of the empire, as well as much landed property. A fairly considerable percentage of senior posts in the provincial administration was in the hands of the local elite, and not a few of the members of this layer attained senior positions in the Ottoman administration outside their own area. For example: 'Abd al-Laṭīf Ṣalāḥ of Nablus served at the end of his Ottoman career as first secretary of the senate;[21] Aḥmad Ḥilmī Pasha 'Abd al-Bāqī was the general director of the Ottoman Agricultural Bank in Syria and Iraq;[22] Muṣṭafā al-Khālidī of Jerusalem served as Beirut's chief of police, public prosecutor, and judge on the Court of Appeals;[23] 'Ārif Pasha al-Dajānī of Jerusalem filled various posts in the Ottoman administration and attained the rank of district governor (mütaṣarrif);[24] As'ad al-Shuqayrī of Acre was a member of the Committee of *Shar'īa* Clarifications attached to the *Shaykhülislām* in Istanbul and, during the First World War, served as *muftī* of the Fourth Army (commanded by Jemāl Pasha and which fought on the Egyptian-Palestinian front);[25] and Mūsā Kāẓim al-Ḥusaynī rose from rather low posts in the administration to subdistrict governor (*qā'im maqām*), district governor, and finally to governor of Yemen.[26] The establishment of an Ottoman Parliament also helped the *a'yān* to strengthen their position; all the delegates to Parliament from the Palestinian districts were from this class, which thus enjoyed an additional source of political and social influence.[27]

The hegemony of the *a'yān* is clearly revealed by an examination of social reality in the various Palestinian cities during the late nineteenth and early twentieth centuries. In Jerusalem the Ḥusaynī and Khālidī families were prominent, with the Nashāshībīs in a process of social and economic rise, while gradually supplanting the Khālidīs. The Khālidīs filled in the main religious positions, and their sons traditionally held the post of chief scribe at the Muslim religious court in Jerusalem.[28] At the start of the twentieth century, there were among the Khālidīs two religious dignitaries: Shaykh Khalīl al-Khālidī, who was eventually to become president of the *Sharī'a* Court of Appeals in Palestine; and Shaykh Rāghib al-Khālidī, founder of the Khālidiyya Library. However, it seems that the members of this family failed to find their way into the new Ottoman administration, and their influence declined accordingly, as well as by virtue of their numerical depletion.[29]

The Ḥusaynī family held, from the mid-nineteenth century on, the office of *muftī* of Jerusalem. In 1864 a municipality was established in Jerusalem, and members of this family served often as mayor, although from time to time a Khālidī – and once even an 'Alamī – won this position.[30] In the 1880s, Salīm al-Ḥusaynī served in this position, while in the second decade of the twentieth century, his two sons, Ḥusayn Salīm al-Ḥusaynī and Mūsā Kāẓim al-Ḥusaynī, were mayors.[31] Members of this family also attained other high positions in the administration of the Jerusalem district and as district and subdistrict governors, and even in the staff of the central government in Istanbul.[32]

The position of *muftī* of Jerusalem gave this family a basis for its country-wide status. The *muftī* of Jerusalem was the central figure in the Nabī Mūsā celebrations,[33] and we have already seen that the importance of these celebrations exceeded the bounds of Jerusalem and affected the entire country. Moreover, the strong tie between the Ḥusaynī family and the Nabī Mūsā celebrations was emphasized still more by the fact that members of this family were the traditional caretakers of endowments set aside for the Nabī Mūsā mosque near Jericho.[34]

The Nashāshībī family, as has been mentioned, began to progress only in the last few generations. The wealthy 'Uthmān al-Nashāshībī was elected to Parliament in 1912,[35] while Rāghib al-Nashāshībī served as the engineer of the Jerusalem district and in 1914 was also elected to Parliament.[36] Members of this family also served on the district's administrative council.

It is no wonder, then, that the position of these families was so solidly entrenched, and that the governor of the district had to manage affairs according to their wishes.[37] In the 1850s, James Finn, the British consul, described their status thus: "It should be mentioned that a closed corporation of Arab families, not recognized by law, but influential by position, usurped all the municipal offices among them."[38] Fifty years later, the situation was unchanged and the governor of the Jerusalem district from 1906 to 1908 attempted to alter it. He described the status of the families in this way: "There are here influential people and notables who have attained wealth and fame through injuring the rights of the people . . . on account of the ascendancy of the Arab [Bedouin?] inhabitants, most of whom are primitive, the notables of Jerusalem have always been famous for their many rebellions against the government . . . from the time when Rauf Pasha was appointed Governor of Jerusalem he put into effect a system aimed at liquidating the domination of these parasites over the common people and showing these influential people of the province, who are called Ḥusaynī, Khālidī, Nashāshībī and Da'ūdī [Dajānī] what their limits are . . ."[39]

In Nablus, also the capital of a district, the status of members of the local families was equally prominent. Members of these families had for generations filled important posts in the traditional army and administration of the district and the empire; but it seems that with the renovation of the empire their participation declined. It seems that this conservative city did not adjust to the new needs as quickly as Jerusalem. We find Amīn 'Abd al-Hādī, alone among the Nablusites, serving as governor of a subdistrict outside his native district.[40] Nor do we find evidence to the effect that the influence of Nablusite families on the management of their district's affairs was comparable to that which developed in Jerusalem.

The important families of Nablus were split into two factions. The origin of the split lay in the division between Qays and Yaman, but with the Egyptian conquest in the 1830s, this split took on new political significance. The Yamani faction, headed by the 'Abd al-Hādī and Nimr families, supported Egyptian rule and served as governors under it, while the Qaysi faction, led by the Ṭūqān family, headed the rebels.[41] This new identification left traces in the names of the two rival factions: the pro-Egyptian faction came to be called *Dār al-Miṣrī* and the other, *Dār al-Bey* – apparently because of the title

"Bey" that the Ṭūqān family carried. This split and these designations were preserved at least until the second decade of the twentieth century.[42]

In the subdistrict cities of Gaza and Jaffa, the situation was no different. There, too, we see the important local offices (mayor, local *muftī*) in the hands of the leading families, and large-scale land grabs by these families stand out.[43] If we recall that the coastal plain was sparsely populated in the nineteenth century and pay attention to the way land registration was carried out in unclaimed desolate areas, we can easily understand this development.

The particularly solid position of the Jerusalem *a'yān* families apparently resulted from the special status of the *sanjaq* of Jerusalem. This was the result, above all, of Jerusalem's sanctity and the international interest which it aroused. In the seventeenth and eighteenth centuries, we see the *qāḍī* of Jerusalem enjoying widespread territorial jurisdiction. There were times during this period when the *sanjaq* of Jerusalem was raised to the status of *eyalet* (province) or at least to that of a *sanjaq* independent of the governor of the province. The formal expression of this was the appointment of a district governor of high rank (*mütaṣarrif*) as its head.[44]

In the 1850s, after the Crimean War, this administrative status was made permanent. It was determined at that time that the governor of the *sanjaq* of Jerusalem was not to be subordinate to the governor of the provinces of Saida or Damascus, but would instead be directly dependent upon Istanbul – the status of the *sanjaq* would thus be equivalent to that of an *eyalet.*[45] The governor of this district would have a higher rank than that of ordinary district governors.[46] When, in accordance with the Ottoman Vilayet Law of 1864, general councils (*majālis 'umūmiyya*) were set up in the new vilayets above the administrative councils (*majālis al-idāra*) of the districts, a general council was also set up in the Jerusalem district.[47]

As a result of these processes, the urban *a'yān* became the decisive power in the Arab community of Palestine, with the Jerusalemites as the central factor within it. This took place at the expense of the previous position of the rural subdistrict *shaykhs,* and to a lesser degree at the expense of the status of the *a'yān* in the Nablus and Acre districts. Among these declining elements, there were those who looked for an opportunity to express their dissatisfaction. This opportunity was given them with the establishment of British mandatory rule, when the political opposition to Zionism of the Arabs of Palestine began to be organized.

THE ORGANIZATIONAL DEVELOPMENT

We do not intend to deal in this article with the motives behind the rise of the Palestinian Arab national movement, but propose to stress several aspects of its social composition and organizational structure.

With the start of organized anti-Zionist action in November 1918, the group known as the "Muslim-Christian Association" (*al-Jam'iyya al-islāmiyya al-masīḥiyya*) appeared in Jaffa and Jerusalem. Its leaders submitted protest petitions to the military governors of these cities on the first anniversary of the Balfour Declaration. The heads of this association were also the leaders of the important urban families and religious communities.[48]

In Jerusalem two more extreme associations were founded, favoring unification with Syria under the crown of Fayṣal, the son of Ḥusayn: *al-Nādī al-'arabī* (the Arab Club) and *al-Muntadā al-adabī* (the Literary Club), the former dominated by the Ḥusaynī family and the latter by the Nashāshībīs.[49] These associations succeeded in establishing branches in other cities in the country, but after 1920 they went into decline – in the wake of the decline of the trend towards unification with Syria. The Muslim-Christian Association (hereafter: MCA) then became the central organization of the Palestinian Arab national movement and gradually spread to other cities.

The center of the organization, the Jerusalem MCA, included until the summer of 1922 most of the public figures in Jerusalem. The dismissal of 'Ārif Pasha al-Dajānī from the post of president of the Executive led to his withdrawal from the Jerusalem branch, and the secretary of the Executive, Jamāl al-Ḥusaynī, became the real director of the association. The hegemony of the Jerusalem MCA in the country-wide framework can be seen by the fact that its leaders also headed the country-wide framework, the Executive met in Jerusalem, and day-to-day management of the secretariat was also entrusted to Jerusalemites. The first secretary was Isḥāq Darwīsh; the second, Jamāl al-Ḥusaynī, with his brother Isḥāq al-Ḥusaynī serving as his aide. When Jamāl al-Ḥusaynī left for India in the autumn of 1923 as a member of the delegation of the Supreme Muslim Council (hereafter: SMC), he was replaced by another Jerusalemite, Khalīl al-Sakākīnī. When Jamāl al-Ḥusaynī rose to a higher position and became one of the heads of the Executive, the post was conferred upon another Jerusalemite Ḥusayni, Ṣafwat Yūnus al-Ḥusaynī.

Another expression of Jerusalem's hegemony was the consigning of the right to represent distant areas (both geographically and politically speaking) at the country-wide congresses to Jerusalemites – although residents of other cities also enjoyed some of these spoils. It is impossible to tell whether the residents of Tiberias, Safed, and other places promoted their representation by Isḥāq Darwīsh, Jamāl al-Ḥusaynī, Ḥasan Abū Sa'ūd, and others, or whether the latter simply exploited the fact that no delegates came from these places. Whatever the reason, the phenomenon of Jerusalem's weight in the all-country congresses having grown because of this is most significant.

The second important center of the Muslim-Christian Association, Jaffa, stood out between 1918 and 1923 because it was less affected in the early 1920s by the internal division between supporters and opponents of the Executive. During this period the Jaffa MCA succeeded in uniting within it most of the respected community leaders in Jaffa, while its power and influence on the public was almost uncontested. However, in late 1923 this united front began to crumble. At that time the Jaffa municipality consented to receive electric power from P. Rutenberg's project, thus arousing the ire of various extremist elements. The mayor, 'Āṣim Bey al-Sa'īd, was a close friend and ally of 'Umar al-Bīṭār, the president of the Jaffa MCA, and the anger directed against the municipality was also aimed at 'Umar al-Bīṭār. The powerful al-Dajānī family utilized this situation to attack him and to undermine his position. As a result of this conflict, the Jaffa MCA slowly disintegrated into two opposing camps, and its former status passed.[50] This development was accelerated further from 1926 on, when 'Umar al-Bīṭār and 'Āsim Bey al-Sa'īd joined the ranks of the opposition. The Jaffa newspaper *Filasṭīn* also switched its political loyalty from the Arab Executive (AE) to its opponents. The weakness of the supporters of the Executive was demonstrated by the June 1927 municipal elections in Jaffa, when 'Āsim Bey al-Sa'īd and his men were victorious, and he became mayor once again.[51]

The reconsolidation of 1928 and the August 1929 disturbances led to a revival of the Jaffa Muslim-Christian Association. From the second half of 1929, the association there stands out by its vigorous activity, extremist positions, and the pressure it directed on the Executive to bring it to the point of extreme activity. At that time – and not by chance! – 'Abd al-Qādir al-Muẓaffar was serving as secretary of the association, and the new character infused into its activities expressed the new spirit in the Palestinian national movement, which would become still more apparent some years later.[52]

Haifa was also an important center for nationalist activity, although a united Muslim-Christian Association did not come into being there. In the last period of Ottoman rule, relations between Muslims and

Christians there had greatly worsened. The economic advancement of the latter left the Muslims behind and aroused noticeable envy.[53] Apparently because of this development, the active nationalists of Haifa were unwilling to set up an intercommunity organization. Instead they set up in the Hijrite year 1337 (which began on 7 October 1918), a "Muslim Association," which was active on the level of nationalist struggle, but not as an organization concerned with religious-community affairs.[54] The Christians set up a "Christian Association" about a year later, which worked parallel to the Muslim Association,[55] although already in the First Palestinian Congress in January 1919, a Christian delegate from Haifa participated. Generally speaking, the two associations worked in common: they sent protest telegrams to the government, brought the petitions of the populace to the attention of the local governor, and organized joint demonstrations, although they organized the representation of the populace at the congresses separately. This separate existence lasted throughout the lifetime of the MCA and the Executive,[56] and it seems that suprareligious nationalist frameworks came into being in Haifa only in the second half of the 1930s.

Another Muslim-Christian Association already in existence in 1919 was that of Nablus. This association, under the presidency of al-Ḥājj Ṭawfīq Ḥamād and the direction of Ḥāfiẓ Aga Ṭūqān (who was *mu'tamid al-jam'iyya,* i.e., director of the association's affairs), was extremely active in Nablus itself, in its district, and on a country-wide scale.[57] Its strength stood out in the first congress, when it constituted a clear alternative to the country-wide center in Jerusalem – in the wake of the refusal of the Jerusalem leadership to fit into the trend of unification with Syria. In the course of the 1920s, it succeeded in grouping most of the Nablus notables around it, and, as we have seen, it was an important factor behind the failure of the elections to the legislative council. Perhaps the height of its achievements and power came in 1926, when the Nablus MCA joined the opposition in its struggle against the Ḥusaynī monopoly of power in the Supreme Muslim Council. It seems that this development caused the growth of an alternative nationalist framework in Nablus in the late 1920s – the Committee of the Arab Congress (*Lajnat al-mu'tamar al-Ārabī*) – although the MCA continued to exist until 1921.[58]

In July 1931 the Nablus MCA decided to change its name to "The Arab Patriotic Association" (*al-Jam'iyya al-'arabiyya al-waṭaniyya*)[59] – a change which was highly significant. Previously, at the fifth congress, 'Izzat Darwaza, the outstanding spokesman for the young militants, had expressed his dissatisfaction with the name "Muslim-

Christian Association." In his opinion, this name gave no expression to the new nationalist spirit and was overly anchored in the communal structure.[60] The change in name of the Nablus MCA, thus, was intended to emphasize the more militant trend which began spreading in 1931 in the wake of the great disappointment over the MacDonald Letter (the "Black Paper", as the Arabs called it, of February of that year).

Alongside the Nablus MCA, *al-Nādī al-'arabī* continued to exist, although it was largely silent and apparently absorbed by the MCA.[61] It is interesting that this structure produced in late 1927 an important initiative which was to influence the further development of the national movement in the 1930s. In December 1927 the Nablus *al-Nādī al'arabī* turned to the various associations of Muslim youth in Palestine with a proposal to establish a country-wide framework of the associations of Muslim youth. While this body did not at first intend to deal in political affairs, its growing strength and political activization a few years later were among the important characteristics of the period. It is important to note that the initiator of this activity was once again Muḥammad 'Izzat Darwaza.[62]

The first evidence of a Muslim-Christian Association in Gaza dates from December 1920, although Gaza sent representatives to the first congress. From then on there is more evidence concerning the active existence of the association.[63] As we have noted, the Gaza MCA was completely successful in stymieing the elections to the legislative council, and the opposition hardly penetrated there. In the municipal elections of 1927, the supporters of the Supreme Muslim Council and the Arab Executive won their only great victory in Gaza.

Jerusalem, Jaffa, Haifa, Nablus, and Gaza – this is the map of the MCA (although in Haifa separate community structures existed) in the first stage of organization, i.e., up till the Third Palestinian Congress in December 1920. Throughout 1921 and the first half of 1922, one could sense a pause in the spread of these associations across the country, and only in the summer of 1922 was it possible to detect renewed organizational efforts. In June 1922 an attempt was made to set up an MCA in al-Bīra,[64] but it never got off paper. Slightly more successful was the attempt made at the same time in Nazareth. This town had not taken an active part in the national movement in its first stage. A delegation from Nazareth had indeed taken part in the first congress, but the town was unrepresented at the third and fourth congresses. Moreover, Nazareth did not in the least satisfy the financial demands made upon it by the Arab Executive for financing the activity of the AE and its delegations.[65] Later in the 1920s,

Nazareth was the location of several influential elements (above all the al-Fāhūm family) which worked hand-in-glove with the rivals of the AE. Nevertheless, an MCA was set up there, basing itself mainly on the rivals of the al-Fāhūm family, the Zu'bī family, and the association even sent delegates to the sixth congress in June 1923.[66]

The first evidence of the existence of a nationalist association in Tiberias dates from the same time, July 1922, although there existed only a Muslim association without a parallel Christian one, such as was set up in Haifa. Tiberias was rather poorly represented at the country-wide congresses. A delegation was indeed sent to the first congress, but at later congresses the local residents forewent their right of representation (except for the instance of sending one delegate to the fourth congress) and permitted residents of other areas to claim that they were acting as representatives of Tiberias.

The Tiberias association, like the one in Nazareth, was not conspicuously active in a district which, generally speaking, stood on the sidelines of the national movement and hardly fulfilled its financial obligations. Indeed, after 1923 – the year marking the climax of the first wave of nationalist activity – it is no longer heard of.[67]

Another region which was still further removed from the national movement and its Jerusalemite leaders was the city of Hebron and its surrounding villages. Representatives of this region took no part in the first three congresses (the first, third, and fourth) and contributed little to covering the expenses of the Arab Executive, so that one can actually say they took no part in the national movement in its early years.[68] In the summer of 1922, a delegation from Hebron participated for the first time in a country-wide congress (the fifth), and from that period approximately dates the first evidence of the existence of an MCA, although it was not overly active and left no impression on the city.[69]

Hebron and its environs were throughout the 1920s and early 1930s an important center of opposition. Conflicts between the administrators of the local endowments and the Supreme Muslim Council over the disposal of the usufruct *awqaf* were, as we have seen, among the important causes of this situation. In the late 1920s this situation changed somewhat. The president of the SMC appointed as local *muftī* one of the opposition's leaders in Hebron, Shaykh 'Abd al-Ḥayy al-Khaṭīb al-Tamīmī; and in this way his family became a supporter of the SMC and the AE. However, this appointment did not do away entirely with elements opposed to the SMC and the AE.

Several *shaykhs* from the tribes of the Beersheba area (the fifth congress) joined the framework of the country-wide congresses and the AE in 1922, but the Bedouin character of the population in this region nullified from the start any possibility of organized activity in a nationalist, country-wide spirit, or participation in the financial burden of such activity.

The situation was different in Safed. At the end of the first organizational stage of the national movement – autumn of 1920 and winter of 1921 – *al-Nādī al-'arabī* was active in this town.[70] However, it seems that this body was neither all-embracing nor particularly active. Actually, until March 1923, nationalist activity in Safed (participation in the country-wide congresses, in demonstrations, sending of protests, the boycott of the elections to the legislative council) was carried on through the social and religious leadership, headed by Shaykh As'ad Muḥammad al-Ḥājj Yūsuf Qaddūra, *muftī* of Safed. A framework as weak as this put difficulties in the way of collecting funds, and Safed too had only a tiny share in the Arab Executive's budget – one far smaller than the quota demanded of it. In the winter of 1923, the Safed Muslim-Christian Association was established, and it survived until the late 1920s, although during the low period of 1925 to 1928 its existence was completely unnoticed, as was the case in the other parts of the country.[71]

Developments in Beisan were to a certain extent similar to those of Safed. In the early 1920s no nationalist organization worthy of the name existed there, and until the fifth congress, Beisan was not represented at the country-wide congresses. Nevertheless, Beisan was not off the map concerning nationalist activity. A number of individuals headed by Jubrān Iskandar Kazmā (a Greek Orthodox who had studied agronomy at Montpelier in France, son of one of the pupils of the Russian schools which had aided the Orthodox community in its struggle against Greek rule of their patriarchate) bore the burden of activity, without setting up an organized association. They succeeded in uniting most of the *shaykhs* of the region in a struggle for their rights to *jiftlik* (government) lands in their area and in large measure became their representatives. However, their power was not unlimited, and there were *shaykhs* who preferred to tie themselves to the other active elements (the opposition's National Muslim Association and the emissaries of the Zionist Executive). There is evidence from late 1924 of the establishment there of a Muslim-Christian Association, which also was to survive, without being very active, until the end of the 1920s.[72]

The nationalist spirit which surged through the country in the wake of the 1929 riots led to the awakening of the various associations which until then had been slumbering. Several attempts were also made at that time to widen the organizational framework. In both Ramallah and Ramleh – two towns in which the leaders of the opposition (Būlus Shiḥāda and Shaykh Sulaymān al-Tājr al-Fārūqī) had considerable influence – MCAs were set up, and the one in Ramleh even began to show signs of activity. An attempt was also made to set up a MCA in Lydda.[73] With the exception of the fourth congress, Ramleh was represented at all the country-wide congresses, Ramallah's representatives were absent from the first and fifth congresses, while those of Lydda took no part in the third, fifth, and sixth.

In three cities (or large towns) no MCAs were set up – Tulkarm, Jenin, and Acre; but with respect to the first two, this failing does not reflect alienation from the national movement. In Tulkarm a local organization called *al-Nādī al-waṭanī* (the Patriotic Club) was set up in late 1918, and throughout the period of "Southern Syria" it was active along with the branches of *al-Nādī al-'arabī* and *al-Muntadā al-adabī.*[74] Afterwards, this organization continued to be the one nationalist framework in Tulkarm and called itself *al-Nādī al-'arabī al-waṭanī.* It was this organization which maintained connections with the AE and which organized local activity. In the second half of 1921, nationalist spirit in Tulkarm died down in the wake of the collective fine imposed on the town, but in 1922 nationalist activity came back to life with *al-Nādī al-'arabī al-waṭanī* serving as its framework.[75] Tulkarm was represented at all the country-wide congresses from the first on.

An attempt was made in May and June 1922 to set up an MCA in Tulkarm to work as a branch of the Nablus MCA. However, this should not be seen as an effort to strengthen the ties of the nationalist circle in Tulkarm with the country-wide framework, but as an attempt on the part of Muḥammad Kamāl al-Jayūsī to come out against the leadership of *al-Nādī al-'arabī al-waṭanī,* which was controlled by members of two other families: Salīm 'Abd al-Raḥmān al-Ḥājj Ibrāhīm, the mayor's son, and 'Abd Allāh Samāra, the son of a large landowner.[76] The attempt failed, and the above-mentioned organization continued to act as the branch of the national movement in Tulkarm. It seems that in the latter part of 1923, the organization began to wither and gradually disappeared.[77] It should be noted that at the end of the 1920s and the beginning of the 1930s, when the thrust of the Palestinian national movement was renewed, this organization was not reestablished there. The two young leaders whom we mentioned were prominent in the efforts of their circle in Nablus and other places to bring about the radicalization of the national movement, and Salīm 'Abd al-Raḥmān stood out as one of the important leaders of the militant stream. It seems that the reservations shown by the men of this trend toward the old associations deterred them from reviving their local organization.

In Jenin, too, no Muslim-Christian Association was set up; no attempt was even made to establish one. Nevertheless, nationalist activity was not unknown in this region. Its notables participated in the various local and country-wide activities, and it seems that the lack of an organizational framework was not always a hindrance.[78] However, it was probably the nonexistence of such a framework that caused Jenin's lack of representation at the fourth and sixth congresses.[79]

It is very likely that the reason no MCA was set up was the strongly entrenched opposition in Jenin and the surrounding villages – a position which was a result of the al-Jarrār family's having joined its ranks. The establishment of an MCA would have revealed the al-Jarrār family's aloofness to the nationalist circles – a possibility which the Jenin activists probably wanted to avert.

Acre, in which no MCA was set up either, was throughout the period (and later, too) the most important center of opposition to the Arab Executive in the north of the country. The reservations felt toward the country-wide nationalist framework could be seen in the minimal participation in the country-wide congresses. Acre had no representatives at the first and fourth congresses. At the third congress one citizen of Acre participated on a personal basis – it being stressed that no structure in Acre had authorized him to represent it at the congress. At the fifth and sixth congresses, only one delegate participated; and only at the seventh congress, which was held by virtue of agreement with the opposition, did a large and representative delegation take part.

A study of the spread of the Palestinian national movement shows clearly just how central the MCA framework was for that movement. In places where branches of the MCA were set up, political-nationalist activity was more systematic and organized. In those places, it was easier to gather funds to finance country-wide activities, and participation in the crystallization of a country-wide political framework was less problematical.

These Muslim-Christian Associations were never set up as organizations based on personal membership by the Arab inhabitants. Wherever they existed, they formed a combination of representatives from the various elements comprising the local elites. In general, one finds in each of them representatives of the important families, the religious functionaries, and the *shaykhs* of the villages in the vicinity of the town, whenever the latter were prepared to take part in nationalist activity. Special representation was always reserved for the Christian communities on the local committees – which usually exceeded their proportionate share in the population. The MCA thus constituted a basic framework of leaders and activists who were able, whenever necessary, to manipulate the masses under their influence.

This organizational character suited the traditional social structure and the accepted status of the local elite, which drew its authority from traditional prestige factors, such as religious status – filling religious posts, belonging to the *ashrāf* (people tracing their descent from the Prophet Muḥammad) – possession of land property, and long-time family claims to positions in the Ottoman administration, along with a consciousness of noble origin (the village and *nawāḥī shaykhs*). The elite thus needed no popular democratic confirmation of its status.

Moreover, the conversion of the MCA into the main nationalist organization further strengthened this organizational trend, at the expense of more personal concepts of membership, such as were prevalent in the militant associations of the "Southern Syria" period – *al-Nādī al-'arabī, al-Muntadā al-adabī, al-Ikhā' wa-'l-'afāf,* and *al-Fidā'iyya.*

A summing up of the many Jewish reports concerning the extent of membership in the various associations in 1919 puts their membership at approximately three thousand. A British police report of December 1920 gives a similar number,[80] although it includes all the Arab associations: philanthropic, cultural, and community organizations. Nevertheless, it seems that this estimate can be accepted, since we have seen that these organizations also took part in political activity and acted as representatives of their members on a political plane. It is not impossible that there was some overlapping of membership in the various associations, and thus the number given should be regarded as the upper limit of active membership in the various nationalist associations. In the course of the 1920s, the layer which carried the burden of nationalist activity grew somewhat and came to include a number of intellectuals who were not always from the traditionally important families, but there was no essential change in the character of membership in the MCA. This statement will be amplified when we discuss below the election and composition of the country-wide congresses.

The following event exemplifies the composition of the Muslim-Christian Association: In February 1919, at the height of the quandary prevailing in the Jerusalem MCA with regard to the orientation toward Damascus, the association convened a meeting. Present were seven heads of Muslim families, five Latin notables, five Orthodox notables, and nine village *shaykhs* from the Jerusalem area. While it is unlikely that all those connected with the association were present, and the proportions of representatives of the various sectors should not be seen as constant, it is still instructive to note that this meeting saw itself as authorized to speak "on behalf of all the inhabitants."[81]

During the abortive attempt to set up an MCA in Tulkarm in June 1922 (see above), about 100 of the village notables took part; while in the Haifa Muslim Association, 114 participated in electing the board, out of the 160 notables from the Haifa Muslim community who had been invited to participate.[82]

It should be noted that the participation of village *shaykhs* in the MCA framework was limited to Judea and Samaria, where rural structures with historical roots (*nawāḥī*) and their own traditional leadership existed.

The boards that directed these associations were elected at meetings of the active members. These elections were not held on fixed occasions, and at times groups competing for leadership would try to convene the notables who supported them in order to elect a different leadership. In any case, there was some degree of turnover in the composition of the boards.[83]

The organizational apparatus of these associations was very restricted. Generally speaking, there existed a board of members which met from time to time to adopt resolutions, while the everyday activity was carried on by the secretary. These bodies were voluntary and without a paid staff. Thus, only individuals with a strong financial position could have the leisure for constant activity, and the membership of these institutions was indeed drawn from the class of landowners, big merchants, and professional people (lawyers and journalists as a rule). Only in Jerusalem did the Muslim-Christian Association have a small permanent staff. The secretary of the Arab Executive acted also as secretary of the Jerusalem MCA from the time when 'Ārif Pasha al-Dajānī, the first president of the Jerusalem MCA, was dismissed from the presidency of the AE in June 1922.

With all the shortcomings of the MCA framework, it nevertheless constituted the organizational base – local and national – of the Palestinian national movement. The local associations were the medium of communication between the Jerusalem AE and the regions of the country. From it the associations received reports of its activities by way of circulars and instructions to carry out various activities (demonstrations, cable protests, presentation of petitions, etc.), and the associations issued reports of their own activities.[84] Nevertheless, it is hard to see the various MCAs as one crystallized, country-wide framework. The nationalists were themselves aware of this and, at the fourth and fifth congresses, brought up various proposals to consolidate the associations into a hierarchical country-wide framework, in which the associations in the large cities would establish branches in the villages and towns nearby.[85] Only in Nablus was such an attempt made. The Nablus MCA and its leaders saw themselves as the leaders of the entire district and tried to further nationalist activity in Jenin, Tulkarm, and the villages of the district. However, specifically the Nablus MCA illustrates the lack of crystallization of a country-wide framework. Not infrequently this association took its own initiatives, sent emissaries to Muslim elements outside of Palestine without consulting the AE, and constituted a factor of constant pressure on the Jerusalem AE in the direction of extremist action.[86]

Despite all these shortcomings, the MCA saw itself as the body representing the entire Arab population.[87] In 1918-20, the MCA was not yet the only body representative of the population. Other elements, more extremist than the MCA, were also active. Later, after these extremist organizations had expired, the MCA did not have the field to itself for long; opposition began to develop and organize. Nevertheless, the extent of the support which the AE and the MCA enjoyed was incomparably greater than that of the opposition, as can be shown by the success in blocking the elections to the legislative council. One must, however, bear in mind that we are dealing here with that part of the urban population which had political consciousness and gave thought to the question of the political and national future of the country. This part was limited, above all, to the urban educated elite, although its influence penetrated other layers, and it was capable of moving still greater masses. By virtue of this phenomenon, the MCA was able to claim that it represented the entire population.

It should also be recalled that the growing strength of the opposition in the latter 1920s deprived the MCA of its title to complete representation. The seventh congress of June 1928 was convened by agreement between the heads of the AE and the heads of the opposition, and the AE elected at it ceased to be identical with the MCA. However, up until then, the AE had been the pinnacle of a pyramid, the base of which was comprised of the MCAs and the center layers of the country-wide congresses. These institutions were the MCA's country-wide instruments of representation and the organizational basis for its attempt to appear as a country-wide representative organization.

Before the assembling of the congresses, the executive members of the local MCA, or of any other association which was active in the area as the framework for nationalist activity, would convene to elect a number of the local active members as delegates. There were never general elections. Moreover, not all the members were invariably connected to the local association convened for the elections.[88] In Jerusalem an attempt was made to convene the local notables to elect delegates to the sixth congress in June 1923, since the local MCA had been paralyzed when its president, 'Ārif Pasha al-Dajānī, had joined the ranks of the opposition. Approximately one hundred and fifty notables were invited, but only some sixty showed up and chose thirty delegates to the congress. The fact stands out that this election campaign was organized by Jamāl al-Ḥusaynī, the secretary of the AE, while the local MCA was completely ignored.[89] This electoral method was also used before the seventh congress, which was in many respects the most representative of all the congresses. However, this time, in the wake of the preliminary agreement between the supporters of the AE and the Supreme Muslim Council and the opposition, it was necessary to maintain numerical equality between the two sides, and the delegates were therefore decided upon in preliminary negotiations among the notables of both camps in each spot.[90]

It is no wonder, then, that from the first the British authorities had doubts about the representative character of this framework and subsequently maintained their dubious attitude. We have seen that after the convening of the third congress, the government voiced doubts as to whether the congress deserved to be considered as truly representative of the Palestinian population. In response, Mūsā Kāẓim al-Ḥusaynī remarked:

> The delegates of the congress convening in Haifa [the third, December 1920] were chosen in part by the Muslim-Christian Associations and the other associations and clubs which were established in orderly fashion and which represented all the inhabitants before the American commission [King-Crane Commission] and the government in all matters; the rest were chosen by the notables and dignitaries of the country (*a'yān wa-wujahā' al-bilād*), the *shaykhs* of the town quarters and the villages and the representatives of the various communities . . . On this basis it should be clear to His Excellency the High Commissioner that the congress was elected by the people, that it represents an absolute majority of the Palestinian people, Muslims and Christians, and that it unites within it the notables and dignitaries of the country, who have always represented it.[91]

In these words, Mūsā Kāẓim al-Ḥusaynī revealed with complete frankness the social concept of the Palestinian aristocracy. The source of this aristocracy's authority was traditional, and not democratic, and it did not see the need to have its status confirmed by other classes. Notwithstanding this fact, it saw itself simultaneously as the representative of the entire population, since according to its conception no other form of representation could possibly develop. It should be noted that even if the masses had been asked at the time to give their opinion as to who should represent them, they would undoubtedly have authorized the representatives of the social elite, whose leadership they accepted without qualification. What is more, from 1876 on, when elections to the Ottoman parliaments began to be held, the electoral method employed had been no different in any meaningful sense from that described by Mūsā Kāẓim al-Ḥusaynī. The reasons for this lay in the property qualifications for franchise required by Ottoman electoral law and in the holding of elections in two stages.

This social concept was, of course, reflected by the composition of the delegates at the various congresses. The delegates came, generally speaking, from that same social elite which saw itself as the true representative of the people: the prestigious urban families which produced religious functionaries, officials in the administration, merchants and landowners, and the families of the village *shaykhs.* In the seventh congress there were slightly more professional people (mainly lawyers), yet most of them also came from these same aristocratic families.

As to the families of village *shaykhs,* it should be stressed that this element did not come from all parts of the country. The only rural areas represented at the congresses, and in the other political structures, were Judea and Samaria and the Carmel. The villages of the coastal plain and Galilee were completely passive and took no part in political activity – since they were relatively new villages lacking a tradition of self-organization.

The religious functionaries had no great weight at the various congresses, although some of them (Shaykh Muḥammad Murād, the *muftī* of Haifa, Shaykh Sa'īd al-Khaṭīb, the main preacher in al-Aqṣā) took part in most of the congresses. However, this phenomenon does not prove that there was little participation on their part in nationalist activity. On the contrary, religious functionaries appeared as representatives of the population when petitions and protests were presented to the authorities, during demonstrations, and at various popular assemblies. The fact that such assemblies were frequently held in mosques and churches and that demonstrations often began or ended in them made the active participation of the religious functionaries inevitable.

The various congresses used to elect an executive to direct activity and carry out the resolutions until the convening of the next congress. This body comprised the highest echelon of the country-wide leadership. A fundamental feature of the election of these bodies at the various congresses was the desire to give representation to the various regions of the country and to that part of the Christian community which continued to take part in nationalist activity after 1920 – the Orthodox community in the main. In the Executive elected at the sixth and seventh congresses, special representation was given the Christians on a country-wide community basis; at the sixth congress the Christian delegates in the Executive were elected by their community, in addition to those Christians who were chosen to represent their towns, while at the seventh congress the Christian representatives in the Executive were elected on a community basis only. At most congresses (until the fifth and afterward), the members of the Arab Executive were elected representatives of their cities, but it was the plenary of the congress that did the electing. However, at the sixth congress the regional character of the AE's composition (alongside its community character) stood out, as the representatives of each region were responsible for electing the representative of their region in the AE.[92] This system was clumsy and made the AE's activities more difficult. It was hard to assemble its members from everywhere in the country for sessions in Jerusalem, and not infrequently sessions were cancelled or held in the most partial fashion because members were unable to attend.

THE SOCIAL BACKGROUND OF THE INTERNAL SPLIT

This consolidation within a country-wide framework was not accomplished smoothly. Already at the First Palestinian Congress, in late January and early February 1919, the Nablusites threatened Jerusalem's hegemony and strove to take over the primacy of leadership.[93] Although this attempt failed, active participants in the national movement in Nablus continued to show bitterness over the monopoly that the Jerusalemites – or rather, part of the Jerusalemites – had acquired over the leadership of the Palestinian community.

Much more serious than this attempt was the constant split that accompanied the Palestinian movement – a split which expressed family and regional conflicts of interest within the urban elite (among the Jerusalem families themselves as well as non-Jerusalem elements versus the Jerusalemites) and the rebellion of some of the rural notables against urban hegemony.

The rise of the Nashāshībī family in Jerusalem at the start of the twentieth century, and its competition with the traditionally pre-eminent families in that city (al-Ḥusaynī and al-Khālidī), made inter-family competition in this city particularly bitter. The Nashāshībī family, which had just recently risen to prominence and whose status was connected more closely than that of the other families to the Ottoman administrative apparatus, was apparently more alarmed than others over the departure of Ottoman rule.

For the Ḥusaynī and Khālidī families, whose members had filled in the course of generations various posts in the urban and local religious apparatus, the coming of a British regime did not mean a loss of status. The position of the Nashāshībī family was primarily a product of the status of Rāghib al-Nashāshībī as a member of the Ottoman Parliament and chief architect of the Jerusalem province.[94] For this reason, the end of Ottoman rule could have meant the end of the family's public position. It is no wonder, then, that the heads of the Ḥusaynīs formed ties, by virtue of their public posts, with the new regime. The younger members of the family, who were prominent in the leadership of *al-Nādī al-'arabī,* also maintained good connections with the British military administration, which at that time was encouraging the Arab national movement connected with Fayṣal, Ḥusayn's son. In contrast, the members of the Nashāshībī family looked upon the imperial rival, the French, for alliance and support. It should, thus, not surprise us that the association which they set up and led in the early days of the British military administration, *al-Muntadā al-adabī,* was tied to the French. These two organizations cooperated with each other because of their common goals, but this idyllic situation ended, as we have seen, in the spring of 1920 with the dismissal of Mūsā Kāẓim al-Ḥusaynī from the Jerusalem mayoralty, and with the first awakening from the dream of a Syria united under Fayṣal's rule.

The dismissal of Mūsā Kāẓim al-Ḥusaynī from the Jerusalem mayoralty in the wake of the disturbances of April 1920,[95] the manner in which it was accomplished, and the personality of his successor certainly contributed greatly to the increased tension between the Ḥusaynī and Nashāshībī families. The appointment involved a change in the orientation of the Nashāshībīs toward the Zionists. So far the Nashāshībīs had enjoyed the support of French agents; now they turned to the British. Those individuals who called for a policy of cooperation with the British, even after the establishment of the civilian regime and the ratification of the mandate, came from among the Nashāshībīs and their followers.

As we have seen, Mūsā Kāẓim al-Ḥusaynī became the outstanding figure in the Palestinian national movement and president of its executive committee. Another rival of the Nashāshībīs, al-Ḥājj Amīn al-Ḥusaynī, past president of *al-Nādī al-ʻarabī,* was elected president of the Supreme Muslim Council in January 1922. It would have been unusual had the personal animosity toward these individuals not turned into opposition to the bodies they headed, just as there was no hope that these bodies would not be turned into tools in the hands of their leaders against their personal rivals. In this way, then, the internal division within the Palestinian community developed, and an element opposed to the leadership and the circles supporting it appeared.

Personal and family reckonings with the heads of the Arab Executive and the SMC were not limited to the Nashāshībīs. From the start of the AE's activity, various individuals who felt themselves deprived or pushed to the side lent a hand to the opponents of the AE and began to be conspicuous. This is a fairly important phenomenon, since in this manner the opposition left the bounds of narrow family conflict and comprised a larger number of elements. These individuals and their supporters claimed unceasingly that their opposition to the AE was a result of their having been thrust aside and of the exploitation of the national movement by its leaders for their private aims.[96] At least at the start, they did not advance political justifications for their opposition, but we will see that in the course of time they also crystallized political stands of their own. Nevertheless, there is no doubt that the haste with which the heads of the AE accused anyone who hesitated to support them of treachery strengthened the feeling of personal bitterness and was an important factor in the appearance of the opposition.

In this context, it is worthwhile to cite several cases out of many. Shaykh Sulaymān al-Tājī al-Fārūqī of Ramleh, who had been the initiator of the Palestinian Congress in December 1920 and had been elected there to the first Arab Executive, later found himself to be without any representative function. When the first delegation was selected at the following congress, he was not among its members – because of the desire to leave the post of president of the delegation free for Mūsā Kāẓim al-Ḥusayni.[97] This learned *ʻalim* was not even reelected to the Executive, charged with handling the affairs of the movement during the delegation's stay in Britain. Reacting to this, he resigned from the congress.[98] In early 1922 he still remained outside the Supreme Muslim Council and its staff. He took no part in the fifth congress in August 1922. An attempt on the part of ‘Umar al-Biṭār of Jaffa to bring about his election to the AE did indeed succeed, [99] but al-Fārūqī still took no part in its activities. It is no wonder, then, that when the opposition party was set up, al-Fārūqī became one of its leaders and main supporters for many years.

A similar development occurred with respect to ‘Ārif Pasha al-Dajānī. He had been the first president of the Jerusalem Muslim-Christian Association. His status as leader of the national organizations had begun to deteriorate with the growth in the importance of the militant *al-Nādī al-‘arabī.* Mūsā Kāẓim al-Ḥusaynī's election as president of the AE took away what was left of his importance as president of the Jerusalem MCA. When the first delegation departed, he was elected to substitute for Mūsā Kāẓim al-Ḥusaynī, who headed the delegation, in the post of president of the AE. But this was far from appeasing him for not having been chosen to the delegation. He responded by propagandizing against the utility of the delegation's activity and by putting difficulties in the way of the collection of funds for it. When a year later it was decided to send a delegation to the Hijaz, he demanded to be at its head; when this time too he failed to be elected, he came out against the decision of the AE to send it and against its policy. The AE responded by dismissing him from the post of head of the AE, and in this way he too was thrust into the ranks of the opposition.[100] It is not by chance that at that very time his brother, Shukrī al-Dajānī, also joined the first body of the opposition, the "National Islamic Association" (*al-Jam‘iyya al-islāmiyya al-waṭaniyya*), and even stood at its head. This move undoubtedly affected the status of ‘Ārif Pasha as well.[101]

The split of the noted families of Nablus into two rival camps facilitated the spreading of the opposition to Nablus. The leader of the first camp was al-Ḥājj Ṭawfīq Ḥamād; of the second, Ḥaydar Bey Ṭūqān. Ḥaydar Ṭūqān had been mayor for a long period and in 1912 had been elected to the Ottoman Parliament; however, in 1914 things changed, and al-Ḥājj Ṭawfīq Ḥamād was elected in his place to Parliament.[102] The causes of this are not clear, but, in any case, Ṭawfīq Ḥamād began to stand out as the main figure in Nablus and its surroundings, and when the national organizations were set up in the early 1920s (the AE and the Palestinian delegation) Ṭawfīq Ḥamād was elected to them. It is not surprising, then, that Ḥaydar Ṭūqān became the prime opponent of the AE in the Nablus area and the pillar of the oppositional organizations there, along with his cronies and supporters.[103]

There are many other cases of individuals who in the past had filled various posts in the civil or religious Ottoman administration and who, now that they were left without any national or religious function, joined the ranks of the opposition. We will note only one more, whose opposition to the Arab Executive and the Supreme Muslim Council probably had a wider significance – As'ad Shuqayr, or Shuqayrī, of Acre. This individual had filled important positions during the Ottoman period, such as delegate to Parliament, head of the Committee for Clarification of *Sharī'a* Affairs in the office of *Shaykh al-Islām,* and *muftī* of the Fourth Army (the army of Syria) during the First World War. He was at that time a fierce opponent of the newly awakening Arab nationalist trend and wholeheartedly supported the integrity and unity of the Ottoman-Muslim Empire.[104] In this he was not, of course, an exception, but rather typical of the vast majority of community leaders who later became nationalists – like Mūsā Kāẓim al-Ḥusaynī and al-Ḥājj Ṭawfīq Ḥamād, for example. Nevertheless, the fact that he had been *muftī* of the Fourth Army under the command of Jemāl Pasha at the time the leaders of the Arab awakening were executed[105] gave his pro-Ottoman stance a special significance. What marked him off from many others was that, even after the disintegration of the empire and the conquest of Palestine, he did not abandon his views. At the beginning of the renewed Palestinian organizational activity, in the autumn of 1920, he not only stood apart, but even opposed this trend.[106] His ties with various Zionist elements were extremely close, and most important of all, he came out publicly in a large number of articles against the Arab nationalist awakening and the dismantling of the empire within which the Arabs had enjoyed complete equality and freedom.[107]

As'ad Shuqayrī was one of the main props of the opposition in the district in the North. His Muslim training and his senior status in the past enhanced the importance of his opposing stands toward the president of the Supreme Muslim Council and his methods. The question thus arises: was there a connection between his anti-nationalist and traditional Muslim stand and the fact that he joined the less extreme of the Arab camps of Palestine, or was this no more than a personal coincidence? The answer to this rather complex question cannot be unequivocal, but it seems that the position taken by As'ad Shuqayrī was more common among the opposition than among the circles of the AE and the SMC. Side by side with Shuqayrī, one finds several additional members of the opposition who maintained their loyalty to the traditional Ottoman-Muslim conception even after the conquest of Palestine, e.g., Ḥaydar Bey Ṭūqān and ʻAbd Allāh Mukhliṣ.[108] We saw above that this position was indeed adopted by numerous circles in the country and reached its peak in 1922, but it is instructive to note that at that time those who demanded to act toward restoring Turkish rule to Palestine came from the circles opposed to the AE. It is not surprising, then, that when the paper *al-Karmil* began (approximately at the end of 1923) to support the opposition, it renounced its anti-Ottoman approach, started extolling the days of the caliphate, and admitted that it had erred when in the past it had supported those "seekers of offices and interests in the name of racism (*unṣuriyya*),"[109] i.e., the Arab nationalists.

It is no wonder, then, that those personalities who were later to be the leaders and spokesmen of the opposition (Rāghib al-Nashāshībī, Ya'qūb Farrāj, ʻĀrif Pasha al-Dajānī, and others) stood apart in the period of the national awakening in the "Southern Syria" spirit and expressed, during the early 1920s, their enmity for the Hashemites and for their activities in Syria in 1918-20.[110]

Another phenomenon which fits into this picture is the pattern of relations which formed, at the start of the 1920s, among the most conspicuous personalities of the opposition and the institutions of the Zionist movement in Palestine. We have already seen how Mūsā Kāẓim al-Ḥusaynī maintained "special relations" with this element through H.M. Kalvarisky; and there is no doubt at all – abundant evidence exists in the files of the Zionist Executive – that the majority of the prominent personalities of the opposition benefited from Zionist financial support, made use of their help for various personal needs, and, when they came to set up their first political framework, enjoyed the active support of this element.[111]

It seems, then, that alongside the personal-family factor that lay at the roots of the opposition to the Arab Executive and the Supreme Muslim Council, there was another, more abstract, factor. Generally speaking, the prominent members of the opposition were not, in the early 1920s – and certainly not before then – caught up in the new spirit of nationalism, whether Pan-Arab or Palestinian, that began at that time to penetrate the Palestinian community. The AE and the SMC gave this spirit a much clearer expression than did the circles of the opposition. The fact that the wealthiest men of the country tended to join the opposition's camp rather than that of the AE – whereas one tends to find the few Palestinian intellectuals largely in the camp of the AE – reinforces our conclusion.

In the years 1920-22, open signs of the split in the Palestinian camp gradually began to appear. Various personalities ceased participating in the Palestinian congresses, and the first organizations opposed to the Arab Executive and its methods began to appear.

The split between the two camps did not develop overnight to the point where the AE and the congresses were completely identified with one of them. Only with the establishment of the opposition party, *al-Ḥizb al-waṭanī al-ʿarabī al-filasṭīnī* (The Palestinian Arab National party), in November 1923, did it receive full expression, with the members of the opposition deserting the AE and the associations connected with it. However, this party was not the first opposition organization. The previous existence of the National Muslim Association and the partial support given it by those who were later to found the National party bear witness to the doubts and hesitations which the members of the opposition underwent before a majority of them dared to unite within their own political organization.

Another important means utilized in establishing this association was the exploitation of Muslim bitterness against the Christians. In the Muslim community there were many who complained that the percentage of Christians in the government administration was out of all proportion to their part in the population. The AE and the MCA, on the other hand, did all they could to present a united front of Muslims and Arab Christians against Zionism. The Zionists, of course, tried to prevent the appearance of a united front: thus, the founders of the National Muslim Association resorted in their contest with the MCA to the argument that the latter organization included Christians and was in reality a tool in their hands.[112] In places such as Beisan, where the local branch of the MCA was headed by Christians, and in places where Muslim religious functionaries lent a hand in this sort of campaign, this approach was most fruitful.[113]

The other side of this approach was the desire on the part of the Muslim notables to take the places filled by Christians in the administration. One of the important factors motivating various Muslims to join the National Muslim Association was the hope that in this way they would win the support of the Zionist Executive for their efforts to attain government offices.[114]

A survey of the areas in which the association was set up says much about the causes of its establishment and the potential for opposition to the AE which existed among the Arabs of Palestine. The association first started in the North – Haifa, Acre, Nazareth, Tiberias, and Beisan – and it was there that it was strongest.[115] It was not by chance that the northern province was an important center of opposition to the

AE. It seems that the hegemony of the Jerusalem elite was not accepted with enthusiasm in a province which in the past had never been connected to Jerusalem. The sense of all-Palestinian solidarity was not yet strong enough to compensate for the bitterness toward Jerusalem's position of hegemony. Several years later this bitterness was still more strongly expressed and, as we shall see, led additional elements to join the circles of the opposition. The fact that an important personality, Shaykh As'ad Shuqayrī, was located in Acre certainly enhanced the power of the opposition in this area. We have already noted how this individual was left without any post, and how the active members of the AE and the MCA treated him with reservation and even hostility. It is not surprising, then, that he and his supporters set up the oppositional organization in Acre and were one of the main factors responsible for turning Acre and the entire district of the north into an important center of the opposition.

Other local elements also contributed to the success of the opposition in the North. In Haifa the sense of Muslim and Christian solidarity was apparently quite weak, and even the supporters of the AE there were organized into separate Muslim and Christian associations. The appearance of a Muslim Association which did not hesitate to come out against partnership with Christians in the AE and which included an important religious functionary, Shaykh Yūnis al-Khaṭīb (past *qāḍi* of Mecca), therefore met with much success.[116]

In Beisan there was a combination of two factors: the ability to come out against the local MCA branch, which was headed by a Christian; and the traditional approach of Bedouin *shaykhs,* who were far removed from any sense of national solidarity with the other components of Palestinian-Arab society.[117] In Nazareth there was a strong local family, the Fāhūms, whose rivals in the area, the Zu'bī family, were inclined toward the AE and its supporters.[118] This combination of local factors with an overall factor in the province made the North into a traditional center of opposition to the AE.

This organization succeeded in spreading to the center of the country as well – the Nablus and Jenin areas. Here the organization based itself on members of the Ṭūqān family and a branch of the 'Abd al-Hādis, who had long opposed the leader of the rival faction in the contest for local hegemony, al-Ḥājj Tawfīq Ḥamād.[119] However, in this area, another important factor stood out – destined to appear more powerfully several years later – the strong village families. When the Palestinian national movement was beginning to organize itself, with its leadership coming primarily from the urban elite, it often happened that members of the rural elite lent their hands to the rivals of this leadership. Thus, in the Jenin and Tulkarm regions, we find the important rural families, Jarrār (in the villages of the Jenin subdistrict) and Abū Hanṭash (Qāqūn), leading the organizers of the opposition association.[120] A similar picture holds true for the Hebron area, where the moving spirit behind all the organizations of the opposition setup were members of the Hudayb family, the *shaykhs* of the village of Duwaima, and in the Ramleh area, the al-Khawājā family from Na'ālīn.[121]

In Jerusalem, where the Nashāshībī family was located, the success of the National Muslim Association was relatively modest. The members of the Nashāshībī family itself did not dare in the early 1920s to come out openly against the Arab Executive and its policy – apparently preferring to accomplish this through emissaries. In any case, in the summer of 1921 Būlus Shiḥāda, owner of *Mir'āt al-sharq* and close friend of Rāghib al-Nashāshībī, and 'Umar Ṣāliḥ al-Barghūthī of the village Dayr Ghassāna and the *shaykh* of the traditional *nāḥiya* of Banī Zayd, began to busy themselves in setting up an opposition organization; they failed, however, and after some time Būlus Shiḥāda went back to supporting the AE, although only for a short time.[122] Kalvarisky himself, therefore, took over the task of establishing the association, finding as his chief support members of the Dajānī family, the head of which, 'Ārif Pasha al-Dajānī, was at the time president of the AE – although he was beginning to come out against the policy of the first delegation in Britain. When the association came into being in Jerusalem in the winter of 1922, it was headed by Shukrī al-Dajānī, 'Ārif's brother, and Fā'iq al-Dajānī – there having been no success in recruiting prominent figures from other families.[123]

In the course of 1923 it became clear that this attempt at organization had ended in failure. The causes were political and therefore not within the limits of this discussion.

An additional attempt to organize opposition was made in November 1923, when the Palestinian Arab National party was established. This was the organization of the circles opposed to the AE from among the urban notables, and we have already seen the social motives for their stand. We therefore move on to a discussion of another organizational attempt – that of the village *shaykhs*. We refer to the appearance of farmers' parties in the course of 1924.

What sets this phenomenon off from its predecessors is the fact that it was based on the families of village *shaykhs* and attempted to give political expression to the peasants. In previous attempts to set up oppositional organizations, this social factor had played an important role. The bitterness of the village *shaykhs* – who in the second half of the nineteenth century had lost their social importance – toward the urban elite which had taken their places was apparently quite deep. When this urban elite gradually became identified with Palestinian-Arab nationalism – the concrete expression of which was opposition to Zionism – its rivals began to lean toward the other side. Not infrequently, they were willing to express their opposition to the urban elite by supporting Zionism or, at least, by demurring from the anti-Zionist movement. Thus, for example, in March-April 1920, a long line of village *shaykhs* in the South, the Ramleh-Jaffa area, Judea, and Galilee dissociated themselves from the strong anti-Zionist wave which was passing through the cities of Palestine at the time and signed petitions supporting Zionist immigration to the country.[124] In organizing this project, several rural *shaykhs'* families were conspicuous – e.g., the Abū Ghūsh family of Qaryat al-'Anab and 'Amwās, which enjoyed the support and encouragement of the Zionist Organization[125] – but the very fact of mass response to this initiative proves the existence of latent rural bitterness toward the urban leadership. Not by chance does one of the petitions of the village *shaykhs* from the regions of Judea, the South and Ramleh-Jaffa, end by stating that the urban political associations have no connection at all with the community outside the cities and that "in the name of the villages we are opposed to all their corrupt activities which hamper the security of the community. We accept all resolutions that the peace conference may adopt and declare that all the demonstrations which they organized were solely on their own behalf. On the other hand, every petition we present is on behalf of the country's base, its notables and its leaders."[126]

The special stand of the village *shaykhs,* who were striving to preserve their social primacy, was maintained for years and was of course supported by the Zionists.[127] However, attempts at separate self-organization were not made until the start of 1924, after the anti-Zionist wave had passed its climax and following the open appearance of other opposition elements on the political scene. This attempt to organize was not lacking in other motives, including regional and familial ones, but the combination of all these factors lent the organization a certain weight. It is worth adding that this complex of factors did not include the miserable state of the impoverished fellahs, sunk in debt to urban moneylenders. While the urban leaders of the national movement were in many cases none other than those same moneylenders, the rural self-organization with which we are now dealing based itself on the village notables and not on the poor. In fact, this was an organizational attempt on the part of one component of the Palestinian social elite against another.[128]

In the first attempt, The Association for Village Cooperation (*Jam'iyyat ta'āwun al-qurā*) in the Ijzim-Haifa area, the regional and familial elements are especially conspicuous. This region had in the past been the *iqṭā'* of the Māḍī family of Ijzim, which had managed gradually to turn considerable parts of it into their private property. Even after part of the family moved to Haifa, the villages of the area continued to be under their social, economic, and political mastery.

Mu'īn al-Māḍī, as we have seen, maintained more moderate positions than the official line during the time he was a member of the first delegation to Britain and afterwards supported participation in the elections for the legislative council. He did not join *al-Ḥizb al-waṭanī* when it was set up, but in 1924 he began giving a political-factional expression to his traditional leadership in the area. The Māḍī family was strong enough to do without Zionist aid in setting up its organization, and, therefore, the platform it adopted was in the common anti-Zionist spirit.[129] However, the establishment of the other rural organizations bore a different character.

In early 1924 there began to form in the Nazareth, Nablus-Jenin, and Hebron regions organizations calling themselves *Ḥizb al-zurrā'* (Party of the Farmers). Generally speaking, they were headed by village *shaykhs* who were influential in their districts, such as Fāris al-Mas'ūd of Burqa and 'Abd al-Laṭīf Abū Hanṭash from Qāqūn (the Jenin-Tulkarm area) and Mūsā Hudayb (Duwaima, near Hebron), while contacts were maintained with urban oppositional elements, such as the Fāhūm family in Nazareth and the Ṭūqān family in Nablus.[130] These men were aided in organizing their groups by the Zionist Executive and H.M. Kalvarisky, and the Zionists covered the party's expenses – although at first Col. F. Kisch was unenthusiastic over the renewed organization of Arab opposition parties by Jewish initiative and assistance.[131] These associations were opposed to the Arab Executive and its methods and political line; they leaned toward cooperation with the government, and even with the Zionists.

The Zionists appraised this party as a fairly serious element which had gained a larger measure of support than *al-Ḥizb al-waṭanī,* the party of the urban opposition elements, although the open stand taken by the party in the Hebron area in favor of the British Mandate had reduced its influence to the supporters of the Hudayb family of Dawā'ima only.[132] However, this party's complete dependence upon the Zionists led in 1927 – when the source of Zionist support dwindled in the wake of the deepening crisis surrounding Zionist activity in Palestine – to its weakening and eventual disintegration.[133] This failure is of great significance when one recalls that it was precisely in that year that the power of the opposition reached a climax unparalleled in the past and, indeed, never to be repeated.

The rising strength of the opponents of the Arab Executive was not merely expressed by the setting up of markedly oppositional parties. Of no lesser importance was the fact that during 1924-25 splits formed in two of the most important Muslim-Christian Associations – in Nablus and Jaffa.[134] On the surface, the opposition camp was not all of one color, and in particular there were differences of opinion over the degree of open support to be shown the mandate. On occasion, the members of *al-Ḥizb al-zirāʿī* were even denounced by other elements of the opposition for their support of the mandate and their ties with the Zionist Executive.[135] Nevertheless, a common front of all the members of this camp gradually crystallized. During the negotiations in late 1924 over the possibility of reaching an agreement between the AE and its rivals, all the factors of the opposition appeared together in united fashion and were represented by a single delegation.[136] This unity took form in the midst of the struggle which all the factors of the opposition were carrying on against the Supreme Muslim Council, and it was this struggle that brought them the support of circles which had previously supported the AE and gave them a large degree of influence which they were not to have in later years.

The success of the opposition in 1925-27 can be seen in its electoral success in the SMC balloting between December 1925 and January 1926, and in its crushing victory in the municipal elections in the spring of 1927. This success was achieved by virtue of the fact that several circles previously connected with the AE now joined the ranks of the opposition. The nepotistic appointments made by al-Ḥājj Amīn al-Ḥusaynī, the president of the SMC, and by its other members; the exploitation of endowment funds for purposes other than the ones intended; and the conversion of the SMC as a whole into an instrument in the hands of its president, his family, and his political allies, the men of the Arab Executive – all these led men who had formerly belonged to the AE and supported the SMC to join the ranks of the opposition. Thus, for example, during the process of the disintegration of the Jaffa MCA, which began in late 1923, when the municipality agreed to let the Rutenberg electric project into its territory, its president, ʿUmar al-Biṭār, joined the camp of the opposition and thus enabled it to penetrate Jaffa, previously the citadel of AE supporters.[137]

It seems that many members of the Nablus MCA, the mainstay of the Palestinian national movement, were disgusted with the methods of al-Ḥājj Amīn al-Ḥusaynī and 'Abd al-Laṭīf Ṣalāḥ, the representative of the Nablus district in the SMC. In April 1924 they wanted to hold a separate procession during the Nabī Mūsā festivities – understanding as they did that the Jerusalem al-Ḥusaynī family was exploiting their participation in the festivities for the purpose of strengthening its status and prestige; the following year they started coming out against the AE, refrained from sending their banners to the Nabī Mūsā procession, and hardly took part in the festivities.[138] 'Abd al-Laṭīf Ṣalāḥ perceived that the support of the nationalist circles of Nablus was slipping away from him. He therefore set up a new association under the name *Ḥizb al-ahālī* in competition with the Nablus MCA; it acted in the main to safeguard its founder's status. This development helped thrust the local MCA with its leaders, al-Ḥājj Ṭawfīq Ḥamād, Amīn al-Tamīmī and Ḥāfiẓ Ṭūqān, into the ranks of the opponents of al-Ḥājj Amīn al-Ḥusaynī.[139]

It seems that the passing of the Nablus MCA into the ranks of the opposition was facilitated by a fairly deep-rooted development. Beginning in late 1922, one senses the growing detachment of its president, al-Ḥājj Ṭawfīq Ḥamād, from the ranks of leadership. He was not elected to the second delegation, which departed at that time for Geneva, and, probably because of this, took no part in the Sixth Palestinian Congress in June 1923. Some time later he announced his withdrawal from political activity, justifying this by declaring that the nation knew not how to value those who worked and sacrificed on its behalf. In the opinion of *Mir'āt al-sharq,* he secretly lent a hand to the new organization, *Ḥizb al-ahālī,* which was fighting the Nablus MCA.[140]

In Hebron too, the opposition to the Supreme Muslim Council began to grow stronger. Behind this lay the ire of the local notables over the SMC's taking over Hebronite endowments and spending their usufruct not in accordance with the original conditions of endowment.[141]

It should be noted that this struggle was supported by several personalities who had previously supported the Arab Executive and its ways and who were later to return to this position, such as 'Izzat Darwaza of Nablus, Ḥamdi al-Ḥusaynī of Gaza (who at the time was beginning a career of political activity in a left-wing nationalist spirit), and the paper *Filasṭīn.*[142]

The highpoint of the opposition's rise in power came in June 1928 with the convening of the Seventh Palestinian Congress. The congress was jointly convened by the AE and the opposition organizations, and the strength of the opposition at the congress and in the Executive elected there was equivalent to the strength of the AE, the supporters of the Supreme Muslim Council, and the Jerusalem al-Ḥusaynī family.[143]

THE SOCIAL BACKGROUND OF THE RADICALIZATION

The balance of power created from 1925 to 1928 between supporters of the AE and members of the opposition began to erode in the late 1920s. One of the important results of the strengthening of the opposition between 1925 and 1928 was the fact that, at the seventh congress in June 1928, the relative strength of the Jerusalemites was far less than at previous congresses.[144] In this manner, the part played by residents of other regions of the country in the Palestinian movement and in its leadership organizations (the Arab Executive) increased.

No less important was the fact that at this congress a new generation – which was later to leave its mark on the Palestinian movement – began to find itself.[145] It was better educated and included individuals who did not come from the traditional aristocratic families, though it was far from homogeneous. Some leaned toward radical pan-Arab ideology, secular in its symbolism, while others based their nationalism on Islam. The former ('Awnī 'Abd al-Hādī, Ḥamdī al-Ḥusaynī, and others) founded in 1932 the Istiqlāl (Independence) party, while the latter ('Izzat Darwaza, 'Abd al-Qādir al-Ḥusaynī) heralded the militant Muslim trend which brought about the 1936-39 revolt.

The Istiqlāl party was a first attempt at setting up a modern political organization grounded in a clear-cut nationalist ideology (an independent and united Arab state as an expression of the unity of the Arab people) and in personal affiliation.

Its founders were relatively young, of European education, and engaged in the liberal professions: lawyers, journalists, doctors, etc. Its active members did not spring from the aristocratic families: if there were such in its ranks, they were individuals who had cut themselves off from their family base (e.g., Ḥamdī al-Ḥusaynī and 'Awnī 'Abd al-Hādī). However, notwithstanding its importance, this party did not survive for long.[146] The family-community-regional nature of Palestinian politics was too strong, and it more or less disappeared after a few years of activity – although several of its leaders continued to stand out in the midst of the Palestinian community by virtue of their character and talent. The split between pro-Hashemites and pro-Saudis, which divided the camp of the pan-Arabists in the 1930s, also contributed to its disintegration.

From the point of view of influence and actual results, the second trend, the Islamic, was more significant.

In the first years of its activity, the Palestinian Arab national movement managed to acquire the image of a joint Muslim-Christian movement, although even then there were Muslims who saw this only as a strategem.[147] However, cracks gradually appeared in this facade. The first signs could already be detected in the early 1920s: Christians leaned more toward cooperation with the government. When the Kemalist Turks triumphed over the Greeks, the Muslims of Palestine rejoiced, while the Christians experienced a wave of solidarity with their suffering coreligionists. Attacks on Christians in Syria during the 1925 revolt aroused fears among the Christians about what awaited them if independence were attained. The influence of the Supreme Muslim Council grew stronger in Palestine, and the Arab Executive came to be identified with it, while the Christians tended to support the opposition to this body.[148] In 1926-28 the Zionist movement weakened, and Jewish settlement in Palestine looked moribund. At this time the Muslims began to express their misgivings with respect to the Christians and to organize themselves in special frameworks.

In the spring of 1928, a world congress of Christian missionaries convened in Jerusalem. The Muslim community feared this congress might become a launching pad for intensive missionary activity in its midst. They therefore raised an outcry against the congress, and some of them failed to distinguish between the foreign missionary element and the local, indigenous, and Arabic-speaking Christians.[149]

In the same period, early 1928, the country-wide structure of Young Muslims' Associations was established.[150] These associations were set up in the course of 1927 throughout the country, and their organization into a united country-wide framework lent them added importance. It seems that the very setting up of this body points to a strengthening of the sense of communal identity. It occurred at a time of crisis in Zionism when, apparently, the urge to demonstrate Muslim-Christian unity had weakened greatly. It is almost certain that a desire to compete with the parallel Christian structures and with the missionary activity was also at work. However, this organization gradually took on an anti-Christian character, as it was combined with another question which then preoccupied the Muslim community to a considerable degree.

From the start of British rule, the Christians had enjoyed an important place in the administration. By virtue of their greater education and knowledge of foreign languages, Christians found far more places in government service than their proportionate share of the population warranted.[151] There was from the start latent bitterness among the Muslims because of this, although during the first years of British rule it was hard for the Muslims to express this. In those years, all was being done to demonstrate Muslim-Christian solidarity, and even to have brought the matter up would have been interpreted as an admission of the importance of community identities and of the existence of conflicts of interests between the two communities. In the mid-1920s, with the weakening of this solidarity, many Muslims began to allow themselves to express their feelings on this point. It is safe to assume that, as a result of the work of the government's educational network, the number of educated Muslim youths grew larger, so that there was more pressure on government offices. Complaints began to appear in the press about discrimination against Muslims with respect to government offices and preferment of Christians.[152] This topic gradually became a public issue of primary importance, agitating spirits and affecting relations between the two communities.[153] Various elements began to organize themselves, to present petitions, and to send delegations to the government with a demand to do justice to the Muslims in this area, while the Arab Executive was requested to organize country-wide activity.[154]

Meanwhile, the August 1929 disturbances broke out and contributed greatly to the strengthening of Muslim sentiment and the Muslim character of the Palestinian movement. The disturbances broke out against a background of a religious conflict in which the Christians were not involved, and in their wake the religious head of the Palestinian Muslims, al-Ḥājj Amīn al-Ḥusaynī, became the most prominent leader of the Arabs of Palestine, and the Muslim coloring of their movement was strengthened.

Subsequently, the organization of the Associations of Muslim Youth adopted the government jobs issue as its own and began to be one of the most important elements active toward enlarging the proportion of Muslims in government service. At the fourth congress, in the summer of 1932, much attention was given to this question, and it occupied an important place in the resolutions.[155] In less public meetings, the heads of the organization did not hesitate to state explicitly that "the Christians are robbing the Muslims of their rights to [government] offices."[156] *Al-Jāmi'a al-islāmiyya,* the paper of

Shaykh Sulaymān al-Tājī al-Fārūqī, which held to a radical pan-Islamic position, dealt with this issue with a ferocity bordering on open incitement against the Christians.

Several young Muslims organized themselves in a special body, the Preparatory Committee of Young Educated Muslims, to fight for their rights. In November 1932 these men convened a country-wide congress in Jaffa and established the Committee of Young Educated Muslims. At their congress they came out fiercely against the Christians, although 'Abd al-Qādir al-Ḥusaynī, the son of Mūsā Kāẓim, tried – apparently under his father's influence – to calm the agitated spirits.[157]

In the wake of these developments, the Christians began to organize themselves in the opposite direction, and there were fears that there would be a public and violent split between the two communities.[158] Still earlier, on 9 September 1932, the Arab Executive had discussed, on its own initiative, the bitter controversy between the two communities and decided to request the government not to employ foreigners, in order to leave room for local residents, "and to maintain a proportionate balance in parcelling out offices."[159] It should be noted that this resolution was proposed by 'Īsā al-'Īsā, a Christian from Jaffa, and it should be seen as a temporary measure taken in light of heavy Muslim pressure. However, this resolution apparently did nothing to cool tempers. On 28 September 1932 the AE again discussed the factional spirit prevailing in the country and met with 'Abd al-Qādir al-Ḥusaynī, the representative of the Preparatory Committee of Young Educated Muslims. In the discussion, the need to put an immediate end to the danger of factionalism and to refrain from attacking the Christians was stressed. However, while the Christian members demanded that the topic be dealt with, that anything which could affect "the good atmosphere which exists among the children of the single homeland" (the words of 'Īsā Bandak, a Greek Orthodox from Bethlehem) be condemned and that the Association of Young Muslims of Jaffa, the "root of the evil" (in the words of Alfred Roq, a Greek Catholic of Jaffa) be restrained, the Muslim members expressed support for the Preparatory Committee and argued that it was not acting against the Christians, but simply in favor of Muslim rights (in the words of Hāshim al-Jayūsī and 'Izzat Darwaza).[160]

In light of these differences of opinion, the Arab Executive was unable to reach any conclusion and had to leave it to its office to issue a manifesto on this matter.[161] However, by this time the activity of the AE and its office was in decline. The AE did not convene again until a year had passed, and the office too convened only once (19 May 1933)[162] before October 1933. As a result, this institution, which was considered the leadership organization of the Palestinian national movement, was unable to deal with this serious question.

It should be noted that on a lower, everyday level, things were no less wearisome. We have seen that fairly successful anti-Christian propaganda accompanied the establishment of the National Muslim Associations in 1921. In various places in Palestine, an anti-Christian spirit continued to exist and, from time to time, received forceful expression.[163] Personal conflicts over land deals, or acts of kidnapping or murder, in which members of different communities were involved, sometimes took on factional significance and were seen by the Christians as indicative of the true attitude of the Muslims toward them.[164] In 1924, when the mayor of Nazareth died, the struggle over the appointment of his successor turned into a conflict between Muslims and Christians in this city.[165]

In the summer of 1930 a Christian journalist, Jamīl al-Baḥrī, head of the Organization of Christian Youth in Haifa, was murdered. This murder was directly tied to a conflict between the Christians and Muslims of Haifa over ownership of the old cemetery area.[166] The murder greatly agitated spirits and affected relations between the communities. The Arab Executive decided to act and did all it could to keep the murder case a personal affair. A high-ranking delegation was sent to Haifa,[167] but the Christians were still left with a weight of bitterness; some of them presented the British government with petitions, in which they disavowed any connection with the national movement and the Muslims.[168]

As a result of all this, tension between the different communities grew more intense in the early 1930s.[169] The HC was able to write: "Christian Arab leaders, moreover, have admitted to me that in establishing close political relations with the Muslims the Christians have not been uninfluenced by fear of the treatment they might suffer at the hands of the Muslim Majority in certain eventualities."[170]

In the summer of 1931, two conventions were held in Nablus to discuss the future of the country. This was an expression of the feeling that the traditional leadership and the Arab Executive were powerless to change British policy. MacDonald's letter to Weizmann in February 1931 ("the Black Paper," as the Arabs called it) and the sale of land to Jews by members of the Arab Executive were proofs that the old way had to be abandoned. The circles present at the conventions which refused to accept the authority of the AE included the pan-Arabist element (which had established the Istiqlāl) and the circles of Muslim youth influenced by al-Ḥājj Amīn al-Ḥusaynī. At these conventions several Muslim religious functionaries and others brought up the idea – for the first time in public – of resorting to arms in order to prevent the fulfillment of Zionism.[171]

The first attempt to realize this idea also came from these circles and was connected with the figure of ʻIzz al-Dīn al-Qassām of Haifa. This man, a religious functionary born in Latakia in Syria, fled to Palestine after Fayṣal's defeat and began to function as the *imām* of one of the mosques in Haifa. He stood out by his preaching for the purification of Islam, for leading a modest life in the spirit of the Ḥanbalite school of law, and for preserving the Arab character of Palestine. In the late 1920s he established and headed the Young Men's Muslim Association in Haifa. In the years 1931 to 1935 he set up a terrorist band in the north of the country, which was active against Jewish settlements and based itself on members of the Young Men's Muslim Association of Haifa and Tzippori. In November 1935 a British military unit managed to surround his band near Ya'bed, and he and several of his men were killed. The survivors escaped and reorganized themselves in the Samarian hills; it was they who began the revolt in April 1936.

This affair has another aspect. What information we possess about the men around ʻIzz al-Dīn al-Qassām indicates that they came from a class which until then had taken no part in nationalist political activity – villagers who for various reasons had left their villages and moved to the cities. The prosperity of 1933-35 drew many villagers to the cities, where they were able to earn far more than in their native villages. Uprooted from their native society, they were not absorbed by new urban structures. ʻIzz al-Dīn al-Qassām's organization provided them with the framework they so badly needed and with Muslim identity symbols with which they were familiar. It should be noted that a similar, though less important, phenomenon occurred in Hebron as well.[172]

This lower-class participation in the national movement took on new dimensions during the 1936-39 revolt. Although, in the early stages of the revolt, the leadership and major activity was located in the cities (the general strike), the fellahs gradually joined it and became the decisive factor in it. The fighting bands were almost entirely composed of fellahs, and during the height of the revolt, in the autumn of 1938, these bands entered the Arab cities, gained control over them, and established their hegemony for a short period. The urban leadership was out of sight (some were exiled, some fled, and some went into hiding because of the murderous internecine struggle); if the fellah bands had been organized under a consolidated leadership, they could have effected a far-reaching change in the political structure of the Palestine Arabs. However, they were not united, and even at the height of their power they were unable to create a single framework.

Moreover, the strengthening of the position of the fellah bands was not without a negative aspect with regard to future organization of fellahs for independent activity. The victory of the bands was attained simultaneously with a fierce internecine struggle. Old conflicts in the villages found new expression in the struggle between different bands. Elements which had wearied of the revolt began to organize counter-bands ("peace gangs"), which began struggling against the guerrillas' control of the villages. The "peace gangs" became a real power supported by the authorities, and a violent and vicious struggle broke out between them and the guerrilla bands. In many villages, bloody, hate-filled scores against the bands developed because of their extortions, forced recruitments, and murders of collaborators. Thus, the victory of the fellah bands in the fall of 1938 held within it the seeds of future controversies and divisions.[173]

In addition to all this, the British began to take firm action at this time. It seems that in the autumn of 1938 the British decided to suppress the Palestinian Arab revolt at all costs – and quickly. Troops were concentrated in the country and began a systematic campaign to liquidate the rebels' nests in the hills. Villages which aided the rebels, or in the vicinity of which acts of sabotage had been committed, were hit with stiff collective punishments, houses were demolished, arrests made, and not a few men sentenced to death and hanged.[174]

As a result of this combination of internal controversy and military suppression, the revolt gradually died out in early 1939. Politically, it was not without fruit: in May 1939 the Malcolm MacDonald White Paper was published, to no small degree as a result of the rebellion.[175] However, it seems that internally the revolt had serious consequences. The fellahs were not again able to work as a force organized within its own framework, and it is unlikely that they were inclined to participate in wider frameworks led by others. The internal controversies were exacerbated still further. Toward the end of World War II, when it was clear that the political future of Palestine was soon to be determined, various elements among the Palestinian Arabs tried to reestablish the Arab Higher Committee as a framework for organization and political representation. However, the internal split was stronger and the attempt failed. All hopes then focused on the newly-formed Arab League, which after several abortive attempts did indeed succeed in June 1946 in appointing an Arab Higher Committee to speak for the Arabs of Palestine. The League, naturally enough, relied on the old political leadership, the heads of the large families and the notables.[176] The newer forces, the Istiqlālists, Mūsā al-'Alamī, and others like him, who tried to act on the basis of nationalist ideology and their personal authority, were in large measure thrust aside. The Ḥusaynī family's hegemony was reinstated by the League without its being weakened seriously by any internal force. A new political force, unwilling to make peace with this situation, did in fact crop up – the League for National Liberation. This organization demanded that democratic elections to the Supreme Arab Committee be held and the masses enlisted in the nationalist struggle, but because it was communist, it failed to influence the community at large – although it succeeded in organizing – in a rather formidable fashion – a considerable portion of the young workers' class and the new intelligentsia.[177]

The Arab Higher Committee was unable to depart from its original nature as "a club for the notables from the important families." Its attempts to organize the urban youth and the fellahs in military organizations for war against the Jews did not have serious consequences. The organized force was not very large, and its efficacy was smaller yet.[178]

Since "salvation" failed to come from the armies of the Arab states, the 1948 war ended in defeat for the Palestinian Arabs – a large part of whom became refugees.

The new situation completely changed the nature of political activity among the Palestinian Arabs. A minority became Israeli citizens; a large part (including the refugees) received Jordanian citizenship; in the Gaza Strip a considerable community of refugees was concentrated in one large camp area, which became a hotbed of militant nationalist feeling; a considerable part of the refugee population in Syria moved in the course of time to Lebanon, where they could more easily find employment.

This reality led to important changes. The Jordanian government worked toward weakening the power of the Ḥusaynī family and its supporters, who were its sworn enemies. Members of this family did not, generally speaking, achieve public office, did not serve in the Jordanian parliaments or governments, and seemed to have been completely eliminated from political life. On the other hand, its Nashāshībī rivals were nurtured and rose to power. These elements had aided King 'Abd Allāh in annexing the West Bank to his kingdom and were therefore generously rewarded. Rāghib al-Nashāshībī and the members of his family, as well as members of the Khālīdī family, reached respected positions in the Jordanian administration. Hebron and Nablus, where many respected anti-Ḥusaynī families were concentrated, were rewarded by economic support for their development efforts, while "Ḥusaynī" Jerusalem suffered discrimination.

However, from the beginning of Jordanian rule, a relatively new element – which was to have no mean influence on the further development of the Palestinian factor – stands out. From the early days of Jordanian rule on the West Bank, young intellectuals tended to organize themselves in opposition frameworks in the form of cultural clubs or the Ba'th party. These intellectuals, who did not necessarily spring from the noted families ('Abd Allāh Rimāwī, Kamāl Nāṣir, etc.) adopted a militant pan-Arab ideology and opposed with all their might the pro-Western Hashemite regime which they suspected of being relatively moderate toward Israel.

Other young men, similar to the others in education and in not belonging to the old aristocracy, were behind another political and organizational attempt to remove the shame of 1948 – the Arab Nationalists Organization *(al-Qawmiyyūn al-'arab).* This organization was established in the early 1950s by Palestinian students at the American University of Beirut with the aim of achieving Arab unity which would lead to the destruction of Israel. Its slogan was "Unity, Freedom, and Revenge."[179] In the late fifties this organization put its trust in 'Abd al-Nāṣir and became in large measure an instrument of the Nasserist regime. However, in the sixties the organization began to free itself more and more of the belief that Arab unity would be the Palestinians' salvation. Instead of this, the organization turned to the left – farther left even than the Nasserist regime – and adopted the view (in 1966) that the Palestinians had to free their land by their own efforts in a war of popular liberation.[180]

A similar process characterizes the birth of *al-Fatḥ*. This organization also sprang from the Palestinian student and intellectual circles in Egypt and Kuwait. While it took its first organizational steps in 1956, it reached major proportions only in the sixties.[181] It is hardly a coincidence that it began its military activities in January 1965. The Arab world was then beginning to free itself of the belief that the process of Arab unity was in the ascendant. The United Arab Republic had broken up; the Egyptian intervention in Yemen had been exposed in all its impotence; the common Arab effort (the summit policy) had failed to keep Israel from diverting the Jordan waters. The beginning of *al-Fatḥ*'s activity was also motivated, it seems, by the recognition that "if I am not for myself, who will be for me?"

In this way a clear distinction was formed with regard to the class of leadership between the Palestinian community which had remained on its land and its segments which had become refugees. On the West Bank (and to a lesser degree in Israel), leadership remained in the hands of the important families who had a tradition of leadership and the prestige of property, while among the refugees traditional prestige and vanished property ceased to have any influence over the composition of the leadership; their place was taken by modern education, readiness for political struggle, and the ability to organize and make sacrifices.

NOTES

1 A detailed list of these *nawāḥī* and the *shaykh* families who ruled them can be found in Muḥammad 'Izzat Darwaza, *Al-'arab wa'l-'urūba taḥta 'l-taghalub al-'uthmānī* (Damascus, 1959), pt. 2, pp. 132-291; Iḥsān al-Nimr, *Ta'rīkh jabal nāblus wa'l-balqā'* (Nablus, 1961), pt. 2 pp. 183-6, 404-27; R.A. Stewart Macalister and E.W.G. Masterman, "Occasional Papers on the Modern Inhabitants of Palestine," *Palestine Exploration Fund Quarterly Statement* (1905): 352-6; (1906): 35-7 (hereafter cited as *PEFQS*); J. Finn, *Stirring Times* (London, 1878), 1: 226-43. See also U. Heyd, *Ottoman Documents on Palestine 1552-1615* (London, 1960), pp.67, 96; M. Ma'oz, *Ottoman Reform in Syria and Palestine, 1840-1861* (London, 1968), pp. 113-22.

2 Mrs. Finn, "The Fellaheen of Palestine," *PEFQS* (1879): 38-40.

3 Heyd, p.99, n.10.

4 Darwaza, pt. 2, p. 141.

5 Mrs. Finn, "The Fellaheen of Palestine," p.38.

6 Macalister and Masterman, pp. 334, 345-6.

7 George E. Post, "Essays on the Sects and Nationalities of Syria and Palestine," *PEFQS* (1891): 106-7; S. Bergheim, "Land Tenure in Palestine," *PEFQS* (1894): 197-8.

8 G. Baer, "The Evolution of Private Landownership in Egypt and the Fertile Crescent," in *The Economic History of the Middle East, 1800-1914,* ed. C. Issawi (Chicago, 1966), p. 82.

9 Gad Frumkin, *Derekh shofet biyerushalayim* (Tel Aviv, 1954), p. 110 (my emphasis, Y.P.). On Gad Frumkin's position in the administration of the Jerusalem district, see this volume, p.187.

10 Ihsān al-Nimr (pt. 2, pp. 261-2) states this unequivocally. And of 'Umar Ṣāliḥ, "Traces of Feudal System in Palestine," *Journal of Palestine Oriental Society* (hereafter cited as *JPOS*) 9 (1929): 70.

11 Ma'oz, pp. 117, 120-2; Macalister, *PEFQS* (1906): 46-50; Bargūthī, *JPOS* (1929): 79.

12 Report by Beshwer, assistant to the official in charge of public security, 18 Jan. 1921, Israel State Archives (hereafter cited as ISA), Chief Secretary Files

(hereafter cited as CS), 157; a petition of about 150 notables to the governor of Jerusalem with respect to the appointment of the *muftī* of Jerusalem, 21 March 1921, *ibid.*, 245.

13 Protest petition of the *mukhtārs* of the Banī-Zayd al-Shimāliyya, *nāḥiya* to the chief secretary, 14 July 1923, *ibid.*, 158.

14 Protocol of the session of the Committee for the Collection of Donations from the Villages, 25 Nov. 1929, ISA, Arab Excutive Committee Files (hereafter cited as AE), 3098.

15 A.H. Cohen, "Seder Hatahalukhot biymai Nabi Musa, 22.4.32-29.4.32," Zionist Archives (hereafter cited as ZA), S/25, 3070.

16 A. Hourani, "The Fertile Crescent in the 18th Century," *A Vision of History* (Beirut, 1961), pp. 35-70; *idem,* "Ottoman Reform and the Politics of Notables," in *Beginnings of Modernization in the Middle East,* ed. W.R. Polk and R.L. Chambers (Chicago, 1968), pp. 41-68.

17 Ma'oz, pp. 34-8; 87-107.

18 S. Shamir, "The Modernization of Syria: Problems and Solutions in the Early Period of Abdulhamid," in Polk and Chambers, pp. 351-82.

19 Frumkin, p. 110; Iḥsān al-Nimr, pt. 2, p. 262.

20 See the sources quoted in f.n. 19 and also M. Asaf, *Hitorerut ha'aravim be'eretz yisrael uvriḥatam* (Tel Aviv, 1967), p. 37; Baer, pp. 80-90; Paul J. Klat, "The Origins of Land Ownership in Syria," *Middle East Economic Papers* (1958): 51-66. Lists of large landowners in Palestine in the years 1918-20, in which the number of urban notables stands out, are found in ZA S/25, 7433. Cf. A. Granovsky, *Hamishtar haqarq'ī be'eretz yisrael* (Tel Aviv, 1949), pp. 34-7; 50-62; 68-70.

21 Biographical sketch in ZA, S/25, 4022.

22 A.H. Cohen, "Meora'ot November bitzfon ha'aretz," 1 Dec. 1935; ZA, S/25, 4224.

23 Ibrāhīm al-Sayyid 'Isā al-Miṣrī, *Majma' al-āthār al-'arabiyya* (Damascus, 1936), p. 124.

24 *Mir'āt al-sharq,* 12 May 1927.

25 See the cover of the pamphlet by As'ad al-Shuqayrī, *Al-risāla al-marfū'a ilā aṣhāb al-jalāla wa'l-sumūw mulūk al-muslimīn wa-umarā'him wa-ūli al-ḥall wa'l - 'aqd* (Acre, 1936).

26 *Al-Jāmi'a al-'arabiyya,* 26 March 1934; Frumkin, p. 283.

27 A list of the candidates who ran in the 1912 elections in the Jerusalem district appears in *Filasṭīn,* 10 Feb. 1912. The results of the elections appear in the issue of 4 May 1912.

28 Iḥsān al-Nimr, pt. 2, p. 405.

29 Frumkin, p.282.

30 *Ibid.*, p. 283, Geoffrey Furlonge, *Palestine Is My Country – The Story of Musa Alami* (London, 1969), p. 29.

31 Asher Druyanov, *Ketavim letoldot hibat Tzion,* pt. 1 (Odessa, 5679), p. 770; *Filasṭīn,* 31 Jan. 1912; Frumkin, p.283.

32 Druyanov, pp. 769-70; Frumkin, p. 104.

33 Iḥsān al-Nimr, pt. 2, p. 330; Tawfiq Cana'an, "Muhammedan Saints and Sanctuaries in Palestine," *JPOS* (1926), pp. 117ff.

34 'Abd Allāh Mukhlis and Ya'qūb Abū al-Hudā to the High Commissioner (HC), 25 Oct. 1923, ISA, CS, 189; *Mir'āt al-sharq,* 7 June 1924.

35 *Filasṭīn,* 8 May 1912.

36 Frumkin, pp. 102, 285.

37 Druyanov, pt. 1, p. 770. On other officeholders in the local administration from the local aristocracy, see document no. 13 from 1908, ISA, 'Alī Akram Bey Archive (governor of the Jerusalem *sanjaq* in the years 1906-8).

38 J. Finn, p. 180. Cf. also p. 181.

39 Letter from 'Alī Akram, governor of the Jerusalem district, to the Ministry of Interior, document no. 11, ISA, 'Alī Akram Bey Archive.

40 *Filasṭīn,* 10 Feb. 1912.

41 For details, see Iḥsān al-Nimr, pt. 2 pp. 417-26.

42 On the basis of the reports in ZA, L/4, IV, 276.

43 The families of Abū Khadrā, Shuwā, and Bīṭār of Gaza and Jaffa are conspicuous in the lists of large landowners in Palestine at the end of the second decade of the twentieth century. The lists are found in ZA, S/25, 7433.

44 Y. Ben-Zvi, *Eretz-Yisrael veyishuva biymai hashilton haothmani* (Jerusalem, 1962), p.99.

45 Ma'oz, pp. 33; 122.

46 *Ibid.* A regular district governor was a pasha of one or two *ṭūghs* (horse-tails), whereas the rank of the governor of the Jerusalem district was a pasha of three *ṭūghs* with the title *mushīr*.

47 *Filasṭīn,* 28 May 1913.

48 On the basis of the material in ISA, CS, 140; Foreign Office (hereafter cited as FO), 371, 3385, and 3386.

49 Along with the many services listed in my *Tzmikhat hat'nu'a haleumit ha'arvit – hapalestinait,* pp. 84ff; cf. *Documents on British Foreign Policy 1919-1939,* 1st series, 4: 361-4.

50 HC to the colonial secretary (secret dispatch) 14 Dec. 1923, CO 733/52; Clayton to the same (secret dispatch) 17 July 1924, CO 733/71. ZE Press Bureau, communiqué no. 427, 11 Aug. 1924, ZA, S/25, 517.

51 *Al-Karmil,* 5 June 1927 and 19 June 1927.

52 For details about MCA in those days, see ISA, AE, 1787.

53 A. Carmel, *Haifa,* pp. 175-6, 181.

54 Aḥmad al-Imām to the AE, 1 Oct. 1922, ISA, AE, 1773.

55 A cable of protest by the Muslim and Christian Associations of Haifa to General Bols, March 1920, ISA, CS, 30.

56 Report on a meeting of a delegation of these two associations with Lord Milner, ISA, AE, 1772; these two associations to the AE, 28 Feb. 1922; *ibid.*, 3046; same to M.K. al-Ḥusaynī, 22 March 1921; *ibid.*, 1058; Aḥmad al-Imām to the AE, 14 August 1930; *ibid.*, 1780.

57 See Nablus petitions in ISA, CS, 140. On the activities of this association and its position, see ISA, AE, 1072.

58 Cable by *Lajnat al-mu'tamar al-'arabī* (Committee of Arab Congress) to AE, 7 Oct. 1929; *ibid.*, 1780; report of the financial committee, 27 Jan. 1930; *ibid.*, 1524; see also the mailing list of the AE, 11 June 1931; *ibid.*, 3595.

59 *Al-Jāmi'a al-'arabiyya,* 15 July 1931.

60 Report on the fifth congress, ISA, CS, 168.

61 See a letter of 'Izzat Darwaza (of 1921), ISA, AE, 1773. In 1925 one of the appeals of the Nablus MCA to the AE was written on the official paper of *al-Nādī al-'arabī* (see Ḥāfiẓ Ṭūqān to AE, no. 2, 6 June 1925; *ibid.*, 1825; *al-Nādī al-'arabī* cable to the AE, 25 March 1925; *ibid.*, 3605).

62 'Izzat Darwaza, secretary of *al-Nādī al-'arabī* in Nablus, to Jamāl al-Ḥusaynī, 23 Dec. 1927 and 10 Jan. 1928; *ibid.*, 2700.

63 CID report, 23 Dec. 1920, ISA, CS, 156. On the activities of the association in 1921, see ISA, AE, 1058. On the later periods, see letter of nomination of the Gaza delegates to the sixth congress, 15 June 1923; *ibid.*, 3596; Gaza MCA to the AE, 17 Dec. 1924; *ibid.*, 1825; cable of Gaza MCA to AE, 25 March 1925; *ibid.*, 3605.

64 'Īsā Shaṭārah and 'Abd Allāh al-Jawdah to the AE president, 15 June 1922; *ibid.*, 1773.

65 See the financial reports for 1921, *ibid.*, 1713.

66 Jubrān Iskandar Kazmā to Jamāl al-Ḥusaynī, 4 July 1922; *ibid.*, 3785; letter of nomination of Nazareth delegates to the sixth congress, 14 June 1923, *ibid.*, 3596.

67 Muslim Association to the AE, July 1922, *ibid.*, 1057; *al-Karmil,* 1 Nov. 1922; letter of nomination of Tiberias delegates to the sixth congress, 15 June 1923, ISA, AE, 3596. On the financial aspect see f.n. 65.

68 See f.n. 65. HC to the colonial secretary, confidential dispatch, 6 Oct. 1922, CO 733/26.

69 'Ilyān Abū Gharbiyya, secretary of Hebron MCA, to the AE, 11 Oct. 1922, ISA, AE, 1773.

70 Safed Protest, 12 March 1920, ISA, CS, 30. See also the list of the association in March 1921, *ibid.*, AE, 1058.

71 As'ad al-Ḥājj Yūsuf (Qaddūra) to AE, 21 March 1923, *ibid.*, 1541; letter of nomination of Safed delegates to the sixth congress, *ibid.*, 3596; cable by Safed MCA to the HC 29 Nov 1923, ISA, CS, 172. As'ad al-Ḥājj Yūsuf to the AE president, 5 Jan. 1924, ISA, AE 3589; cable by Safed MCA to the AE, 23 March 1925, *ibid.*, 3605; same to the same, 16 Oct. 1929, *ibid.*, 2482.

72 Yūsuf Zamarīq to M.K. al-Ḥusaynī, 19 Dec. 1924, *ibid.*, 1825; cable by Beisan MCA to the AE, 25 March 1925, *ibid.*, 3605; same to the same, 20 Sept. 1929, *ibid.*, 1715.

73 For Ramallah, see Salīm Salāma to the AE president, *ibid.*, 1716; for Ramleh, cable by Ramleh MCA to the AE, 16 Oct. 1929, *ibid.*, 1780; protocol of the AE Bureau session, 11 Feb. 1930, *ibid.*, 3797; report of the financial committee, 27 Jan. 1930, *ibid.*, 1542; cable by Ramleh MCA, 12 Nov. 1930, *ibid.*, 1022. For Lydda, see *ibid.*, 1782.

74 See 'Abd Allāh Samāra to the AE, 11 Oct. 1922, *ibid.*, 1773. ZA, L/4, 276

IV. Haganah Archive, Shneorson Papers, nos. 5, 6. *Do'ar ha-yōm,* 9 Dec. 1919.

75 ISA, AE, 1059. Tulkarm petition concerning the muftī of Jerusalem, April 1921, ISA, CS, 245; Tulkarm petition to the Foreign Secretary, May 1921, *ibid.*, 224. Salīm ['Abd al-Raḥmān] al-Ḥājj Ibrāhīm to the AE, 23 June 1921, ISA, AE, 1773.

76 'Abd Allāh Samāra to the AE, 30 May 1922, *ibid.*, 1059; Muḥammad Kamāl al-Jayūsī to the AE, 26 Feb. 1922, *ibid.; mukhtārs* of Tulkarm subdistrict to the AE, 26 June 1922, *ibid.*, C.F. Reading, the governor of Tulkarm, to Tulkarm mayor, 19 June 1922, ISA, CS, 158.

77 *Al-Karmil,* 29 Aug. 1923.

78 ISA, AE, 1061; *al-Karmil* 16 Dec. 1922.

79 Cable by 'Abd al-Qādir Yūsuf 'Abd al-Hādi and Nāfi' 'Abūshī to M.K. al-Ḥusaynī, ISA, AE, 1058.

80 CID report, 23 Dec. 1920, ISA, CS, 156.

81 Jerusalem MCA to the governor, 10 Feb. 1919, *ibid*.

82 *Al-Karmil,* 22 April 1928.

83 Salīm al-Ḥājj Ibrāhīm to AE, 23 June 1921, ISA, AE, 1773; Ḥumaydān Kātiba Badr to M.K. al-Ḥusaynī, 13 Oct. 1925, *ibid.*, 3591; Salīm Ḥijāzī to same, *ibid.,* Ṭālib Marāqa to the same, 17 Oct. 1925, *ibid.*; Ḥasan Sidqī al-Dajānī to the delegates of the sixth congress, 20 June 1923, *ibid.*, 1771.

84 See *ibid.*, 1057, 1058, 1059, 1061, 1072, 1525, 1722, 1773, 1782, 1787, 1810, 2482, 3591, and 3785.

85 See the various proposals in *ibid.*, 1771.

86 See *ibid.*, 1072 and the AE report to the sixth congress, 16 June 1923, *ibid.*, 1026.

87 Memorandum to the League of Nations, 1922, *ibid.*, 1810; AE announcement regarding "The Palestinian Administration and the Alleged Establishment of an Advisory Council," 15 Aug. 1923, *ibid.*, 2425.

88 The various notices of the societies on the election of their delegates in *ibid.*, 1072, 3596. and 3714.

89 Ḥasan Ṣidqī al-Dajānī to the sixth congress, 20 June 1923, *ibid.*, 1771. Jamāl al-Ḥusaynī's note on the election of Jerusalem delegates to the sixth congress, *ibid.*, 3596. Report on the sixth congress, 25 June 1923, ISA, CS, 171.

90 Ḥamdī al-Ḥusaynī, pp. 7 ff; *al-Karmil,* 11 March 1928.

91 M.K. al-Ḥusaynī to Deedes (end of 1920), ISA, CS, 244.

92 See *al-Karmil,* 19 Dec, 1920. Report on the fourth congress, 21 June 1921, CO 733/13. Cox to the Assistant Chief Secretary for Political Affairs ACS (P), 25 Aug. 1922, ISA, CS, 168. Letters of election of the AE members, ISA, AE, 3596. Hamdī al-Husaynī, p. 15.

93 See the material in ISA, CS, 156.

94 Frumkin, pp. 282-6.

95 R. Storrs, *Memories* (New York, 1937), p. 351.

96 See *al-Karmil,* 23 Jan. 1924.

97 *Ibid.*, 19 Sept. 1926.

98 Report on the fourth congress, 21 June 1923, CO 733/13.

99 'Umar al-Biṭār to the fifth congress, 15 Aug. 1922, ISA, AE, 1711; al-Fārūqī's cable to the same, 20 Aug. 1922, *ibid.*, 1058.
100 Kāmil al-Budayrī to the AE, 2 June 1922, *ibid.*, 1773; protocol of the AE session held on 26 June 1922, *ibid.*, 1058. 'Ārif Pasha al-Dajānī's announcement that he had resigned from his position in the AE owing to his objection to its methods was published in *Mir'āt al-sharq*, 1 July 1922. For the AE letter on his dismissal, his reaction, and the notice to the government, see ISA, AE, 1773. 'Ārif al-Dajānī's nephew and close assistant, Ḥasan Sidqī al-Dajānī then wrote an article denying the right of the AE to decide upon sending a delegation to Hejaz (see *Bayt al-maqdis*, 10 June 1922, and 21 June 1922).
101 Eder to the secretary of the ZE in London, 17 July 1922, ZA, Z/4, 1053. ZE in Jerusalem to Eder, 16 Aug. 1922, ZA, S/25, 4377.
102 See reports in ZA, L/4, Z76IV, *Filasṭīn*, 10 Feb. 1912, 17 April 1912. *Mir'āt al-sharq*, 7 Feb. 1924. D. Miller to Eder, 9 June 1922, ZA, S/25, 4380.
103 AE Bureau, "The 35th Newsletter," 24 March 1922, ISA, AE, 1722; Ḥāfiz Ṭūqān to Jamāl al-Ḥusaynī 9 Oct. 1921, *ibid.*, 1072; last source in previous note.
104 On his jobs, see Khālidī, *'Ahl al-'ilm*, p. 39, and As'ad Shuqayrī, *al-Risāla al-marfū'a* on the internal part of the cover. On his political views, see Tawfīq Barū, pp. 507-8, 543.
105 *Al-Karmil*, 22 Oct. 1924.
106 *Ibid.*, 31 Oct. 1920.
107 *Ibid.*, 25 Oct. 1924.
108 Document no. 15A (August 1920), ISA, CS, 33; *Mir'at al-sharq*, 4 Aug. 1927.
109 *Al-Karmil*, 8 Aug. 1926. See also *ibid.*, 17 May 1930 and 10 Aug. 1930.
110 For 'Ārif al-Dajānī and Ya'qūb Farrāj and the stand of the Jerusalem MCA which they headed, see my doctoral dissertation, *Zmichat Hatnuach Haleumit Haravit Hapalestinait 1918–1929* (Jerusalem, 1971). The English version, *Growth of the Palestinian Arab National Movement*, is being published in London (summer 1973). On Rāghib al-Nashāshībī, see *Al-Jāmi'a al-'arabiyya*, 29 Nov. 1932 and *Mir'āt al-sharq* 21 April 1927. See the articles by Ḥusnī 'Abd al-Hadī (a prominent opposition leader from Nablus) in *Bayt al-maqdis*, 7 July 1920, 17 July 1920, 24 July 1920, 31 July 1920, 7 Aug. 1920, 12 May 1921; *al-Karmil*, 22 Aug. 1931, tells about a group of Palestinians who clashed with Faysal during his rule in Damascus. All these Palestinians became supporters of the opposition later on. See also *Mir'āt al-sharq* 27 Feb. 1924.
111 The files of the political department of the Zionist Executive prove this.
112 Memorandum to Eder, 5 May 1920, ZA, Z/4, 2800 II. *Filasṭīn*, 26 Nov. 1921. Kalvarisky to the political department of the Zionist Executive, 24 March 1923, ZA, S/25, 4379; report on the meeting of the members of the "National Muslim Association" with Dr. Eder, 3 April 1922, *ibid.*, 4380. Jubrān Iskandar Kazmā to the AE, 24 Aug. 1921, ISA, AE, 3785; same to same, 12 Sept. 1921, *ibid.*
113 Same to Jamāl al-Ḥusaynī, 24 Aug. 1921, *ibid.*; same to same, 29 Nov.

1921, *ibid.;* same to same 20 Feb. 1922, *ibid;* Farīd Fakhr al-Dīn to same, 30 July 1923, *ibid.*, 1057.

114 Conversations between members of the "National Muslim Association" and Dr. Eder, 30 March 1922 and 3 April 1922, ZA, S/25, 4380.

115 AE Bureau, "The 2nd Newsletter," 10 Aug. 1921, ISA, AE, 1722.

116 CID report, signed by E.H. Howard, 16 Aug. 1923, ISA, CS, 158.

117 See note no. 113. See also Jubrān Iskandar Kazmā to Jamāl al-Ḥusaynī, 13 April 1922, ISA, AE, 3785; same to the AE president, 7 July 1921, *ibid.*, 1058.

118 Same to Jamāl al-Ḥusaynī, 4 July 1922, *ibid.*, 3785.

119 See note no. 116. See also Ḥāfiẓ Ṭūqān to Jamāl al-Ḥusaynī (no date), *ibid.*, 1072.

120 Nāfi' 'Abūshī to the same, 17 Aug. 1921, *ibid.*, 1061; AE Bureau, "The 5th Newsletter," 28 Aug. 1921, *ibid.*, 1722.

121 For details on this family, see ISA, CS 151. A list of the active members of the National Muslim Association all over the country can be found in ZA, S/25, 6310.

122 AE Bureau, "The 3rd Newsletter," 10 Aug. 1921, ISA, AE, 1722; "The 4th Newsletter," 18 Oct. 1921, *ibid.;* "The 36th Newsletter," 30 March, 1922, *ibid.*

123 "The 21st Newsletter," 16 Dec. 1921, *ibid*; "The 42nd Newsletter," 19 May 1922, *ibid*; "The 47th Newsletter," 14 July 1922, *ibid*.

124 The petitions are kept in ISA, CS, 30. Communiqué of the Zionist Commission Press Bureau, no. 325, 1 June 1920, ZA, Z/4, 1454; report no. 37, 17 April 1920, *ibid.,* 2800 II; report no. 41, 21 April 1920, *ibid.;* report from Haifa, 24 May 1920, *ibid*.

125 Secret memorandum to Eder, 5 May 1920, *ibid.* See also *al-Quds al-sharīf,* 29 July 1920.

126 Petitions and letters signed by 'Abd al-Ḥamīd Abū Ghūsh and others, of March-April 1920, ISA, CS,30.

127 See, for example, Nāfi' 'Abūshī to the AE, 17 Aug. 1921, ISA, AE, 1061; same to same, 4 Jan. 1922, *ibid.*

128 Cox to ACS (P), 25 Aug. 1922, ISA, CS, 168.

129 Mir'āt al-Sharq, 9 July 1924; *al-Karmil,* 19 July 1924. On the activities of this organization against the SMC and its part in the negotiations held at the end of 1924 between the rival factions, see Maḥmūd al-Māḍī to the HC, 11 Sept. 1924, ISA, CS, 189. "Resolutions of the Reconciliation Committee," ISA, AE, 1825; *al-Karmil,* 15 Sept. 1925.

130 Cox to the ACS (P), 17 Jan. 1924, ISA, CS, 173. See also the various petitions in *ibid.,* 189; Darwaza, pt. 3, p. 41; *Mir'āt al-sharq,* 1 Dec. 1923.

131 See his claim in his book, p. 89, but the huge amount of letters, reports, and summaries included in ZA, S/25, 517, 518, and 665 proves our argument.

132 F. Kisch, "The Political Development of the Arabs in Palestine," 6 June 1925, ZA, S/25., 517; Kalvarisky, "Remarques sur la situation politique," 9 Oct. 1924, *ibid.,* 518; same to Kisch, 27 June 1926, *ibid.*, 665; Clayton to Colonial Secretary, 17 July 1924, CO 733/71.

133 Memorandum by Mr. Hason, 1927, ZA, S/25., 517.

134 A leaflet signed by Jamāl al-Ḥusaynī, "The Policy of Imperialism – Divide and Rule," ISA, AE, 1825; Ḥāfiẓ Ṭūqān to AE, no. 2, 6 May 1925, *ibid.*; *Filastīn,* 29 Jan. 1926.
135 *Mir'āt al-sharq,* 14 June 1924.
136 On this issue, see ISA, AE, 1825.
137 See opposition petition to the Colonial Secretary, ISA, CS, 189 and *al-Karmil,* 9 May 1925. On the dissolution of this branch, see ZE Press Bureau communiqué (according to *Mir'āt al-sharq,* 12 July 1924, and *Lisān al-'arab,* 16 July 1924), no. 427, 11 Aug. 1924, ZA, S/25, 517. HC to Colonial Secretary, secret dispatch, 14 Dec. 1923, CO 733/52; Clayton to the same, secret dispatch, 17 July 1924, CO 733/71.
138 HC to the colonial secretary, secret dispatch, 23 May 1924, CO 733/68; Clayton to the Colonial Secretary, secret dispatch, 24 Oct. 1924, CO 733/74; HC to the same, secret dispatch CO 733/93.
139 *Al-Karmil,* 25 Feb. 1925; *Mir'āt al-sharq,* 1 Feb. 1925, 25 Aug. 1927; *Filasṭīn,* 2 Oct. 1925, 29 Jan. 1926; leaflet signed by Jamāl al-Ḥusaynī, "The Policy of Imperialism," ISA, AE, 1825; Ḥāfiẓ Ṭūqān to the AE, no. 2, 6 May 1925, *ibid.*
140 *Mir'āt al-sharq,* 23 June 1923, 1 Feb. 1925. It is not surprising, therefore, that Colonel F. Kisch discerned this process already at the beginning of 1924. See his book, p. 92.
141 *Mir'āt al-sharq,* 2 Dec. 1925, 5 Dec. 1925.
142 *Filasṭīn,* 8 Dec. 1925, 29 Dec. 1926; *al-Karmil,* 23 Dec. 1925, 31 Jan. 1926, 14 Feb. 1926; see also Darwaza, pt. 3, pp. 50-1.
143 On this congress, the preparations for it, its composition, and character, see my doctoral dissertation, pp. 292-5.
144 Detailed lists of participants in the above-mentioned congresses appear in the supplement to my doctoral dissertation.
145 On this congress, see *Al-Jāmi'a al-'arabiyya,* 21 June 1928; *Sawt al-sha'b,* 23 June 1928; Ḥamdī al-Ḥusaynī, *Kalima ilā al-sha'b al-'arabī al-filasṭīnī ḥawla 'l-mu'tamar al-'arabī al-filasṭīnī al sābi';* 'Izzat Darwaza, *Ḥawla 'l-haraka al-'arabiyya al-ḥadītha* (Sidon, 1950), 3: 54.
146 Y. Shimoni, *Arvei Eretz-Yisrael* (Tel Aviv, 1947), pp. 288-9.
147 See ZA, S/25, 3405.
148 See my doctoral dissertation, ch. 8.
149 *Al-Jāmi'a al-'arabiyya,* the series of articles which began to be published on 22 March 1928. See also *ibid.*, 7 May 1928, 21 July 1932, 15 Aug. 1933. Protocol of AE session, 9 Sept. 1932, ISA, AE, 3797.
150 *Al-Jāmi'a al-'arabiyya,* 26 April 1928.
151 Frumkin noted (p. 324) that in 1918, when the courts of law were reopened, no young Muslims who knew how to write English could be found.
152 *Al-Ittihād al-'arabī,* 27 June 1925; *Mir'āt al-sharq,* 10 Oct. 1925.
153 *Al-Karmil,* 6 Feb. 1928, 13 Feb. 1928, and 1 April 1928; *Al-Jāmi'a al-'arabiyya,* 7 May 1928.
154 'Abd al-Qādir al-Muẓaffar to the AE, 27 Dec. 1930, ISA, AE, 2700.

155 *Al-Jāmi'a al-'arabiyya,* 21 July 1932.
156 Protocol of AE session, 9 Sept. 1932, ISA, AE, 3797.
157 Report on the congress, 7 Nov. 1932, ZA, S/25, 4122.
158 Report from 4 Nov. 1932, *ibid.*
159 Protocol of AE session, 9 Sept. 1932, ISA, AE, 3797.
160 Protocol of the AE session, 28 Oct. 1932, *ibid.*
161 *Ibid.*
162 According to the book of protocols, *ibid.*
163 Farīd Fakhr al-Dīn to Jamāl al-Ḥusaynī, 30 July 1932, *ibid.*, 1057. HC to the Colonial Secretary, secret dispatch, 14 Dec. 1923, CO 733/52. Eder to the secretary of the ZE in London, 17 July 1922, ZA, Z/4, 1053.
164 Fu'ād Shaṭāra to M.K. al-Ḥusaynī, 18 Aug. 1924, ISA, AE, 3520; Young-men's Association of Bīr-Zayt to the same, 18 Aug. 1924, *ibid*; Dā'ūd Majā'id to the same, 21 Aug. 1922, *ibid.; al-Karmil,* 15 June 1921; D. Miller to Eder, 9 May 1922, S/25, 4380.
165 *Al-Karmil,* 20 Feb. 1924.
166 *Al-Karmil,* 10 Aug. 1930.
167 Protocol of AE session, 26 Sept. 1930, ISA, AE, 3797. Protocol of AE Bureau session, 9 Sept. 1930, *ibid.*
168 Reactions of Christians from various places in the country who objected to these petitions, *ibid.*, 1052.
169 See, for example, *al-Jāmi'a al-'arabiyya,* 4 Sept. 1932, 13 Aug. 1933.
170 J. Chancellor to the Colonial Secretary, confidential dispatch, 15 Aug. 1931, CO 733/202.
171 *Al-Jāmi'a al-'arabiyya* and *Mir'āt al-sharq,* 23 Sept. 1931; ZA, S/25, 4108.
172 See the material in ZA, S/25, 4224, Ṣubḥī Yāsīn, *al-Thawra al-'arabiyya al-kubrā fī Filasṭīn* (Cairo n.d.), and Yuval Arnon, "Felahim bamered ha'aravi be'eretz Yisrael, 1936-1939," (M.A. Diss., The Hebrew University, 1970), pp. 4-5.
173 This description is based on the above-cited work by Yuval Arnon and on *Te'udot udmuyot – miginzei haknufiot ha-'arviot* (Hamagen Haivri, 1944).
174 See Yehuda Slotzki, *Seger toldot hahaganah* (Tel Aviv, 1963), 2: 759-78.
175 See Y. Bauer, *Diplomatiah umaḥteret bamdiniyut hatzionit 1939-1945* (Merhavia, 1963), pp. 11-61.
176 See Y. Shimoni, *Arvei Eretz-Yisrael* (Tel Aviv, 1946), pp. 315-28.
177 See Y. Porath, "Haligah leshihrur leumi – tequmatah, mahutah, vehit-parqutah (1943-1948)," *Hamizrah Hehadash* (The New East) 14 (1964): 354-66.
178 Y. Shimoni, "Ha'aravim Liqrat Milhemet Yisrael-'Arav," *Hamizrah Hehadash* 22 (1962): 206-7.
179 On the establishment and development of this organization, see Michael Suleiman, *Political Parties in Lebanon* (New York, 1967), pp. 155-72.
180 For the turn to the left of this organization and the turning point it under-went, see *Limādhā munaẓẓamāt al-ishtirākiyyīn al-lubnāniyyīn* (Beirut, 1970).
181 On this organization, see Ehud Ya'ari, *Fatḥ* (Tel Aviv, 1970).

REGIME AND OPPOSITION IN JORDAN SINCE 1949*

URIEL DANN

INTRODUCTION

Jordan is no self-evident entity like Egypt, or even like Syria or Iraq. Yet the state, created by Churchill and the Sharif ʻAbd Allāh for their common convenience, has by now existed for two generations – time enough to set a socio-political pattern. One should, therefore, regard with caution the easy commonplace that Jordan is "artificial"; that its raison d'être is self-perpetuation in the interest of the king and a handful of his supporters, protected by a "Bedouin army"; and that this interest is opposed to the interest and wishes of the majority of the population, and the more progressive and better educated majority at that.

This concept is clearly too dependent on subjective values to be proved or disproved at present with the historian's tools. This study moves on a different plane; it examines its theme inductively, by analyzing the role and the background of the main actors at certain turning points over the last twenty-one years.

In detail the method will be as follows:

a. The "image of Jordan" will be delineated as it has imprinted itself over the years on a consensus of well-wishers, ill-wishers, and detached observers alike.

b. The "population of Jordan" will be briefly described in terms of objectively determinable sectors which have played a significant role in the political history of the country.

c. The "politically active public" will be classified in terms of its attitude toward the "image of Jordan": the "establishment" – those persons or groups who have been active and effective in maintaining and advancing the "image"; and "anti-establishment elements" – those who endeavored to supplant it.

---

* This paper is published as originally composed late in 1970; the author believes it to be essentially up-to-date in early 1973.

d. These two criteria will then be confronted as they appeared at different times, in analytical notes followed by tables. This is the main body of the study.

e. Finally, "observations" will be made on the strength of the material presented.

Obviously, certain assumptions will have to provide the starting point of much of the argument. However, the far-reaching breakdown into facts should render the analysis as safe as can be expected in a story where so many imponderables must always remain.

The "image of Jordan" can be defined at its highest denominator still acceptable to a wide consensus as follows: A kingdom, hereditary in the Hashemite family, successor to the British-mandated emirate of Transjordan, and heir, as far as possible, to the emirate's political, social, and psychological values; hence, the king as linchpin of the political machine; the trappings of monarchy possessing real significance; an establishment jealous for the independence of the state and fearful of "liberated" pan-Arabism, whatever the origin of its appeals; determined to lean on the West and dependent on its aid; a professional army in the background, to be called out on comparatively slight provocation and used ruthlessly if need be. The disappearance of any of the components would mean a fundamentally different Jordan – provided it survived at all – posing a fundamentally different challenge to the observer and to the world at large.

The population of Jordan within the country's de facto boundaries is about 1.5 million; it is unprofitable for our purpose to try and arrive at more than an approximation.[1] Of this number the "political public" is certainly a small percentage, if the criteria applicable to the West are taken as the sole yardstick. However, it will be shown that on occasion "the masses" exerted an influence in contexts which are not devoid of a genuine political rationale. Also, it must be kept in mind that the political public of today's West Bank is much involved, emotionally at least, in East Bank politics, though this factor cannot as yet be estimated by the inductive method used here.

The population sectors considered relevant to this study have ethno-religious, geographical, or ecological criteria, with the exception of one which is defined by occupation. Age, education, and party membership, so far as they appear at all, figure in a secondary capacity.[2]

Once the "image of Jordan" as delineated above is accepted, the first sector demanding attention is the population native to the East Bank, the Transjordanians proper – rather less than one half of the population. However, some qualifications are necessary. For one, the nomad and seminomad population, the Bedouin proper, must be bracketed out. Their way of life, their needs, values, and history under the emirate, establish them as a sector to be assessed separately. Secondly, the term "native" cannot be taken literally. At the least, hundreds of families originating in Palestine, and to a lesser degree in Syria and the Hejaz, settled in Transjordan between 1921 and 1949. They came to play an important part in the administration and economy of the emirate. On purely pragmatic grounds, they must be considered "Transjordanians" in our context. Thirdly, though the inhabitants of Transjordan are in their vast majority Sunni Muslims who think of themselves as Arabs, there are two minority groups important enough to be considered here: the one is the Circassians, Sunni Muslims who originally emigrated from their native Caucasia to Transjordan and other frontier regions of the Ottoman Empire during the last quarter of the nineteenth century.[3] They settled as farmers, with Amman, Wādī al-Sīr, and Jarash as their main concentrations in Transjordan. With a language of their own, vividly conscious of their national distinctiveness, socially and economically ahead of their neighbors, the Circassians have played so far, as individuals and as a group, a part in the history of the country far greater than their modest number of about fifteen thousand would warrant. There are signs that the younger generation tends toward assimilation among the "Arabs," but for the time being the community must still be considered a factor in any political assessment. The other minority group, though larger by far in numbers, has played a less impressive role. These are the Christians native to Transjordan, most of them Greek Orthodox, rather less than ten percent of the population in 1948; their main communities are at Salt, Kerak, and Madaba. In line with their traditional role in the Ottoman Empire, they have not made themselves conspicuous in extra-communal affairs; it is, however, of interest to examine whether their special status has tended to align politically-minded individuals with the establishment, or with its enemies.

An important subdivision of the "Transjordanian" population for the purpose of political analysis runs along regional lines. Climate, topography – the lateral cleavage of the settled country by a number of deep canyons – and one instance of near chance – 'Abd Allāh's choice of Amman as his capital in 1921 – account for at least three distinct regions, each with its own traditions, loyalties, and aversions. The north centers about Irbid, the second city of the kingdom, and Jarash. It has a compact agricultural population, sedentary since times immemorial. There is a tradition of self-reliance that goes back to closely knit associations for local defense, *nāḥiyas,* which still did duty two generations ago and which have survived in the attitude of the population toward outside interference. Further south lies al-Balqā' around Salt, long the most important town of the East Bank; it has a tradition of hostility to Irbid, family ties with Nablus, and distrusts the central administration in Amman – the upstart rival which has displaced Salt from its relative eminence within living memory. Amman, the young metropolis, shelters one-third of the country's population. However, its mushroom growth – fifteenfold over the last thirty years – has so far precluded the emergence of the "Ammani" as a meaningful category of political citizen. In contrast, the countryside south of Amman definitely constitutes a recognizable unit in this sense. Its comparative remoteness from the centers of social and political unrest in the contemporary Arab world, its closeness to the conservative Hejaz, the paucity of prospects for economic advancement, and, most important, a kinship system which preserves tribal identifications and values give this region a peculiar significance relative to the "image of Jordan."

The second primary sector are the Palestinians, for our purposes the inhabitants of Jordan born in Palestine under the mandate. The young generation, born to Palestinian parents since 1948, does not yet concern this study – though it will pose a major problem to the state, and to the political analyst, very soon. The Palestinians were about two-thirds of the population when 'Abd Allāh took possession of the West Bank. Their part in the population of the East Bank has grown steadily ever since, and today they constitute half the population of Jordan in its post-1967 frontiers. The position of the Palestinians in Jordan, their attitudes, advantages, and handicaps, has too often been described to justify repetition. Yet a few points must be made. The Palestinians have been citizens of Jordan in the full legal sense since 1949–50. It is an impermissible generalization that they were, because of their background, "more progressive" politically than the Transjordanians; in advanced administrative experience, they lagged behind Transjordanians of comparable status. Lastly, although throughout the last twenty-two years many Palestinians were entrusted with high office, these cases bear on the theme of this study only when the officeholders were invested with a share in high-level decision making or decision enforcing. The subject will come up later on.

It is meaningful to subdivide the Palestinians into three subsectors: (a) natives of the Jordanian West Bank, including those who moved their homes to the East Bank between 1949 and 1967; (b) refugees in the wider sense, i.e., Palestinians born in what was by 1949 Israel, whatever their circumstances at the stage under survey; (c) refugees in the narrower sense, i.e., inhabitants of refugee camps.

The Bedouin have been important in the history of the state since the establishment of the emirate. Their notables had been on terms of intimacy – not necessarily of friendship – with the Hashemite ruler from the first. Since the 1930s they have provided the core of the fighting units of the army. The number of "pure" Bedouin – tent-dwelling, camel and sheep-raising nomads with only marginal recourse to agriculture – has been steadily diminishing for decades. But it is established that Bedouin *mores* keep alive for a generation or more after a community becomes sedentary, and thus the term "Bedouin" must comprise for the present purpose more than nomads proper. It is therefore difficult to arrive at even an approximation of their number: 100,000 may be near the mark for the wider interpretation.[4] It is further advisable to distinguish between the two chief tribal groups, the Banū Ṣakhr and Ḥuwayṭāt, in view of the rivalry between them for political influence and royal favor. As each of the two groups has a periphery of client tribes, they have been loosely referred to below as "northern" and "southern" Bedouin, respectively.

The Jordanian army, still popularly known as the Arab Legion, has been identified with the established order in the state to an extent that few armies have achieved anywhere, whenever the regime was not outright military in nature. There were stages when active disloyalty was not uncommon among individual officers. They have never succeeded, so far, in inspiring a movement in the army which became a serious threat to the regime. Since its inception as a fighting force the army has never, as an institution, disappointed the trust which the rulers of the state put in it. Its very reputation for loyalty has probably deterred would-be plotters in more cases than will ever be known. The instances when it took action against domestic enemies of the regime must be numbered in scores. The causes for this devotion are reasonably clear: long-term service under excellent material conditions; a carefully nurtured ésprit de corps and good leadership from the throne downward; fear for its position under a regime which rejects the "image of Jordan." The widely accepted explanation of a Bedouin army alienated from a *ḥaḍarī* population is too simple, though it contains some truth, especially with regard to the rank and file. The following may serve to introduce some differentiation. Apart from the rare eruption of the rank and file as a primary political factor, three aspects of the role of the army will be probed: the communal background of its chiefs, on the one hand; that of defectors and conspirators, on the other; the part senior officers have played on occasion in the councils of the ruler outside their substantive appointments.

The last sector is undoubtedly the smallest, but not the least significant: Few royal families can nowadays be as closely knit as the Hashemites, descendants in the male line of the Prophet's daughter. All three kings of Jordan were the offspring of marriages between cousins: Ḥusayn himself took a kinswoman as his first wife. It is only to be expected that members of the family should occupy positions of political importance, official and otherwise. This phenomenon will also be observed.

The "establishment," for the purposes of this enquiry, has been narrowly defined. It comprises the high-level decision makers and the high-level decision enforcers; the manipulators, but not the manipulated. It does not comprise holders even of exalted office – if it can be fairly shown that the office, or the appointment, conferred administrative responsibility, wealth, or prestige, but no primary political power.

The first place, according to the "image of Jordan" as defined, goes to the king. From among the cabinet, only the prime minister, the deputy prime minister, the minister of the interior, and, since the inception of his office, the minister of information always belong to this group. (The Nābulsī cabinet of 1956–57 is an anomaly, in this respect as in others.) But it is important to realize that the foreign minister and the minister of defense as such never did: the former is expected to interpret the king's day-to-day policy to the outside world and to supervise the diplomatic staff for the same purpose; the latter executes some of the functions of a director-general at his ministry, with far less responsibility and elbow-room than career directors-general at the Ministry of Defense enjoy in most countries.

The heads of the army inside the "establishment" are: the commander-in-chief and his deputy; the chief of the General Staff and his assistant for operations; the commanders of the top formations, brigades until the mid-sixties and divisions afterwards; the director of military intelligence; and, finally, the director of public security, the chief of police.

Outside these functional categories, there is a circle of "king's friends" who may or may not hold official appointments, but who have the king's ear and who are apt to be entrusted with missions of political importance. Among the former are the chief of the royal cabinet and the senior aide-de-camp; the latter are usually identified by common report.

The "anti-establishment elements," that part of the political public which essentially rejects the "image of Jordan," for long fell into two categories: civilian politicians who generally owed what weight they had to their membership in the House of Representatives; and army officers engaged in conspiracy or other acts of fundamental protest. Both categories were opposed to much or all that Jordan represented, but they had no clearly considered concept to replace the Jordanian entity as such, or even a strong motivation to do so. Thus, with all their enmity to the regime, often deeply felt and sometimes dangerous, they remained members of the body politic in whose framework they struggled. With the Palestine organizations, a different category of "anti-establishment elements" emerged. The development is of importance, not merely for its own sake, but also for its rebound on the older type of opposition. The problem will be treated in its place below.

I. 'ABD ALLĀH'S LAST DAYS: NOTE

When 'Abd Allāh annexed the West Bank to his kingdom, he furthered an ambition which he had nursed since his first establishment in Amman: that of becoming, in the fullness of time, ruler of a Greater Syria extending over the mandated territories of Syria, Lebanon, Palestine, and Transjordan. A number of seeming opportunities at earlier dates had turned barren, usually as soon as the first feelers were stretched out. This time fortune appeared to smile: Britain considered 'Abd Allāh's plan the best, and nascent Israel considered it the least obnoxious, of all possibilities for Arab Palestine; the anti-Hashemite front among the Arab states, Egypt, Syria, and Saudi Arabia, was incapable of effective action. The complex array of allies and clients which 'Abd Allāh had managed to set up over the years within the chaos and turmoil of Palestinian politics served its purpose: the Palestinians, thrown into the depth of despair, were readily turned toward the only protector in sight. When the armistice with Israel was signed on 3 April 1949 all seemed over but the shouting, and the factual integration a matter of formalities to be carried out at leisure. The various roots of the difficulties that followed have been identified, though their relative significance will always remain a matter of dispute. It is even arguable to what extent 'Abd Allāh, at the end of his life, saw the annexation as an achievement: temperamental optimist that he was, there is evidence that he died a tired and disappointed man.

One point which tends to get blurred with the passage of time is the extent to which the attitudes of the preceding decades determined the relations between 'Abd Allāh and the Palestinian political public: most of the high appointments 'Abd Allāh made for the West Bank were *mu'āriḍūn* – Nashāshībīs, their allies, and followers – and were appointed for that reason. A substantial case can also be made out that 'Abd Allāh's murder was more of a last link in his feud with the Ḥusaynīs than punishment for his readiness to come to an arrangement with Israel. This important aspect of the "Palestinians' problem" in its beginnings still awaits research. For this study it may be neglected, since it disappeared as a matter of primary significance with 'Abd Allāh's death.

TABLE I. 'ABD ALLĀH'S LAST DAYS

A. The establishment

1. The king	
'Abd Allāh b. Ḥusayn	b. Mecca; Transjordanian[1] 1921; Hashemite.
2. The inner cabinet (Dec. 1950)	
Prime Minister: Samīr al-Rifā'ī	b. Safed; Transjordanian since 1920s.
Interior Minister: 'Abbās Mīrzā	Transjordanian; Circassian.
3. Army and police	
Chief of General Staff: J.B. Glubb Heads of branches and commanders of formations: All British	Regular officers seconded for service in Jordan or serving under personal contract. No case is known where a British officer did not conform to the "image of Jordan" while serving in Jordan.
Deputy Chief of General Staff: 'Abd al-Qādir al-Jundī Director of Public Security:[2] Aḥmad Ṣidqī al-Jundī	Former Ottoman officers who served with the Arab Legion since its beginnings.

4. "King's friends"

Chief of Royal Cabinet: Sulaymān Tūqān	Nablus. "Nashāshībī" appointment; family tradition of cooperation with Hashemites discernible till today.
Chief Aide de Camp: Muḥammad Sa'dī Shāhīn	Ramleh. Till 1948 senior police officer in Palestine.
Amīr Na'if b. 'Abd Allāh	Younger son of king and favorite of his father.
Sa'īd al-Muftī	Transjordanian; Circassian.
Ibrāhīm Hāshim	b. Nablus; Transjordanian since 1920s. (Alternated with Rifā'ī as Prime Minister since late 1930s)
Tawfīq Abū'l-Hudā	b. Acre; Transjordanian since 1920s.
Sir Alec S. Kirkbride	British minister in Amman; personal friend of 'Abd Allāh.

B. Anti-establishment elements

1. Within army

'Abd Allāh al-Tall	Irbid: family of local notables. Involved in a "plot"; anti-British and vaguely Arab nationalist. Civilian kinsmen also implicated.

2. Within House of Representatives

(elections of April 1950)	(Based on their debating and voting records[3])
'Abd al-Ḥalīm Nimr	Transjordanian; representing Salt
Anwar Nusayba	West Bank;[4] representing Jerusalem and Jericho
'Abd Allāh Na'wās	West Bank; Christian; representing Jerusalem; Ba'thī
Rashād Maswada	West Bank; representing Hebron
'Abd Allāh al-Rīmāwī	West Bank; representing Ramallah; Ba'thī

Mūsā Nāṣir	West Bank; Christian; representing Ramallah
Khlūṣī Khayrī	West Bank; representing Ramallah
Shafīq Rashīdāt	Transjordanian; representing Irbid; family local notables

3. Involved in 'Abd Allāh's murder[5]

Muṣṭafā al-'Ushī	Jerusalem; the murderer; killed on the spot
'Abd Allāh al-Tall	Irbid; anti-British army officer from a family of local notables; sentenced to death *in absentia*
Mūsā al-Ayyūbī	Jerusalem; sentenced to death *in absentia*
Mūsā al-Ḥusaynī	Jerusalem; hanged
'Abd al-Qādir Faraḥāt	Jerusalem; hanged
Zakariyyā 'Ukka	Jerusalem; hanged
'Abd al-Maḥmūd 'Ukka	Jerusalem; hanged

4. Mass action — In West Bank towns north of Jerusalem were sporadic riots, which were of significance insofar as they deterred leaders of the establishment from putting their weight behind 'Abd Allāh's policy of seeking accommodation with Israel.

1 Transjordanian Sunni Muslim unless otherwise stated.
2 Director of Public Security is the equivalent of the national Chief of Police.
3 Based on Y. Algom in *Hamizrah Hehadash (The New East)* I: 302.
4 West Bank residents are not refugees unless specifically stated.
5 It may be taken as established that all the Palestinians were active in the Husaynī interest before 1949.

II. ṬALĀL'S REIGN (SEPTEMBER 1951 – AUGUST 1952): NOTE

Ṭalāl's brief reign is often regarded as an interlude, in the sense that it eliminated, while it lasted, the "image of Jordan" as defined here. This view is based on the following points: Ṭalāl had been known as a prince for his self-effacing shyness, and, as a king, he did nothing to strike another, more aggressive pose in public. He was rumored to hate the British and to be uncompromising toward Israel. He was also believed to see in Arab nationalism something else than an occasion of aggrandizement for his house, as his father had done; or, putting the same idea with greater fairness to ʻAbd Allāh, Ṭalāl's concept of Arab nationalism was believed to be more in accord with modern strands of opinion. He joined the Arab League Defense pact and demonstrated his wish to bury the feud with Ibn Saʻūd. Domestically, Ṭalāl as a prince was reputed to be anti-authoritarian and "democratic." As king his grant of a new constitution, which for the first time accepted the principle of ministerial responsibility to Parliament, and some relatively progressive social legislation tended to confirm this reputation. That ʻAbd Allāh's trusted collaborators were believed with some reason to have intrigued first against his succession and then in favor of his removal lent further color to the picture of Ṭalāl as "different."

The bases of this speculation are not very sound, quite apart from the scarcely disputed fact that Ṭalāl was incurably deranged. His liberalism as crown prince may be explained as defiance of a father with whom he was on bad terms – a common phenomenon in such cases. As king, Ṭalāl showed in one or two cases that he could be vindictive and tyrannical in vengeance of personal slights. The constitution was hardly his own inspiration: ʻAbd Allāh had already promised ministerial responsibility and died before he could be fairly accused of bad faith. In any case, the two-thirds majority required from the Chamber of Deputies for a vote of nonconfidence made parliamentary supremacy illusory in practice.[5] Ṭalāl kept his father's Transjordanian ménage intact with insignificant exceptions; Glubb and his British subordinates remained as firmly in charge as ever. No attempt to dislodge either is known, and together they certainly conserved the principles of ʻAbd Allāh's rule. Under these circumstances, the limited rapprochement with the League and Ibn Saʻūd can be regarded as useful adjustments, certainly connected with the change of regime, but without historical significance.

In one respect Ṭalāl's personal image made itself felt. Though the establishment remained unshaken, tension along the armistice line was rising, and a harsh economic crisis made life for the poor even more of a misery than usual, and despite individual protest and occasional demonstrations, the domestic scene was basically more relaxed than at any other period since 1949 and until now. During the brief year of his reign, Ṭalāl did not exhaust the vague expectations of the largely amorphous opposition that a fundamental change would soon be decreed from above. No doubt this euphoria could not have lasted for much longer had Ṭalāl remained on the throne. On the available evidence, it is unprofitable to speculate in which direction the kingdom would then have moved.

TABLE II. ṬALĀL'S REIGN

A. The establishment

1. The king	
Ṭalāl b. ʻAbd Allāh	b. Mecca
2. The inner cabinet (July 1951)	
Prime Minister: Tawfīq Abū'l Hudā	b. Acre; Transjordanian since 1920s
Deputy Prime Minister and Interior Minister: Saʻīd al-Muftī	Transjordanian; Circassian
3. Army and police	No significant change
4. "King's friends"	Not a meaningful category under Ṭalāl; Muḥammad Saʻdī Shāhīn remained Chief Aide de Camp; Sir Alec S. Kirkbride left Jordan toward the end of 1951.
B. Anti-establishment elements	Not a meaningful category under Ṭalāl; see note

III. THE REGENCY (AUGUST 1952–MAY 1953): NOTE

At the time of Ṭalāl's deposition, the heir apparent, Amīr Ḥusayn, was a minor, and a regency became necessary until his coming of age nine months hence. For the first time, and until now for the only time, the state had to cope with the protracted absence of a Hashemite ruler, physical as well as constitutional.

The establishment did not change in personnel. The temporary rulers attempted to combine conciliation of "the modern spirit" evoked by Ṭalāl with firmness wherever the established principles of government were called into question, and on the whole they were successful. It was then, to give an example, that the time-honored titles of pasha and bey were abolished.[6] Also under the regency, attempts of the Ba'th and Taḥrīr parties to achieve recognition, supposedly guaranteed by the new constitution, were put down with a firmness that had lost nothing for 'Abd Allāh's exit.

Inevitably, the question arises to what extent the regency is relevant today, when the survival of a Transjordanian state without the Hashemites but otherwise retaining essential characteristics of the old image is a possibility worth considering. In one important respect a parallel exists. The regency proves that at a certain time, ages ago in terms of Middle East political history, the establishment could keep on top in the rough-and-tumble of domestic challenges, without the Hashemite ruler as a continuous prime mover. It will be seen that men of similar background, political complexion, and, above all, determination to survive are not lacking today. Should the present ruler be removed from the scene, these men may have the determination to take over and try to carry on as did their forerunners. But here the parallel breaks down. The essentials of the 1952–53 situation included Glubb and his array of British commanders, detested by the opposition, but with a fearful prestige for readiness to crush all physical challenges to the regime. That this repute seems almost comical in the light of after-knowledge detracts nothing from its validity then. Today's essentials include a Palestinian community whose basic dissociation from the state has not changed, but which has grown immeasurably in assertiveness, self-importance, and powers of organization. Lastly, the world around Jordan has changed: a concept of inter-Arab and international alignment which was accepted – grudgingly in many cases – as a given fact then is an intolerable challenge now, unless carefully camouflaged.

TABLE III. THE REGENCY

A. The establishment

1. The Regents

Ibrāhīm Hāshim	b. Nablus; Transjordanian since 1920s; President of the Senate.

Sulaymān Ṭūqān	Nablus; senator
'Abd al-Raḥmān al-Rashīdāt	Irbid; senator
2. The inner cabinet	
Prime Minister: Tawfīq Abū'l-Hudā	b. Acre; Transjordanian since 1920s
Deputy Prime Minister and Interior Minister: Sa'īd al-Muftī	Transjordanian; Circassian
3. Army and police	No significant change
B. Anti-establishment elements	
1. Within House of Representatives[1]	
Vote of confidence, 11 Nov. 1952, on the speech from the throne	The Prime Minister refused to apologize for two Bedouin members who had insulted the Palestinians. Of the twenty West Bank members, fifteen walked out. The speaker and two ministers abstained. One Christian member for Bethlehem and one Muslim member for Jenin voted with the government.
2. Extra-parliamentary opposition[1]	
Ba'th party:	
Munīf al-Razzāz	Amman; b. Syria. Arrested during razzia, November 1952.
Amīn Shuqayr	Amman; b. Syria
Bahjat al-Gharbiyya	Jerusalem
Sulaymān al-Ḥadīdī	Salt
Aḥmad Kharīṣ	Irbid
'Abd al-Raḥmān Shuqayr	Transjordanian
Taḥrīr party:	The party resembles the Muslim Brethren in its principles but has been unrelenting in its enmity to the regime.

Taqī al-Dīn al-Nabhānī	Ramallah; founding member
Dā'ūd al-Ḥamdān	Lydda; founding member

1 Based on Sh. Shina in *Hamizrah Hehadash,* IV: 112.

IV. THE BAGHDAD PACT CRISIS: NOTE

The last months of 1955 brought the sharpest confrontation of Western and neutralist concepts which Jordan has ever faced. The Eden government, under attack from a vocal and influential minority of the Conservative party for its supposed softness toward Egypt, and in mounting irritation over 'Abd al-Nāṣir – his politics *and* his personality – was eager to make the Baghdad Pact as spectacular a success as possible in the Arab world. To 'Abd al-Nāṣir it became, in consequence, an overriding necessity that the Pact should be a spectacular failure. In the case of Jordan at least, an element of irrationalism creeps into the issue when regarded from the Western view: at best, the contribution of Jordan to the declared purpose of the pact – the military defense of the Middle East against the Soviet Union – could not be very significant. Ḥusayn's attitude was decidedly favorable. Young as he was, his conviction that his fate and the well-being of his country were tied up with the West was as firmly rooted as his grandfather's had been. This being so, the political, diplomatic, and monetary advantages promised to Jordan in case of her adherence were a neat bonus; he had no experience as yet of 'Abd al-Nāṣir's anger and the rage of a hysterical "street." Ḥusayn's established advisers were in their majority fair-weather supporters: they did not object to the principle; appreciated the bargaining position it gave Jordan opposite Britain; were fearful of domestic trouble from the start; and did not consider the issue worth running unusual risks for. A visit of the Turkish president, Bayar, put the public on the alert. When the British chief of the Imperial General Staff, General Templer, arrived in Amman on 6 December 1955 to clinch the deal, tension neared the explosion point.

The prime minister, Sa'īd al-Muftī, soon thought it prudent to resign in view of the atmosphere. His resignation, and the appointment as his successor of Hazzā' al-Majālī, reputedly the most determined of the Baghdad Pact supporters, taught the opponents of the pact a double lesson: that time was short and that pressure paid. Within a day, Amman and every town on the West Bank erupted in riots which have never had their equal in Jordan in violence and extent. They were certainly fanned from Cairo and, in no small measure, managed by Egyptian personnel within Jordan. But this point should not be overrated. The passion was genuine. The threatened accession of Jordan to the Baghdad Pact actually spelt to much of the public – intelligentsia and masses – surrender, treason, and utter humiliation, and they rose in fury and despair. The student of history must register the phenomenon without being capable of fully explaining it in rational terms. It is, however, ironic that the grand prize Britain held out to public opinion – the strengthening of the army through increased aid – was as responsible as any secondary factor for the hostility to the Templer mission. It reflects on the penetration of British Middle East experts at the time that they did not grasp the real menace which the British-led Arab Legion meant to Arab nationalists in the circumstances of 1955.

The establishment – king, army, inner cabinet – reacted feebly. Counter mass demonstrations were considered and rejected, though they were feasible without doubt. After four days of pandemonium, Majālī resigned in turn, and, though no positive statement was made, the public knew that the Baghdad Pact was out. Undoubtedly, mass action had deflected the regime from a major policy. Yet one reason for this outcome was that the stakes were unequally distributed. Once the establishment realized what it was up against, the game was no longer worth the candle.[7] It is for this reason that this particular history has not repeated itself. A month later violent riots broke out again. The Baghdad Pact issue being practically dead, anti-establishment slogans as such came much more to the fore. This time the authorities reacted forcefully, and the riots petered out.

TABLE IV. THE BAGHDAD PACT CRISIS

A. The establishment

1. The king

Ḥusayn b. Ṭalāl	b. Amman, 1935; installed 2 May 1953

2. The inner cabinet

Of 30 May 1955:

Prime Minister and Minister of Foreign Affairs: Sa'īd al-Muftī	Transjordanian; Circassian
Interior Minister: Hazzā' al-Majālī	Kerak; tribal but not Bedouin. For generations the leading family of town and district.

Of 15 Dec. 1955:

Prime Minister and Minister of Foreign Affairs and Economy: Hazzā' al-Majālī	Interior Minister in previous cabinet.
Interior Minister: 'Abbās Mīrzā	Transjordanian; Circassian. Resigned when riots were at their peak of violence.

Of 21 Dec. 1955:

Prime Minister: Ibrāhīm Hāshim	b. Nablus; Transjordanian since 1920s
Deputy Prime Minister and Minister of Foreign Affairs: Samīr al-Rifā'i	b. Safed; Transjordanian since 1920s
Interior Minister: 'Umar Maṭar	Amman; in state service since 1924

3. Army and police

Director of Public Security: Rāḍī 'Ināb	Nablus; Arab Legion since 1920s: succeeded Glubb as Chief of General Staff in March 1956 and retired in May.
	No other significant changes

4. "King's friends"

Queen Mother Zein	Hashemite; first cousin of her husband King Ṭalāl. Of great political influence during first years of Ḥusayn's reign.
Chief of Royal Cabinet: Bahjat al-Talhūnī	Ma'an; family of local notables

Chief Aide de Camp; ‘Alī Abū Nuwār	Salt; early boon companion of king
Hashemite family:	
Sharīf Ḥusayn b. Nāṣir	Uncle of Queen Mother
Sharīf Nāṣir b. Jamīl	Brother of Queen Mother

B. Anti-establishment elements

1. Ministers who resigned during crisis

From Mufti cabinet:	
‘Alī Ḥusnā ‘Aẓmī al-Nashāshībī Na‘īm al-Hādī Sam‘ān Dā’ūd	All from West Bank. Resigned when cabinet majority rejected their demand that Egypt give prior consent to Jordan’s accession to Baghdad Pact.
From Majālī cabinet:	Resigned when riots were at their peak of violence.
‘Abbās Mīrzā	Transjordanian; Circassian
‘Ārif al-‘Ārif	West Bank
‘Umar al-Barghūtī	West Bank
Muḥammad ‘Alī al-Ja‘barī	West Bank
Jalīl Badrān	West Bank

2. Army and police

Director of Public Security: Aḥmad Ṣidqī al-Jundī	Former Ottoman officer who held this position under ‘Abd Allāh. Dismissed for negligence in carrying out the official policy of honoring armistice with Israel.[1]

3. Mass action

Destructive riots after 16 Dec. 1955; no mob leaders can be identified.	The centers of action were Amman and Jerusalem, and the starting points were refugee camps everywhere. However, the urban student population also was deeply involved, whatever its social background. See also note.

1 No cases of active disloyalty have come into the open.

V. THE NĀBULSĪ GOVERNMENT (OCTOBER 1956 – APRIL 1957): NOTE

The Nābulsī government is a singular phenomenon in the history of Jordan. It was a cabinet, the senior members of which rejected the "image of Jordan" – consciously and publicly – point by point. The Hashemite tradition was nothing to them; the king, if permitted to reign, should certainly not rule. Arab nationalism meant alignment with Egypt and Syria under 'Abd al-Nāṣir's leadership. "Positive neutralism" was accepted in its full implication of hostility to the West and friendliness to the Communist bloc. The army was to be weaned from its traditional values through its least tradition-bound sector, the urban officer.

It is astonishing that such a government should ever have come into office without a coup d'état. And yet, under the circumstances, the king had no choice. On 1 March 1956 he had dismissed General Glubb and expelled him from Jordan; within three months the other British officers also left. The background has often been analyzed. One rational factor involved usually receives too little attention: Ḥusayn realized, as a moral of the Templer affair, that Glubb and his British associates had become a mortal political liability, outweighing any advantage which could be derived from their reliability and professional competence.

The risks were soon obvious. The sudden need to replace an entire leadership put to the fore what had so far been the second rank with few chances of promotion. It was a dazzling vista that opened all of a sudden and, it must be realized, it was a situation which was then almost without parallel in the Arab world.[8] Above all, it affected the officer who was in any case less likely to value the "image of Jordan" – the young, the well educated, the adaptable, the ambitious, the officer with an eye for the political chance. This type of officer knew, of course, to what forces he owed this boon. It is little wonder then that throughout 1956 the most active elements of the officers' corps saw their fortune tied to the civilian anti-establishment sector. It was apparently the combined pressure of the new command group, headed by the new chief of the General Staff, 'Alī Abū Nuwār, which ensured the holding of new elections for the Chamber of Deputies on party lines, with guarantees for honest scrutiny without army intervention. In the prevailing atmosphere an anti-establishment majority was a foregone conclusion, and it is worth stressing that the establishment candidates fared better than might have been expected.

The elections took place on 21 October 1956. The anti-establishment parties were (with the number of successful candidates in a house of forty): the National Socialist party, 11; the Communists, in the guise of a National Front, 3; the Ba'th, 2; the Muslim Brethren, 4; the Ṭahrīr party, 1. The Muslim Brethren by then hated 'Abd al-Nāṣir too much to be effective against Ḥusayn. The Islamic-fundamentalist Ṭahrīr party, though uncompromisingly hostile to the establishment, had nothing positive in common with the secular opposition. The first three parties mentioned here shared, however, the characteristics outlined at the head of this chapter, and to that extent they had a common positive policy. Accordingly, the leader of the National Socialist party, Sulaymān al-Nābulsī, found no difficulty in forming a coalition government with the other two.

Yet the National Socialist party occupied its own place among the opposition. It was "historical" within the terms of the country: its past went back to the National Congress, the first opposition party, however rudimentary, under the Organic Law of 1928. Its leaders, as a rule, were not pushing newcomers, but respectable citizens whose families were sometimes of older standing in the country than the Hashemites and conscious of the fact. They were little interested in social questions. And for all their identification with Nasserite nationalism – accepted by the public as genuine – they had no affiliations abroad. It is therefore not surprising that alone among the coalition parties, the National Socialists gained seats on the East Bank. That they should also have gained so great an advantage over their coalition partners suggests that even in its oppositional moods, at a time when 'Abd al-Nāṣir's prestige was nearing its zenith, the electorate did not lack a certain soil-bound stolidity. The National Socialists certainly owed nothing to the authorities.

The record of the Nābulsī cabinet during its six months in office is of little interest here. Its most spectacular act, the abrogation of the 1948 treaty with Britain, was a matter of little controversy; the treaty had indeed been emptied of its content. Ḥusayn's main charge against the Nābulsī cabinet, that it opened Jordan to Communist penetration, should not be dismissed as mere demagogy, but it was obviously only one aspect of the situation. In truth, Ḥusayn realized that what is called here the "image of Jordan" was rapidly dissolving, and that further resilience would soon leave him with nothing to be resilient about.

It is of greater interest to enquire what brought the anti-establishment cabinet down. Its constitutional position was very strong (notwithstanding Ḥusayn's later assertions to the contrary), it had the support of articulate public opinion, and it was eminently acceptable to Egypt and Syria – the most aggressively vocal Arab states of the period. In a nutshell, the answer is that the Western powers known to stand by Ḥusayn were still feared as much as hated, that Ḥusayn had a better hold on the army than Nābulsī's officer allies, that Ḥusayn developed tactical gifts unsuspected in him so far, and above all, that in the hour of crisis Ḥusayn showed courage and determination of a high order while his opponents showed none.

The outline of events is quickly drawn. When first dismissed on 10 April 1957 Nābulsī correctly assumed that the king would not find a cabinet representing the establishment; when the king refused to appoint Nābulsī's nominees instead, Abū Nuwār made a pitifully inept attempt to coerce the king by sending up to the palace a Bedouin regiment from Zarqa recently put under the command of a personal friend. The Bedouin, suitably enlightened by the king's uncle and others, went berserk. Ḥusayn appeared in their midst, carrying with him Abū Nuwār, by now shaking with fright. The Bedouin wept for joy and were dissuaded from lynching Abū Nuwār. The latter disappeared over the Syrian frontier, followed within three days by his friend and successor, 'Alī al-Ḥiyārī. The peak of the crisis was over. In the meanwhile, Ḥusayn had appointed a colorless interim cabinet headed by the elderly Ḥusayn Fakhrī al-Khālidī, one of the three West Bankers ever to serve as prime ministers, all ephemeral. Nābulsī himself accepted the Foreign Ministry – perhaps because he interpreted the "interim" in his favor, more probably because by now he was frightened and saw the summons as a pardon. When the interim government could not prevent riots on the West Bank, it resigned, or was dismissed, on 24 April. With the new government installed the following day, a new chapter opens in the history of Jordan.

TABLE V. THE NĀBULSĪ GOVERNMENT

A. The establishment

1. The king

   Ḥusayn

2. Army and police (as of October 1956)

   Chief of General Staff:

'Alī Abū Nuwār	Salt; succeeded Raḍī 'Ināb in May 1956

General Staff Branch:	
Ṣādiq al-Shara'	Irbid
Director of Military Intelligence:	
Maḥmūd Mūsā	Transjordanian
Formation commanders:	
Alī al-Ḥiyārī	Salt
Shāhir Yūsuf	Salt
Ma'an Abū Nuwār	Salt; cousin of Chief of General Staff, 'Alī Abū Nuwār (see above); in command at Zarqa
Raḍī al-Hindāwī	Irbid
Turkī Ḥusayn	Amman
Director of Public Security:	
Bahjat Ṭabāra	Transjordanian; with Arab Legion since its beginning.

3. "King's friends"

Chief of Royal Cabinet:	
Bahjat al-Talhūnī	Ma'an
Chief Aide de Camp:	
'Akāsh al-Zabin	Northern Bedouin. Briefly under arrest after Glubb's dismissal for incitement against supplanters.
Adviser to Minister of Defense:	
Sharīf Nāṣir b. Jamīl	Hashemite family; brother to Queen Mother
Sa'īd al-Muftī, Samīr al-Rifā'ī, Ibrāhīm Hāshim	Members of establishment under 'Abd Allāh; active in king's interest (see Table I, A-2 and A-4)
Senior functionaries retired by Nābulsī on political grounds	
Bahjat Tabāra	Transjordanian
'Abd al-Mun'im al-Rifā'ī	b. Safed; Transjordanian since 1920s; brother of Samīr; action cancelled by king
Muḥammad Amīn al-Shanqīṭī	b. Medina; Transjordanian since 1920s; action cancelled by king.

4. Mass action

Regiments stationed at Zarqa, 14 April 1957	Bedouin troops staged riots in favor of the king which undoubtedly put the senior commanders allied with Nābulsī in fear of their lives.

B. Anti-establishment elements

1. The cabinet (Politically active members only)

Prime Minister and Minister of Foreign Affairs: Sulaymān al-Nābulsī	Salt; National Socialist party
Minister of Interior and Defense: ʻAbd al-Ḥalīm al-Nimr	Salt; National Socialist party
Minister of Public Works: Anwar al-Khaṭīb	Hebron; National Socialist party
Minister of Justice, Education: Shafīq al-Rashīdāt	Irbid; National Socialist party
Minister of Economy: Naʻīm ʻAbd al-Hādī	Nablus; National Socialist party
Minister of Health and Social Affairs: Ṣāliḥ al-Maʻshar	Salt; Christian; National Socialist party
Minister of State for Foreign Affairs: ʻAbd Allāh al-Rīmāwī	Bayt Rīmā (north of Ramallah); Baʻth
Minister of Agriculture: ʻAbd al-Qādir Ṣāliḥ	Nablus; Communist

2. Chamber of Deputies (elections October 1956)

National Socialist party:

Saʻid al-ʻIzza	Member for Hebron; party secretary
Aḥmad Maḥmūd Ḥajja	Member for Hebron
Najīb Muṣṭafā al-Aḥmad	Member for Jenin
Naʻim ʻAbd al-Hādī	Member for Jenin
Ḥikmat al-Maṣrī	Member for Nablus
Ḥāfiẓ Ḥamd Allāh	Member for Tulkarm
Muḥammad Sālim al-Dwayb	Member for Bethlehem
ʻAbd al-Qādir Ṭāsh	Member for Amman; Circassian
Shafīq al-Rashīdāt	Member for Irbid
ʻAbd al-Ḥalīm al-Nimr	Member for Salt
Ṣāliḥ al-Maʻshar	Member for Salt; Christian

Baʻth:

ʻAbd Allāh al-Rīmāwī	Member for Ramallah
Kamāl Nāṣir	Member for Ramallah; Christian

National Front (Communists):	
Ya'qūb Ziyā al-Dīn	Member for Jerusalem; Christian
'Abd al-Qādir Ṣāliḥ	Member for Nablus
Fā'iq Warād	Member for Ramallah
Taḥrīr party:	
Aḥmad al-Dā'ūr	Member for Tulkarm
3. The army	Prominent officers who deserted or were arrested after the collapse of the Nābulsī government
'Ali Abū Nuwār	See above (A-2)
'Ali al-Ḥiyārī	See above (A-2)
Ma'an Abū Nuwār	See above (A-2)
Maḥmūd Mūsā	See above (A-2)
Maḥmūd al-Rūsān	Irbid
Ghāzī 'Arbiyāt	Salt
Nadhīr Rashīd	Salt; commander of regiment detailed by 'Alī Abū Nuwār to coerce the king
Shahīr Yūsuf	See above (A-2)
Maḥmūd al-Ma'ayṭa	Kerak; in 1970 commander of Syrian-sponsored al-Ṣā'iqa
Qāsim Nāṣir	Transjordanian

VI. THE PERIOD OF MILITARY GOVERNMENT (1957–1958): NOTE

On 25 April 1957 Ḥusayn appointed a cabinet dominated by the Old Guard. The same day emergency regulations put the country under the rule of a military governor general. The emergency regulations stayed in force for a year and a half, until 1 December 1958. This period gave the "image of Jordan" – in essence as old as the state – the specific turn-out which has stuck to it till now. It is a turn-out which largely centers about Ḥusayn's person: to the West the youthful king, true to duty and ancient friendships, battling against impossible odds with daredevil courage ("I regard assassination as a professional risk" – it was a public relations man of genius who put the words into Ḥusayn's mouth); to the Arab nationalists, the traitor and paid agent, walking in his grandfather's steps toward his grandfather's fate. The fanciful distortions of either contain a true kernel common to both. What they ignore is Ḥusayn's propensity for having his pudding as well as eating it; his untiring attempts to gain the approbation, or at least the toleration, of new-style nationalists while he stuck to the basic tenets of his policy. His success was at times surprising. Whether the sacrifices he has chosen to make for this purpose have improved his chances of long-term survival – it is even now impossible to judge with confidence.

However, in 1957–58 the situation left no room for maneuver. The excitement engendered by the nationalist tide under Nābulsī, the crash that followed, the open substitution of the United States for Britain as protector and guarantor of the regime, the union of Egypt and Syria, the Lebanese civil war, and the revolution in Iraq – all made a strong hand imperative. Within days the army stamped out disorder. So far as we know, its rank and file were enthusiastic. The combination of urban politician and urban officer aspiring to supremacy in the state had evidently shocked them beyond anything the challengers foresaw. It was a constellation which, in different circumstances, returned after thirteen years with comparable results.

Once the immediate danger from violence was past, arrests, purges, and censorship, all vigorously applied, did the rest. The "opposition" – yesterday's government coalition – virtually disappeared from the Chamber of Deputies through resignation, flight, or expulsion.

So far as it is possible to assess "atmosphere," these nineteen months held less tension than might at first be imagined. There was no doubt where the power lay. It was exercised resolutely and consistently, brutally on occasion, but not vengefully. Here, too, Ḥusayn took after his grandfather. A number of incipient plots among would-be Free Officers were nipped with ease. The West Bank was quiet for once. By the end of 1958 Ḥusayn felt sure enough of his position to restore civil liberties – for what they were worth.

TABLE VI. THE MILITARY GOVERNMENT, 1957–1958

A. The establishment (as of turn of 1957-1958)

1. The king

2. The inner cabinet

Prime Minister:	
Ibrāhīm Hāshim	In 'Abd Allāh's circle of "friends" (See Table I, A-4)

Deputy Prime Minister:	
Samīr al-Rifā'ī	Prime Minister under 'Abd Allāh (See Table I, A-2)
Interior Minister:	
Falāḥ al-Madādaḥa	Kerak
3. The military government	
Military Governor-General:	
Ḥābis al-Majālī	Kerak
Local Military Governors:	
Of Amman: Sa'ad Jum'a	Ṭafīla
Of al-Balqā': Waḥīd 'Ūrān	Ṭafīla; took office June 1958
Of 'Ajlūn: 'Umar Maṭar	Interior Minister during Baghdad Pact Crisis (See Table IV, A-2)
Of Jerusalem and Hebron:	
Ḥasan al-Kātib	b. Mecca, lived in Palestine; Transjordanian in 1946
Of Nāblus: Bahjat Ṭabāra	Former Director of Public Security (See Table V, A-2)
4. Army and police	
Chief of General Staff:	
Ḥābis al-Majālī	See above (A-3)
General Staff Branch:	
'Abd Allāh Majalī	Northern Bedouin
Director of Military Intelligence:	
Muḥammad Sa'dī Shāhīn	'Abd Allāh's Chief Aide de Camp (See Table I, A-4)
Formation commanders:	
'Izzat Ḥasan Qandūr	Transjordanian; Circassian
Fuwāz Māhir	Transjordanian; Circassian
Muḥammad al-Baṭayna	Irbid
Adīb Qāsim	Ramtha (east of Irbid)
Sharīf Nāṣir b. Jamīl	Hashemite; brother of Queen Mother. In command of Royal Guards Brigade formed in this period (See Table IV, A-4)
5. "King's friends"	No significant changes

B. Anti-establishment elements

1. Within cabinet[1]	
Walīd Ṣalāḥ	West Bank; Minister of Justice and Development who was dismissed in December 1957 for "statements contrary to government policy."
2. Chamber of Deputies[1]	Members who abstained from voting on speech from the throne, 1 Oct. 1957. No member voted "no".
Fā'iq al-'Anabtāwī	For Nablus (Independent)
'Abd al-Qādir al-Ṣāliḥ	For Nablus (National Front)
Ḥikmat al-Maṣrī	For Nablus (National Socialist)
Ḥāfiẓ Ḥamd Allāh	For Tulkarm (National Socialist)
Aḥmad al-Dā'ūr	For Tulkarm (Tahrīr)
Na'īm 'Abd al-Hādī	For Jenin (National Socialist)
3. The army	Prominent officers involved in plots against the regime, 1958-1960
Turkī Ḥusayn	Amman. Formation commander under Nābulsī (See Table V, A-2)
Māzin al-'Ajlūnī	'Ajlūn
Adīb Qāsim	See above (A-4)
Raḍī 'Abd Allāh	Irbid
Ṣādiq al-Shara'	Irbid; General Staff Branch under Nābulsī (See Table V, A-2)
Sharīf Zayd b. Shākir	Hashemite family; distant relation of the king. "Reformed" within months of his fall from grace.

1 Based on N. Sofer in *Hamizrah Hehadash (The New East)* IX: 84.

VII. THE EVE OF THE 1967 CRISIS: NOTE

The nine years that passed between the forced settlement of 1957–58 and the catastrophe of 1967 are no void in the history of Jordan. Underneath their seeming confusion they are full of meaning; unravelling the thread which gives them direction and a measure of unity is a profitable task which has yet to be taken up. Yet for our present purpose, development was slow and uniform. The relationship between the regime and the political public can be probed as it was at the end of the period without omitting a significant stage.

As to the establishment/anti-establishment dichotomy, the establishment kept its character and continuity throughout the period – political, environmental, and to a large extent personal. If there was a change, it was one of stress: the importance of the king's role increased until it assumed an overall significance which even ʿAbd Allāh – under British tutelage – had never possessed. With the anti-establishment forces the case lies differently. Here the historical change is the appearance, since about 1964, of a frame which, in the Palestine Liberation Organization, presumed to represent "the Palestinians" in a positive sense, as a nation prepared to take charge of its own destiny; a nation no longer content with appearing as petitioners or protesters making demands, however violent at times, on the decision processes of mightier friends. It is outside the purpose of this study to describe the genesis of the PLO, or to analyze the relation between its presumptions and its achievement. It is, however, relevant here that the PLO succeeded to no mean degree in being accepted by the Arab world at its own evaluation. Paradoxically, at first sight, this changed the character of the anti-establishment forces in Jordan in a way which was not entirely to the disadvantage of the regime. Alongside the PLO, other opposition moulds lost much of their relevance and attraction. Yet those older moulds – clans and families traditionally hostile to the regime, political parties, Free Officers, or just fleeting combinations of malcontents – had worked from within and had placed before the establishment a challenge difficult to assess and consequently uncertain and, in the view of the moment, dangerous. The PLO, however, claiming to represent a people of equal status with others inside the Arab community, and assuming as many of the trappings of statehood as circumstances would permit, made it easy for the Jordanian regime to bring to bear its enormous preponderance in material resources. By the same token, the PLO could not afford to reject out of hand overtures which the regime found it politic to make, though obviously a show of coexistence gave the regime an alibi and made the PLO more vulnerable whenever open hostilities broke out afresh. It also worked in favor of the regime that the PLO, by its nature, had many tasks to consider, even if its rejection of the "image of Jordan" was fundamental and unwavering.

For these reasons, the personal background of the PLO leaders is of little interest to our study. Suffice it here to state that Aḥmad al-Shuqayrī, the chairman, and Wajīh al-Madānī, commander of the PLO armed forces, were both refugees in the wider sense (see pp. 148-149); of the eleven members of the PLO executive (excluding Shuqayrī) formed in July 1966, nine were refugees, and one a West Banker.[9]

TABLE VII. THE EVE OF THE 1967 CRISIS

A. The establishment

1. The king	(see note)
2. The inner cabinet (formed April 1967)	
Prime Minister: Sa'ad Jum'a	Ṭafīla
Interior Minister: Raḍī 'Abd Allāh	Irbid
Information Minister: Sharīf 'Abd al-Ḥamīd Sharaf	Hashemite; distant relation of king
3. Army and police	
Commander in chief: Ḥābis al-Majālī	Kerak
Deputy Commander in Chief: Sharīf Nāṣir b. Jamīl	Hashemite family; brother of Queen Mother (See Table IV, A-4)
Chief of Staff: 'Āmir al-Khamāsh	Salt
Director of Military Intelligence: Muḥammad Rasūl al-Kaylānī	Salt
Commander of Eastern Front: Muḥammad al-Baṭayna	Irbid
Commander of Western Front: Mashhūr Ḥadītha	Southern Bedouin
Director of Public Security: Ma'an Abū Nuwār	Salt; former formation commander at Zarka (See Table V, A-2)

4. "King's friends"

Chief of Royal Cabinet:	
Aḥmad Ṭūqān	Nablus
Bahjat al-Talhūnī	Ma'an (See Table I, A-4)
Waṣfī al-Tall	Irbid
	Al-Talhūnī and al-Tall alternated as Prime Minister in 1960s; they were personal rivals, but both in the king's counsel.
Hashemite family:	
Amīr Ḥasan b. Ṭalāl	Youngest brother of king and heir presumptive

B. Anti-establishment elements (see note)

VIII. THE PRESENT: NOTE

Among the results of the Six Day War, the one which concerns us most is that which has turned Jordan back into "Transjordan" in more respects than the territorial. It is not a result the regime has acknowledged, or which it is likely to acknowledge in the foreseeable future. It is also a result which was not realized in its full implications until recently, with more than three years' delay.

There was an attempt after 1967 to revive an opposition which still accepted the frame of a Jordanian state, though not the traditional image or the establishment which embodied it. This was the *al-Tajammu' al-waṭanī,* the National Grouping (chaired by Sulaymān al-Nābulsī), essentially a continuation of the National Socialist party in ideas, background, and membership. For some time, the National Grouping endeavored – without much encouragement from either side – to form a bridge between the regime and the Palestinian organizations, with a decided bias in favor of the latter. When Ḥusayn appointed a new cabinet in June 1970, at the height of the Palestinian tide, he included about eight members of the Grouping. What was probably meant as no more than a sop to prevailing trends turned out as a political success of the first order. The Grouping, which had so far "explained" the organizations to the regime, promptly reversed its attitude. Since the September 1970 crisis, the National Grouping as such has not been heard of, though its members have not apparently been harassed by the authorities. It is a mistake to attribute this drying-up merely, or mainly, to opportunism. The last four years have seen the acceleration of a process which started even earlier, and the September crisis acted as the catalyst which crystallized the opposing fronts. Today there is no room for anti-establishment forces which reject the traditional "image of Jordan," but accept the state as a desirable, or at least a workable, framework of political existence. The pull of the polarized forces – the regime, on the one hand, and the Palestinian organizations, on the other – has left a no-man's land in between. And it is natural that yesterday's opposition – with a stake in the country as it grew over the last fifty years – should find itself arraigned on the side of the regime, not merely as the smaller evil, but as the side with which it holds more in common.

Whatever turn the fortunes of the Palestinian organizations may yet take, they have ceased to be part of the "public in Jordan" in any meaningful sense. Their leaders' refusal to attempt a takeover of the state – at a time when the chances of success were rated high – may not have been based merely on considerations of utility. It was alien territory, and so long as it did duty as a base there was little temptation to push on. It was the leaders' misfortune that they could not coerce their followers into respecting the coexistence which the regime was then only too willing to accept. It is noteworthy that one major Palestinian organization, which positively urged the immediate overturn of the established state and which deliberately started the chain reaction that led to the confrontation of September 1970, was led by one of the few Transjordanians prominent among the organizations, Nā'if Hawatma, leader of the Democratic Front.

On the other side, this "homelessness" has recently led – for the first time since 1949 – to fairly general outbursts of physical hostility against the Palestinians throughout the Transjordanian countryside. No doubt these outbursts were not unwelcome – putting it mildly – to the regime, and they are directly connected with the arrogance and ruthlessness which the guerrillas showed in their day of glory. But part of the explanation must lie with the image of the Palestinian organizations as strangers to their host country; many reports show that the villagers of the East Bank tend to regard the guerrillas today as intruders undeserving of sympathy. The part which this attitude has in the decline of morale among the Palestinian organizations, which has been noticeable since October 1970, cannot be negligible.

It only remains to examine the identity and background of today's establishment leaders and to trace the strands which lead them backward to the remote past of twenty years ago.

TABLE VIII. THE PRESENT[1]

A. The establishment

1. The king

2. The inner cabinet (formed 28 Oct. 1970)

Prime Minister and Minister of Defense: Waṣfī al-Tall	Former Prime Minister and confidant of the king (See Table VII, B-3)
Interior Minister: Māzin al-'Ajlūnī	Once involved in anti-Ḥusayn plot (See Table VI, B-3)
Information Minister: 'Adnān Abū 'Awda	West Bank

3. Army and police

Commander in Chief: Ḥābis al-Majālī	Kerak; Military Governor General, 1957-58 (See Table VI, A-3)
Deputy Commander in Chief: Qāsim al-Mu'ayṭa	Kerak
Chief of Staff: Muḥammad 'Abd al-Dā'im	Ma'an
Asst. Chief of Staff for Operations: Sharīf Zayd b. Shākir	Once involved in anti-Ḥusayn plot; member of Hashemite family (See Table VI, B-3)
Director of Military Intelligence: Muḥammad Bushīr Ismā'īl	Transjordanian; Chechen
Division commanders:	
'Atallah Jāsim Ḥamdān	Northern Bedouin
Salīm 'Oudeh al-Najādāt	Southern Bedouin
'Alāwī Jarād al-Najādāt	Southern Bedouin
Kāsib Ṣfūq	Southern Bedouin
Director of Public Security: 'Abd al-Majīd al-Sharīda	Dayr Abū Sa'īd (west of Irbid)

Deputy Director of Public Security:	
Turkī Ḥusayn	Once involved in anti-Ḥusayn plot (See Tables V, A-2, and VI, B-3)
4. Military Governorate during September 1970 Crisis	
Military Governor-General:	
Ḥābis al-Majālī	Held same position, 1957-58 (See Table VI, A-3)
Deputy Governor-General:	
Māzin al-'Ajlūnī	Once involved in anti-Ḥusayn plot (See Table VI, A-3)
Local Military Governors:	
Of Amman:	
Kāsib Ṣfūq	See above (A-3)
Of al-Bālqā'-Kerak:	
Qāsim al-Mu'ayṭa	See above (A-3)
Of Irbid:	
Bahjat al-Muḥaysin	Ṭafīla
Of Zarka:	
Muḥammad Idrīs	Transjordanian; Circassian
Of Ma'an:	
Salīm 'Oudeh al-Najādāt	Southern Bedouin
5. "King's friends"	
Chief of Royal Cabinet:	
Aḥmad al-Ṭarāwana	Kerak
Director of General Intelligence:	
Nadhīr Rashīd	Salt; took part in anti-Ḥusayn movement under Nābulsī government (See Table V, B-3)
"Special representative":	
'Alī Abū Nuwār	Salt; Chief of General Staff under Nābulsī government (See Table V, A-2 and B-3)
Zayd al-Rifā'ī	Amman; son of Samīr; reputedly close collaborator of king
6. Mass action:	Demonstrations of hostility toward Palestinian organizations in countryside. See note.

B. Anti-establishment elements

1. "The National Grouping":[2]

(Al-Tajammu' al-waṭanī)	
Sulaymān al-Nābulsī	Prime Minister of anti-Ḥusayn cabinet (See Table V, B-1)
Rūḥī al-Khaṭīb	Jerusalem
'Ākif al-Fā'iz[2]	Paramount Chief of Banū Ṣakhr Bedouin
Ṣubḥī Amīn 'Amrū[2, 3]	Hebron
Najīb al-Rashīdāt[2]	Irbid
Dā'ūd al-Ḥusaynī[2]	Jerusalem
'Abd al-Qādir Ṭāsh[2]	Former Deputy; Amman; Circassian (See Table V, B-2)
Ja'far al-Shāmī[2]	Salt
Sulaymān al-Ḥadīdī[2]	Salt; member of Ba'th opposition in parliament 11 Nov. 1952 (See Table III, B-2)
Ṣāliḥ al-Ma'shar	Salt; Christian; National Socialist cabinet member under Nābulsī (See Table V, B-2)
Shafīq al-Rashīdāt	Irbid; National Socialist cabinet member under Nābulsī (See Table V, B-2)
'Abd al-Hamīd al-Sā'iḥ	Nablus

2. The Palestinian organizations — See note

1 Situation of early 1971, unless otherwise stated.
2 Member of 'Abd al-Mun'im Rifā'ī cabinet (June 1970)
3 Member of al-Tall cabinet (October 1970)

OBSERVATIONS[10]

The commonly accepted view that Jordan is governed by East Bankers is demonstrated to a startling degree. Throughout the tables West Bankers figure hardly at all in the "establishment" sections; refugees, even in the wider sense, are entirely absent.[11] Among the Transjordanians there is a marked, but not an overwhelming, preponderance of southerners over northerners; this is also no surprise. Christians are absent. Whatever their merits in the eyes of the regime – and as a group they have certainly not been characterized by disloyalty –

capacity for rule is not one of them. Circassians and the less known Chechens play a prominent role – again a recognized fact. However, it is not generally realized that the "sharifian" origins of the regime are still noticeable in sensitive appointments, though plain Hejazis have no longer a special claim to be admitted to the king's counsel, as they had under ʻAbd Allāh. Bedouin officers fill the majority of the highest army appointments – *of late*.

Much more rewarding is a search for trends. The point is that *there is no trend*. The king and his family retainers, the Kerak and Maan notables, the sharifs and the Circassians make up the bulk of the establishment as they did twenty years ago; if anything, more so. This phenomenon cannot be put aside as fossilized immobility. The establishment has been exposed to incessant challenges of different description and in permanently changing circumstances. It has found the proper response to them all so far, without changing its character. Its evident success in the struggle for survival entitles it to be regarded as a living political organism, well-adjusted to its surroundings. It is a verdict valid for the present, whatever the future may bring.

The astonishing number of one-time rebels returned to favor and position is further testimony to the vitality of the establishment. When they strayed from the fold, the rebels broke a pattern; they restored it when they returned.

No socio-political formula works without blemish. ʻĀkif al-Fā'iz, the Banū Ṣakhr chief who sympathizes with the Palestinian organizations; ʻAbd al-Qādir Ṭāsh, the Ammani Circassian who has ever been a faithful supporter of Nābulsī; Maḥmūd al-Muʻayṭa, the Kerak officer of ancient family and leader of al-Ṣāʻiqa – they are all genuine exceptions to the pattern. But they *are* exceptions, and the tag that the exception proves the rule may be fairly applied to so complex an equation as the recent history of Jordan sets to the observer.

It will have been noted that Bedouin officers have only recently appeared among the highest army appointments, much later than their comrades of *ḥaḍarī* background. However, this is no change in trend. It merely took the Bedouin longer to master the requirements which a modern army makes on its command. That the Bedouin officer belonged to the "establishment" long before he was appointed to top positions is proven by the Zarqa incident mentioned above.[12]

Among the "anti-establishment elements" the almost total and continued absence of southern East Bankers, ethnic minorities, and Bedouin leaps to the eye. The constituents of the "anti-establishment" – West Bankers, refugees, and northern East Bankers, mainly from Salt and Irbid – fall into two distinct patterns. The political groups which reject the set "image of Jordan" without putting up an alternative to the Jordanian entity, are represented by West Bankers and northern East Bankers – the latter also playing a considerable role in the establishment, the former next to none. These groups, as described earlier, have been replaced in recent years by others in whose concepts Jordan takes no positive part at all; here refugees predominate, after many years of absence from the leading ranks even of the anti-establishment.

The foregoing study cannot lay claim to revelations which radically overturn accepted views. But it may help to make the interpretation of Jordan's political society less dependent on impression and generalization than has often been the case in the past.

BIBLIOGRAPHICAL NOTE

The data in this study have been collected from the press, broadcasting monitorings, and various compendia. Among the latter, *Hamizrah Hehadash* (*The New East,* publication of the Israel Oriental Society) and the chapters "Jordan" in *Middle East Record 1960, 1961, 1967, 1962, 1968* (the last two in manuscript) have been particularly useful (published for The Shiloaḥ Center for Middle Eastern and African Studies, Tel Aviv University).

The history of Jordan between 1949 and 1957 is covered in the well-known works of Abidi, Dearden, Glubb, Harris, Māḍī and Mūsā, Patai, Shwadran, Vatikiotis, and others. Little historical research has been published on the last thirteen years. University Microfilms, Ann Arbor, has brought out three doctoral theses which deserve notice: Clinton Bailey, *The Participation of the Palestinians in the Politics of Jordan* (1966); Naseer Aruri, *Jordan: A Study in Political Development, 1921–1965* (1967); Jamil E. Jreisat, *Provincial Administration in Jordan* (1968). None of the three takes into account the 1967 war.

FOOTNOTES

1 So far as I know, the Jordanian Government has not yet published population statistics adjusted to the East Bank after 1967 – for political reasons.

2 Compare the contrast, e.g., with Phebe Ann Marr, "Iraq's Leadership Dilemma," *Middle East Journal,* vol. 24, no. 3 (Summer 1970).

3 Followed by a smaller number of Shiite Chechens from the eastern fringes of Caucasia.

4 The official Jordanian Statistical Yearbook of 1968 gives an estimate of 101,000 "scattered tent dwellers and nomads." This is far higher than recent guesses of "true" Bedouin. Of course, there are no hard-and-fast definitions of either category.

5 In 1954 an amendment to the constitution reduced the two-thirds to an absolute majority.

6 'Abd Allāh first ran afoul of the Colonial Office when he created a "pasha" within weeks of his installation at Amman.

7 The parallel with the Portsmouth episode in Iraq in early 1948 is striking, excepting the role of Egypt.

8 With the possible exception of Syria – not really a precedent. In Egypt the young officers had become political masters as well; in Jordan the ejection of the British elite did not, as such, touch the established order.

9 I have not been able to establish the background of one member.

10 Attention must be drawn to the fact that no absolute negatives are possible on the strength of the preceding tables, since these only show static situations at certain stages. But the relatively large number of probings over a relatively short period, together with the particular significance of each stage, give the observations a fair degree of general relevance.

11 Muḥammad Shāhīn, the chief ADC of 'Abd Allāh and Ṭalāl, is only technically an exception. The man was a lifelong security officer – obviously the determinant of his personality.

12 An additional point may be made – admittedly a speculation. The British leadership of the Arab Legion was peculiarly successful in inculcating British traits in the Bedouin, both trivial and essential. Even now we may listen on occasion to a Jordanian Bedouin officer over wireless or television, speaking a very passable imitation of Sandhurst/Camberley English, clipped, careful, and with a remarkably "British" accent, much in contrast to that of the non-Bedouin. In the present context it is not impossible that, after the sudden departure of the British officer, the Bedouin should have felt inhibitions regarding his own competence for high command. The politically-minded group around Nuwār had no inhibitions at all – quite rightly from their point of view.

THE TUNISIAN PATH TO MODERNIZATION

L. CARL BROWN

If one wished to be mildly malicious he could argue that it has now become traditional to study the modern Near East[1] within the framework of "modernization." At least two or three generations of scholars – both Western and Near Eastern – have approached the subject in this fashion. Earlier, of course, such words as "westernization" and "awakening" were preferred, but these differences are mere terminological trifles, not likely to obscure the continuity of the modernization theme.

For this reason, a paper entitled "The Tunisian Path to Modernization," submitted as part of a general series devoted to modern Arab society, would probably occasion few arched academic eyebrows. Noting the title, most readers would feel themselves on sufficiently familiar ground that they would see no need to challenge the author to define his terms or justify his interpretative approach.

Use of the term modernization seems even more conventional when the subject is Tunisia, where scholarly attention has been especially attracted to the modernization or, a synonym, developmental approach.[2] Why this seems to have been the case can most easily be explained in terms of a series of negatives. The Tunisian struggle for independence did not, as in Algeria, monopolize scholarly and public attention for over a decade, to the exclusion of other concerns. The Tunisian political leadership has not, as in Syria, been subject to continuous – if seemingly erratic – change through coups and cabinet crises. And, finally, unlike the United Arab Republic, Tunisia has not been tempted – or thrust (for both factors have been at work) – into playing an important role in international politics.

Instead, contemporary Tunisia presents a picture of relative stability and uniformity of national purpose. The country boasts what is perhaps the most effective political party in the Arab world, the Socialist Destour – whether measured in terms of durability, popularity, or ability to stimulate and guide social mobilization. There has been a continuity of leadership personified by Ḥabīb Bourguiba for well over a generation. Moreover, it is a group leadership with organizational roots extending back to the 1920s. This leadership has evolved – and been shaped – in the dialectics of everyday socio-political confrontation. It is not a leadership by default – as is necessarily the case when hitherto apolitical forces grasp power from the incapable hands of those doomed to failure.

These and other characteristics of modern Tunisian society are best explained historically, and more particularly in terms of developments during, roughly, the past century and a half. For the central theme of modern Tunisian history – indeed the only theme that appears capable of providing overall interpretative intelligibility to a welter of complex and, at times, seemingly contradictory changes – is that of a long-term organic process with definable stages of development following one after the other in a comprehensible fashion.

To speak, then, of modernization in discussing Tunisia is not just to adopt the current scholarly fashion, since the Tunisian case cries out for treatment in terms of modernization theories. This, coupled with Tunisia's advantages of size, relative cohesiveness, and a cluster of other attributes that might be collectively labelled "analytical manageability" (to be explained more fully below), thrusts the country into a potentially very important role as yardstick for comparative studies of modernization.

If, however, Tunisia is to be presented as a yardstick, or model, then at least some passing attention to what is meant by modernization (and, equally important, what is not meant) is in order. For only with somewhat greater attention to measurement and definition can the comparative possibilities, implicit in Tunisia's modern history, be utilized fully.

All theories of modernization contain the assumption of comprehensive societal change with structural and organizational reverberations at all important levels of human activity. It is a revolutionary process in the sense that it sets in motion fundamental change, and, accordingly, many label the present historical period as the "modernization revolution," just as earlier ages are now encapsulated in the Industrial Revolution, Commercial Revolution, Scientific Revolution, or the revolution that ushered in urban-based bureaucratic empires, i.e., in the literal-etymological sense, civilization itself.

Like earlier fundamental revolutions, modernization is, thus, also a transcultural phenomenon. Although originating in one cultural area, it spills over into others. More than that, modernization acts as a solvent of existing cultural boundaries, dissolving them in part and in the process setting the stage for new organizing principles. Many would argue, and they make a strong case, that modernization is the first truly world-wide revolution.

There is no scholarly consensus on the general characteristics of modernization. Among the critical variables that have been suggested are: (1) the degree of reliance on inanimate as opposed to animate sources of power, (2) "the unprecedented increase in man's knowledge, permitting control over his environment," and (3) the socio-psychological adaptation to a situation of constant change.[3] The first two, especially the former, put forward at least a potentially quantifiable scale for measuring the degree of modernization. Yet, they both deal with factors that have always been at work in human society – technological and scientific advance.

Further, both technological and scientific improvements, at an accelerating rate, have been *major* desiderata in human history since at least the beginning of the Industrial Revolution. Application of these two criteria, in short, would provide only hazy notions of when modernization "began," or what rule is to be applied in determining that a certain society is "modernized" or " modernizing." Nevertheless, this apparent inadequacy may well be a source of strength, for it serves to emphasize historical continuity and directs attention to a complex developmental process rather than to turning points.

Both of these variables may be fitted into a larger general category – a decisive increase, often a quantum jump, in an organized society's effective power. This power accumulation will, in every case, spring from several sources (including technology and knowledge), not the least of which being newer, stronger patterns of organizing individuals for group endeavors. This, the political aspect of the modernization revolution, is most in evidence in the Third World, and it is quite likely, as several scholars have suggested, that the political breakthrough is the essential precondition for modernization.

The third variable, institutionalizing adaptability to constant change, is perhaps more nearly a good heuristic insight, for it does not readily lend itself to empirical verification.

Such variables and their possible limitations would deserve more attention if a general treatise on modernization theories were being attempted. For present purposes it will suffice to accept that all merge to provide a rough-and-ready (although imprecise) fleshing out of the idea of modernization.

In societal terms, many modernization theories are adaptations of the celebrated distinction between *gemeinschaft* and *gesellschaft,* between "small, organic pre-industrial, close-knit status Society . . . and big, impersonal, industrialized, bureaucratic contract society."[4] This too may be integrated into our modernization collage: Modernization brings, at least in part, a process of transition from *gemeinschaft* to *gesellschaft*.

Politically, modernization always involves an increase both in governmental power and in the scope of what is deemed legitimate governmental activity. A major characteristic of increased governmental potential is that it cannot be actualized and institutionalized unless society's rank and file are brought into a new, more intimate relationship with government. To use Karl Deutsch's term, "social mobilization" underpins increased governmental power.

Modernization makes obsolete the notion of government as a small political elite, content to exercise power in a very limited field of activities, and presiding over a segmentary society (i.e., over semi-autonomous communities). One gauge, then, of modernization is the extent to which governments grow in power, use that new power to engage in hitherto undreamed of activities, and set in motion a process whereby the fate of governors and governed become (for better or worse) intimately intertwined.

In the first historical example of modernization (or, as other theorists would have it, the preliminary stage to modernization) which took place in Western Europe, the resulting social mobilization led to the creation of nation-states.

The well-known history of Western nationalism suggests the first distinction concerning what modernization is not. Modernization is not necessarily democratization. Nor does it lead ineluctably to totalitarianism. Modernization clearly increases the potential for individual freedom in many respects. The process, just as obviously, increases the organizational potential for a more intimately oppressive control of the individual's freedom. It cannot be asserted that modernization necessarily leads to a net increase (or loss) of individual freedom.

Modernization does involve, as we have seen, an increase in governmental activities and actors. Beyond them are to be found even greater numbers who come increasingly to be identified with government. Instead of a situation in which the great masses of people want only to be left alone by government (and government, in turn, does not choose to "mobilize" the masses), a new value system is substituted. The subject becomes a citizen, and when something goes wrong he is inclined to demand remedial action. One leaves the world of "that government governs best which governs least" to enter the new world of "there ought to be a law." Segmentary autonomies tend to be melted down and poured into the mold of a single, more powerful, more comprehensive political system. The resultant mass mobilization can lead to a populist, or democratic, political culture, but this is not the inevitable result. Democracy is not a necessary attribute of modernization. The many powerful mass mobilization regimes of the totalitarian left or right prove that modernization can take various political forms.

Modernization, in other words, works to undermine ascriptive socio-political elites – be they monarchs (unless playing formal roles as in constitutional monarchies), landed aristocracies, village and tribal notables, or religious old families. The anthill of stratified and relatively fixed hierarchy is kicked down, and the resulting swarm increases the possibilities for upward mobility. The new system to develop out of this modernization revolution can be an even more efficient authoritarianism (totalitarianism), a more complete, participatory, and socially mobile democracy, or some point in between these two extremes.

All of which indicates another matter which modernization is *not*. Modernization is not a teleological system. It is not a political philosophy (even less, a political program) hiding ever so coyly behind the skirts of scientific method. Modernization theory involves nothing more than an effort to describe and interpret patterns of fundamental change. The theory, if well constructed, can help the historian and social scientist understand and interpret the world. It can even give the politician or planner a better appreciation of available options. It is not, however, a secular religion or a prescription for action.

Finally, modernization is not just the transition from tribalism to centralized, urban-based politics. It is *not* the move from provincialism to cosmopolitanism. To have any significance, modernization must be distinguished from these themes, as old as human civilization. Since the dawn of history, all areas of the world have experienced the processes of unification into a larger cultural arena, whether in response to the rise of a new universal religion or by being absorbed into a rising "bureaucratic empire."[5] All areas of the world have also witnessed the breakup of such larger entities into smaller parts, organized according to different principles and to meet different exigencies.

Usually, the creation of new, larger entities is accompanied by scientific and technical advance – made possible by a better organization of human control over the environment and an enhanced security position vis-à-vis the stranger and potential enemy beyond.

And, often, the breakup of empire can lead to a technological decline or even, *in extremis,* a lapse into primitive tribalism – which is, after all, nothing more than a highly colored way of describing a subsistence level economy that generates no surplus to support government, cities, or to stimulate functional specialization. This creates a political culture wherein security is sought at the smallest unit, the family or clan, which works out fluid defensive alliances to avoid being dominated by other clan combinations.[6] Such a radical dissolution of the bureaucratic empire is most likely to take place following a series of cataclysmic blows administered by man or nature.

Yet, the breakup of old empires is not necessarily a step backward in terms of society's power to master its environment. The rise of European nation-states out of the ashes of the Holy Roman Empire and the ideal of unified Christendom, demonstrate that at certain historical junctures there is strength in division.

Indeed, one could eclectically borrow from such diverse thinkers as Gibbon, Ibn Khaldūn, and Toynbee to suggest a constant process, or dialectic, of division and unification – a process best understood as being neither intrinsically cyclic nor progressive.

This line of approach evokes two considerations, important for any discussion of modernization theory. First, the process of modernization may involve the creation of a new universal, of a new "world culture." What is known in a somewhat different context as the "convergence theory" may be seen as based on the implication that modernization has this unifying, homogenizing effect. Such, however, is not necessarily the outcome; and for purposes of the present discussion we prefer a more modest, more technical (and less teleological) definition of modernization: It is a process that will have (or is having) a revolutionary impact on all cultures and will accordingly radically change the contours of these cultures. This much can be said with confidence. To suggest that the result will be a new world culture is, at this time, unwarranted prophecy. Indeed, the meager empirical evidence now available would tend to suggest, for the forseeable future at least, the creation of a variety of new modernized (and modernizing) cultures.

Second, the very process of modernization may intrude upon certain cultures when they are at a historic stage of fissiparous provincialism (as in sub-Saharan Africa). Or, it may confront other cultures united in a premodern form of cosmopolitanism, i.e., united politically by a bureaucratic empire and ideologically by a religious system.

Tunisia and most of the Near East fitted into the latter category. When the modernization process began in Tunisia, that small country was a province (beylik) of the Ottoman Empire, and however loose the de facto ties between Tunis and Istanbul, there can be no doubt that the beylik was part of the Ottoman political world. The ruling class in Tunisia may be seen as a small model of the greater Ottoman political class, sharing the same basic notions of political theory and practice. Tunisia was also at that time religiously and ideologically linked to the greater Islamic *umma* (community of Believers).

The Tunisian case is therefore an example of modernization marching to the historic beat of imperial decline (the breakup of the Ottoman Empire) with the concomitant challenge to the religio-ideological world view that had always buttressed the imperial system (the greater community of the Sunni Muslim *umma*). To this extent the Tunisian (and, grosso modo, the Near Eastern) experience seems at least superficially comparable to the rise of modern Europe. The first stages of modernization in Tunisia (as in the Near East) involved, therefore, a breakaway from a larger universal entity, or in a sense a move from the cosmopolitan to the provincial, both spatially and ideologically.

In other ways the narrowing of Tunisia's political and cultural world under the impact of modernization was accompanied by a new integration into a larger world, and this latter process touched an infinitely greater number of people. That is, what the very small cosmopolitan class of the earlier system lost in scope was outweighed by the rural and urban masses who came to be jarred and enticed out of their earlier parochialism into a sense of identity with (or, at the very least, wary concern about) the increasingly comprehensive Tunisian government and society.

We are now in a position to clarify the earlier assertion that modernization involves, *in part,* a transition from *gemeinschaft* to *gesellschaft.* The world view of the masses is enlarged, but, if the modernization process strikes a moribund empire, it may present the existing elite with the challenge of adapting to a narrower world view, at least temporarily. The added psychological strain this places on the existing elite – especially when the ideas and artifacts of modernization are being imposed by the old politico-cultural enemy – have perhaps not yet been adequately assayed in scholarly study of modern Near Eastern history.[7]

Such then, with all its sketchiness and imprecision, is the general notion of modernization to be applied here. Modernization is a process leading ultimately to an increase in organized human power over the environment (and over those groups not so organized) so vast as to be distinguishable from earlier times. The gross power increase, at one and the same time, (a) is made possible by radical changes in human relations, institutions, and ideologies, and (b) renders such radical changes irresistible. Only greater human integration, functional specialization, and an increase in the scope and responsibility of government can achieve modernization. It can result either in greater individual freedom or the opposite. What is more predictable is that modernization will steadily eliminate whatever advantages or liabilities accrue in circumstances of relative human and societal isolation.

The value of Tunisia's experience in modernization as a model and yardstick can now be more precisely fixed. The Tunisian case offers comparative utility for all parts of the Third World where the challenge of modernization came arm-in-arm with the impact of the West. The link of common experience is even closer with those countries that endured some variety of formal Western colonial rule. Beyond this the Tunisian experience is most pertinent within its own cultural context of the Muslim world, and especially the Arab states.

And probably the best fit of all, blending conventional historical methodology with comparative studies, is to place the Tunisian case alongside the story of the other two independent or autonomous units of the greater Ottoman political world – the central Ottoman Empire and Egypt – to form a historical triptych.

It is to be hoped that this lengthy prolegomena lends added significance and relevance to the general interpretative essay now to follow on the Tunisian path to modernization.

MODERNIZATION IN TUNISIA: SPECIAL CHARACTERISTICS IMPOSED BY HISTORY AND GEOGRAPHY

History is a seamless web, and, accordingly, the notion that major new developments began at a precise point in time does violence to a more complex, nuanced reality. Indeed, an overly persistent quest for origins should readily reveal the limits of the biological metaphor in history. Individual men are born, mature, and die, but operative ideals, societies, institutions, and epochs are not equally graced with birth-dates and tombstones. There was no day or year when it may be said that Tunisia crossed the threshold and took the first step on its journey to modernization.

Societies enter new epochs, not as a child is born, but as a young lad attempts to walk the length of a seesaw. At first, the seesaw is held in stable repose by the weight of the boy at one end, but then, as he proceeds toward the middle, the seesaw begins to move, and the boy uses arms, legs, and body to maintain balance. If he does not fall off, he can reach the middle and keep the seesaw in precarious balance. Then, when he decides to move on, his own weight quickly brings the seesaw to its new, stable position.[8]

It cannot be said precisely when Tunisia started walking up that seesaw (or was both pushed and dared), but the historian can with greater confidence pick up the point in time when there is some movement from the board – as the Tunisian political leadership lurched and groped upward toward the fulcrum. The long reign of Tunisia's Aḥmad Bey (1837-1855) clearly stands out as a period of early modernizing activity. These dates, enclosing the long reign of an energetic would-be innovator, should immediately suggest comparison with the Ottoman Empire's Sultan Maḥmūd (1808-1839) and Egypt's Muḥammad 'Alī (1805-1849). Like them, Aḥmad Bey was attempting to break with tradition, centralize, and consolidate. Like them, he was faced with the task of "defensive modernization,"[9] or of quickly strengthening politico-military capacity at home in order to be able to face an increasingly threatening Europe. And, like them, he adjusted his innovations to accord with his own world view of a political elite controlling a society of subjects. His was one more example of manipulative reform from the top. And, finally, just as with his fellow Muslim modernizers, his reforms met only scattered successes in terms of his own goals, but they set the stage for ultimately revolutionary change both in values and social organization.

Aḥmad Bey's reform measures will therefore sound a familiar refrain to those who know the modern history of Egypt or Turkey. But to completely appreciate the variations on the modernizing theme, it is important to know the instrument, Tunisia, that Aḥmad had in his hands.

The Beylik of Tunis which Aḥmad Bey began to rule in 1837 could look back on roughly two and one-half centuries as part of the Ottoman Empire. Beyond that stretched almost three centuries of Hafsid rule, itself an offshoot of the most extensive North African Muslim dynasty, the Almohades. The Hafsid tradition represented, in short, the ultimate development of late medieval political culture in Western Islam. The later blend of Hafsid and Ottoman ideals and practices concerning government gave Tunisia its own distinctive style of bureaucratic polity.[10]

Even farther back in time stretched the historical legacy of a Tunisia which spawned the Fatimid dynasty before it transferred to

Egypt in the late tenth century, of the Aghlabids, the first major autonomous political unit within the Abbasid Empire, and, farther still in time, the heritage of Byzantine, Vandal, Roman, and Carthaginian rule.

Several important aspects of Tunisian culture may be teased from this cursory historical carding: What was the Beylik of Tunis and is now the Republic of Tunisia possessed a considerable geographical cohesiveness throughout time. The boundaries at times expanded to include portions of what is now the Constantine area of Algeria, and at other times contracted within Tunisia's present borders. Nevertheless, there was always a core area revolving around a single capital and dominant metropolitan center – Carthage and later Tunis – during most of Tunisia's history. The importance of Kairouan in early Muslim history is to be explained by a new political system that was yet to find its sea legs, and the brief role of Mahdiyya as capital under the Fatimids represents the rear-guard action of a regime that had lost control of the interior.

Tunisia never offered anything comparable to the great urban center and regional rivalries that set Aleppo against Damascus or that divided Fez, Meknes, and Marrakesh, not to mention later entrants, such as Rabat and Tangiers. Geography did not conspire, as in Algeria, to impose a three-way regional breakdown in the Ottoman period, carried over in French times as the separate *départements* of Oran, Alger, and Constantine.

Tunisia is a small country of approximately sixty thousand square miles, or somewhat less than the state of Missouri. It can be thought of as smaller still if the vast southern semidesert and desert region (thinly populated and until very modern times only lightly yoked to Tunis) is excluded. Even within this modest territory, nature avoided the exuberance of geographical and ecological variety that she treated herself to in the rest of North Africa. There is relatively little of the awkward juxtaposition of plains, mountains, and desert to be found in Morocco and Algeria to the West. Nor do Tunisia's best natural harbors abut on forbidding mountain ranges. The richest and most cultivable areas of Tunisia form a continuous whole, all within easy reach of the capital at Tunis. A mere 90 miles separate Kairouan and Sousse from Tunis. Le Kef, the traditional garrison town on the Algerian border, is 105 miles southwest of Tunis, and the major port city to the south, Sfax, is a manageable 162 miles away (plus being accessible by sea). Even before a modern communications system was installed, the slow-moving military expedition to collect taxes (the *maḥalla*) could reach the end of its journey in two weeks.

Nor did Aḥmad Bey's Tunisia offer that elaborate mosaic of races, religions, and languages so characteristic of the Near East. By the nineteenth century, the Arabic language had virtually eradicated Berber except for a few surviving pockets, especially in the extreme south. This is in striking contrast to Algeria and Morocco, where to this day even modest estimates would find twenty percent and thirty percent native Berber speakers, respectively.

There was no great split within Islam dividing Sunni from Shiite as in the Fertile Crescent. Nor were there any great heretical groups that had broken away from Islam as the Druze and Nuṣayris. Except for the small Ibadite community (descended from the seventh century Kharijite movement) concentrated on the island of Djerba, native Tunisia was uniformly Sunni of the Mālikī school. Of course, the Ottomans were Ḥanafī, and this school was given official precedence in Ottoman Tunisia, but there was no effort to "convert" the native Tunisians. Instead, the Ḥanafī/Mālikī distinction served as yet one more way to classify governors and governed, to the apparent satisfaction of both sides.[11]

No native Christian population had existed for centuries, probably not since the Almohade period – thus again setting Tunisia in sharp contrast to the Fertile Crescent or even Egypt with its roughly ten precent Coptic element.

The Jews, accounting for perhaps two to four percent of the total population and concentrated mainly in Tunis and Djerba, were the only native non-Muslims.[12]

Nor were there in these early decades of the nineteenth century, any great population movements into, or within Tunisia, to disturb the country's cohesion (or, from another perspective, to challenge a sluggish traditionalism). Even the importation of young men from the Levant and other parts of the Mediterranean to serve as *mamlūks* or as recruits in the regular (Turkish) army had come to a virtual halt by Aḥmad's reign, and the slow trickle of Blacks via the slave trade was destined to cease completely when Aḥmad first abolished the slave trade and later slavery itself in the 1840s. The small increment of Blacks was absorbed into a traditional Islamic pattern of domestic slavery. There was nothing comparable in Tunisia to the New World system of plantation slavery with its formidable economic and demographic imperatives that imposed legal segregation. As a result, although Blacks tended to be found in lower social or economic status in traditional Tunisia, there were no caste barriers to mobility or social integration.[13]

Tunisia in the 1830s was also of manageable size and proportion in terms of population. The country contained at that time an estimated 1,000,000 to, at the very most, 1,500,000 inhabitants. Of that number roughly twelve to twenty percent may be counted as urban.[14] Further, it may be estimated that two-thirds to three-fourths of the population were sedentary, the remainder being nomads.

The proportion of those having a fixed abode, whether in towns, villages, or on farms, was in itself reasonably high by comparison with other Near Eastern countries at that time. This, too, was a factor favoring public order and central government control, for the positive correlation between the size of the sedentary population and the ability to maintain a centralized bureaucratic polity has been accepted as axiomatic from at least the time of Ibn Khaldūn to this day.

The advantage was further enhanced by the placement of the nonsedentaries who, as we have noted, tended to be on the geographical fringe, rather than interspersed in a way that would have divided and isolated the towns and sedentary areas from each other.

These several elements, making for relative geographical cohesion, matched by an ecological, ethnic, religious, and linguistic consistency rare for the Near East, did not, of course, coalesce to automatically make of Aḥmad Bey's Tunisia a nation in the modern sense.

Even less did all this make Tunisia a modernizing nation-state. Tunisian society remained segmented in its essentials; and, equally important, the traditional separation between state and society (which can be seen as the very antithesis of the nation-state) survived completely intact both as ideal and reality.

Nevertheless, the items enumerated above provided a fortunate combination of circumstances that made Tunisia more responsive to the innovations of any ruler or political class. As a result, any government setting in motion the process of modernization would be working with a somewhat more malleable clay. Even more important, the central government would be offered a mercifully greater margin of error. At the first failure, the first "time of troubles," there would be nothing comparable to the Moroccan "land of dissidence" (*blād al-sība*) always ready to challenge a central government that had temporarily lost its moorings.[15]

This last point leads to the most elusive theme which confronts the historian or social scientist – the description of a people's basic character and values. At its worst such efforts degenerate into unthinking, and often highly prejudicial, "national stereotypes," in which a society is pigeon-holed as militaristic, xenophobic, carefree, authoritarian, achievement-oriented, deferential, violent, or the like.

Yet, these crucial cultural differences must not be avoided just because they are so easily distorted or misinterpreted.

With all due caution, this much can be hazarded as an enduring cultural trait characterizing Tunisia from the time we pick up the thread of modernization in the 1830s to the present: Tunisia may be thought of as the open end of a funnel leading into a considerably less inviting and penetrable Maghrib. Historically, Tunisia has been the natural conduit for the movement of men and ideas into North Africa. As a relatively small socio-political unit with a limited hinterland from which resources and manpower may be mobilized, Tunisia has often been absorbed into other bureaucratic empires but seldom the base itself for such an imperial effort.[16] Tunisia is also sufficiently removed in space from the more "natural" geographical bases for imperial center (e.g., Iberian peninsula, Nile valley, Fertile Crescent, Anatolia, the French hexagon) that it has usually been able to maintain some degree of autonomy.

As a result, the historically-determined Tunisian tactic in facing the outside world has been that of a relatively small society that has learned to achieve its ends through accommodation and eclectic borrowing. Tunisia has possessed neither the bold particularistic zeal and xenophobia that characterize much of Albania, Algeria, and Morocco, nor the haughty self-sufficiency of China.

This pattern of measured resistance, accommodation, and middle-of-the-road adjustment to reality provides a dominant motif in the Tunisian path to modernization. In the following sections it will be shown that those political and social leaders who picked up and played this motif were the most successful. Those who acted as if they were dealing with Albanians or Chinese left a record of frustrated plans and were denied entry to the national pantheon of heroes. Some – such is the human condition – reveal a career pattern wavering between these two extremes. This brings us back to Aḥmad Bey and his work.

REFORMIST ATTEMPTS FROM WITHIN THE SYSTEM

Aḥmad Bey, the tenth ruler of Tunisia's Ḥusaynid dynasty (1705-1957), came to the throne seven years after the French conquest of Algeria and two years after the Ottomans had reestablished direct control over Tripolitania. His natural interest in things military (e.g., he was happiest when on campaign with the army, adorning the walls of his palace with tableaux of Napoleon's most famous battles) was heightened by the awareness that his regime faced two formidable threats – to the East and to the West. A precarious diplomatic balancing of the Great Powers helped assure continued Tunisian autonomy, but realists in Tunis must have sensed that the Great Powers were unlikely to restore the Ḥusaynid dynasty if it succumbed to a lightning military blow, either from within or without.

Here, then, was a case of defensive modernization in its purest form. Aḥmad turned to an ambitious program of military reform in order, as he saw it, to insure the survival of his dynasty. There were, of course, other motivations. He wanted to be accepted by his European peers as a very modern monarch. Even without the stimulus of an outside threat, he would have relished the task of converting all Tunisia into a militarized hierarchy responsive to his command just as he would have taken pleasure in innovation for its own sake. Still, the defensive imperative gave cohesion to his overall program.

Aḥmad was not, however, a very consistent planner or performer in his modernizing efforts. The reason is quite simple. By birth, background, and education Aḥmad was still very much a traditional man. His mother had been a Christian slave, captured as a young girl in one of the last successful Tunisian corsair raids on Sardinia. Aḥmad was born into this earlier age – by then hopelessly anachronistic – of corsairs and concubines.

He grew up in the constricted palace life surrounded by family, cousins, and *mamlūks.* He was trained along with those *mamlūks* destined to form his own loyal retainers in the Bardo *madrasa.* He was being groomed as a possible candidate to preside over the small ruling elite, largely of alien origin, which passed for government.

And it was a government consistent with traditional Islamic political values, responsible *for* the governed only to the extent of providing the minimal security and public order that would enable the individual Muslim to live out his life in accordance with the precepts of Islamic Law. Government was in no way responsible *to* the governed. Indeed, as the alien origins, the preferred marriage alliances, and the official adoption of the Ḥanafī (rather than Mālikī) school all indicated, government was not even closely identified with the governed.

All this was a far cry from the ideals and the new reality ushered in by the French Revolution and the Napoleonic period. Aḥmad Bey, in short, had a very incomplete (and therefore distorted) notion of the European model upon which he based his would-be reforms. The results obtained betrayed this ill-fitting combination of traditional and modern.

The accomplishments of Aḥmad Bey's eighteen year reign, if reported with the sharp eye for efficiency and rational links between plans and performance that a management consultant might provide, may be tersely and bleakly reported:

(a) He created a new, westernized *niẓāmī* army with a projected strength of approximately twenty-six thousand, but an actual strength that seldom reached two-thirds that number.

(b) He initiated several ancillary industrial concerns with the aim of making Tunisia more nearly self-sufficient in its military needs. These included a textile mill to produce uniforms at Tabourba, a cannon foundry, powder mills, tanneries, and a small arms factory. Most plants were placed under the supervision of European specialists charged with setting up the enterprise and training Tunisian cadres. All, however, had been completely abandoned or were in an advanced state of decline even before the end of Aḥmad's reign.

(c) His naval efforts, although not so ambitious as the army reforms, were, unfortunately, symbolized by the silting up of the harbor at Ghār al-Milḥ (Porto Farina) and by the frigate, Aḥmadiyya, which, having been built on the Lake of Tunis before the channel to the open sea was widened, was destined to remain imprisoned in its basin "like a wooden island"[17] until destroyed years later.

(d) In 1840 he founded the Bardo Military School – pompously, and erroneously, called "école polytèchnique" by certain European observers. The institution was, at best, the equivalent of a high school for classes numbering perhaps forty to sixty officer candidates.

(e) The cumulative financial strain of these many efforts (exacerbated by the dispatch of a ten thousand strong expeditionary army to fight alongside the Ottoman Empire and the Allies in the Crimean War) imposed upon a still traditional economy created great social unrest, provoked a flight from the land, and paved the way for the later revolt in 1864 and state bankruptcy in 1869.

This adds up to a harsh indictment not lightly to be dismissed by some historicist flourish about "the wave of the future." Since Western historiography of the Third World is especially prone to adopt a "Whig interpretation of history," favoring innovators over conservatives and westernizers over traditionalists, it is especially apt to pose the question whether Tunisia might have been able to move toward modernization with greater speed and less cost if spared the excessive enthusiasms of Aḥmad Bey (or Egypt without Muḥammad 'Alī).

Yet there is another side to the story. Even if Aḥmad Bey had not existed, Tunisia would no longer have been free to maintain the traditional socio-political system (which for all its weaknesses was at least familiar). The economic and political pressure coming from an expansive Europe was already making itself felt. The economic difficulties experienced by Tunisia during the period 1815 to 1830,[18] when no major domestic reforms were being tried, had already proved the vulnerability of the old system. The choice, in short, was no longer whether to maintain the old, and the only practical question was what form the new was to take.

From this viewpoint a somewhat more charitable appraisal of Aḥmad's reign seems justified. Admittedly, the picture is still far from rosy. He, his government, and the Tunisian people paid an unnecessarily high price for his poor administrative leadership. The crucial importance of appropriate organizational structures to implement bold new innovations is painfully illustrated, time and again, by the events of his reign.

Aḥmad, in effect, tried to load a conscripted mass army on a traditional economy; and he tried to squeeze the extra money out of the people by means of a traditional tax-collecting apparatus that could not do the job without self-defeating inefficiency and injustice. He ignored almost completely the need to create a more responsible, and hierarchically structured, bureaucracy to implement the more powerful and more centralized government his reforms ineluctably involved. Instead, he relied almost exclusively on the "old school tie" system of working through an intimate clique of *mamlūks*, friends and retainers. The flight to France of his old friend and chief tax farmer, Maḥmūd bin 'Ayād, taking with him several million piastres embezzled from the state treasury, pointed up the fatal flaw in Aḥmad's approach.

His military and modest "industrial" reforms were all terminated before they had time to change appreciably the life style of many Tunisians. The several thousand peasants conscripted, or recruited, into the army faded back into the countryside. The smaller numbers brought into the military-related industries had only a fleeting brush with modern factory methods, not enough to create any kind of new outlook.

Aḥmad's ambitious but erratic efforts were, at the level of the masses, largely negative and disruptive. They served to move a reasonably large number of people out of their traditional patterns, obliging them – at least temporarily – to wrestle with new ways and to consider the possibility of change. The financial burden of his reforms certainly accelerated the decline of the traditional economy, but this is only a matter of degree. European pressure was taking care of that in any case. In sum, none of Aḥmad's reforms became sufficiently rooted among any portion of the Tunisian people to make it possible to speak of self-sustaining growth, or even of a multiplier effect.

So much for the imposing debit side of the ledger. When, however, one turns from the masses to the existing political and social elite, when one thinks, not of revolutionary change reaching out into the countryside, but of reform filtering down from the top, it can be seen that Aḥmad made his mark on Tunisian history.

He gave the Tunisian political elite their first practical experience in working with European military and civilian advisers, thus providing a small group with a "window to the West."

He started the necessary process of symbolic adjustment to the West with its concomitant implicit concession that *Dār al-Islām* (the areas ruled by Muslims) could no longer survive in self-sufficient isolation. U.S. Consul Hodgson, reporting his first audience with Aḥmad Bey in 1842, wrote: "The Bey was seated in an European armed chair. Musulman princes who have adopted the European system of military tactics, no longer sit cross-legged."[19] Aḥmad Bey did even more: He imposed the western-style *niẓāmī* uniform upon his army and his court.[20] He had European architects build a thoroughly European palace complex at Muḥammadiya. He established good relations with Catholic prelates residing in Tunisia, permitting them to establish new private schools. He made a lavish state visit to France in 1846.[21] He even – the seemingly banal incidents are often more telling – invited the French Consul, Marcescheau, to bring his wife to see the display of gifts that were to be sent to the Sublime Porte.[22]

The Bardo Military School, created by Aḥmad, did manage to survive the later retrenchments that brought the other reforms to grief; and, in spite of its relatively modest academic or technical standing, the school served as a worthy successor to the former Bardo *madrasa* (for training *mamlūks* and Ḥusaynid sons). It was the first official educational institution in Tunisia inspired by western notions of curriculum with French, in addition to Arabic, as a language of instruction. It should come as no surprise to discover that the next generation of modernizers rallying around Khayr al-Dīn al-Tūnisī were graduates of the Bardo Military School.

One of Aḥmad's major achievements was to instill a growing sense of Tunisian national identity among the Tunisian political elite and, even to some extent, among rank and file Tunisians. He inherited a governmental apparatus dominated at the center by *mamlūks*, Turks, and their descendants.[23] Turks and Berber Zouaves (Zwāwa) were expected to form the manpower for the military.[24] To nine-tenths of the Tunisian population government was an alien "them."

With military conscription came the notion that soldiers need not be Turks or Zouaves. This was a potentially revolutionary change resisted by both the conscripted Tunisian peasants (no effort was made to conscript the nomadic tribesmen deemed, quite rightly, less tractable to organized military discipline) and the old Turko-Mamluk officer class. It cannot be said that either group had been completely won over to the new idea by the end of Aḥmad's reign, but the "received wisdom" that an ethnically distinct political and military class was in the natural order of things had been challenged by almost two decades of basically different policy. Remnants of the old world view with its political class distinctions would, of course, long survive, but the seeds had been sown for a more modern notion of national cohesion, political and social.

Aḥmad's measures to bring the official status and perquisites of the Mālikī *'ulamā'* (religious scholars) in line with the Ḥanafīs represented another breach in the walls dividing state from society.

Aḥmad also promoted Arab tribal and regional leaders "to positions and ranks they had never thought of nor aspired to,"[25] undermining thereby, in yet another major arena of governmental relations with society, the notion that leadership belongs ethnically to Turks and Mamluks and, spatially, to those residing at the court in Tunis.

"He regarded all sons of the country as qualified for any post . . . showing no preference for one group over the other." Such was the appraisal of Aḥmad Bey's own private secretary, Bin Diyaf, who added that Aḥmad himself was wont to insist, "The source of kingship is the subjects' affection. There can be no affection where there is special consideration for one class to the exclusion of others. Now, if the group feeling (*al-'aṣabiyya*) disintegrates, the bonds linking king and kingdom are dissolved. It is therefore necessary to treat all persons equally without distinction, even the Hashemite." And Bin Diyaf cites as further evidence of Aḥmad's approach his decision to marry his sister to Muḥammad al-Murābiṭ of a leading native Kairouan family, whereas his predecessors had tended to marry among their *mamlūks* and clients.[26]

"*Hubb al-waṭan min al-imān*" (Love of the homeland is part of the faith) – so goes the *ḥadīth* later to become popular among early Arab nationalists. The phrase is to be found in Aḥmad's beylical letter to the people of the Sahil in 1841 announcing military conscription. In the following year he inaugurated the new Fifth Infantry Regiment, noting with pride that it was an army "completely composed of our sons." The same emotional speech contained references to "love of the homeland and the land," "our land, where our fathers are buried and our sons will be born," and "Tunisia, our blessed home."[27]

And Aḥmad's farewell speech to his troops departing for the Crimea contained the following charge: "Do not forget what is due your homeland and your country, the resting ground of your fathers, the birthplace of your sons, and the abode of your hearts and bodies. . . The flag of your homeland and territory will reveal to all eyes your honor."[28]

Here was, indeed, a new political ideal. Not everyone was convinced, but a handful from among the political elite did come to embrace this new vision. Nor did they do so uncritically. They noted the gap between Aḥmad's plans and the results. Commenting on Aḥmad's later loss of interest in the Tebourba textile project, Bin Diyaf observed: "If only he had considered that the greatest profit was in clothing his soldiers and people of his country by this factory so that the value of cloth which is bought from others would remain in the country not to mention the benefits gained by those living near the factory and those working in it, all of which would increase the country's prosperity and stimulate the local markets, etc., then he would not have lost interest. . . This is unlike the Frankish nations. They spend money for a profit likely to be realized only years later. In their activities they are concerned with the benefit to be derived from this approach and of their ability to dispense with the need to rely on others."[29]

The same Bin Diyaf, who accompanied Aḥmad Bey on his state visit to France, could sum up the trip from Marseilles to Paris in the following lyrical terms: "The traveller on this easy road wishes only that the journey might continue for he sees good roads, is surrounded by buildings, trees, fertile lands and rivers, and there are many other travellers of all kinds. He cannot hear the voice of the oppressed unless it be from one who had brought this state upon himself. And this is indeed an almost unheard of wonder in view of the many taxes and levies. The secret is that these taxes are not unfair. The inhabitants know exactly what is required, and the revenue collected is spent for the benefit of all without distinction." As for Paris, it was "all you could wish of sciences, industries, wealth, good administration, elegance, civilisation and justice."[30]

For all his errors, Aḥmad Bey had managed to give Tunisia a decisive push along the road to modernization. At his death in 1855, the majority of his subjects were not yet effectively linked to the emerging new patterns. Even most of the small political elite would have preferred a return of the old traditions, but that was no longer possible. Most important, Aḥmad's reign had trained and converted a small, dynamic minority committed to change and westernization. They would be heard from later.

At first, however, there was a pause, if not indeed an effort to turn back the clock. Aḥmad's cousin Muḥammad Bey, who reigned from 1855 to 1859, may be compared to Egypt's 'Abbās I, who followed the hectic, dynamic years of Muḥammad 'Alī. Like 'Abbās I, Muḥammad Bey wanted nothing more than a return to a traditional Muslim autocracy undiluted by any European ideas and practices. He even tried to restore slavery, abolished by Aḥmad, until dissuaded by his ministers.[31]

He had little interest in Aḥmad's *niẓāmī* army and showed no inclination to undertake expensive innovations in other fields. One happy result, although only temporary, was that the hard-pressed peasantry obtained some tax relief. If Muḥammad Bey's policy of conservatism and retrenchment had been matched by adminstrative reform, his reign could have diverted the innovative current remaining from Aḥmad's reign into more effective channels.

Instead, Muḥammad Bey offered no acceptable alternative that would attract the handful of reformers produced during Aḥmad's reign. At the same time, his own nostalgic preference for traditional autocracy was doomed to failure as a result of forces which neither he nor Tunisia could control. By mid-1850 the European economic and political domination was even stronger than it had been a generation earlier. Muḥammad Bey proved unable to swim against this tide.

An incident in 1857 provoked the first joint European intervention – itself a precursor of things to come. A Jewish carter, one Batto Sfez, ran over a Muslim child in the streets of Tunis. A scuffle followed during which Sfez allegedly insulted the Prophet Muḥammad. Sfez was brought before a *Shari'a* (Islamic Law) court, sentenced to death, and summarily executed.[32] A scandalized Europe, following British and French lead, remonstrated, and the Bey was obliged to show that such arbitrary action could not happen again by issuing a charter of rights, (or the *'ahd al-amān*) patterned on the Ottoman *Hatti şerif* of *Gulhane.*

The 1857 *'ahd al-amān* symbolized Tunisia's political vassalage to Europe, just an an increasingly domineering European merchant class and the declining native class of artisans and merchants bore witness to the beylik's economic subordination.[33] A succession of other measures followed, all bearing telltale "made in Europe" signs: the removal of sumptuary laws and customs imposed upon the Jews, the establishment in 1858 of a municipal council for Tunis, and, during the reign of Muḥammad al-Ṣādiq Bey (1859-1882), the drafting of the first modern constitution for the Arab or Ottoman world. This constitution went into effect in early 1861.[34] The previous year Muḥammad al-Ṣādiq Bey had taken advantage of Napoleon III's presence in Algiers to visit him there and secure his approval. "Muhammad al-Sādiq's visit, draft constitution in hand, to the head of state of a foreign, non-Muslim country sufficiently epitomizes the power relations surrounding the birth of 'constitutionalism' in Tunisia."[35]

From the Sfez incident until the French Protectorate was imposed in 1881, the Tunisian government lived on borrowed time, carefully measuring out its maneuverability in terms of what Europe would find acceptable. The situation was not unlike that faced by the central Ottoman Empire, where, throughout the entire *Tanẓīmāt* period, Western-inspired reforms were implemented, both to placate Europe and to build up internal strength in the hope of warding off Europe. Contemporary Western observers, and even some later historians, saw only one side of the story, claiming that the "tanzimat stopped at the doorstep of the Sublime Porte".

Such an interpretation is to be faulted not so much for its cynicism as its superficiality. It is, rather, more important to discern in Tunisia – as in the Ottoman Empire – the unbroken but evolving tradition of the westernizers. Yes, they were to some extent collaborators with European powers. They were opportunists. They occasionally played a double-game.[36] In the context of the times this was normal. Equally important was the purpose for which they played the risky game of seeking European support. Some, such as Maḥmūd bin 'Ayād (who absconded with state funds to France in 1852) and Muṣṭafā Khaznadar (who served as chief minister from 1837 to 1873) used European support for personal interests or to defend the traditional system. Others, such as Khayr al-Dīn and his school, risked reliance on outside support as a means of achieving reforms. And the "game" itself gave this small corps of modernizers precious time to familiarize themselves with the European model of modernity and to internalize some of its values.

The central theme of the Tunisian story is that of continuity, of reformist efforts fought within the existing political elite and only very slowly filtering down to the masses. Eventually, by the 1930s a new national elite was created that was in a position to mobilize the entire nation; but unlike the developments in many other Third World societies, this stage was reached without at any time a radical political or social break with the past. There was no revolution.

The abortive 1864 revolt clearly illustrates this central theme. The revolt, starting among the tribes but spreading even to such sedentary and normally orderly regions as the Sāḥil, came close to bringing down the Ḥusaynid dynasty; but within a year the shrewd policy of divide and rule emanating from Tunis had sundered the briefly coalescent forces and stifled the revolt.

This was a classic "time of troubles" – an imposing mass revulsion against excessive taxation (the major tax having been arbitrarily doubled in 1863) rendered even more powerful by the increasing general malaise, the hopeless feeling that the system was not working and no one was acting to make things better. If the revolt's leader, 'Alī bin Ghadhāhim, had toppled the Ḥusaynid dynasty, the continuity of Tunisia's political development toward modernization would surely have been shaken, if not decisively broken.

The result, however, would not necessarily have made a revolution. More likely, it would only have accelerated European intervention (somewhat like what happened to the 'Urābī Pasha movement in Egypt or the events in Morocco during the last few years before 1912). 'Alī bin Ghadhāhim, himself, had quickly learned to seek out European support,[37] and there is little reason to believe that he had the political sophistication or the power base to avoid becoming a helpless shuttlecock in the European diplomatic game.

There was, in short, a revolutionary climate in 1864 but no revolutionary apparatus to utilize it. The thoroughly traditional bias to be found in the petitions and propaganda emanating from the 1864 revolt and the segmentary, tribal outlook of its leadership explain how even a weakened and discredited regime in Tunis was able to survive the challenge.[38] Tunisia was fated, for better or worse, to continue on its tortuous path guided by the same political elite.

However, like most wars and revolutions, the 1864 revolt had served as a catalyst. The old regime was even more thoroughly discredited – and bankrupt. The fiscal axe fell five years later, in 1869, when the Tunisian government was placed under the control of an Anglo-French-Italian Financial Commission. Only the balanced rivalries of the Great Powers preserved Tunisia's precarious autonomy, and when this essentially European question was settled by the mid-1870s in favor of France, it was only a matter of time before the French exercised their option and established the protectorate in 1881.

Before that event there was a rather short, but impressive, second round of reform from within the beylical system, during the brief period, 1873 to 1877, when Khayr al-Dīn served as chief minister.

Khayr al-Dīn's administration represented a last-ditch stand of those who had become committed to reform during Aḥmad's long reign. Many had been connected with the Bardo Military School and the intricacies of military modernization. Others, such as Bin Diyaf, until his death in 1874, and Shaykh Muḥammad Bayrām al-Khamīs, represented the *'ulamā'* and "men of the pen" who had been previously converted to reform.[39]

The Khayr al-Dīn reforms were not linked to constitutional or democratic issues. The idea of representation – of breathing some new life into the moribund Constitution of 1861 – interested him not at all. His was still a stewardship mentality.[40] He aimed to make government more efficient and capable of providing for the needs of the people. In a sense his approach represented the marriage of Aḥmad's sporadic and often uncritical enthusiasm for westernization with administrative rationalization. He reorganized taxes and general economic policy to encourage economic growth rather than, as had so often been the case, stifle initiative. He began, with an identical aim in mind, an organization of habous[41] administration. He gave equal attention to making the bureaucracy better organized and more accountable. He even installed a complaint box – a fitting symbol for a Weberian model of rational bureaucracy.[42]

Khayr al-Dīn's most important long-term contribution was to establish Ṣādiqī College in 1875. It was to be a college in the French sense of a secondary school, and, in terms of present-day standards, it appears as only a modest effort to provide rudimentary training in Western languages and Western ways to the next generation destined for the state bureaucracy. It was intended to achieve, starting twenty-five years later, for the "men of the pen" what the Bardo Military School was designed to accomplish for the "men of the sword." Even for the times this was a cautious blend of old and new, indigenous and alien. A westernized bureaucratic elite was the aim, but the 150 students during those first years were actually guided by twenty-one teachers of Arabic and Koranic studies as opposed to only thirteen teaching all other subjects.

Yet, after all reservations are recorded and the reality separated from latter-day myth-making, the founding of Ṣādiqī College stands as a bold, new departure – a truly seminal event. Ṣādiqī College survived both the decline following Khayr al-Dīn's dismissal and the new regime brought by the French Protectorate. It did more than survive. The college became the Eton and Harrow for subsequent generations of the Tunisian political elite. They met and were molded at Ṣadīqī. Following 1906, when admission came to be governed by competitive examination,[43] Ṣādiqī College became the goal of bright young provincials. Those who made it received, in turn, the Ṣadīqī stamp. They became part of the old political elite even while changing and challenging it.

In 1877, Muḥammad al-Ṣādiq Bey removed Khayr al-Dīn from office for trivial reasons; and the reformers, shorn of their power base, were thrown into disarray. Khayr al-Dīn himself left Tunisia for Istanbul where for a short time he was to serve as Sultan ʻAbd al-Hamīd's grand vizier (yet another indication that the great Tunisian statesman was more a "management expert" than a liberal). Ṣādiqī College, itself, barely survived the neglect and poor administration that followed.

The limited success achieved by Khayr al-Dīn and his followers demonstrated that the old regime remained very much alive for all its anachronistic lumbering. It would not freely give way to necessary structural change. This would have to be imposed upon the Ḥusaynid system either from forces within Tunisia or from abroad. The failure of the 1864 revolt and the shaky successes of Khayr al-Dīn's years revealed the limitations on possible further change from within. The next development was destined to be that of outright Western control in the form of the French Protectorate.

THE COLONIAL PERIOD

The period of French colonial rule[44] in Tunisia, from 1881 to 1956, is to be treated here from a special perspective that will seem at times whimsical, perverse, or machiavellian (or all three) by comparison with earlier accounts. There will be no effort to explain (praise or condemn) how France got into Tunisia or how she got out. The complex of alien forces that made up the Protectorate (both the government and the "colons") will not be appraised on its own terms, but rather as a newly-imposed part of the "environment" to which native Tunisia had to adjust. The nationalist movement will be analyzed according to the several stages of its adjustment to this new "environment." The aim, in short, is to understand this colonial period of Tunisia's path to modernization with the same dispassion one could normally be expected to bring to a study of the Romanization of Gaul. It is hoped, by this approach, to avoid refighting old battles without, however, completely squeezing out the human drama and the dynamics of individual variation.[45]

Two interrelated conditions shaped the early years of the Protectorate period: (1) Armed resistance was minimal. Both the intrusive "protectors" and native society quickly sensed that the Protectorate was not to be effectively challenged from within. (2) The existing native political institutions were preserved, at least in form.

The establishment of the French Protectorate with a minimum of violence and resistance stands in stark contrast to the colonial period in both Algeria and Morocco. The long, heroic resistance by Algeria's 'Abd al-Qādir and the harsh French response organized by Marshal Bugeaud set a pattern of violence and mutual incomprehension never completely broken. A century and a quarter later Algeria was to regain her independence with the same violence with which she had lost it.

The French Protectorate in Morocco may be divided into two equal periods of 22 years each: from 1912 to 1934, when "pacification" was finally completed, and the postpacification period from 1934 to 1956. There was nothing of the same violence that characterized French Algeria. Some aspects of the pacification followed a typically Moroccan *baroud d'honneur* geste. Even so, this protracted pacification campaign did distract both French and Moroccan attention from other concerns.

Tunisia's acceptance of colonialism was more like that of Egypt – a brief military skirmish for several weeks or months and then recognition of the fait accompli. Not the stuff of heroic sagas, perhaps, but the result was to keep the existing native political elite intact and to concentrate its attention on how to make the best of the new situation. The native elite was understandably disorganized and baffled following the imposition of outside rule, but the rapid establishment of a seemingly unshakable colonial regime narrowed down their range of choices, sparing them the illusion, costly in time and manpower, that armed resistance would be effective.

If the native political elite could not lead an armed resistance to the occupier (either because native forces were not available or because the elite realized that it could not long maintain its leadership over a guerrilla movement), they were obliged to choose some form of collaboration or passive resistance, which, under the circumstances, amounted to withdrawal from the political arena.

The traditional forces in both Egypt and Tunisia offered a grudging, tactical collaboration with colonialism *faute de mieux*, but the modernizers – eager to play a more active role – gambled on the possibility of achieving enough through cooperation with the new authorities to offset the taint of "collaboration with the enemy." The early years of colonial rule in both Egypt and Tunisia spawned what might therefore be called "collaborationist modernizers."[46]

This was the group that rallied around Shaykh Muḥammad 'Abduh and the *Umma* party in Egypt. In Tunisia, they were the men who later came to be called the "Young Tunisians." Both sprang from the existing political elite but both represented a tendency toward enlargement of that elite – if not, indeed, ultimately a veritable "circulation of elites" à la Pareto. Both had links with the immediately preceding generation of political leadership. In Tunisia this continuity of political generations was most clearly discernible. Bashīr Sfār, the leader of the young Tunisians, was called "the second father of the reawakening." Khayr al-Dīn had been the first.[47]

In these important matters Tunisia's colonial experience resembles that of Egypt and stands in sharp contrast to what took place in either Algeria or Morocco. On the other hand, in other equally important determinants of change in the colonial situation, Tunisia is found squarely lined up with Algeria and Morocco in contrast to Egypt and, for that matter, the rest of the colonized Arab East. French North Africa was an area of settler colonization. Masses of Frenchmen, or other Europeans capable of absorbing French culture and becoming French citizens, flocked into North Africa with official French blessing.

Algeria, the first to be colonized and the only part of French North Africa legally absorbed as part of France, was the extreme example. In 1906 the *colons* accounted for thirteen percent of the total Algerian population, and as late as 1954, after over two generations of a demographic explosion among the native Algerians, the French population remained almost ten percent of the total.

Yet, it is sometimes forgotten that Tunisia, although only a protectorate, was also a great haven for European settlement. As early as 1906 French and Italians combined accounted for 6.4% of Tunisia's total population. The figure climbed to 8.2% in 1931 and had leveled off to 6.7% at the time of independence in 1956.[48]

What did it mean to native Tunisians to have thousands of Europeans pouring into their country? What was the significance of this challenge to the still intact, but beleaguered, native political elite? How is such a colonial experience to be contrasted with what transpired in Egypt, Sudan, and the Fertile Crescent?[49] A few brief indications here may help to clarify the more significant differences.

For example, in 1938 Tunisia had seven thousand European functionaries out of a total 11,500; and at the end of the Protectorate one-fourth of the Europeans gainfully employed worked in government.[50] This imposing domination of the governmental apparatus by French personnel left little room at the top, or even in middle ranks, for aspiring native Tunisians.

The European presence also overshadowed the representative institutions established during the Protectorate. The *Conference Consultative,* established in 1896, had *only* French representation until 1907 when sixteen Tunisian members were added to give native Tunisia minority representation. Significantly, the French community elected its representatives (after 1905) by universal suffrage. The Resident-General appointed the Tunisian members.

Later steps toward "liberalization" of representation were in the same pattern. The *Grand Conseil,* established in 1922, had two sections – one with fifty-six French members, the other with forty-one Tunisians. Suffrage was indirect for the Tunisians; the French and Tunisian sections deliberated separately; some of the representation for both sections was reserved for *intérêts économiques* (twenty-two of fifty-six French, eighteen of forty-one Tunisians); the *Grand Conseil* had limited jurisdiction, and – as if these were not sufficient safeguards – a *Conseil superieur,* dominated by the Protectorate Executive, decided the issue in the event the French and Tunisian sections disagreed.[51]

After the Second World War the *Grand Conseil* was modified to grant equal membership to the French and Tunisian sections (fifty-three each), and the economic interests groups were abolished. Even so, the Tunisian section represented a carefully restricted electorate,[52] the *conseil's* prerogatives were scarcely expanded, and in any case the government could always take emergency measures without consulting the *conseil.*

Comparable, if not more severe, restraints were placed on regional and municipal representative bodies.

The fine points of this representative system and the last-ditch efforts to establish what was known as "cosovereignty" of French and Tunisians are now of only antiquarian interest. It is, however, still useful to consider how such a representative system influenced the Tunisian political culture during the protectorate period. It was clearly a less attractive system to the native Tunisians than the several systems prevailing in nonsettler colonial situations, e.g., some combination of indirect rule or a national parliament, but with restricted prerogatives.

Even after the actual systems connected with the names of Lugard, Sandeman, Minto-Morley, Allenby, Percy Cox and Douglas Newbold are exposed to the harsh light of reality, it remains true that many politically concerned people in these areas detected certain political potential in these colonially imposed representative schemes. These systems, in short, appealed to other than a class of *beni oui-oui,* at least at certain stages in the colonial process.

At first sight it might seem that the Tunisians were deprived of precious experience in modern representative institutions, but second thoughts are perhaps in order. By the time of the Neo-Destour, the young, westernized leaderhip around Ḥabīb Bourguiba were content to stake their claim on representing the *pays réel* as opposed to the *pays légal.*[53] Perhaps in Egypt they would have been drawn into the Wafd only to have their reformist zeal converted to cynicism and opportunism as they lived the demeaning sham that passed for a representative system in a supposedly independent country which the British still controlled by neatly balancing off king and popular party.

Perhaps the colonial dialectic nudged the Tunisians – by the time of the Neo-Destour at least – into a more genuine exercise in representation, whereby they set for themselves the task of organizing peasants, workers, and others beyond the narrow, legal orbit of the *Grand Conseil.*

Colon orginally, and literally, had the sense of homesteader, the European who settled on the land with his family and took up farming. Only later did the term come to be used for all Europeans. The early meaning highlights another distinguishing feature for Tunisia and other settler-colonies. In Tunisia, French and Italian settlers moved out into the country, eventually securing possession of 750,000 hectares, or twenty-one percent of the country's cultivable land.[54] There was, admittedly, during the years of the Protectorate a decreasing relative number of European farmers living on the land, for the tendency was toward large, capitalistic farming – often by joint-stock companies. Nevertheless, the model of technological modernity on the land backed up by seemingly unlimited credit facilities and a solicitous state apparatus was there to taunt and impress Tunisian rural society.

And they responded in many ways. Some became agricultural day laborers working on the European holdings (not a proportionally large number for mechanized agriculture uses less labor). Even more became adjusted to the notion of fixed boundaries and agriculture as a commercial enterprise, taking advantage of the Protectorate land registration laws (originally passed in response to *colon* pressure).[55]

In many nonsettler colonies the colonial power was often inclined to support a rural land-owning class as the most economical way to establish control in the countryside. The result could sometimes be to convert a traditional *shaykh*-like class into provincial despots who had learned only the profit motive from their colonial patrons. After independence such forces could be in a strong position to resist modernization, whether the pressures came from the capital or their own peasantry.

The *colon* challenge left a different legacy in Tunisia. No native latifundia were supported or created. Instead, there was a disorganized rural population, from agricultural laborers to small holders, who faced a common threat in the *colons* and sought only an effective means to combine against that threat. This the Neo-Destour provided.[56]

With eventually over a quarter of a million Europeans living in Tunisia under the French Protectorate, it is understandable that not all of the *colon* class were prosperous, "establishment," and of bourgeois background. On the contrary, the strong European presence created thriving Socialist and Communist parties as well as a militant wing of the *Confédération Générale du Travail* (C.G.T.). From the vantage point of European history, it can be seen that European leftism in the colonial situation was doomed. Its rank and file membership, enjoying an advantageous position just by being Europeans in a colony, inevitably broke ranks and joined the colonial establishment in resistance to the rising nationalist movement. Nevertheless, the impact of this short-lived European leftism on native Tunisia was immense. Young Bourguiba and his followers worked out much of their tactics and ideology in journalistic conflict with the group editing *Tunis Socialiste,* and the Tunisian trade union leader Ferhat Hached learned the ropes in the C.G.T.[57]

The presence of so many Europeans also had its impact on Tunisian education during the Protectorate period – not that any greater number of Tunisians were educated than in other colonial situations. On the contrary, as late as 1930 only 7.4% of primary-school-age Tunisians were actually in school. The figure crept up to a modest 9.5% by 1945. On the eve of independence in 1955, after a decade of special effort, only twenty-six percent were in school. At that latter date, three percent of the secondary-school-age population were attending classes. Even so, the existence of a network of French schools serving the French population (and a handful of Tunisians) did provide an important yardstick by which the Tunisians could measure their own demands and goals. The resulting Franco-Arab system and the continued vitality of Ṣādīqī College insured an excellent education to the slowly expanding Tunisian elite. It also provided a good foundation for the rapid educational expansion following independence.

The intensity of French colonial rule in Tunisia can also be seen in the survival of French as a language of culture and administration almost a generation after independence. The problems of bilingualism and the underlying biculturalism are not lightly to be ignored, but from another perspective this continued role of French is significant. That a great number of Tunisians rely on *Le Monde, L'Express, Le Canard Enchainé* for their news, continue to model their education on French patterns, appreciate and even participate in Francophone cultural activities – all without feeling in any way uprooted from their Tunisian heritage – suggests a more than superficial process of acculturation. French and French ways have to a considerable extent been "nationalized" in Tunisia. Whether this is a completely healthy phenomenon or whether the now deep-rooted biculturalism may be an obstacle to that national unity of purpose earlier posited as a major requisite of modernization remains to be seen. In any case, it is irrefutable evidence of the strong French imprint that the Protectorate period left on Tunisia.

These aspects of the French colonial presence in Tunisia provide both background and partial explanation for the staged development of Tunisia's political elite since 1881, culminating in a modernizing elite, capable both of winning independence and mobilizing the masses for needed reforms.

Schematically, the process went somewhat as follows:[58] In the early years following the establishment of the Protectorate, the existing political elite reacted very cautiously, while trying to learn just what this new French-imposed political system involved. Then, cautiously, a few disciples of the Khayr al-Dīn school began to sense the possibility of attaining part of their aims by working with and through the Protectorate. When a neglected Sādiqī College was about to be abolished, they were able to convince the French authorities that they would need the bilingual, bicultural graduates of such an institution as interpreters and junior officials in the Protectorate administration.

The same group, with the blessing of the Resident General, organized the *Khaldūniyya*, an institution intended to provide a bridge to French language and modern ways for Zitouna mosque/university students. They met with only slight success in their immediate aim, but they were well on their way to jelling into a cohesive group – the Young Tunisians.

These Young Tunisians, almost all of whom had been born into the existing political elite, played a mediating role between the more liberal elements of the Protectorate administration (and in France itself) and native Tunisian society. They asked of the former only the chance to work with them in implementing France's *mission civilisatrice,* insisting that native Tunisia would be responsive. And they urged the latter, their own compatriots, to defer their chagrin at being dominated and learn the modernizing ways from the French in order to catch up with the world around them.

Denied the opportunity to become a mass political party (native Tunisia was not yet ready for such a westernizing and secularizing ideology), the Young Tunisians were obliged to play the role of teachers (to Tunisia) and advocates (representing Tunisia to France); and they played this imposed role to perfection.[59]

The Young Tunisia movement had been disrupted following a banal confrontation with the protectorate authorities in 1911. Little more overt activity was seen from them or from other proto-nationalist groups until after the First World War. By that time the mood had changed – the war itself serving as a catalyst, speeding up developments in the colonial process. The time had come to move beyond a small, powerless native elite who, not being able to "represent" anyone, could rely only on reason and cajolery. The next stage in the nationalist development required a group that could bring some power to the bargaining table by claiming to speak for great numbers of Tunisians.

This was the role of the Destour party founded in 1919, the first Tunisian effort to create a mass political party. Organizationally, in the context of the times, it was a considerable success. Ideologically (or, one might even say, developmentally), it was a step backward from the modernizing zeal of the Young Tunisians.

Leadership of the Destour party was more traditional and less westernized as a group than the Young Tunisians. The Destour party represented an organizational effort that reached beyond those in the tradition of the old, narrowly drawn political class, separate from the rest of society. The Destour brought in nonpolitical or, at least, hitherto ambivalently political groups – especially the *baldiya* class, or the bourgeoisie of Tunis and the major towns. These were the good "old families" whose sons traditionally provided Tunisian society with its middle and upper-level *'ulamā'*, merchants, and artisans.

The *baldiya* had always been less cosmopolitan and more resistant to change than the traditional political class, and the Destour, ideologically, betrayed signs of this move into the more conservative mainstream of Tunisian society.

It can readily be seen that the relative organizational success and the ideological conservatism of the Destour were intimately linked. The Destour was a "popular" party because its leadership did not dare (in most cases did not wish) to get out beyond the "received wisdom" of traditional Tunisia. It was, for this reason, comfortable and acceptable to the *baldiya* class and the many other Tunisians who had long been accustomed to look to the *baldiya* as the legitimate guardians of societal values. As a result, many more Tunisians were brought into the political process, receiving through the Destour their basic training in party organization.

Yet, in terms of modernization, this is all that can be entered on the positive side of the ledger for the Destour. Its leadership was unheroic, uninspired, and unrealistic. They represented in full measure the smugness, aloofness, and narrow-mindedness so often associated with a traditional bourgeoisie.[60] If Tunisia was to push further along the road to modernization, it would need considerably more daring scouts than would be provided by the Destour.

Herein lies the crucial importance of the Neo-Destour's challenge to the Old Destour in the 1930s. Those destined to organize and lead the Neo-Destour represented the first great influx of provincial parvenus into the Tunisian political system. Coming mainly from the cohesive *Ṣāhil* region, where numerous holders of olive groves had long since developed a work-save-achieve ethic, these young provincials were among the first to take advantage of the new opportunities offered by the French Protectorate.

They flocked into Ṣādiqī College and other new educational opportunities then available (in very limited numbers, of course) to those who did best in competitive examinations. They earned more than their share of these plus, in some cases, the even rarer opportunity of higher education in France. It was *la carrière ouverte aux talents, à la tunisienne.*[61]

The handful of young Tunisians from this kind of background who began to converge on Tunis in the late 1920s – soon to find their leader in Ḥabīb Bourguiba – changed the course of modern Tunisian history. And, in credit to the young Bourguiba and his colleagues, it must be emphasized that the course they adopted was neither the easiest nor the most natural under the circumstances. They had been accepted into the Old Destour party. They had only to wait a few years before emerging as leaders of the existing party. A bit of carefully circumscribed agitation within the party might even have accelerated their upward movement without risk. Either they or their sons would have been accepted as promising marriage prospects by the oldest Tunis families. Within the constraints imposed by the French Protectorate they were assured promising social and economic careers. And they were in a position to inherit the "political kingdom" whenever the French Protectorate faded away.

Instead, these young parvenus chose not to play it safe. They challenged the Destour on all fronts – its old family, *baldiya* social bias, its enervating "golden age" mentality, its traditionalist exploitation of Islam, and its fraudulent political tactics vis-à-vis the Protectorate – leonine in word, ovine in deed.

The Neo-Destour leadership, instead, took a deliberately populist stance, calling attention to the plight of the powerless rural poor, championing the efforts to organize a native trade union movement on which the Old Destour had turned its back, and boasting of their own modest origins.

They expressed a commitment to modernize their own society and had the fortitude to admit openly that this meant borrowing from the very culture whose political representatives dominated Tunisia and whose citizens resident in Tunisia lorded it over them. Nor did they sugarcoat the bitter pill with lucubrations about Christendom having borrowed the fundamentals of its present technical superiority from Islam. Avoiding the "golden age" placebo, they were better able to see their own strengths and weaknesses with clarity and "inner-directedness."

The Neo-Destour leadership chose to fight what they saw as the two-front war: against foreign domination and against underdevelopment. They had the foresight to see, and the courage to state, that victory in the former was of no great moment unless achieved in such a way as to prepare for victory in the latter.

Accordingly, this group was not only willing to be, but made a virtue of being, tactically supple in dealing with the *prépondérance* (the cover word used to describe the Protectorate, the *colons,* and all those forces for the continuation of a dominant French position in Tunisia). It would have been, indeed, a pyrrhic victory over the Protectorate that left the *vieux turbans* in charge. They were, of course, interested in wresting concessions from the Protectorate, but they were even more interested in organizing Tunisians behind their long-term aims. They, therefore, never compromised this imperative of organizing Tunisia's rank and file in order to gain some short-term advantage.

In this last development of Tunisian nationalism under the Protectorate, a modernizing ideology was wedded to a modernizing organization. "The link sketched by our Bach Hamba" (a Young Tunisian leader), proclaimed a young Neo-Destourian leader in those early years, "has finally been established between the people and their intellectuals."[62] And, in many ways, the Neo-Destour, that achieved independence and has since provided the organizational apparatus to implement impressive modernization, did represent the resurgence at the popular level of the bold Young Tunisian approach to the world around it. Never is the Tunisian theme of staged development more in evidence: first, the ideology enunciated by a small political elite (Young Tunisians), then, the first attempts at mass organization with its concomitant politization of hitherto apolitical groups (Old Destour), followed by a new group – and a new elite, itself the product of the protectorate situation – who knew how to combine and improve upon the earlier ideology and organization (Neo-Destour).

"Organization," Michels had insisted, "is the weapon of the weak in their struggle with the strong."[63] The Neo-Destour was able to go beyond the role of humble petitioner in dealing with the Protectorate because it developed and maintained organizational strength. By 1937, the leadership claimed a membership of 100,000. Even if the much smaller estimate, advanced by Henri de Montety, of twenty-eight thousand was closer to the truth, it was an impressive achievement.[64] The party, even by that early date, was organized into over four hundred local branches – a clear demonstration of the Neo-Destour's national character. On the eve of independence, the Neo-Destour was able to rely on 325,000 trained and fully-committed party regulars, grouped in local branches to be found in the largest cities and the smallest hamlets, and organized in a classical hierarchy.[65]

The Neo-Destour was also able to do more than organize mass protests *against* the Protectorate. Several nationalist groups in the colonial situation have been able to "control the streets." This is a not insignificant organizational feat, but by itself it is useless – perhaps worse than useless, creating as it does a politics of checkmate and irresolution. The genuine test of organizational loyalty and cohesion is the ability to keep in serried ranks during times of compromise or defeat. With its pragmatic tactics, its problem-solving mentality, and its modernizing ideology the Neo-Destour was able to meet this test.

For organization is more than the weapon of the weak against the strong. It is also the means by which all peoples can overcome the inertia of their traditional ways. Organization provides the human vessel that will contain and sustain a new ideology. In a sense, then, the story traced here of Tunisia's path to modernization has shown one part of the development – the move in a process of evolutionary stages from political potential to political reality, or the creation of a nation-state. This is not, of course, the same as the creation of a modernized society, but it is a necessary early step. And the postindependence record suggests that Tunisia may well be able – true to its historical legacy – to keep up the pace, not without problems and false starts, but avoiding, for all that, the agony of social and political breakdown.

CONCLUSION AND PROSPECT

Tunisia as a study in modernization? Is this, in retrospect, the best way to tell the story? Has there been that much accumulation of new knowledge, that great a switch to inanimate sources of power? Or has there been sufficient change in the other indices to warrant speaking of Tunisia as having moved into the ranks of a modernizing society, of having entered the modernization process?

Anyone who has studied what Tunisia was like in the 1830s and sees the present scale of mechanization and education (to name only these two critical factors) would be inclined to answer the above question positively. Although Tunisia is still underdeveloped in relation to standards set by the West, the country has received and absorbed such changes during the past century and a half that one can speak of the new structures. And these changes are of the nature to be clustered under the rubric "modernization."

Even so, the Tunisian case traced here is not an example in which economic or technological innovations emerge as the dynamic variables. Indeed, the postindependence period, for all its innovations and seeming progress in other fields, continues to record a rather sluggish economic development. The structural economic changes have been among the least successful – witness the ill-fated agricultural cooperatives scheme that brought the dismissal and disgrace of Aḥmad ben Saleh.

Tunisia's modernization record to date is to be seen much more in terms of human organization – of creating a sense of political interest and commitment among groups where it had not existed, strengthening the sense of identity with a Tunisian entity, giving Tunisians the feeling of participating in a going concern, enhancing opportunity according to merit,[66] and providing the organizational apparatus (government and party) to channel this newly created human power. In terms of Dankwart Rustow's interesting triad, it may be asserted that modern Tunisia has recorded considerable change and development in authority, identity, and equality.[67]

This Tunisian leitmotif may clearly be seen in the measures adopted over the past decade and a half since independence. These suggest a combination of classical nineteenth century European nationalism and populism – a president to replace the bey, the goal of universal education, female emancipation, secularization, a bit of "soak the rich" in the early days, equality of opportunity, attention to less developed areas of the country, public health projects, and the like.

Although the party changed its name to Socialist-Destour in 1964 and much has been made of Destourian socialism since that time, it may be argued that the political culture created by Ḥabīb Bourguiba and his followers is still to be characterized as nationalist and populist.

The Tunisian case, in short, is one of the several to be found in the Third World where political organization as a handmaiden to modernization gets far ahead of economic and technological change. There is no intention to claim that such is the best way, and even less that this is the only way, for countries such as Tunisia to proceed. Suffice it to point out that this is an option often adopted in the Third World, and in Tunisia the results *thus far* have been promising. And this working hypothesis alone makes Tunisia an interesting study in comparative modernization.

But, some critics might well seek to ask if this emphasis on organization and politicization of a mass society has not been overdrawn. Has Tunisia benefited by an overly favorable, and somewhat uncritical, "press"? Doesn't this rather unseemly emphasis on the leader, on "Bourguibism," bespeak the authoritarian control of a dynamic individual rather than democratic organization?

Bourguiba, in the view of this author, is one of the most impressive leaders in the Third World. He has presented Tunisia with an ideal of national unity, dignity, and modernization which is demanding but realizable. Anyone who has followed his long speeches to the Tunisian people is quite likely to be impressed with this man playing the role – even more than Ataturk – of schoolmaster to a nation.

Yet, after all is said, it must be admitted that Bourguiba is an autocrat, and in his latter years, his life style is rather more like that of a reincarnated Aḥmad Bey than he would ever admit or even realize (e.g., palaces, parades, keeping his ministers in attendance like a neo-traditionalist court, abruptly bestowing and withdrawing his political favor, etc.).

Even so, the Socialist-Destour, leadership and mass, does exist. Other organizations, trade unions, students, agriculturalists, business and women's associations are still going concerns – even if in some cases they have lost part of their autonomy to an almost oppressively paternalistic party and government. Tunisia appears to be especially well-endowed with modernized political and social leadership by comparison with other countries in a roughly comparable situation.

The question of how much Bourguibism will survive Bourguiba is now in the process of being answered as the ailing leader is obliged to relinquish his tight grip on Tunisia and prepare for his succession.

The answer will be found not just in effectiveness of organization, but in the blend of organization and ideology. Now, the history of ideas is the most capricious of Clio's daughters, and it requires some temerity to assert that Tunisia has now consolidated a genuine change in political ideology and world view. Yet, many outside observers, including the present author, who have had the opportunity to know Tunisian leaders in political, educational, and economic fields and to compare their approach to daily problems with that demonstrated by leaders in other countries of comparable developmental standing, are inclined to make such an assertion. Here, then, is perhaps one more provocative theme that recommends Tunisia as a case study in comparative modernization.

Assuming the above analysis is correct, what is the likely, or desirable, next stage beyond the Bourguiba era? The very success of Bourguiba and his generation – who built, as we have seen, on the earlier stages of Tunisian development – has created requirements for new structural change. The challenge for the next generation might be seen as that of maintaining sufficient modernizing zeal and central control while permitting the flowering of a plural society. The task will not be easy. It is the problem that Turkey had been wrestling with ever since Ataturk, and a workable adjustment is still being sought.

In Tunisia, the Socialist-Destour party can no longer attempt to extend its smothering embrace to all aspects of Tunisian society. Any such effort at this juncture of Tunisia's development will only drive the more creative individuals into disaffection, leaving control in the hands of organizational drones.

This does not necessarily mean a two-party or a multi-party system in the near future. It does mean that the qualified Tunisian must be able to make a career for himself in administration, business, education, the trade unions, or farming without having his work goals and advancement determined by the party.

This does not amount to depolitization of Tunisian society. It is, rather, the next step in the functional specialization required of a modernizing society. In such a development, those able Tunisians given the option to carve out for themselves other than politicized careers are more likely to remain stalwart supporters of a modernizing program. And, accordingly, those who choose a strictly political career are both more likely to possess the necessary political skills and be appropriately circumscribed in their ideological choices by the burgeoning modernizing sectors of society. For all these reasons, students of development in the Third World should be drawn to follow events in contemporary Tunisia just as they have observed, and learned from, Turkey's efforts over the past generation.

Finally, the Tunisian case as a model or yardstick suggests one further major methodological consideration:

Tunisia offers a classic example of staged development: no revolutions, no complete breakdowns, but a process of change that lacks these violent swings of the socio-political pendulum. An earlier historical tradition tracing the development of political modernity in Europe was to compare and contrast the history of Britain and France since the late eighteenth century. By this scale Tunisia is to be classified among the evolutionary "British" examples in the Third World.

And the Tunisian case suggests what all but the most monocausal fanatics have long known: There are many paths to modernization. Tunisia suggests that the Fanonian catharsis of violence is not a universal solvent to escape the fate of being, not only colonized, but "colonizable." Tunisia shows that, contra Mao, political power does not always grow out of the barrel of a gun. Gandhi, one might have thought, had made that clear long ago, but the most basic historical "lessons" need to be reiterated.

The Tunisian way is not to be seen as, for these reasons, better or worse than others. Indeed, it is almost certain that the Tunisian approach could not have been replicated in, for example, neighboring Algeria, and it may well not offer much of relevance for certain other parts of the world. Nevertheless, many elements in Tunisia's modern history do fit into the mainstream of modernization theory – and experience. In this sense the Tunisian path to modernization can be of interest, not only to Tunisians themselves and to those studying the modern Arab world, but to all concerned with the common human problem of adjustment to modernity.

NOTES

1 The Near East is here defined as the entire Arab world, Turkey, Iran, and Israel. A more accurate term, consistent with current usage, might be "the Near East and North Africa," but this seems cumbersome. Near East has been chosen over the now more common usage "Middle East" essentially for reasons of institutional *'aṣabiyya*. Near East is the term that has always been used at Princeton University. On the whole elusive problem of naming, see the witty and stimulating article by Roderic Davison, "Where is the Middle East? " *Foreign Affairs,* July 1960.

2 The title of the book by Charles A. Micaud, Leon Carl Brown and Clement H. Moore, *Tunisia: The Politics of Modernization* (New York, 1964), sets the tone. Moore's other works treating Tunisia – *Tunisia Since Independence – The Dynamics of One-Party Government* (University of California, 1965) and *Politics in North Africa* (Boston, 1970) – reveal the same orientation and are inclined to give high marks to Tunisian modernization achievements by comparison with other North African countries. The creditable study by Lars Rudabeck, *Party and People: A Study of Political Change in Tunisia* (London, 1967) also emphasizes Tunisian adjustment to new modern institutional structures. Among French writers the theme of an effective Tunisian accommodation to modern ways is also very much in evidence. See, for example, the several works by R.P. André Demeerseman, Henri de Montety, *Femmes de Tunisie* (The Hague, 1958), Jean Lacouture's chapter on Bourguiba in *Cinq Hommes et la France* (Paris, 1961), and André Raymond, *La Tunisie* (Paris, 1961). There is, by contrast, very little scholarly or popular writing on traditional structures, Islamic movements including Islamic reformism, or even classical anthropological village or tribal monographs. There is nothing comparable to the works of Richard P. Mitchell or Christine Harris on the Muslim Brethren in Egypt, to Ali Merad's study of the Algerian Association of Ulama, to Ernest Gellner's stimulating *Saints of the Atlas* (University of Chicago, 1969). It is, perhaps, significant that one of the few Tunisian village studies, by Jean Duvignaud, deals with a confrontation in mutual incomprehension between "old" and "new," and the English translation is entitled *Change at Shebeika* (New York, 1970).

This tendency to filter modern Tunisian history through the screen of modernization and also to offer a moderately favorable verdict on results achieved to date is, as this paper will argue, understandable and largely justified. Nevertheless, as a corrective, attention to other organizing themes plus a more hard-bitten skepticism concerning what has allegedly been accomplished would be healthy developments.

3 See Marion J. Levy, Jr., *Modernization and the Structure of Societies* (Princeton, 1966), pp. 9-15; Cyril E. Black, *The Dynamics of Modernization* (New York, 1966), p. 7; and Manfred Halpern, unpublished manuscript.

4 W. G. Runciman, *Social Science and Political Theory* (Cambridge, 1963), p. 152. It is sobering to reflect that this distinction, first formulated by Ferdinand Tönnies in 1887, is now almost a century old.

5 S. N. Eisenstadt, *The Political Systems of Empires* (New York, 1963). Often, of course, new religion and new empire evolve together.

6 Or, in the felicitous phrase of Ernest Gellner, a system of "divide that ye need not be ruled." *Saints of the Atlas,* pp. 41 ff.

7 To restate the case in a broad schematic comparison: Western Europe in early modern times had to face the trauma of loss of political and religious unity (as an ideal at least) but was able to move toward the new world of nation-states at its own pace without bullying from an intrusive outside enemy. China and Hindu India were both jostled along by outside forces but were able to avoid the agony of seeing a solution only in terms of political and cultural disunity (the "ghost of empire" posed an added burden on the remnants of the old Muslim Moghul ruling class). Sub-Saharan Africa could at least seek some encouragement in the awareness that the dialectic process was creating a new unity of the sort which often had not existed for centuries. The Muslim Near East was both bullied from outside and haunted by the fear that the solution seemed to involve an abandonment of the existing (ideal) unity.

8 An even more accurate metaphor of social change would have a changing number of children at both ends of the seesaw (the interaction of societies in history) with their movement toward and away from the center or falling off the seesaw determining the motion of the board. Further, since there is never a condition of stable repose (this is the error of certain social scientists who tend to posit a uniform premodern "traditional society"), and since changes in the balance set up new conditions to be faced, the seesaw of human history might be seen as connected at each end to others – on to infinity or the millennium.

9 This is an adaptation of Black's term. He describes defensive modernization as "calculated to satisfy the demands of a rapidly changing society without destroying the traditional privileges," citing as two classic examples the Ottoman Empire and the Russia of Peter the Great (Black, *Dynamics of Modernization*, pp.70-1). The term, it seems to us, can be better employed to describe defensive measures taken by autocratic rulers against a more definable opposition, viz. menacing foreign governments and pockets of provincial strength within the country. Nor were these "defensive modernizers" intent on maintaining all traditional privileges, but only those of the central government. Indeed, they evoked tradition (e.g., back to the good old days of Sulaymān the Magnificent) to justify radically innovative patterns of central control. The crucial point at issue is that political leaders respond only secondarily, if at all, to social forces or the "challenge of modernity." They respond instead to the challenges and opportunities presented them by other political actors, domestic and foreign.

10 The classic work on Hafsid Tunisia is Robert Brunschvig, *La Berbérie Orientale sous les Hafsides,* 2 vols. (Paris, 1940-46). Brunschvig also has demonstrated in one important field, that of law and the administration of justice, the way in which Hafsid and Ottoman governmental practice merged following the Ottoman conquest. See his "Justice religieuse et justice laique dans la Tunisie des Beys et des Beys, jusqu'au milieu de XIX° siécle," *Studia Islamica* 23 (1965).

11 That is, until Aḥmad Bey's reign, when he began to take steps to grant equal rights and privileges to the two schools, setting in motion a process to achieve even greater national cohesion.

12 See Jean Ganiage, *Les origines du protectorat français en Tunisie (1861-1881)* (Paris, 1959), pp. 152-61.

13 We are poorly informed of the extent to which Black Africa has made an ethnic contribution to Tunisia for several reasons, not the least of which being that Tunisian society, while not "color-blind," is far from color conscious. On this subject, see Leon Carl Brown, "Color in Northern Africa," in *Color and Race,* ed. John Hope Franklin (Boston, 1968). Except for the southernmost Djerid area, where the French geographer Robert Capot-Rey has estimated that Blacks account for about one-fourth of the population, it is probable that Blacks in modern times formed a smaller proportion than the Jews, were more scattered geographically, and were constantly in a process of absorption into the racially (and, of course, religiously) undifferentiated Mālikī Muslim population. See Lucette Valensi, "Esclaves chretiens et esclaves noirs à Tunis au XVIII siecle," *Annales: Economies Societes Civilisations,* no. 4 (Nov.-Dec. 1967); Jean Ganiage, "La Population de la Tunisie vers 1860," *Etudes Maghrebines Mélanges Charles-André Julien* (Paris, 1964); and Robert Capot-Rey, *Le Sahara français* (Paris, 1953), pp. 167 ff.

14 There is a confusing variety of population estimates to be gleaned from European consular reports and travel literature during the period from the early nineteenth century until 1881. Listed below in tabular form is an indication of how such information (or, quite likely in many cases, misinformation) was used to arrive at the estimate of twelve to twenty per cent urban population, based on the arbitrary minimum population of five thousand to define a city.

Column I lists the total number of estimates recorded for each city.

Column II gives the lowest estimate recorded and Column III the highest. These two columns clearly reveal the elusiveness and imprecision of such data.

Column IV is our own *conservative* estimate of the urban population. This figure is *not* an average of all estimates recorded for any particular city. It has been arrived at after an evaluation of the sources themselves, their overall reliability, their likely competence to make reasonable estimates, and their access. This is, admittedly, a very subjective, if not at times intuitive, approach.

The entire exercise should not be taken seriously, representing as it does scarcely more than a grudging votive offering to the Western *deus ex numero.* These are derived from second-hand estimates. They can, at best, provide a crude working hypothesis, pending more adequate exploitation of controllable sources, such as tax records. See, for example, Ganiage's interesting estimate of the total population from the 1860/61 *majbā* tax records (*Protectorat français,* pp. 130-1). Ganiage's monograph, *La Population Européenne de Tunis au milieu de XIX° siècle* (Paris, 1960), is a good example of what information can be extracted from parish registers for the European population. The challenge now is to find equivalent or, as required, substitute data for the Muslim population.

City	I No. of Estimates	II Lowest Estimate	III Highest Estimate	IV Conservative Estimates
Tunis	25	70,000	200,000	85,000
Beja	6	4,000	9,000	6,000
Bizerte	9	4,000	12,000	6,000
Djemmal	2	6,000	8,000	6,000
Gabes	7	7,500	30,000[1]	7,500
Gafsa	5	3,800	8,000	[2]
La Goulette	3	3,000	30,000	[3]
Kairouan	10	12,000	60,000	20,000
Le Kef	9	5,000	8,000	6,000
Mahdiyya	6	3,000	10,000	5,000
Msakin	2	10,000	10,000	7,000
Monastir	9	4,000	12,000	7,000
Nabeul	4	4,800	15,000	6,000
Nefta	4	5,000	10,000	6,000[4]
Sfax	11	6,000	12,000	10,000
Sousse	13	5,000	15,000	7,000
Tozeur	5	2,000	15,000	10,000[4]
Zaghouan	5	2,500	12,000	[5]
			TOTAL	194,500

1 The highest estimate includes the entire oasis.
2 Not counted. Less than five thousand.
3 Not counted. Permanent population probably considerably less than five thousand. Highest estimates includes summer population (already included under Tunis).
4 Actually, a cluster of village oases.
5 The center of *shāshiya* manufacturing, Zaghouan, was surely over five thousand early in the nineteenth century, but had probably declined to less than five thousand by mid-century.

15 Or Kurds and Druze in the Fertile Crescent, Baggāra and other tribesmen in the Sudan eagerly passing on the word of governmental weakness in Khartoum (*mā fīsh hukūma*), nomads coalescing around a religio-political message such as Wahhabism, Kabyles making a bid for autonomy in the name of new doctrine, as they have done from the time of the Donatists to that of the F.L.N., etc.

16 For example, the commercial and maritime oriented Carthagenian Empire was an impressive enterprise, but it did not send deep administrative or economic roots into the Tunisian hinterland or, for that matter, the other coastal points colonized along the Mediterranean. This lack of in-depth hinterland support for the sea-going empire was probably Carthage's fatal flaw.

17 Aḥmad Ibn Abī Diyāf (Bin Diyaf), *Ithāf ahl al-zamān bi-akhbār mulūk Tūnis wa-'ahd al-amān,* 8 vols. (Tunis, 1963-1966), 4: 142-43.

18 See the excellent article by M.H. Chérif, "Expansion européenne et difficultés tunisiennes de 1815 à 1830," *Annales: Economies, Sociétés, Civilisations,* no. 3 (May-June, 1970).

19 *U.S. Consular Reports* (Tunis) 7 (15 February 1842).

20 Historical accounts have long emphasized these symbolic changes initiated in the Ottoman Empire by Sultan Maḥmūd (e.g., the fez) and his successor in the *Tanẓīmāt* period, and rightly so. In a very profound sense clothes do make the man. It requires no trained psychologist to appreciate the following: After his first stroke in July 1852, Aḥmad Bey reverted to wearing native clothes. Broken in health, his reforms a shambles, he was disappointed and even frightened. Then came his bold decision to send troops to fight in the Crimean War, and the French consul who called on Aḥmad reported to his government, "Au lieu du costume arabe qu'il s'est habitué à porter depuis le début de sa maladie, il avait revetu un habit à la mode d'Europe" (*Affaires Etrangères* [Tunis] 14, no. 113 [29 June 1854]).

21 Setting something of a precedent, for the first Ottoman sultan to come to Europe other than at the head of an army was 'Abd al-'Azīz who made a state visit to France in 1867. Shah Nāṣir al-Dīn broke the ice for Persian rulers with his European visit in 1873. Egypt's Ibrāhīm Pasha had visited Europe earlier in 1846, but he was at that time only the man slated to succeed his father, Muḥammad 'Alī, who still ruled Egypt.

22 The consul reported that Mme. Marcescheau was graciously received by the Bey. Earlier, Aḥmad ordered his court to attend the Christian wedding of Count Giuseppe Raffo's daughter (Raffo was his foreign minister while maintaining Sardinian citizenship), where these Muslim dignitaries found themselves "melés à la société européenne des sexes" (*AE Tunis* [Politique] 11, no. 43 [18 June 1849]).

23 As a summary estimate for purposes of the present argument this seems a fair statement, but it should be pointed out that the actual situation was more complex and nuanced. Native Tunisians were integrated into the political system in the bureaucracy (the *kātib* class), the religious offices (teachers, judges, *muftīs,* mosque officials, habous [*waqf*] administrators), and local and tribal government. There were also a few old Tunisian families (e.g., Marabit, Jalluli, Bin Ayad, Lasram) holding high positions. Finally, in many important ways the process of

"nationalizing" the Ḥusaynid dynasty had begun well before Aḥmad's reign. These aspects of the Tunisian political culture on the eve of modernization are treated in the author's forthcoming study on Tunisia in the reign of Aḥmad Bey.

24 Note, for example, the agitation and near-riot among the *baldiya* (bourgeois) of Tunis in 1837 when Aḥmad's father, Mustafā Bey, first attempted a census with an eye to military conscription. Their arguments against this measure as paraphrased by Bin Diyaf included the following: "The sons of Turks are the soldiers . . . God did not command the use of this [*niẓāmī*] uniform. . . We are not able to give our sons to spend their lives in hardship, all in the same place, like beasts attached to a millstone with no hope for anything else, for they are our support in earning a living. Nor can we bear a usage which your ancestors did not impose upon ours. The soldiers of Tunis are Turks and Zouaves." The census was immediately abandoned. Aḥmad did not forget this incident, and in his later military conscription he always exempted those living in Tunis. Bin Diyaf 3: 208-10.

25 Bin Diyaf, 4: 169.

26 Bin Diyaf, 4: 170. Aḥmad also refused special treatment for *mamlūks,* at least in principle. When Aḥmad suggested that a young fugitive *mamlūk* be placed in the band, a leader *mamlūk,* Farḥat, remonstrated, "How can a *mamlūk* be put in the band? " This angered Aḥmad who retorted, "People are all the same to me. If I am to consider a *mamlūk* too important to be placed in the band then I must similarly treat native sons of which I am one." Admittedly, Aḥmad was over-stating his own feelings, for he later told a few intimates, "Farḥat is impolitic. Otherwise he would not have made such a statement before a group." Bin Diyaf 4:171. This, however, is incidental. The anecdote illustrates that Aḥmad, whatever his innermost feelings, realized which way the wind was blowing (to recapture the metaphor of the original Arabic).

27 Bin Diyaf, 4:57, 63-4.

28 Bin Diyaf, 4:158-60.

29 Bin Diyaf, 4:78.

30 Bin Diyaf, 4:99.

31 Bin Diyaf, 4:266.

32 For more detail, see Leon Carl Brown, *The Surest Path: The Political Treatise of a Nineteenth-Century Muslim Statesman* (Harvard, 1967), p. 27 and the other references cited there.

33 See, for example, L. Valensi, "Islam et capitalisme: Production et commerce des Chéchias en Tunisie et en France aux XVIII° et XIX° siècles," *Revue d'histoire moderne et contemporaine* 16 (July-Sept. 1969), which shows that the very important Tunisian *shāshiya* trade was able to hold its own against European competition until the 1820s. Precise economic study of the post-1830 decline comparable to what Mme. Valensi and Mohammed Cherif are engaged in for the earlier period remains to be done. Suffice for the moment these few impression-istic straws in the wind: A member of the notable Andalusian family of *shāshiya* merchants of al-'Arūsī who lived during this period (d. 1868) broke with the family tradition of exclusive business concerns, becoming in turn governor of Sfax

and then governor of different Arab tribes. Did he perhaps need the extra money government service provided? A member of another old *shāshiya* family became a notary when the *shāshiya* trade became stagnant. He was later appointed *wakīl* of Zitouna Library. Then there was the member of the 'Asfūrī family, with a tradition of state service going back to Hafsid times, who lost all his fortune by going into business "imitating Frankish ways." See Bin Diyaf, vols. 7 and 8, biographies nos. 389 ('Alī al-'Arūsī), 390 (Muḥammad al-Wazīr), and 400 (Muḥammad al-Shādhilī al-'Asfūrī). All three died in 1868.

34 A brief sketch with references is found in *Dustur: A Survey of the Constitutions of the Arab and Muslim States* (reprinted with additional material from the second edition of the *Encyclopaedia of Islam* [Leiden, 1966]).

35 Brown, *The Surest Path,* p. 28.

36 There is, for example, evidence to suggest that Khayr al-Dīn and other reformers "used" the European powers during the Sfez incident to get the *'ahd al-amān* promulgated.

37 See Marcel Emerit, "La révolution de 1864 et le secret de l'empereur," *Revue tunisienne,* 1939.

38 Mme. Bice Slama, in an interesting monograph on the 1864 revolt which is clearly favorable to the insurrectionists, reached essentially the same conclusion, viz. it was not a revolution but it was more than a simple tribal movement. It was "une grande insurrection populaire" (*L'Insurrection de 1864 en Tunisie* [Tunis, 1967], pp. 159-71).

39 See both on the immediate subject of Khayr al-Dīn's coterie and the more general theme of the "generations" of political leadership in Tunisia, the excellent work by Shaykh Muḥammad al-Fādil ibn 'Āshūr (Bin 'Āshūr), *al-Ḥaraka al-adabiyya wa'l-fikriyya fī Tūnis* (Cairo, 1956). The only basic demurrer the present author might register is against Bin 'Āshūr's tendency to exalt the role of Zitouna graduates in Tunisian nationalism and reformism.

40 Indeed, aspects of Khayr al-Dīn's agricultural policy (yet to be studied in depth) suggest that he was willing to tie the sharecropper (*khammās*) to the land in a quasi-serf relationship if that would increase production. To put the most charitable interpretation on the matter, it can be said that an authoritarian, organic political theory gave coherence to his reforms. His mentality was an easy Muslim match for the outlook expressed in the nineteenth century Anglican hymn, "The rich man in his castle. The poor man at his gate. God made them high or lowly, and ordered their estate."

41 Habous – literary Arabic *hubus,* religious endowment. *Hubus* is the term used in the Maghreb instead of *waqf.*

42 For more detail see Brown, *The Surest Path,* pp. 31-5, and the references cited there. We have not yet seen the new work recently published in Tunis by Mongi Smida, *Khereddine, Ministre réformateur, 1873-1877.* The complaint box, alas, came to grief. Too many officials with reason to feel threatened managed to inundate the box with crank letters. Khayr al-Dīn reluctantly abandoned the project.

43 Leon Carl Brown, "Tunisia," in *Education and Political Development,* ed. James S. Coleman (Princeton, 1965), p. 149, and references cited there.

44 Colonial rule is used here as a generic term to describe all types of formal control by a single power over a dependent territory. The usage would embrace everything from outright legal absorption (as the French position in Algeria) to the system of mandates. Colonial rule is therefore to be distinguished from the several different kinds of diffuse and informal control exercised by a stronger power constellation (i.e., more than one "state") over one or several weaker areas outside of the "system" (e.g., the situation of the Ottoman Empire or Iran or the present situation of "neo-colonialism" – to the extent that this is employed as a descriptive term rather than a polemical weapon). Our use of "colonial rule" is to be seen as an attempted *first step* toward a more useful classification of the various political patterns governing relations between the West and the non-West in modern times. The next step (not developed in this paper) would be to work out more precisely the various types of "colonial rule" as measured by their impact on the colonized society. That is, we strongly oppose the lazy assumption to be found in present-day polemical writing (and, alas, occasionally scholarly writing as well) that all colonialism is more or less the same.

45 The account given here of Tunisian developments during that long period of the French Protectorate will be even more summary and abstract than the earlier treatment of Tunisia from the reign of Aḥmad Bey to 1881. This is in no way a judgment of the relative importance of the two periods in Tunisia's modernization. On the contrary, developments during the Protectorate period were, by any measure, infinitely more important. Or to state the case in the most conservative terms, the Protectorate period represents the flowering of processes that were, at best, seeds or shoots in the earlier period. The reason for the changed emphasis in this paper is more prosaic: For the Protectorate period considerably more factual data and interpretative analysis is available, and, further, the author's own argument for this period has already been set out in *Tunisia: The Politics of Modernization.* Good monographic or interpretative works for the period before 1881 are only beginning to appear. One should note again the excellent work in progress by Lucette Valensi and Mohammed Cherif. Both are doing pioneering work for Tunisian history in their thorough use of the Tunisian official archives and in their adoption of quantitative techniques. Jean Ganiage's work (*Les origines du protectorat français en Tunisie*) is, by contrast, a first-rate work of conventional European diplomatic history (with a useful emphasis on the activities of financiers and adventurers), but it does not offer the kind of perceptive appraisal of the native Tunisian political culture which is so badly needed.

46 Use of the word "collaborationist" with its highly pejorative connotations is deliberate. It is also worth noting that Western historiography has generally dealt favorably with the colonial "collaborationists" while it has generally condemned similar political options within the West (except in treatment of remote, premodern periods). There is no need to explore here the many reasons for this difference, or double standard. It is, rather, not without value to see the collaboration-resistance scale as a useful analytical tool for comparative history provided it can be utilized without normative overtones. Needless to say, there is no effect here either to praise the "collaborationists" for their "reasonableness" or

condemn them for not having joined the *maquis*. Suffice it to assert that theirs was a plausible political choice, even more readily understandable given their socio-political class background. Also, that events in their country took this form rather than some other was clearly a major determinant of later developments.

47 Bin 'Āshūr, p. 55. Bin 'Āshūr also draws the comparison between Egypt and Tunisia at this time, suggesting as well 'Abduh's direct influence (he visited Tunisia in 1884) upon the Tunisian reformers. Bin 'Āshūr, pp. 43-4. See also, on the 'Abduh visit to Tunisia, al-Munṣif al-Shanūfī (Moncef Chenoufi), "Masādir 'an rihlatay al-ūstādh al-imām al-shaykh Muḥammad 'Abduh ilā Tūnis," *Hawlīyāt al-Jāmi'a al-Tunīsīyya*, no. 4 (1966).

48 Morocco, too, was a settlement colony. In French Morocco alone there were 205,000 Frenchmen by 1936 or approximately 3.3% of the total population. At its peak, following the Second World War, the European population in all of Morocco (French and Spanish zones) ranged between six and eight percent of the total.

49 Except for Palestine, where the growing Jewish Yishuv presented Palestinian Arabs with an even more imposing demographic challenge.

50 André Raymond, *La Tunisie* (Paris, 1961), p. 34, and the official Tunisian *Annuaire Statistique* (1956).

51 Paul Sebag, *La Tunisie* (Paris, 1951), pp. 196-8.

52 I.e., male Tunisians, twenty-five years and older, listed on direct tax registers or veterans and *diplomés* were eligible to vote – not directly, but for five electors in each *cheikhat* or *quartier*. The electors from the several *cheikhats* and *quartiers* forming an electoral district would then assemble to elect their *Grand Conseil* representatives. When electoral schemes get this complicated, there must always be exceptions and "seule, la population tunisienne israélite, soumise aux mêmes conditions d'électorat et d'éligibilité que la population tunisienne musulmans, élit directement ses déleques au Grand Conseil" (Sebag, p. 210).

53 Micaud, Brown, and Moore, *Tunisia: The Politics of Modernization*, p. 88.

54 Jean Despois, *L'Afrique du Nord*, 4th ed. (Paris, 1958), pp. 355-6; René Gallisot, *L'Economie de l'Afrique du Nord* (Paris, 1964) p. 37.

55 Micaud, Brown, and Moore, pp. 15-18.

56 In one sense, the Neo-Destour was spared the temptation (that arose in, for example, quasi-independent Egypt and Iraq during the twenties and thirties) of gaining immediate political muscle by relying on the rural "haves," but in the process sacrificing their reformist, modernist goals. Even so, the early Neo-Destour leadership, itself, deserves credit. They relied heavily on the rural small holder, especially in the *Sāḥil*, but they did champion the then powerless agricultural and laborer sharecroppers at some risk of vexing both the protectorate authorities and the native Tunisians who employed agricultural laborers and sharecroppers. Also, they did not adopt an emotionally satisfying, but ineffective, "Luddite" type of opposition. The early leadership preached both protection of native rights and agricultural modernization. The technical aspects of agricultural colonization in Tunisia are well set out in Jean Poncet, *La colonisation et l'agriculture européennes en Tunisie depuis 1881* (Paris, 1961), but the more human dimension

of the Tunisian rural response and the Neo-Destour organizational activities in the countryside have yet to be adequately treated.

57 A good general account of trade unionism in North Africa is Eqbal Ahmad, "Trade Unionism" in *State and Society in Independent North Africa,* ed. L. C. Brown (Washington, 1966).

58 The following paragraphs represent a distillation of what has been presented in Micaud, Brown, and Moore, pp. 3-66.

59 See, also, the excellent article by Charles-André Julien, "Colons français et Jeunes-Tunisiens 1882-1912," *Revue française d'histoire d'outre-mer* 54 (1967).

60 The qualifier "traditional" in describing this *baldiya* class is important for, as early modern Western history has demonstrated, a bourgeoisie can be dynamic and innovative.

61 The pioneer study on this fundamental social revolution (the term is, perhaps, not too strong) was made by Henri de Montety in a confidential official document entitled "Enquêtes sur les Vieilles familles et les Nouvelles Elites en Tunisie" (1939). A slightly abridged version was later published by the Centre des Hautes-Etudes d'Administration Musulmane, *Documents sur l'Evolution du Monde Musulman,* Fascicule 3 (8 August 1940). An English translation is to appear in the forthcoming *Man, State and Society in North Africa,* ed. I. William Zartman.

62 Bahri Guiga in *L'action tunisienne,* 13 January 1933, a statement made before the formal split of the Neo-Destour from the Old Destour, but what was to emerge as the Neo-Destour leadership had already been working together for several years, using (since November 1932) *L'action tunisienne* to express their ideas.

63 Robert Michels, *Political Parties,* as cited in Dankwart A. Rustow, *A World of Nations* (Washington, 1967), p. 91.

64 Clement H. Moore, *Tunisia Since Independence* (University of California, 1965), p. 108, citing de Montety's unpublished essay on Tunisian nationalism.

65 There was an impressive rise in party membership in the last few years before independence, some of which should be discounted as the usual "bandwagon" psychology. Soon after independence the membership rose to 600,000. In this great mushrooming "the party's public image naturally suffered," and this accounts for the tightening-up and weeding-out process inaugurated in 1958. See Moore, *Tunisia Since Independence*, pp. 112-3. By 1965-66 membership "seems to have stabilized at slightly below 400,000." (Lars Rudabeck, *Party and People: A Study of Political Change in Tunisia* [London, 1967], p. 33.)

66 Adapting Napoleon's famous phrase to the Tunisian situation – where Westernized education loomed so important – it might be said that modern Tunisia has engendered the *mystique* that every schoolboy carries a minister's portfolio in his satchel.

67 Dankwart A. Rustow, *A World of Nations.* especially ch. 4.

POPULAR ISLAM AND TRIBAL LEADERSHIP IN THE SOCIO–POLITICAL STRUCTURE OF NORTH SUDAN

GABRIEL WARBURG

PREFACE

Since I started my studies on the modern history of the Sudan, I was struck by the central role of the tribes and popular Islam in the emergence of the Sudanese political community. However, in choosing this subject as a basis for discussion at the Colloquium on Arab Society, I faced several difficulties. Firstly, despite the fact that the colloquium is primarily concerned with contemporary events, I felt that historical perspective was essential for even a partial understanding of the problems involved – hence, the rather lengthy introduction. Secondly, I had to limit myself to what I hoped would be a manageable and meaningful treatment of the subject. To do so I chose to examine both tribal society and popular Islam from the point of view of the central government and tried to analyze their impact on the emerging nation-state. In consequence, I have neglected several important aspects which undoubtedly rate careful examination. Firstly, how do the tribes and the leadership of popular Islam view their own role in the socio-political development? Secondly, in discussing a period of some one hundred and fifty years, there is certainly room to examine the changes which occurred in the structure and functional framework of the tribes and the image and contents of popular Islam. These parameters are certainly not the same today as they were at the end of the nineteenth or at the beginning of the twentieth century. Thirdly, in referring to the swing of the power pendulum between government, popular Islam, and the tribes, I deliberately ignored the rise of the new political factors, especially since World War II, and the status of the army in the Sudan since 1958. It was not possible within the framework of this paper to deal with these problems with the degree of seriousness they deserve.

An additional difficulty I had to face was that of sources. Whereas several important works deal with this subject in the earlier period, until the end of the nineteenth century, relatively little research has been undertaken on the Condominium period and practically none on that of independent Sudan. I thus could borrow heavily from the works of P.M. Holt and R.L. Hill, covering the nineteenth century, and to a lesser extent from the more general works of Muddathir ʻAbd al-Rahīm and K.D.D. Henderson, covering the period of the Condominium. These I could complement with additional archival material in my possession. I must, however, point to the dearth of reliable sources available at present, particularly for the period since independence. My statements regarding the latter period are, therefore, very hesitant and are intended to indicate possible trends of development, rather than to give a verdict.

INTRODUCTION

THE FUNJ SULTANATE

Prior to the Turco-Egyptian conquest in 1820–21, the Sudan was not a uniform political and governmental unit, and the rule of the Funj Sultanate, from its center in Sennar, was rule in name alone. The centers of power that arose in various areas of the country were based on the tribal and religious structure prevalent in the country at that time. The exact number of Sudanese tribes during that period is not clear, but can be assumed to be not less than the 572 tribes counted during the first census in 1956. Most of these tribes (approximately thirty percent of the population) were in the South, and are, therefore, outside the framework of our discussion. In the area extending north of Baḥr al-ʻArab, the tribes were mostly composed of Arabic-speaking Muslims. However, even the population of that area was not homogeneous. Near the Egyptian border lived the Barābra, who spoke Nubian dialects in addition to Arabic. To the south of them, on both sides of the Nile, were a number of tribes related to the Jaʻaliyyīn group. Although these tribes were largely Arabized and claimed a common forefather – Jaʻal, a descendent of ʻAbbās, uncle of the Prophet Muḥammad – there is no doubt that their origin is Nubian. The most northern tribe of the Jaʻaliyyīn are the Danāqla, who inhabit the district of Dongola. The area south of them, near the bend of the Nile up to Abū Ḥamad, is inhabited by the Rubaṭāb and the Manāṣīr. One of the Ja'aliyyīn tribes, which occupies the area close to the junction of the 'Aṭbarā and the Nile, bears the name of the whole group. Within the Ja'aliyyīn, though not belonging to them, dwells the confederation of the Shāyqiyya in the area between the fourth cataract of the Nile and al-Dabba to the north. All these tribes are mainly sedentary and are consequently known by the general name of *awlād al-balad.* Most of the other tribes claiming to be of Arab origin are nomads or seminomads. The most important among them are: the Kabābīsh, camel-breeding nomads who roam between the Nubian desert and northern Kordofan; the Baqqāra (colloquial, Baggāra), cattle-breeding nomads who inhabit south Kordofan and south Dārfūr; along the Upper Blue Nile are the Rufā'a – one of whose leaders established the dynasty of the 'Abdallāb, which during the Funj sultanate became a center of power among the Arab tribes. Another tribe of this group which began its rise to greatness during the Funj period are the Shukriyya – whose leader Aḥmad Abū attained the rank of bey and the position of governor of Khartoum during the Turco-Egyptian period.[1]

In order to complete this short survey of the northern tribes, three non-Arab tribal groups still have to be mentioned. Firstly, the Fūr, founders of the sultanate of Dārfūr, in western Sudan, who, despite being Muslims, retain their own language up to the present. The second group inhabits the hill region of south Kordofan, known as the Nuba mountains. The origins of the Nuba are not clear, but it is certain that they, in common with the Fūr, found shelter in the hill regions following the penetration of Arab tribes into the Sudan. These tribes speak various dialects and have for the most part retained their pagan beliefs into the twentieth century. The third group, also living in a hill region, are the Beja of the Red Sea Mountains whose origin is Hamitic. As with the Barābra in the North, the Beja have accepted Islam, and to some extent also the Arabic language. The most Arabized of the Beja tribes are the 'Abābda, who control the Nubian desert pass between Egypt and the Sudan. The most famous and militant amongst the Beja are the Hadendowa, nomads inhabiting the southern area of the Red Sea Mountains up to the 'Aṭbarā River and the delta of the Gash. These tribal groups retained a great deal of independence, recognized even by the Funj sultans. The power of the tribes grew during the hundred years preceding the Turco-Egyptian conquest, as the central authority of the sultanate broke up. The supreme position attained by certain families, such as the ʻAbdallāb and the Abū Sinn in the Blue Nile region, has already been mentioned. Similarly, the confederation of the Shāyqiyya was practically independent, while the Jaʻaliyyīn created for themselves a political-religious center in al-Dāmir, at the junction of the Nile and the ʻAṭbarā. Funj rule in western Sudan, particularly amongst the nomad Baqqāra and Kabābīsh, was even more nominal, while the sultanate of Dārfūr had maintained an independent political status since 1596.

Another phenomenon unique to the Sudan is the place of popular religious leadership in the governmental hierarchy. This phenomenon is undoubtedly connected with the character and methods of Islamic penetration into the Sudan. Islamization commenced in the seventh century, following the conquest of Egypt by the Arabs and continued slowly until the fourteenth century. At that time, the Christian kingdom of al-Maqurra fell under the control of the Banū Kanz and broke up into a number of Muslim sultanates. Islam continued to penetrate southwards and in the sixteenth century the tribes under the protection of ʻAlwa – the southern Christian kingdom – had also been Islamized. Islamization progressed gradually during the era of the Funj sultanate, its frontiers stabilizing along the twelfth parallel north. During this period – which lasted some three hundred years up to the Turco–Egyptian conquest – "holy families," both immigrant and indigenous, started to play a central role in forming the special character of Islam in the Sudan.[2] The "holiness" of these families was recognized in that their members – apart from being teachers of law and religion, active in deepening and broadening the scope of Islamic influence – were also regarded as possessors of *baraka,* a power whose source lay in holiness and which brought its holders spiritual and physical happiness. According to belief, *baraka* was inheritable and its beneficiaries tended to claim that they were *ashrāf* (people tracing their descent to the Prophet Muḥammad). It can thus easily be understood that the functions of these leaders far exceeded the teaching of Islam, and they acquired political and social importance in their most ample meaning. By settling amongst the tribes of the northern Sudan, these "holy families" became part of the ruling hierarchy. One of the best known amongst them was the "Sons of Jābir," who, during the second half of the sixteenth century, settled among the Shāyqiyya and established a school for teaching Islamic law according to the Mālikī school. One of the Jābir brothers attained a position of power and wealth which enabled him to maintain forty slaves as bodyguards. Another member of the same family married one of the queens of the Shāyqiyya, while Muḥammad Ṣughayyirūn, also a descendent of Awlād Jābir, settled on the banks of the Nile, south of its junction with the ʻAṭbarā, and opened yet another school for the Ja'aliyyīn. But, while the "Sons of Jābir" were teachers of law, who by virtue of their status achieved wealth and power, other saintly families were teachers of religion and heads of Ṣūfī *ṭarīqas* (orders) at one and the same time. One of the most notable examples of this phenomenon were the Majādhīb. Their progenitor was Ḥamad b. al-Majdhūb, a teacher of Muslim Law, who, during his pilgrimage to Mecca, had joined two Ṣūfī *ṭarīqas.* Upon his return to the Sudan, he founded a center for the teaching of Muslim Law in al-Dāmir, south of the junction of the Nile and the ʻAṭbarā. Aside from his teaching, he also founded a Ṣūfī order, the Majdhūbiyya, a sub-order of the Qādiriyya. At the beginning of the nineteenth century, al-Dāmir was described as a spiritual center, attracting students from all corners of the Sudan seeking to acquire knowledge and to be accepted, at the same time, into the ranks of the Majdhūbiyya. It is clear that a religious center with such power acquired a significant socio-political status, not only among the Ja'aliyyīn where it was located, but also in the Red Sea Mountains, among the Beja who roamed between the ʻAṭbarā and the port of Suakin. It must be added that the disintegration of the Funj sultanate reached its peak exactly in this period, with the rise of the Hamaj dynasty in 1762. The instability of the governing dynasties, as opposed to the stability of the "holy families," and of the tribes in whose shadow they dwelt, brought about the rise in tribal-religious power centers as an alternative to political vacuum.

In conclusion, it must be remembered that the eighteenth century witnessed the revival of Sufism throughout the Muslim world, and primarily in the Arab provinces. New Ṣūfī orders were founded in the Hejaz and spread quickly into other regions, which in many cases led to conflict with local orders. One of these new orders was the Sammāniyya, which was founded in the Sudan in the last quarter of the eighteenth century. Its founder, Aḥmad al-Ṭayyib b. al-Bashīr, established the order's center near Sennar at the invitation of one of the Hamaj regents. The founder's closeness to the authorities helped the growth of the order's influence, but also aroused the jealousy of the older established "holy families" of Sennar, primarily the Ya'qūbāb, who had settled in the area as early as the sixteenth century. Hence the Sammāniyya was forced to move its center further north. Another order established shortly before the Turco–Egyptian conquest was the Khatmiyya, whose founder, Muḥammad ʻUthmān al-Mīrghanī, was a student of Aḥmad b. Idrīs al-Fāsī in the Hejaz. After the death of al-Fāsī, he founded his own Ṣūfī order, called the Mīrghaniyya, or the Khatmiyya, with the object of combining Wahhābī principles of puritan reform with Ṣūfī mysticism. The Khatmiyya found its supporters in the northern and eastern Sudan immediately coming into conflict with the more established orders, and especially with the Majdhūbiyya.

TURCO–EGYPTIAN RULE 1821–81

At the time of Muḥammad ʻAlī's conquest in 1820–21, there was no real central government in the Sudan, and the Funj sultanate collapsed without resistance. However, the two alternative power centers, the tribes and popular Islam, had become stronger with the disintegration of the Funj kingdom. The sixty years of Turco–Egyptian rule were characterized by the government's attempts to undermine the power of the local leadership and integrate it into the new Egyptian administration.

It is not surprising, therefore, that while the Funj sultanate vanished from the stage of history without any attempt at resistance, a number of tribes showed violent opposition to the new rulers. The first to oppose the Turco–Egyptians were the Shāyqiyya, who were defeated in battle in November 1820. The results of this battle were important, not because of the defeat itself – hardly surprising in view of the relative strength and the technological superiority of the Egyptians – but rather because relationships between the Turco–Egyptians and the Shāyqiyya were established in an atmosphere of defeat. The courage and fighting ability of the tribe caused the new authorities to decide to exploit them for their own needs. Members of the Shāyqiyya were exempted from tax and conscripted as irregular cavalry (*bāshī būzuq*) into the army of the conquerors. Their main function henceforward was the collection of taxes imposed on the other tribes – a function which they fulfilled with great cruelty. The hostility of the riverain tribes, such as the Jaʻaliyyīn and the Danāqla, to the Shāyqiyya became an important factor in the Turco–Egyptian regime. Even more important was the rebellion which broke out among the Jaʻaliyyīn in October 1822 and rapidly spread to other tribes. The causes were rooted in the Egyptian attempt to impose an administration and a tax system alien to the Sudanese – which undermined the existing political-economic frameworks and the authority of tribal leadership. While the Funj sultans had been satisfied with a nominal tribute sufficient to maintain their modest capital in Sennar, Muḥammad 'Alī sought to use the Sudan in furthering his plans for the economic and military aggrandizement of Egypt. However, his hopes of finding gold in the Sudan could not be realized, while large-scale slave hunting would have necessitated conquering the South, which was beyond his power. Thus, the only remaining way to satisfy the administration's need was heavy taxation, which would force the tribes, who lacked money, to pay the authorities with slaves or cattle. The suppression of the rebellion took until 1824 and undermined the tribal frameworks, especially of the Ja'aliyyīn, as well as causing part of the riverain tribes to flee the Sudan. Turco–Egyptian policy did not seek the destruction of the tribes since there was no substitute for them in the realities of the Sudan. However, the new regime was not prepared to recognize centers of power not subject to its authority. The tribes had, therefore, of necessity, to be regarded as administrative units, subject to their *shaykhs,* not because of leadership qualities possessed by the latter, but because they represented central government. One of the Jazīra *shaykhs* was first appointed advisor on tribal affairs to the governor and later became *shaykh mashāyikh al-Sūdān,* but without being given any executive power.[3] While the authorities' control could not be extended to the nomads, the tribal heads of the settled, or semisettled, tribes became dependent on the central government. The task of collecting taxes was given to the Copts, who acted as assessors, tax collectors (with the help of irregular soldiers), and bookkeepers. Junior Coptic officials lived with the tribes themselves – thus undermining the *shaykhs'* position even further. *Shaykhs* who showed an excessive degree of independence were deposed or taken as hostages to Khartoum, and their successors learned the lesson. In some cases, two *shaykhs* of rival families were appointed to different factions of the same tribe, with the clear purpose of politically weakening the tribe.[4]

The position of the tribes worsened towards the end of Turco–Egyptian rule, especially during the period of the Khedive Ismā'īl. On the one hand, the burden of taxation was increased due to the desperate situation of the Egyptian treasury as a result of wars in Abyssinia and pressure from European creditors. On the other, many tribes were hurt by restrictions imposed on their slave hunting and trading activities. This policy reached its peak with the signing of the Anglo–Egyptian Convention for the Suppression of the Slave Trade in 1877, which was enforced in the Sudan by Gordon Pasha, then governor general, with the help of European officials. The war on slavery hit three main groups, the first two of which had been almost beyond the authorities' scope of control until then. The first were the slave traders themselves with their private armies, mainly composed of the *awlād al-balad* of the dispersion, such as, the Danāqla, the Ja'aliyyin, and the Shāyqiyya – part of whom had been forced away from the Nile by population pressure or other economic factors, and had gained control of the slave trade mainly in the Baḥr al-Ghazāl. The second group included some of the nomad tribes, such as the Baqqāra and the Kabābīsh, who had helped in transporting the slave convoys northwards and received payment for allowing convoys to pass through their territories. The third group included almost all the settled population living off agriculture, since attempts to restrict the slave trade caused a sharp rise in the price of domestic and agricultural slaves. Therefore, at the time of Ismā'īl's removal in 1879, and just before the 'Urābī rebellion in Egypt, a large section of the Sudanese tribal population was in a state of ferment and opposition to Turco–Egyptian rule was rife.[5]

It is difficult to ascertain the extent to which Turco–Egyptian rule succeeded in undermining the foundations of tribal loyalty in the Sudan. It seems that the settled tribes were more affected because of their proximity to the central government and because of their dependence on the Nile. Until the last decade of the Turco–Egyptian regime, the nomads hardly felt the heavy hand of the administration. The authorities had made no attempt to organize administration among the nomads; neither had they interfered with the powers of their *shaykhs.* It is, however, known that the authorities did support certain tribal leaders who did not control the entire tribe in order to acquire more influence for central government by dividing the tribes into factions. Examples of this can be found both amongst the Baqqāra of Kordofan and in the confederation of the Kabābīsh, which, during the second half of the nineteenth century, was divided into two groups; one in Kordofan and the other in Dongola. The undefined position of the *shaykhs* of the two groups was illustrated by the fact that the central authorities organized punitive action against a subtribe of the Kabābīsh without even consulting the tribe's supreme *shaykh.*[6] Central government interference reached its peak during the rule of Gordon Pasha as governor general, when other tribes, such as the Fūr and the Beja, were affected by the heavy hand of the central administration, particularly by taxation and the war against slave trading. In any event, the power of the tribes decreased – as compared with the beginning of Turco–Egyptian rule – and the tribal map was greatly disrupted by the dispersal of strong tribes, such as the Ja'aliyyīn, and by the blows dealt to the dispersed *awlād al-balad* at a later date. Conversely, a number of tribes improved their position as a result of their close cooperation with the authorities. In addition to the Shāyqiyya, the 'Abābda along the Egyptian–Sudanese border also increased in strength by participating in governmental punitive campaigns against other tribes. Their *shaykh,* Ḥusayn Bey Khalīfa al-'Abbādī, was even appointed governor of Berber. Another tribe which benefited economically and politically as a result of Turco–Egyptian rule were the Shukriyya along the Blue Nile, whose leader, Aḥmad 'Awaḍ al-Karīm Abū Sinn, was appointed governor of the district of Khartoum.

Thus, the authorities tried to integrate the tribes into the administration, but for lack of an alternative were forced to accept their existence. With popular Islam, however, the conquerors had an alternative, which was already activated during the conquest. Three Egyptian *'ulamā'* were attached to the expeditionary force, with the function of explaining to the Sudanese Muslims that their conquest by the Turco–Egyptians was a legitimate act by the lawful ruler of the Muslims, the Ottoman sultan and caliph. It is difficult to suppose that this propaganda was successful among the leaders of popular Islam in the Sudan, especially since from the beginning, the so-called orthodox Egyptian Islamic *'ulamā'* were openly contemptuous of the local *fakīs*[7] and of the heads of the Ṣūfī *ṭarīqas.* Matters developed very quickly into open conflict following the Ja'aliyyin uprising. It will be remembered that the Majdhūbiyya center was founded in al-Dāmir under the protection of the Ja'aliyyīn. The uprising that broke out in 1822 thus also engulfed the *ṭarīqa,* and, after its suppression and the destruction of the Majdhūbī center in al-Dāmir, the head of the order, Muḥammad al-Majdhūb al-Ṣughayyir, fled to Suakin and from there to Mecca. He was only permitted to return to the Sudan in 1830 when he discovered that his place amongst the Ja'aliyyīn had meanwhile been taken by the rival order of the Khatmiyya. He was compelled, therefore, to be satisfied with the Red Sea Mountains as his area of activities. The hostile attitude of the Majdhūbiyya to the authorities sprang, therefore, from the latters' preferential treatment of another *ṭarīqa.*[8]

Similarly, the heads of most other *ṭarīqas* soon understood that their influence and sources of livelihood were being reduced under the new regime. Firstly, *Sharī'a* courts were established by the new authorities. These had previously been unknown in the Sudan, since the heads of the *ṭarīqas* and the "holy families" had carried out all the religious-judicial functions. The new courts, subordinate to government and headed by Egyptian *qāḍīs,* undermined the status of the Sudanese *fakīs* and damaged them economically. Secondly, under the Funj sultanate, the heads of the *ṭarīqas* had enjoyed certain economic benefits, such as exemption from taxes, granting of lands (*ṣadaqa*), and even the maintenance of slaves as bodyguards at the expense of the ruler or the head of the tribe in whose area they dwelt. All these were now cancelled, and the *fakīs* became ordinary citizens paying taxes and no longer enjoying any privileges. Thirdly, in the field of education, although the hold of the *fakīs* continued until the rise of the Khedive Ismā'īl, the schools which they headed were now subordinate to the central administration, and Ismā'īl's attempts to create state schools in the Sudan threatened the status of the *fakīs* in this field as well. However, the authorities' policy of creating in the Sudan a local strata of orthodox *'ulamā'* was an even more serious threat. To this end, youngsters from the Sudan were sent to al-Azhar, where a special center had been set up for them, *al-Riwāq al-Sinnāriyya.* Upon returning to their homeland after a few years of study, these Azhar graduates were integrated into the frame of the *Sharī'a* courts and into teaching positions in the Koran schools. The growth of a generation of Sudanese *'ulamā'* with roots in Orthodox Islam – Egyptian style (and not in the popular Islam of the Sudan) – produced a convenient channel for confrontations between the representatives of the two trends. In certain cases this even brought about a rift within the "holy families," the outstanding example of which is the Ismā'īliyya order of al-Ubayyiḍ, which was founded as a sub-order of the Khatmiyya in Kordofan by Muḥammad Ismā'īl b. 'Abd Allāh al-Walī in 1842. One of his sons, Aḥmad Ismā'īl, was sent to study in al-Azhar on the initiative of the Egyptian authorities and, on completion of his studies, remained in this institution as a teacher of Mālikī law. On his return to the Sudan, Aḥmad Ismā'īl al-Azharī was appointed *qāḍī* of al-Ubayyiḍ and quickly came into conflict with his brother, al-Makkī Ismā'īl, who had become head of the Ismā'īliyya order after the death of his father in 1864. The Mahdist uprising, therefore, found the two brothers in rival camps. Aḥmad al-Azharī rose against Muḥammad Aḥmad – *"al-mutamahdī"* (one assuming the title *mahdī* "the heavenly guided") – and found his death in battle against the supporters of the Mahdi in Kordofan. His brother, al-Makkī Ismā'īl, was amongst the first adherents of the Mahdi – even before "The Revelation" – and brought all the members of his order to the ranks of the *Anṣār.*[9]

The Khatmiyya, alone among the Ṣūfī orders, enjoyed the clear favor of the authorities. The coming of Muḥammad 'Uthmān al-Mīrghanī to the Sudan almost coincided with the Turco–Egyptian invasion. In the eyes of the inhabitants of the Sudan, the two happenings therefore appeared to be interconnected. In addition, the Turco–Egyptian authorities found no common language with the old established orders of the Sudan, nor with the leaders of the "holy families," whom they considered superstitious fanatics and ignorant of Islamic law; not so the educated Mīrghanī family, descended from the *ashrāf,* who had come to the Sudan from Mecca. This family's customs and education soon brought about a closer relationship between them and the rulers. The banishment of the Majdhūbiyya leaders from the Sudan at this time created a vacuum which the founders of the Khatmiyya well knew how to exploit. Their influence grew among the riverain tribes, and particularly the Shāyqiyya, who, as protégés of the Turco-Egyptians, were quick to come to an understanding with the Khatmiyya order. Thus, the Khatmiyya's center, which had been established near Kassala, became a source of spiritual support for the Turco–Egyptian authorities, who in turn expressed their gratitude by subsidizing the order's activities. But far from limiting itself to the vicinity of Kassala, the Khatmiyya succeeded within a relatively short period in gaining adherents in many parts of the northern Sudan.

The process of undermining the status of popular Islam reached its peak during the reign of Khedive Ismā'īl, when the central government tried, by means of economic and educational policies, to drive the Ṣūfī leadership from their traditional positions and enforce Azharite Islam, imported from Egypt. However, the Mahdi's uprising put an end to this process before it had ripened.[10] *'Ulamā'* al-Azhar – or, in the language of the Mahdi, *'ulamā' al-saw'* (corrupt *'ulamā*) – vanished as though they had never been. Some of them fled with their Egyptian masters or fell in battle, others adopted the teachings of the Mahdi and became his disciples. The process of undermining popular Islam was stopped by the Mahdi in its first stages and before it had lost its influence. The evidence of Lieutenant Colonel Stewart, who was sent in 1883 by the British Government to report on the situation in the Sudan at the beginning of the Mahdi's uprising, is revealing. Stewart stated that the ignorance of the inhabitants upset all the efforts of Orthodox Islam to penetrate the Sudan, and hence, in his words: "the enormous influence of the Fakis, or spiritual leaders, who are credited with a supernatural power, and are almost more venerated than the Prophet . . ."[11]

THE MAHDIST STATE 1881–98

The appearance of the Mahdiyya in the Sudan, its success and crystallization into a political entity, were largely based on the tribal structure of the Sudan and the strength of popular Islam. Faith in a *mahdī* is fairly prevalent in *Sunnī* Islam, but, unlike in the *Shī'a,* it never became an integral part of *Sunnī* faith. The appearance of a *mahdī* was therefore usually restricted to areas of *Sunnī* Islam far from centers of government and from the influence of Orthodox Islam. It is thus not surprising that the Sudan, soaked in popular mystic beliefs, was ready and prepared for the appearance of the Mahdiyya. During the nineteenth century, several claimants to the throne of the *mahdī* appeared in the Nile Valley and their number increased at the beginning of the twentieth century after the conquest of the Sudan by the Anglo–Egyptian army. The Mahdi himself, Muḥammad Aḥmad b. 'Abd Allāh, possessed a clearly Ṣūfī background and before his "revelation" belonged to and even was appointed *shaykh* of the Sammāniyya order. His call to *jihād* against the infidel was primarily aimed at the "Turks," representatives of foreign rule and so-called Orthodox Islam in the Sudan.[12]

As a Ṣūfī *shaykh* and member of the Danāqla tribe, the Mahdi understood that his success depended on the support of two central elements in Sudanese society – the heads of the tribes and the leaders of popular mystic Islam. Thus, at the beginning of his way, the Mahdi's letters to the heads of the Ṣūfī *ṭarīqas* are full of symbols taken from Sufism. During the first visit to Kordofan in 1880, even before he had declared his mission, the Mahdi acquired the support of Muḥammad Ismā'īl al-Makkī, head of the Ismā'īlī order, and was active among the dispersed *awlād al-balad* who formed the most important social stratum in al-Ubayyiḍ.[13] Three major elements that supported the Mahdi at the beginning of his way were, therefore, members of his own family, the so-called *ashrāf,* some heads of Ṣūfī *ṭarīqas,* and sections of the *awlād al-balad* of the dispersion in Kordofan and Dārfūr.

The migration *(hijra)* of the Mahdi and his supporters from the island of Abā to Qadīr in the Nuba Mountains on 31 October 1881 brought an additional element to his camp – the Baqqāra of Kordofan and Dārfūr. In his letters to the tribal *shaykhs* and heads of the Ṣūfī *ṭariqās* during this period, the Mahdi recognizes them as his disciples amongst their loyal followers and as the leaders of their respective *ṭarīqas* and tribes. Thus, at this stage, the Mahdi was not yet attempting to enforce his mission as the single focus of authority and leadership, but was prepared to accept the existence of additional centers of power, on condition that they declared their loyalty to his movement. This tolerance was already somewhat weakened in 1883 after the Mahdist conquest of al-Ubayyiḍ and their defeat of the Egyptian army under Colonel Hicks in Shaykān. The Mahdi, now controlling all of Kordofan and Dārfūr, and assured of his power, called the leaders of the tribes that were still vacillating to join him and carry out the *jihād* in their areas. The undertone of the threat in the letters was clear, since he who did not join the Mahdi would henceforward be considered an infidel belonging to the enemy camp. The rebellions in the Jazīra, south of Khartoum, and in Berber, to the north, were the results of the Mahdi's success in the West and the activities of his agents among the tribes. An outstanding example of this was the mission of 'Uthmān Diqna to the Red Sea Mountains in 1883. The success of the Mahdiyya in this area was dependent on recruiting the Beja tribes into the ranks of the *Anṣār.* Two Ṣūfī *ṭarīqas* were active in the Red Sea Mountains – the Majdhūbiyya and the Khatmiyya. 'Uthmān Diqna was therefore supplied with letters from the Mahdi to the two leaders of the *ṭarīqas,* in which they were called upon to join the ranks of his movement together with their supporters. The response of the Majdhūbiyya was immediate, since their hostility to the authorities who had destroyed their center at al-Dāmir, and their jealousy of the Khatmiyya, who enjoyed Turco–Egyptian patronage, caused them to regard the Mahdi as an ally against the common enemy.[14] This brought to the Mahdi's camp an element which was important from both the religious and political-military aspects, since the recruitment of the Majdhūbiyya brought many warriors of the Beja, and primarily the Hadendowa, to the ranks of the *Anṣār.* The leaders of the Khatmiyya refused to join the Mahdi, and their head, Muḥammad Sirr al-Khatim al-Mīrghanī, was compelled to leave the center of his movement near Kassala and go into exile in Egypt. There is a basis for the supposition that the Mahdi's approach to the Khatmiyya did not spring from naiveté, as it was difficult to assume that the order's head – so closely connected with the authorities and the orthodox *'ulamā'* – would support an uprising. However, the Mahdi's letters could at this stage, by relying on his great military victories, bring about a split amongst the members of the *tarīqa* and undermine their faith in the order's leadership.

The military administrative organization of the Mahdist state was also on a tribal basis. While the appointment of the Mahdi's four *khalīfas* was made in order to emphasize the parallel between the Mahdi and the Prophet Muḥammad, the division of the Mahdi's armies in practice represented the major tribal and cultural divisions of the Sudan: *awlād al-balad* under the red flag of the fourth *khalīfa,* Muḥammad Sharīf and the Baqqāra under the command of the first *khalīfa,* 'Abdallāh al-Ta'īshī, of the black flag. The military-political power of these two camps and the friction between them played a decisive role in the development of the Mahdist state up to its destruction. It has been noted that the first powerful groups to join the *Anṣār* were those of the *awlād al-balad* who had been badly hurt by the repression of the slave trade in Baḥr al-Ghazāl, Dārfūr, and Kordofan, and brought to the Mahdi's camp their private armies, consisting of slaves. This tribal element, therefore, fulfilled an important role in the first stage of the Mahdiyya, and the majority of the military commanders of the *Anṣār* were drawn from its ranks. But the recruitment of the Baqqāra tribes after the *hijra* to Qadīr upset the tribal balance, and the strength of the black flag grew. The attempts of the *ashrāf* and of *awlād al-balad* – based on their tribal-familial closeness to the Mahdi – to achieve supremacy in the state caused the Mahdi to condemn his relatives and the men of his tribe in public and declare his full trust in 'Abdallāh al-Ta'īshī as *khalīfat al-mahdī.*[15] Nevertheless, it was clear, even before the death of the Mahdi, that the tribal coalition which had united for the purpose of war on the foreign ruler was destined to bring about open conflict between the two camps, since the religious mission of the Mahdiyya was not sufficient to bridge tribal differences.

The *khalīfa* 'Abdallāh's rise to power constitutes a turning point in the Mahdist state and in its relationship to the two main components of Sudanese society – the tribes and the *ṭariqās.* While the Mahdi enjoyed an aura of holiness – thanks to his mission and his victories in battle – the *khalīfa* was considered by the *ashrāf* and *awlād al-balad* as a member of a western tribe, ignorant of religious matters, and so primitive that he was not sufficiently proficient in Arabic and did not even know how to read and write. From the beginning, therefore, the *khalīfa*'s foundation of power involved a struggle with his opponents and attempts to neutralize or even destroy them. In the first stage, the *khalīfa* split up the army of the *awlād al-balad,* deposed most of its leaders, and put it under the command of loyal members of the Ta'āīsha. In the second stage, he confronted the members of the *ashrāf,* and particularly their *khalīfa,* Muḥammad Sharīf, restricted their power, and turned them into a group deprived of governing functions. At the end of 1886, a year after the Mahdi's death, only two of the *awlād al-balad* commanders were left in their position, and even they did not threaten 'Abdallāh's rule because of their remoteness from Omdurman.[16]

The next stage of 'Abdallāh's tribal policy was to organize a mass migration of the Baqqāra – headed by his own tribe, the Ta'āīsha – from the West to the central areas of Omdurman and the Jazīra. Two main reasons apparently motivated this step: firstly, the safeguarding of his direct control over the Baqqāra, who being independent nomads were not inclined to accept the orders of central government. The Abū Jummayza uprising in 1887–89 showed clearly that the loyalty of the western tribes to the Mahdist state could be easily upset, should a new religious leader appear who could promise them their freedom. The migration of the Baqqāra to the capital was likely to undermine the powers of their tribal leaders and make them dependent on central government. Secondly, as a son of the West, the *khalīfa* probably preferred the proximity of members of his own tribe to that of the *awlād al-balad,* who were his declared enemies. The migration of the Baqqāra to the East was achieved by means of threats and pressure on their leaders, and in 1888–89 they came to the Jazīra driving some of the local tribes from their lands.[17]

After the battle of Ṭūshkī in 1889 (in which the last military commander of the *awlād al-balad,* 'Abd al-Rahmān al-Nujūmī, was killed) all Mahdist armies were under the command of the Baqqāra, excepting the Beja tribes in the East, whose commander, 'Uthmān Diqna, stayed in his position up to the Anglo–Egyptian conquest. Parallel with the deposition of the military commanders, 'Abdallāh also got rid of the tribal heads who were showing too much independence. Madibbū 'Alī, head of the Rizayqāt – one of the strongest Baqqāra tribes in Dārfūr (who had been among the first to join the Mahdi in that area, thereby helping directly in the downfall of the Turco–Egyptian regime) – was executed in 1886. When it became clear to the *khalīfa* that Madibbū was showing too much independence, and trying to seize power in south Dārfūr, he ordered him brought to Omdurman. On the way to the capital, he was executed by the commander of the Mahdist army in Kordofan. Shortly thereafter, a section of the Kabābīsh in northern Kordofan rebelled, and their leader, Ṣāliḥ Fadl Allāh Sālim, refused to obey the orders of the *khalīfa*'s messengers. Ṣāliḥ was killed in battle in May 1887, and tribal opposition was broken following a punitive expedition which lasted a year and was assisted by tribes hostile to the Kabābīsh.[18] An additional attempt at resistance to 'Abdallāh's rule and to the Ta'āīsha also took place against a tribal-religious background. In November of 1891 the *ashrāf* rebelled – supported by the *awlād al-balad* who were led by the Danāqla, the Mahdi's tribe. The *khalīfa,* Muḥammad Sharīf, and the Mahdi's family had become aware that under 'Abdallāh's regime, not only were their rights and status as leaders affected, but they were also dependent on the charity of the Ta'āīsha for their livelihood. Tribal support for this group was guaranteed by the fact that the *awlād al-balad* had not only lost its military superiority, but had also been directly hurt by the tax policies and by the loss of lands taken by the Baqqāra. The *khalīfa,* 'Abdallāh, was informed of the plotted rebellion and on the night of 23 November 1891 the rebels, who had found shelter by the Mahdi's tomb, were surrounded and compelled to agree to a compromise – the practical interpretation of which was an end of their hopes of return to power. Father Ohrwalder, one of the Catholic missionaries imprisoned by the Mahdi, who had fled Omdurman during the rebellion, noted justly that the rule of the *khalīfa,* 'Abdallāh, was total and that anyone intending rebellion was doomed to failure.[19]

The situation of the heads of the *ṭarīqas* and of the "holy families" was not much better. The decline of status of the *ashrāf* after the rise of the *khalīfa* has already been noted, and the fate of other religious leaders was no different. *Fakīs* who showed too much independence, or who for any reason whatsoever aroused suspicions of the *khalīfa* were wiped out or brought as hostages to Omdurman. Thus, al-Manna Ismā'īl, a Sammāniyya *shaykh* active among the Baqqāra, was executed. At the beginning of the Mahdiyya, he had fought by the Mahdi's side and gained great influence. But, in 1883, when it appeared to the *khalīfa* that al-Manna's influence was undermining his own status, he had him executed. Al-Ṭāhir al-Ṭayyib al-Majdhūb – whose support for the Mahdi had been vital in bringing the Beja tribes to the Mahdist fold – was also compelled to accept the *khalīfa*'s rulings and to desist from any show of independence. The *ṭarīqas*' centers and the graves of their saints were destroyed wherever a suspicion arose that they could become centers of power endangering the supremacy of central government.

If we remember that the supreme judicial power was also in the hands of the *khalīfa* and that the *qaḍīs,* including the *qāḍī al-Islām* were subservient to his authority, then it becomes clear that the Mahdiyya succeeded exactly where the Turco–Egyptian regime had failed. Over the ten years since their rise to power, the Mahdi and his heir, the *khalīfa*, were able to undermine the two traditional power centers of Sudanese society and impose their rule upon them. By this means the Sudan was united around a new center of power. The new rulers were assisted in the beginning by the "holy families" and the traditional tribal framework. But, when the regime had become established, these seemed superfluous, and their removal justified. Thus, a new tribal-religious autocracy was created, which succeeded, by means of temptations, threats, and acts of violence, to unite around itself all the previous frameworks. In 1895, Slatin Pasha was able to sum up his ten years of close connection with the *khalīfa*, 'Abdallāh, in Omdurman by saying that the power of central government and the fear of the inhabitants of the Sudan was so great that even the most downtrodden amongst them would not rebel unless the *khalīfa*'s final defeat could be guaranteed in advance.[20] Thus, when the Mahdist state came to its end in 1898, it was not the result of internal disintegration, but rather because of the superior military and technological power of the Anglo–Egyptian Army.

THE ANGLO–EGYPTIAN CONDOMINIUM 1899–1955

After the conquest of the Sudan in 1896–98, the British authorities were confronted with several problems regarding the status of the Sudan and its form of government. Because of international circumstances and financial considerations, the British government adopted the "two flags policy," which meant the hoisting of the Egyptian flag alongside its own in the Sudan, but with no actual intention of letting the Egyptians participate in the government. Following the conquest, the local population was stunned and impoverished as a result of taxation, years of drought and war, and lacking in governing institutions on which the new administration could be based. The British, therefore, believed that the Sudan presented them with a political-administrative vacuum in which it would be possible to create the regime most suitable for local needs – according to British understanding and in line with Britain's interests.

The British officers had formulated three basic assumptions during the period of the Mahdiyya, when they had served as senior officers in the Egyptian army encamped on the Sudanese borders. These assumptions formed the basis for their policies after the conquest when they were called upon to rule the Sudan. In a letter to Lord Cromer in spring 1897, Kitchener, then *sirdār* of the Egyptian army, formulated his understanding of the Sudanese and of the type of government they required. First, he claimed, the inhabitants of the Sudan hate and are contemptuous of Egypt. Second, there are powers within Sudanese society which are not to be found in Egypt and which are capable of undermining a weak government. Thirdly, the

Sudanese (as opposed to the Egyptians) are a proud people, overexcitable, and, therefore, easy to lead astray. Conversely, the stronger the regime becomes and the more based on justice it is, the greater the respect the Sudanese will have for it and the less likely they are to attempt to overthrow it.[21] These assumptions were based on Sudanese history – as understood and defined by Wingate while serving as head of the Intelligence Department of the Egyptian Army. According to this understanding, the Mahdiyya arose out of the failings of the Turco–Egyptian regime and the eternal hostility of the inhabitants of the Sudan for the Egyptians. Centers of power found in the Sudan and nonexistent in Egypt included tribes and Ṣūfī *ṭarīqas* whose loyalty could only be won by a strong regime. The policy formulated as a result of this concept was expressed both in the relationships to the Sudanese tribes and the *ṭarīqas.* The tribes appeared to the British officers to be the most stable and conservative element in society and should, therefore, be strengthened under an established leadership. The *ṭarīqas,* on the other hand, especially the *fakīs,* were considered to be fanatics, tending to superstition, and accordingly prone to rebellion and religious movements of the type of the Mahdiyya. The conclusion was that the utmost must be done to restrict the activities of the *fakīs* and the Ṣūfī orders and to educate a young generation of Sudanese *'ulamā'* for spiritual and religious leadership.[22]

THE TRIBAL POLICIES

In the first period, up to the end of the First World War, it was held that the tribal map of the Sudan must be reconstituted and that tribal leadership should be integrated into the administration. To this end, the tribes were encouraged by means of propaganda, pressure, and financial subsidies to resettle in the areas which they had been compelled to leave during the Mahdiyya. The migration of Baqqāra tribes from Omdurman and the Jazīra back to the West was one of the major expressions of this policy. Tribal leadership was fostered by means of finding men loyal to the government among the tribes, rather than seeking them among the notables – many of whom had been tainted by their activities during the Mahdiyya. The *shaykhs* were appointed by the government and received "robes of honor," exemption from certain taxes, and other small benefits for their services. These included the assessment and collection of taxes, the maintenance of order, and the bringing of malefactors to justice. However, alongside the *shaykhs* and above them hovered the Egyptian and the British administrators, whose presence undermined the authority of the tribal heads even further, since the latter's decisions could always be appealed to the higher level of the Egyptian *ma'mūr*[23] or the British inspector. Apart from a small number of exceptional cases, such as that of Shaykh 'Alī al-Tōm, head of the Kabābīsh, the majority of *shaykhs* became inefficient sycophants and had to be frequently replaced by the central government. 'Alī al-Tōm was unique in that, as head of a nomad tribe, he was less dependent on the government. He won trust because of his leadership abilities and because of his tribe's opposition to the *khalīfa* during the Mahdiyya. In the field of tribal education, a policy was followed similar to that which guided Lord Cromer in Egypt, i.e., the traditional *kuttāb* (school for elementary religious education) was kept, while efforts were made to raise its standards by training teachers from among the sons of the tribal heads. This policy, which was formulated by Slatin Pasha, the inspector general, and Sir Reginald Wingate, the governor general, was revised after the First World War.[24]

The disintegration of the tribal framework and the further decline of tribal leadership were noticeable during the beginning of the 1920s – particularly when seen against the rise of a new strata of young men, graduates of Gordon Memorial College in Khartoum, who began to present Sudanese national claims. Fear of possible collusion between these young men and their colleagues in the Egyptian Wafd, together with the belief that the group was only a vociferous minority not representative of the main trend of thought in Sudanese society, moved the British authorities towards a renewed effort to strengthen the tribes and raise the standard of their leadership. This policy, inspired by that of Lord Lugard in Nigeria, was applied by the second generation of British administrators in the Sudan. This group, exemplified by men such as Sir Harold MacMichael, was composed mostly of Oxford and Cambridge graduates who came to the Sudan in the first two decades of the century. The experience of some of these young Englishmen, starting their way in the administration as inspectors in outlying districts, taught them that exaggerated intervention by government officials in the administration of tribes was doomed to cause a total breakup of tribal society. There was, therefore, a need for decentralization and delegation of powers to the heads of tribes or, in other words, the application of Lugard's principles of devolution to the realities of the Sudan.[25] The first official step in this direction was taken by 1922, when an ordinance was promulgated determining the powers of the nomad *shaykhs* and giving them a legal status in the judicial field. From the beginning, MacMichael, who was then civil secretary, intended to enforce this law among all the tribes of the North, but the conservatism of some of his colleagues compelled him to progress gradually, and only in 1927 was the law broadened to include the northern tribes, apart from the province of Dongola.[26] There is no doubt that the realization of the new policy was assisted by the riots of 1924 in Egypt and the Sudan and by the removal of the majority of the Egyptian officials from the Sudanese administration, following Sir Lee Stack's assassination and Lord Allenby's ultimatum. In the absence of a cumbersome bureaucracy, it was easier to strengthen the power of tribal leadership. Nevertheless, British resistance against more active participation of the rural population in the provincial and district administration continued. A 1929 proposal to create "native advisory councils to assist the Governor and district commissioners of the provinces" was rejected as unnecessary and undesirable. The prevailing opinion of the British governors was that excessive powers of the tribal *shaykhs* should be prevented for so long as it had not been proven that the *shaykh* was capable of "the absorption and digestion of the richer diet." Lord Lloyd, the British high commissioner in Egypt, who by virtue of his position was responsible also for the Sudan, was also happy to report that the "same reservation of *festina lente* as regards the extension of powers" was fully supported by Sayyid ʻAlī al-Mīrghanī, the leader of the Khatmiyya. It is not difficult to guess at Sayyid ʻAlī's reasons, since the appearance of the tribes as a competing political power was undesirable and likely to become a negative factor in the Khatmiyya's conflict with the *Anṣār.*[27]

In any event, the policy delegating judicial and administrative powers to the tribal leaders remained in force. In 1930 there were already more than three hundred tribal courts in the northern Sudan, and the authorities optimistically reported that the *shaykhs* had, to a great extent, improved their status in society and had proven that they were capable of taking upon themselves additional administrative responsibilities.[28] However, Sir James Currie, a one-time director of the department of education of the Sudan, was highly critical of this policy and of the apparently improved status of the tribal leadership. Following a comprehensive tour of the Sudanese provinces in 1934, Currie wrote that in the Sudan young administrators engaged with great enthusiasm in searching for "lost tribes and vanished chiefs and trying to resurrect a social system that had passed away for ever."[29] Currie's statements must be taken with certain reservations since, as has been mentioned above, in specific areas of the Sudan, not only had the tribal framework been preserved, but the *shaykhs* had even succeeded during the years to acquire real power. Without a doubt, first and foremost amongst these was Shaykh ʻAlī al-Tōm, *nāẓir ʻumūm*[30] of the Kabābīsh until his death in 1937. During the thirty-eight years of his rule, ʻAlī al-Tōm succeeded in concentrating in his hands most of the administrative powers and gradually reduced the authority of the *shaykhs* who headed the subtribes under his jurisdiction. His status, both among the tribes and in government circles, was undisputed. Other families of *shaykhs* who acquired powers as a result of this tribal policy also arose amongst the Baqqāra, although their status cannot be compared to that of Shaykh ʻAlī. Thus, for example, the family of Shaykh ʻAlī Julla ruled as *naẓir ʻumūm* of the Ḥumr and the ʻAjaira tribes in Kordofan from the beginning of the century, and two of ʻAlī Julla's grandchildren were even elected as members of Parliament and the Senate on the eve of independence.[31] However, these were exceptions, since normally the tribal policy could not resuscitate tribal leadership and in many cases even hastened the loss of the *shaykhs'* powers and the decline of their political status. This policy also had an impact on the lower level of government officials of Sudanese origin. While previously there had been a tendency to see Gordon College graduates as the main source of officials, there was now a growing trend to recruit officials directly from amongst the tribes and educate them on the job in order to prevent the spread of damaging city influences among the rural population.[32]

The policy of "indirect rule" continued throughout the period of office of Sir John Maffey and Sir Stewart Symes as governors general of the Sudan. In 1937 a number of laws were passed under which the country was divided into districts of local government, with clear distinction between tribal-rural areas and urban areas. The purpose of this division was to enhance local government and to prevent, as far as possible, unnecessary dependence on central government. To this end the formation of urban and rural (district) councils was begun in order to create an infrastructure for central government. However, the implementation of this policy proceeded exceedingly slowly, and the first councils were only created at the end of World War II.

In February 1938 the Graduates' General Congress was founded, inspired by the example of the Indian Congress, not only in its name. The main focus of political struggle was now in the cities, with the leaders of popular Islam and the representatives of the young intelligentsia at its center.[33] The government's tribal policy also came under attack, as in the view of the intelligentsia this policy was directed against them and prevented them from holding the kind of government positions for which they thought themselves qualified, since it gave powers to the most conservative element in the population – the tribal heads. At the center of government in Khartoum, the British continued to hold all senior positions while preventing the appointment of Sudanese to any meaningful posts. The first attempt to include Sudanese in their own government was made in 1944, forty-five years after the reconquest. Tribal and religious leaders, as well as members of the educated class, were invited to join the Advisory Council of the northern Sudan. However, as a result of a boycott against the council by the Graduates' Congress, only the two traditional elements participated, the tribal leaders being the dominant group. Within the council a front formed, composed of the tribal leadership and the *Anṣār*, led by Sayyid 'Abd al-Raḥmān al-Mahdī, the [Mahdi's posthumous son]. The tribal leaders, seeing themselves as spokesmen of the passive majority of the population, sought a political platform, such as a daily newspaper, from which they could propound their opinions and fight against what they regarded as the extremist ideas of the vocal urban intelligentsia. When it became apparent that publishing a newspaper involved considerable investment, the tribal leaders started to negotiate with Sayyid 'Abd al-Raḥmān al-Mahdī, with the result that in March 1945 the *Umma* party was founded. When the Sudan Administration Conference was convened in April 1946 – with the object of raising proposals for associating the Sudanese more closely with the central government and recommending methods to enhance the position of the Advisory Council – the *Anṣār* and the tribal element were preponderant in the conference as a result of its boycott by all the pro-Egyptian parties. Thus, it appeared to the British that the transition to independence would proceed in quiet waters.[34]

After 1947 it was apparent that, because of international circumstances and the entanglement of Anglo–Egyptian relations, the transition of the Sudan to independence would have to proceed at an accelerated pace. The policy of indirect rule and the erection of the desired pyramid, at the base of which stood the district councils, involved a transition period of several decades until the granting of independence. This period was now shortened considerably due to outside pressures and despite the opinions of those holding the reins of government in the Sudan. The latter were therefore forced to stick to the only political power which, in their opinion, was likely to bring the Sudan to independence. Such a power was to be found in the cities and was based on the political parties and the religious leadership. The last attempt of the tribal elite during the period prior to independence to recapture some of its influence was made in 1951. The Socialist Republican party, founded in that year and enjoying British support, was established to undermine the supremacy of the political-religious leadership. The party included a fairly large tribal element which, in wanting to increase the weight of rural population in the future governing bodies of the Sudan, had left the *Umma* party. This attempt failed, and in the first elections to Parliament in 1953 it became finally clear that the tribes, as a political framework, were no longer able to fulfill a central function in the Sudan.[35]

POPULAR ISLAM

British policy after the conquest of the Sudan was to control the influence of the Ṣūfī *ṭarīqas* and of the *fakīs,* while at the same time trying to form a new spiritual-religious leadership composed of Sudanese loyal to so-called Orthodox Islam. This attempt, which continued up to World War I, encompassed a number of practical steps. Firstly, *'ulamā'* were brought from Egypt to rehabilitate the *Sharī'a* court system and guide the Sudanese Muslims in the precepts of Orthodox Islam. Secondly, a "Board of Ulema" was established, with the function of advising the authorities on all religious matters, especially those concerning the campaign against the new *mahdīs* and other "false prophets" (primarily *nabī* 'Isā) who arose frequently throughout the first twenty years after the defeat of the Mahdiyya. Finally, a college for *qāḍīs* and religious teachers was established in order to educate a young generation of Sudanese *'ulamā'* as quickly as possible – thus avoiding the necessity of employing Egyptians, who, together with Orthodox Islam, were liable to inculcate the Sudanese with Egyptian nationalism, unwanted by the British authorities.[36]

While the attitude towards the Ṣūfī *ṭarīqas* was predominantly negative, the Khatmiyya enjoyed special treatment because of their pro-Egyptian stand throughout the Madhist period. During the Anglo–Egyptian campaign, British intelligence officers allowed Sayyid 'Alī al-Mīrghanī to return to Kassala, the center of the Khatmiyya, and to rebuild, with British support, the mosque of the order which had been destroyed during the Mahdiyya.[37] Shortly thereafter, in 1899, Sayyid 'Alī became the first Sudanese to receive a title (C.M.G.) from Queen Victoria. The British hoped to achieve two purposes in supporting the Khatmiyya. Firstly, they regarded it as the only *ṭarīqa* not composed of zealots nor imbued with fanaticism, whose leadership could be relied upon in the campaign against the *fakīs* and the "false Messiahs." Secondly, they hoped for the help of the

Khatmiyya leadership against excessive influence by Egyptian *'ulamā'*. Sayyid 'Alī al-Mīrghanī fulfilled their hopes in both fields, and in spite of the Khatmiyya's historical connection with Egypt, he became the principal and most outspoken opponent of the Egyptian "partner" in the Condominium administration.

When World War I broke out, the Khatmiyya's loyalty was further proven. Sayyid 'Alī al-Mīrghanī used his influence in the Sudan to upset Turkish and Egyptian attempts at undermining the loyalty of the inhabitants to its British rulers. He also used his connections with the family of the Sharīf Ḥusayn in Mecca and became Wingate's emissary in his negotiations with the Sharīf, which were going on parallel to the McMahon–Ḥusayn correspondence. However, Turkey's joining of the German camp and the Ottoman sultan's declaration of *jihād* against Britain and its allies brought about a change in the religious policy of the Sudanese government. The British, in their efforts to recruit any possible support amongst the Sudanese Muslims, were forced to approach the same elements which they had previously attempted to control, namely, the leadership of popular Islam. Despite the fact that rulers of the Sudan ever since Muhammad 'Alī's conquest had fostered Orthodox Islam in order to weaken Sufism, it now became clear that the influence of the latter was still many times stronger than that of the "imported" institutionalized Islam.

Three of the leaders of popular Islam now stood out and were given the unofficial title of "the three Sayyids." Sayyid 'Alī al-Mīrghanī continued to be the most trusted leader in the eyes of the authorities. In addition to al-Mīrghanī, the British were now assisted in their propaganda against the Ottoman *jihād,* and later on against Egyptian nationalism, by Sharīf Yūsuf al-Hindī and by Sayyid 'Abd al-Raḥmān al-Mahdī. The latter had been until then under constant surveillance by the intelligence department, which feared a revival of the Mahdiyya by an offspring of the *imām*'s family. However, following the outbreak of the War, Sayyid 'Abd al-Rahmān was best suited to serve Britain's aims. He was permitted to tour throughout the Sudan and to preach to his followers that the Turks were heretics and that the Sudanese Muslims would do well to remain loyal to their rulers and not pay heed to the Ottoman call for *jihād.* The revival of the *Anṣār* as a religious–political power was, therefore, a direct result of British war interests. These caused the authorities to use the prestige and strength of the Mahdists, still extant, especially amongst the tribes, despite the destruction of the Mahdist state by the same foreign infidel conqueror, whom the *Anṣār* were now called upon to support.[38]

By the end of World War I, the status of the leaders of popular Islam had become a recognized fact. The delegation of notables who went to London in 1919 to demonstrate the Sudan's loyalty to Great Britain and to disassociate themselves from Egyptian nationalism and its claims, as expressed in the 1919 uprising, was first and foremost a delegation of the "three Sayyids." It was headed by Sayyid 'Alī al-Mīrghanī, accompanied by the two other Sayyids, and by a long list of *'ulamā'* and tribal chiefs.[39] But Sayyid 'Abd al-Rāḥmān al-Mahdī derived the greatest political advantage from this delegation. In presenting the sword of his father, the Mahdi, to King George V, Sayyid 'Abd al-Raḥmān demonstrated the bond between the *Anṣār* and the British rulers of Sudan. This act also initiated the beginning of mistrust between Sayyid Alī al-Mīrghanī and Sayyid 'Abd al-Raḥmān – which quickly developed into an open rift. Sayyid 'Alī considered the handing over of the sword as an act undermining his status and as evidence of a desire to raise the family of the Mahdi to a position of political power leaning on British protection.

At this stage, the "three Sayyids" were regarded by the Egyptian nationalists as traitors "who have sold their conscience during the war for British money." At least these were the words used to describe the Sayyids to two Egyptian notables who were sent to the Sudan in 1919 to examine Sudanese attitudes to the Egyptian national struggle.[40] Shortly thereafter, the "three Sayyids" approached the British governor general of the Sudan with a request to permit them to start a kind of political propaganda amongst their followers. Their purpose was to propagate the case for a separate Sudanese national identity and to refute the charges of servitude to England made by their opponents.[41] These ideas were expressed in the first political newspaper of the Sudan, *al-haḍāra,* which started to preach the expulsion of the Egyptians from the Sudan and the attainment of independence under British guardianship. The paper, acquired in 1920 by the "three Sayyids" constituted a milestone in the rise of the leaders of popular Islam to the rank of political leaders.

During 1919–24, as national ferment in Egypt started to leave its mark in the Sudan, the Sayyids continued to be the center of all anti-Egyptian forces in the Sudan. When Lord Allenby visited the Sudan in April 1922, he met with the local notables in order to make it quite clear that the unilateral British declaration of February 1922 regarding Egyptian independence would in no way change the status of the Sudan. Sayyid 'Alī al-Mīrghanī, the uncrowned leader, answered for the Sudanese notables and stressed that the Sudan was a separate country and that the Sudanese had their own national identity and must therefore be permitted to develop and achieve their independence under British protection.[42] Letters from religious leaders and tribal chiefs associating themselves with the British standpoint on Egypt and the Sudan – the spontaneity of which can be doubted – flooded the governor general.[43] But most important of all was the increased activity of Sayyid 'Abd al-Raḥmān who, following his first success during the war, had now begun to put all his energy into organizing his supporters, the *Ansār.* In 1918 the Sayyid erected a private mosque for his followers in Omdurman. In the three years following the war, he appointed agents, who included tribal leaders, rich merchants, and notables, in all districts of the Sudan. These agents collected *zakāh* (alms tax) from all the supporters of the new sect and were the representatives of Sayyid 'Abd al-Raḥmān in his contacts with the authorities, on the one hand, and his supporters, on the other. Already in 1921, reading of the *rātib* (the Mahdi's prayer book) was permitted by the authorities, and new editions were printed in the Sudan and in Egypt. If it be remembered that up to the First World War the use of the *rātib* had been forbidden and whoever preached or prayed in the style of the Mahdiyya was arrested under the law, then it will be understood that the change in the political status of the sect was highly significant. In 1923–24 Sayyid 'Abd al-Raḥmān's political status was thus used by Britain to neutralize Egyptian nationalist influence on the young Sudanese generation.[44]

Sayyid 'Abd al-Raḥmān's rise in influence had a deep and lasting impact on the politico–religious frame of the Sudan. Already in September 1924, Sayyid 'Alī al-Mīrghanī declared (in a conversation with the British governor of Kordofan) that he would prefer to see the Sudan under Egyptian rule, rather than be subject to a Sudanese monarchy headed by Sayyid 'Abd al-Raḥmān.[45] Others, and chief amongst them Sudanese army officers and members of the young intelligentsia, were not happy with the renewed rise of the traditional forces as a leadership recognized by Britain and began to preach the "Unity of the Nile Valley" under the Egyptian crown. The White Flag League, the first political organization to be created in the Sudan since the Anglo–Egyptian conquest, was an expression of this movement. Its members also included representatives of religious families who had not found their place in the new confrontation between Sayyid 'Alī and Sayyid 'Abd al-Raḥmān. For example, Muḥammad al-Mahdī, the son of the *khalīfa* 'Abd Allāh, as well as other members of the *khalīfa*'s family, did not merge into the *Anṣār* sect, since this sect saw the *khalīfa* and his rule as being responsible for the destruction of the Mahdist state.[46] However, already in 1924, some leaders of this new political trend recognized that only the patronage of one or the other of the two Sayyids could convert them from an organization with no influence into a body of political power that the authorities would take into account. Sayyid ʻAbd Allāh Khalīl, an officer in the Sudanese army who had been a close associate of the White Flag League, split away from the league at this stage and adopted the opposite view: "The Sudan for the Sudanese." His political way thenceforward, up to his becoming prime minister in 1956, was that of alliance with Sayyid ʻAbd al-Raḥmān and later with the *Anṣār* dominated *Umma* party. Others, who feared that the way of the *Anṣār* meant British domination, sought the patronage of Sayyid ʻAlī al-Mīrghanī and continued to wave the banner of the "Unity of the Nile Valley."[47]

When, in 1925, following Allenby's ultimatum and the removal of the Egyptian army from the Sudan, Sayyid ʻAbd al-Raḥmān's anti-Egyptian mission was completed, the British authorities again started to restrict his movements. British apprehensions regarding aggrandizement of the *Anṣār* had awakened already before, when it became clear that pilgrimages to Abā Island – the sect's center and residence of its leader – were turning into large-scale demonstrations of political power. In May 1923 the number of pilgrims in Abā was estimated at five to fifteen thousand, and the number of *muhājirūn* (pilgrims from West Africa who had permanently settled on the island and its surroundings) reached twelve hundred. Although there was no reason for the authorities to be suspicious of Sayyid ʻAbd al-Raḥmān or of his loyalty to the British, the fear that his increased strength might bring about an anti-British turn in his policy resulted in repeated attempts to limit the extent of his influence. He was asked to stop the pilgrimage of his supporters to Abā Island and to dismiss all his agents amongst the tribes. In 1926 the authorities even exploited the Sayyid's economic difficulties in order to libel him amongst the *Anṣār.*[48] The new policy inevitably influenced recruitment to the new units of the Sudan Defence Force, which had been established after the removal of the Egyptian army from the Sudan in 1924. Steps were taken to prevent the penetration of *Anṣār* into the army – by means of stopping recruitment from certain tribes where Sayyid ʻAbd al-Raḥmān's influence was dominant.[49]

The most extreme example symbolizing the turn in British policy was the affair surrounding the resignation of Sir Geoffrey Archer, governor general of the Sudan, in 1925–26. At the beginning of 1926, Sayyid ʻAbd al-Raḥmān received from Sir Geoffrey the order of the K.B.E., awarded him by King George V for his services during the war and for his anti-Egyptian activities in the years that followed. When Sir Geoffrey visited Abā Island in March of that year, he made a speech extolling the Sayyid's loyalty and the bond between him and the British administration. This speech incensed senior British officials, who at that stage wished to clip the wings of the *Anṣār* and their leader and rebuild the power of Sayyid 'Alī al-Mīrghanī, who viewed the ascent of the *Anṣār* with increasing suspicion. British officialdom saw in Archer's speech a kind of formal recognition of the status of Sayyid 'Abd al-Raḥmān as a leader and contended that this speech was tantamount to undermining the declared British policies in the Sudan. Despite attempts at mediation by Lord Lloyd, the British high commissioner in Egypt, Archer was compelled to submit his resignation – ostensibly for reasons of ill health – and the anti-Mahdist policy received a new lease of life.[50] Sayyid 'Abd al-Raḥmān's movements were once again restricted, and he was forbidden to leave Khartoum or Omdurman without the permission of the governor general. He was ordered to refrain from all religious–political activity and to instruct his supporters on Abā Island and in all the provinces to dissolve their organizations.[51] The British saw confirmation of their suspicions when a manuscript about the Mahdist sect, written by a pilgrim from the Yemen who had visited Abā Island, fell into the hands of the intelligence department. The author of the manuscript, 'Abd al-Raḥmān al-Jābirī, contended in his book that it was the *Anṣār* who would bring about the end of British rule when the true *khalīfa* of the Mahdi, Sayyid 'Abd al-Raḥmān, would take his place at their head.[52] The gravity with which the British viewed the rise of the Mahdiyya was reflected by a special discussion held on this subject at the Committee of Imperial Defence in February 1927. The conclusions were that a Mahdist uprising was liable to occur as a result of weakness by the administration or of mistaken economic policies – and not necessarily against a religious background. Therefore, the stationing of an additional unit of the Royal Air Force and the reduction of taxes would be a suitable antidote to the rise of Mahdism.[53] Due to lack of data it is difficult to assess the impact of measures taken against the *Anṣār*, but it seems that Sayyid 'Abd al-Raḥmān continued his activities despite the restrictions, since the movement was so deeply rooted throughout the Sudan that it was no longer possible to suppress it by administrative measures. Similarly, ways had been found by the Sayyid to circumvent the instructions of the government without directly violating them. It is known, for example, that in place of his agents in the districts, whose activities had been forbidden, the Sayyid established direct contact with the *shaykhs* of tribes and the *'umad* (administrative heads of villages), who, as representatives of the authorities, could act unhindered as "servants of two masters."[54]

The most important development in popular Islam between the two world wars was its divergence from the sphere of religion, to which it had been relegated by the authorities, and its appearance as a central political power recognized both by the government and by the population. Two years after the 1924 riots, young Sudanese renewed their organization, the Graduates' Club, as the main tool for fostering Sudanese nationalism. In the founding conference of the organization, both Sayyids, who were present as invited guests, were called on to support the demands of the intelligentsia – it being clear that without such support there was no chance to organize.[55] At this stage, the difference of opinion between those claiming "Unity of the Nile Valley" and those believing in "Sudan for the Sudanese" became a dividing line in Sudanese politics. In reality, everyone wanted independence, but each of the sides believed that its way was the shortest and surest. While the pro-Egyptian camp wanted to get rid of British rule with the help of Egypt, its opponents saw the British as a temporary factor who, sooner or later, would leave the Sudan. Conversely, the Egyptians were seen as more dangerous since their historical demands for "Unity of the Nile Valley" were likely to convert Egyptian help in removing the British into permanent conquest of the Sudan by the Egyptians themselves. The consolidation of the two camps was, without doubt, helped by the existing division between the Khatmiyya and the *Anṣār*. When Sayyid 'Abd al-Raḥmān took his place at the head of the "Sudan for the Sudanese" camp, his opponent, al-Mīrghanī, gave his support to the adversaries of the *Anṣār* in order to ensure that his movement would not come out the loser. There is no evidence for the contention that Sayyid 'Alī – the pillar of the British regime and the most bitter opponent of Egyptian domination of the Sudan until after the First World War – all of a sudden became a spokesman for the historical rights of Egypt in the Nile Valley and a believer in the cultural–religious unity of the two peoples. The change was tactical and was made in order to serve the religious political interests of the Khatmiyya, as was proven by the Sayyid's retreat from the pro-Egyptian line on the eve of independence.

Examples of this rift are not lacking. In 1931, when the first strike of graduates of Gordon College broke out against the background of wage demands, the graduates split between the two religious camps, despite the fact that their demands had in fact no political or religious significance.[56] The rift became even deeper when discussions took place on political problems affecting the future of the Sudan. When the Anglo–Egyptian negotiations on an agreement between the two countries were renewed, both camps sharpened their swords in preparation for the struggle. This was the case in 1927 and 1930 even though the problem of the Sudan had been removed from the agenda of the discussions. It is, therefore, hardly surprising that the negotiations in 1936 and the actual signing of the Anglo–Egyptian agreement caused great tension between the two camps in the Sudan and disillusion in their British and Egyptian patrons. The supporters of "Nile Valley Unity" saw in the agreement the perpetuation of the Condominium and betrayal by the Egyptians (i.e., the Wafd) of their nationalist mission, while their opponents, the *Anṣār,* criticized the British for their concessions and were angered that the future of the Sudan had become, by virtue of this treaty, an Anglo–Egyptian problem. Both camps were united on one point – that Egypt and Britain had sinned in deciding the fate of the Sudan without consulting its inhabitants.[57]

The 1936 agreement did not bring about any real change in practice in the status of the Sudan. The agreement had stipulated the return of Egyptian officials and of Egyptian army units to the Sudan and had further promised free immigration of Egyptians to the Sudan, limited only by considerations of health and security. However, Egyptian officials did not appear, the anticipated Egyptian migration did not take place, and the Egyptian army unit – permitted to return to the Sudan as a symbolic gesture of appeasement – was compelled to remain in Port Sudan and became something of a joke. It was not surprising, therefore, that the Egyptians tried their luck in the political–religious field, where they could see their only opportunity to establish their status. On the one hand, renewed attempts were made to penetrate into Sudanese Islamic leadership, primarily through the agency of the rector of al-Azhar, Shaykh Muṣṭafā al-Marāghī, previously the Grand *Qaḍī* of the Sudan; on the other hand, the title of pasha was granted to the two Sayyids in order to bring them closer to Egypt and in the hope of undermining what Egypt regarded as the loyalty of Sayyid 'Abd al-Raḥmān to Great Britain. These steps were seen by the British authorities as not only violating the spirit of the agreement, but also the specific obligations of Egypt. However, apart from British displeasure, there was nothing in the Egyptian action that was sufficient to bring about a change in the traditional political–religious divison of the Sudan, for, as the British themselves knew, the Egyptians "cut very little ice with their Sudanese contemporaries."[58]

The founding of the Graduates' General Congress in 1938 seemed to herald a new departure in Sudanese politics. This was the third attempt by the Sudanese intelligentsia to create for themselves an independent socio–political framework, free of the traditional foci of power. The Sayyids again tried to intervene, proposing the creation of a common council in which the graduates, the *muftī* and the *shaykh al-'ulamā'* of the Sudan, as well as they themselves, would be represented. This proposal was rejected by the graduates, and on the face of it the young generation had finally succeeded in becoming independent of the religious sects and the traditional leadership. However, by 1942 the Graduates' Congress had already split into two factions – moderate and extremist – each of which sought the support of one or the other of the two Sayyids, without whose backing it was bound to fail in its political struggle. The details of that struggle between the movements are not within the framework of this discussion and have been adequately described elsewhere.[59] But the reasons for the rift prove that, even at this late stage, no political force could arise in the Sudan if it attempted to cut itself off from the patronage of popular Islam. For, so long as the congress restricted itself to activities in the cultural, social, and professional fields, the Sayyids left it alone, despite their suspicions, since these spheres of activity did not endanger the Sayyids' positions and, furthermore, almost prevented the possibility of outside interference. But in 1941, when elections took place for the executive committee of the congress, the rift between the supporters of the *Anṣār* and the Khatmiyya was already clear. Matters came to a head in 1942 when the congress's demand to be recognized as the political representative of the inhabitants of the Sudan was severely criticized by the authorities. The division of the congress into moderates and extremists now became an open split and compelled both parties to seek patrons with whose backing they could continue their struggle. The huddling of the so-called moderates in the shadow of Sayyid 'Abd al-Raḥmān al-Mahdī brought about an alliance between the so-called extremists, representing the majority of the congress, under the leadership of Ismā'īl al-Azharī and Sayyid 'Alī al-Mīrghanī, the leader of the Khatmiyya. The latter – who even at this stage would be difficult to identify as extremist in his opinions or even politically motivated – was pushed into this alliance by fear of the rise of the *Anṣār* under British protection. This fear was expressed by the Sayyid on more than one occasion, when he stated that he would prefer to live under the Christian King of Ethiopia, rather than be ruled by a sultan of the Mahdi's family.[60]

Sayyid 'Alī, though he did not hesitate in asserting his authority, refrained from actively interfering in politics until his death in February 1968. Various political parties which arose after the establishment of the *Ashiqqā'* under the leadership of al-Azharī in 1943 sought the Sayyid's patronage, yet they never really won his full support. On the other hand, Sayyid 'Abd al-Raḥmān was a religious leader who did not avoid taking definite stands in fields which were clearly political. The entire political leadership which developed in the Sudan during the period of the Condominium came under his influence at one time or another and continued to take his view into account even after their ways had parted. His status in the eyes of his Sudanese contemporaries was accurately – if somewhat naively – described by one of the architects of education in the new Sudan, Shaykh Bābikr Badrī, who told one of the British officials: "In my eyes Sayyid 'Abd al-Raḥmān's standing is identical to that of Sir [James] Robertson in your eyes."[61] (Sir James Robertson was civil secretary and actually wielded decisive influence in the Sudan during 1945–53). With the foundation in March 1945 of the *Umma* party – which from the start was obviously the political arm of the *Anṣār* – mutual suspicions between the opponents intensified, and overlapping of the religious and political fields became a decisive factor in the formation of the socio–political character of the Sudan. The attempt of both camps to cooperate during the Anglo–Egyptian negotiations in 1946 ended in renewed conflict. On 31 October 1946 thousands of demonstrators marched under the tri-colored flag of the *Anṣār* – black, red, and green, symbolizing the flag colors of the Mahdi's three *khalīfas.* Opposition to the Anglo–Egyptian Protocol on the future of the Sudan reached its peak in November, when a delegation of the *Umma* party clarified to the British authorities that any attempt to impose Egyptian rule on the Sudan would be met with armed opposition and would end in bloodshed.[62] It may be symbolic that exactly at that time the cornerstone was laid for the restoration of the Mahdi's tomb in Omdurman – some fifty years after its destruction had been ordered by Lord Kitchener, conqueror of the Sudan.[63] The fact that the Sudan problem was put before the United Nations Security Council in 1947, as part of Egypt's complaint against Britain, also did not help to improve the atmosphere in the Sudan. Apart from the official delegation of the Sudan government, two additional delegations, representing the *Ashiqqā'* and *Umma* parties and supported by the two Sayyids, went to the United Nations. Each hoped that the line that it represented would win the support of the United Nations, and all three returned to the Sudan disappointed.[64]

Naḥḥās Pasha's unilateral abrogation of the Condominium agreement and the 1936 Anglo–Egyptian treaty in October 1951 restored unity between the two Sayyids for a short while. The proclamation of Fārūq as "King of Egypt and the Sudan" with sovereign powers in the fields of legislation, foreign relations, and defense in both territories; even worse, the submission for ratification by the Egyptian Parliament of a new constitution for the Sudan without consulting the Sudanese leaders themselves (apart from Ismā'īl al-Azharī), provoked the formation of a united anti-Egyptian front, at the center of which stood the religious leadership.[65] The rapprochement of the two Sayyids was also facilitated in a roundabout way by British support which was ostensibly given to the Socialist Republican party, founded in 1951 under the leadership of the tribal chiefs. This step, receiving the covert support of Sayyid 'Alī, was described by Sayyid 'Abd al-Raḥmān as a British betrayal of those who had helped them in their struggle against Egypt and hence provoked a split between the *Anṣār* and the British.[66] From here to the agreement between the Sudanese parties and Muḥammad Najīb, the new ruler of Egypt, the road was not long. The Sudanese viewed the agreement as a personal victory of Sayyid 'Abd al-Raḥmān, who had proved to his British "trustees" that the fate of the Sudan could not be determined without him. Moreover, he had succeeded in getting Egypt to recognize his claim to Sudanese self-determination and to prefer agreement with him to an agreement with his opponents, the supporters of the "Unity of the Nile Valley."[67]

To regard the first general elections held in the Sudan in 1953 as a victory of the pro-Egyptian camp is therefore mistaken. John Duncan, who had served in the Sudan since 1942, saw matters correctly – even before the elections – when he wrote in 1952 that, except for a negligible minority, no one in the Sudan truly supported unification with Egypt. According to him, the so-called pro-Egyptian camp was nothing but a faction of the opponents to Mahdist supremacy, motivated, not by love for Egypt, but by the Khatmiyya's competition with the *Anṣār* for leadership of the Sudan.[68] It is against this background that the election results should be viewed. Most of those opposing Mahdist domination supported al-Azharī's National Unionist party, while such unity could not be achieved within the *Anṣār*'s camp primarily because of the feud between different tribal leaders and the religious leadership. Thus, the supporters of independence went to the elections split into seven parties whose only achievement was in helping their adversaries to win the elections.[69] Furthermore, the long-established tradition of tacit agreement between the *Anṣār* and the British authorities had inevitably damaged the position and political expectations of the *Umma* party on the eve of independence. Thus, the *Umma* received in the elections only twenty-three out of the ninety-seven seats in the Sudanese House of Representatives, compared with the fifty seats won by the National Unionist party. But the fleeting unity which had put Ismāʿīl al-Azharī into power did not last long. In 1955, when it became clear that the danger of Mahdist domination had passed, three of the leading members of the Khatmiyya, headed by Sayyid Mīrghanī Ḥamza, founded the Republican Independence party which enjoyed the Khatmiyya's support. The slogan of the "Unity of the Nile Valley" had served the purpose for which the Sudanese had adopted it, namely, the right of self-determination. Henceforward, it could only serve Egyptian aims – which implied domination of the Sudan by means of unification with Egypt. Even those politicians who sincerely believed in the concept of unification retreated from it after the bloody events of 1954 in Khartoum when it became clear that the *Anṣār* would not hesitate to take up arms against anyone trying to renounce independence for the Sudan.[70]

Henceforward, and up to the Sudanese declaration of independence on 1 January 1956 the central role of the two Sayyids was demonstrated anew. In August 1955 the Sayyids suggested that, in order to prevent chaos and the danger of Egyptian intervention – which seemed more acute since Nasser's emergence to power – the future of the Sudan be determined by means of a plebiscite. The fact that the two Sayyids took a common stand on this proposal was proof that the Khatmiyya had also joined the clamor for independence. On 30 November 1955 the two Sayyids met for the first time since the end of the Second World War to consult on the Sudan's future and published a joint statement in which they called on all their supporters to facilitate a tranquil transition to independence. When the first Parliament of the independent Sudan met in session on 1 January 1956 the center of the dais was not occupied by politicians, but by Muḥammad ʿUthmān al-Mīrghanī and Siddīq al-Mahdī, who were called on to greet the people of the Sudan in the name of the two main centers of power – the Khatmiyya and the *Anṣār.*[71]

The close of the Condominium took place, therefore, against the background of the clear supremacy of the traditional leadership. The tribal heads had suffered a major defeat in their attempt to create an independent political force, and tribal society had largely integrated into the new political structure as protégés of the religious leaders. Even the new political parties which had been established during and after the Second World War were compelled to adapt to the existing framework of sectarian politics, despite the fact that their establishment had been the protest of the young generation against the superiority of the religious orders. This was true, not only for the *Ashiqqā'* and the *Umma* parties, but also, though to a lesser extent, for the Muslim Brothers and the Communists, who had founded their parties in 1946. The Communists drew their power mainly from amongst the urban population of the northern and eastern Sudan, the source of influence of the Khatmiyya. The Communists' extreme opposition to the *Umma* drew to their ranks many of the supporters of the Khatmiyya for whom Communist ideology was completely alien. The Muslim Brothers were active amongst the intelligentsia, and primarily the students. Unlike their Egyptian comrades – who by virtue of their penetration into the urban lower middle classes and the proletariat and their success amongst the fellahs had become a mass politico–religious movement – the Muslim Brothers in the Sudan operated as a pressure group which, because of its being an elite, was able to attain serious political achievements through the existing Islamic groups, and primarily the *Anṣār.* Therein lies the root of the paradox, since the Muslim Brothers, in their war for a state based on pure Islam, were forced, just as the Mahdists had been in their struggle for power in 1881–85, to make use of the assistance of popular Islamic sects, which were the prime factor of divergence from the pure Islam which they sought.[72]

THE INDEPENDENT SUDAN

The paucity of open sources prevents thorough research into the period following the Second World War. It is, nevertheless, possible to recognize two major, and still undisputed, processes relative to the subject under discussion. One process indicates the further decline of the status of the tribes to such an extent that they have ceased to be an independent factor in the political map of the Sudan. The little evidence there is regarding the attempts of certain tribal groups to influence political moves during this period clearly shows their weakness. On the eve of General 'Abbūd's coup, a section of the Ja'aliyyīn and the Shāyqiyya established an independent political framework, whose function it was to undermine the supremacy of the religious and urban elements in Sudanese politics. Shortly thereafter, thirty-five chiefs of tribes congregated and founded the "Shaykhs' Alliance," whose purpose was to ensure that the interests of the tribal population would not be neglected.[73] These efforts came to naught, due to the military coup which took place a few months later. However, there is basis for the assumption that, even had the parliamentary regime continued without interference, the tribes did not have sufficient power or unity to become an active pressure group. This does not relate to the tribe as a socio-economic framework, or to the status of the *shaykh* as a permanent factor in the daily life of those under his control. There were certainly changes in this field, too, since the process of urbanization and the weakening of the family's authority did not omit the Sudan. Nevertheless, it appears that the tribal framework was maintained to a great degree, not only in primitive tribal areas, such as Dārfūr, the Nuba Mountains, and the Red Sea Hills, but also amongst the better educated riverain tribes. The actual attempts at political organization would not have been possible had the tribes been crumbling. The failure of the attempts proves that the tribe had ceased to be a political unit, but does not indicate its disintegration as a socio-economic factor.

Ibrāhīm 'Abbūd's regime between 1958 and 1964 to a certain extent attempted to reach a renewed balance between village and city. The program of Muḥammad Abū Rināt – member of the Shāyqiyya tribe and former chief justice, who was amongst the ideologues of the 'Abbūd revolt – included, inter alia, a new structure for Sudanese democracy by giving suitable representation to the rural population. The Provincial Administration Act of July 1961 was promulgated in order to exchange the old parliamentarianism – Westminster style – for parliamentary institutions on a much wider base suited to the village-tribal structure of the Sudan. However, this did not reach full realization by the end of 'Abbūd's regime, and the tribal leadership did not succeed in becoming a substantial factor even during this period. In May 1965, in the first elections to take place after the civil uprising of October 1964, Nuba and Beja tribal lists did participate and even won nineteen seats in Parliament. But the main struggle took place between the traditional parties, with trade unions and organizations of workers, farmers, and the free professions going together with the Communist party, since by this means they hoped to gain representation appropriate to their numbers and status in the Sudanese population. The results, however, were a victory of sectarianism – with the *Umma* and National Unionist party gaining 131 out of 175 seats in Parliament.[74]

The second process which started in the period before independence, but only ripened after 1956, was the rise in the importance of the two traditional centers of power which came to influence all political steps in the Sudan, even when they were not active partners in the regime. An example of the power of the Sayyids was already given in the summer of 1956, when on 26 June the leaders of the Khatmiyya, meeting in the house of Sayyid ‘Alī al-Mīrghanī, decided to abandon al-Azharī’s National Unionist party and to create a party of their own under the leadership of Mīrghanī Ḥamza. This was the first occasion on which Sayyid ‘Alī had come out from behind the scenes and onto the political stage, giving his support to the new People’s Democratic party (PDP).[75] The fall of al-Azharī’s government and the creation of an *Umma*–PDP coalition backed by the *Ansār* and the Khatmiyya split Sudanese society into two camps: all the branches of popular Islam on the one side and the other political parties on the other. The victory of the Sayyids at this stage was undoubted evidence of the weakness of the united camp of their opponents. It is possible that the attempt to split the *Anṣār* by means of creating a party of supporters of the late *khalīfa* ‘Abdallāh, *ḥizb al-taḥrīr al-waṭanī,* was a desperate attempt by ‘Abd al-Raḥmān’s opponents to undermine his power.[76] However, the general elections of 1958 proved that, as long as unity prevailed between the Khatmiyya and the *Anṣār,* the opposition had no chance. The two religious sects divided the constituencies between them and, for the first time in the history of the Sudan, gave their support to candidates of the opposing sect in order to prevent the election of representatives of other parties. Thus, the representatives of popular Islam won 104 out of the total 170 seats in the Sudanese Parliament, and their control was beyond question.[77]

However, brotherly love did not prevail in the traditional camp and the signs of disintegration of the popular Islamic front appeared shortly after the 1958 elections. Disagreement broke out over the composition of the state’s presidency. While the *Anṣār* were in favor of a single president, the Khatmiyya preferred a Presidium of three – mostly because of their suspicions of the ambition of Sayyid ‘Abd al-Raḥmān al-Mahdī. There were further major differences of approach between the two sects regarding the foreign policy of the Sudan. The supporters of the Khatmiyya favored rapprochement with Egypt and the Arab world and were therefore prepared for compromise in the dispute with Egypt over the northern borders of the Sudan. The *Anṣār,* on the other hand, preferred a policy of balance between the Arab world and the African continent. They objected to border concessions for Egypt and, according to their opponents, even damaged the policy of neutrality by requesting help from the United States during the cotton crisis of 1958.[78]

The result of the governmental crisis was ‘Abbūd’s coup of 17

November 1958 and the army's accession to power less than three years after the achievement of independence. According to 'Abbūd himself, this was the only possible "sound and blessed step," since the army alone could put an end to the "state of corruption, maladministration, instability, and individual and community fear," which parliamentary government had left behind it in the Sudan.[79] Two years of so-called representative government had proven that no political party or coalition of parties could create stable government in the Sudan for as long as real power lay in the hands of the *Anṣār* and Khatmiyya. However, 'Abbūd could also not free himself from this dependence, and it is doubtful whether the coup could have been carried out without the tacit agreement of the Sayyids. It appears that Sayyid 'Ali al-Mīrghanī saw in the army's accession to power an end to friction among the politicians and therefore gave his support to 'Abbūd. It must be added that 'Abbūd himself and a great number of the officers who stood with him were loyal to the Khatmiyya. Sayyid 'Abd al-Raḥmān, on the other hand, did not rush to give his blessing to the plotters of the coup. When 'Abbūd and his deputy, 'Abd al-Wahhāb, came to get the Sayyid's blessing on his yacht on the Nile, 'Abd al-Raḥmān al-Mahdī directed them to the heads of the *Umma* party in Khartoum, who duly complied with the officers' request. Relationships between Sayyid 'Abd al-Raḥmān and the heads of the coup remained tense up to his death on 24 March 1959.[80] The interesting fact in this is that the military regime – as had parliamentary government before it – needed the blessing of the Sayyids in order to achieve legitimacy for itself in the eyes of the Sudanese people.

The force of popular Islam expressed itself throughout the whole period of 'Abbūd's regime. The law for the dispersal of the parties and the confiscation of their property did in fact hit the *Umma* and the People's Democratic party, the political arms of the two sects. However, the *Anṣār* and the Khatmiyya themselves were, not only unhurt by these measures, but in fact fulfilled some of the functions that had previously belonged to their parties. The *Anṣār,* under their new leader Ṣiddīq al-Mahdī, reorganized and created a hierarchy of party-like institutions, both at the center and in the provinces. Siddīq's power and self-confidence rose to such an extent that in October 1959 he demanded of 'Abbūd that he end military government and revive democratic parliamentary institutions. The leaders of the *Anṣār* did not even hesitate to attack 'Abbūd for, in their opinion, selling the rights of the Sudan by signing the Agreement for the Division of Nile waters with Egypt on 8 November 1959.[81] Siddīq's declaration of the *Anṣār*'s loyalty to 'Abbūd in May 1960, stressing that his activities and the activities of the *Anṣār* were solely religious, was lip service only.[82] In November of the same year, Ṣiddīq's name appeared at the top of a list of twenty religious and political leaders on a petition to the military authorities, demanding that they return to their barracks.[83] In March 1961 Ṣiddīq reiterated his demand, stating that the military regime had extracted the state from a crisis, but that its continuation in power was now doing more harm than good.[84] Despite his repeated demands for the cessation of military government, the authorities refrained from attacking Ṣiddīq or the *Anṣār* and, apart from attempts to restrict their economic power, left them alone to operate unhindered. Even in June 1961, following a railwaymen's strike, when a letter of protest from all the veteran political leadership, including Ṣiddīq, was sent to 'Abbūd, the authorities still did not dare to harm the head of the *Anṣār*. All the other leaders were arrested and exiled to Juba, capital of Equatoria, while Ṣiddīq continued his activities unhindered.[85] Only in August of the same year, after a bloody clash at the Mahdi's tomb between young demonstrators of the *Anṣār* and the army, was Ṣiddīq placed under house arrest for a short period, and a number of leading *Anṣār* were imprisoned.[86]

Till mid-1961 cordial relations prevailed between the leaders of the Khatmiyya and the military junta. The majority of officers in the Revolutionary Council were supporters of the Khatmiyya and the army's policies, particularly regarding foreign relations, were in line with the viewpoints of the sect's leaders. However, the economic situation worsened in 1961, and pressure of Khatmiyya supporters, especially among the Railwaymen's Union, brought about a change in the line. In April Ṣiddīq and his son al-Ṣādiq al-Mahdī visited the leader of the Khatmiyya, Sayyid 'Alī, with the intention of reviving a unified front of the two orders against the military regime. Consequently, Muḥammad al-Mīrghanī, who had signed the June 1961 letter of protest to 'Abbūd in the name of the Khatmiyya, was among the Sudanese leaders who were exiled to Juba.[87]

Ṣiddīq died in October 1961 and the leadership of the *Anṣār* passed to his brother al-Imām al-Hādī al-Mahdī. Ṣiddīq's son, al-Ṣādiq, was designated to lead the *Umma* party and was ordered by his father, before his death, to continue the struggle for the return of political freedom and democratic rule to the Sudan.[88]

The caretaker government, headed by Sirr al-Khatim al-Khalīfa, which took power after the deposition of 'Abbūd in October 1964, was the first nonsectarian government in the history of the independent Sudan. Independent public personalities, as well as representatives of the Communists and of the Muslim Brothers, were prominent in it. This government also turned over a new leaf in its policy by attempting, for the first time, to solve the problem of the South with maximum consideration for the claims of the southerners themselves. It also began a campaign of purging the administration of officials who had shown too much loyalty to the military regime and of others who were described as lacking suitable qualifications. But even during the short period when this government ruled, the influence of the *Anṣār* and the Khatmiyya continued behind the scenes. Ṣādiq al-Mahdī and Dr. Aḥmad al-Sayyid Ḥamād, the representatives of the *Anṣār* and the Khatmiyya in the United National Front – which had been organized against 'Abbūd's regime – censured every activity of the caretaker government and sharply criticized all its failures. It was obviously anticipated that, at the first general elections to be held, power would return to the hands of the traditional forces who had not ceased to argue against the unrepresentative nature of Sirr al-Khatim's government. At the same time, the *Anṣār* feared that power would slip from their fingers as a result of changes in the electoral law and the widening of the constituencies. Indeed, the Trade Unions Federation and the Jazīra Tenants' Organization demanded (with Communist support) that half of the seats in the new Parliament be reserved for them. Similar claims were advanced by the students, who demanded the allocation of special constituencies. A National Front of the Free Professions also arose and declared its intention to stand for election with its own list. The caretaker government did not accede to most of these demands, but even the few that were accepted indicated to the leaders of the traditional parties that continuation of their supremacy was in danger. The students and the professionals were promised several additional special constituencies and, by granting the vote to eighteen year olds (instead of twenty-one), the electorate was increased by some 750,000 new voters of both sexes.

In this state of affairs, when tension between the United National Front of the traditional forces and the Left and its allies reached its peak, the caretaker government resigned in February 1965. The Communists, the People's Democratic party, and their supporters demanded that the office of prime minister be given to their candidate, Chief Justice Bābikr 'Awad Allāh, who had actively participated in the antimilitary coup of October 1964. But the *Anṣār* were not prepared to take the risk of having a hostile government carry out the preparations for general elections. In opposition to the

United National Front of the traditional forces, the Communists, the People's Democratic party, and their followers founded the Social-Democratic Rally, which declared a general strike against what was called "domineering by Islamic parties." This strike was a fiasco, since the Jazīra tenants and the railway workers continued their work – clearly indicating that they were not interested in political conflicts. Thus, it became clear that even in sectors which the Communists considered to be their bastions, their real political influence was minimal. The control of the traditional parties in the new government of Sirr al-Khatim al-Khalīfa was guaranteed, while the Communists had only one minister.[89] In May 1965, as the date of the elections drew near, the Communists and their supporters suggested a postponement. The representatives of the southern districts also opposed the elections since the situation in the South did not permit holding elections. Opposition also came from the People's Democratic party, which, under the influence of the Khatmiyya, decided to boycott the elections. This was probably due, among other reasons, to fear of *Anṣārī* domination and the election of a member of the Mahdī's family to the presidency of the Sudan. The election results showed anew that only the *Umma* and the National Unionist party could win mass support. Out of the 170 seats in the new Parliament, the *Umma* won seventy-six and, together with the fifty-five representatives of al-Azharī's party, was able to rule as it pleased. Among the other parties, the Communists won eleven places – all of them in the special constituencies – and the Islamic Front, composed mainly of the Muslim Brothers, won only five places. For the first time in a long period tribal lists also participated in the elections. Thus, the Beja tribes succeeded in seating ten representatives in Parliament, while the independent list of the Nuba Mountains won nine places.[90] The reasons for the traditional parties' decisive majority are not clear-cut. Apparently, most voters had more faith in the old leadership, based on the religious-political tradition, than in modern parties whose ideology was for the most part alien, and who had proven themselves only as a revolutionary force, but not as capable of ensuring order and solving the problems of the people. Furthermore, the chances of the Communists and even of the Muslim Brothers among the tribal population were slim. Independent tribal lists, like those of the Beja and Nuba, were primarily at the expense of the *Anṣār* and should be regarded as part of the traditional conservative camp. In tribal districts par excellence, such as Dārfūr, the *Anṣār* succeeded in defeating all their opponents – the independent Dārfūr list winning only one seat in Parliament. It appears, therefore, that the combination of Islamic leadership deeply rooted in the population and a mainly tribal and rural society, guaranteed supremacy of the traditional parties in any political confrontation. However, the Communists' achievements should not be regarded as a failure, since the winning of eleven out of the fifteen special graduates' constituencies and polling 17.3% of the total electorate doubtless constituted considerable progress in comparison with the period before 'Abbūd. Communist success may be partly attributed to the People's Democratic party's boycott of the elections, which caused its supporters to split between the Communists and the National Unionist party (NUP) – the latter probably receiving the bulk of Khatmiyya support.

The traditional coalition's regime continued for four additional years. However, after one year its stability had already been undermined, not because of the rise of new forces, but as a result of disagreement among the *Anṣār* themselves. The ascendancy of Ṣādiq al-Mahdī – an Oxford graduate and grandson of the sect's founder – to the rank of political leader of the *Umma* party met increasing opposition from his conservative uncle, al-Hādī al-Mahdī, the religious spiritual leader of the *Anṣār*. In July 1966, Ṣādiq exploited a vote of no-confidence in Parliament in order to overthrow the NUP–*Umma* coalition of al-Azharī and Maḥjūb and established a new government with himself and Mīrghanī Ḥamza at its center – a kind of alliance between the more progressive wings of the *Anṣār* and the Khatmiyya. It is noteworthy that Ḥusayn al-Sharīf al-Hindī, representing the "Third Sayyid's" family, participated in the new government, alongside leading members of the two principal sects, as minister for local government. Al-Ṣādiq's government fell after one year, as a result of the struggle for the presidency, and the conservative wing of the *Anṣār* returned to power. The election campaign of March–April 1968 brought the struggle between the two wings of the *Anṣār* to its peak. The Democratic Unionist party, which united the two Khatmiyya-supported parties (the People's Democratic party and the National Unionist party), for the first time since 1956 now took part in the campaign. Meanwhile, the two factions of the *Umma,* headed respectively by al-Ṣādiq and al-Hādī, competed with each other for support within the *Ansār*. Matters reached the point of bloody clashes between members of the *Anṣār* on Abā Island, the sect's center. The result was an outstanding victory for Khatmiyya-supported representatives, who, for the first time since 1953, won the majority of seats in the general elections. The Democratic Unionist party won 101 places in the new Parliament while the two factions of the *Umma* took only 68. The other parties – which included the Communists, the Muslim

Brothers, two tribal parties, and three representing the South – divided the remaining seats amongst themselves and did not have the power even to form a strong opposition. The new coalition government, headed by Muḥammad Aḥmad Maḥjūb, was again, therefore, a government leaning on the traditional hierarchy of popular Islam, while one wing of the *Anṣār,* headed by al-Ṣādiq, joined the opposition. The 1968 elections were convincing proof that in the political struggle within a parliamentary framework, there was still no power in the Sudan which could undermine the supremacy of the conservative religious political leadership.

Numayrī's coup in May 1969 was, therefore, caused by the fact that the new political forces in the Sudan despaired of ever taking power by legitimate means and attempted, therefore, to break the power centers of popular Islam with the army's help. The revolt thus won the unrestrained support of the Communists and broke out after the *Anṣār* reunited – thereby strengthening even more the power of Islamic leadership. Between May 1969 and March 1970, no less than four attempted revolts were reported from the Sudan. The *Anṣār* and what was called "Sudanese reactionary forces" stood at their center. The most important of these was, without doubt, the attempt of March 1970, which took place in the bastion of the *Anṣār* in Abā Island and which ended in the massacre of approximately twenty-five thousand *Anṣār,* including their leader, al-Hādī al-Mahdī. The ruling military junta's version of the affair was that the *Anṣār,* with the aid of the United States, Israel, and other imperialistic powers had attempted to destroy the Sudanese revolution. However, it seems somewhat more likely that, since all other means of destroying the bearers of religious-political power had failed, it was decided to annihilate them physically. Did the military succeed where the politicians failed? It would be presumptuous to venture an answer, the matter depending on the stability and unity of the military regime and on its political acumen. A wrong step in the direction of unification with Egypt or in the solution of the southern problem could reverse everything and bring the traditional political forces back into power for a third time.[91]

CONCLUSION

Despite the many changes which occurred, tribal society in the Sudan was preserved due to geo-political, economic, and social factors. Up to the Turco–Egyptian conquest, the tribe was an administrative-economic unit whose importance was only emphasized by the weakness of central government. Economic backwardness of the Sudan during the nineteenth and twentieth century prevented the disintegration of the tribe in spite of the creation of a modern state frame. Furthermore, because of political considerations by the three regimes which ruled the Sudan up to independence, the tribe was made into an administrative unit which the government was interested in preserving. However, the decline of the tribes as a political force, especially during the period of the Condominium, derived from the mistaken assumption that a strengthening of the tribal heads' authority was possible even under a strong central administration. The viewing of the *shaykhs* as docile administrative clerks to be dismissed and appointed according to criteria of efficiency and obedience brought about their decline as an independent political power. Conversely, the preservation of the tribes as socio-economic units was due to their remoteness from the centers of government, poor communications, lack of economic incentives, and, hence, a slow process of urbanization. If we add to this that, during the whole period, only very small budgets were allocated to expanding the educational system amongst the tribal population, it will be understood that undermining of the tribe from inside, by its own younger generation, was largely prevented, since those tribal members who received a modern education generally left for the cities and integrated into the urban intelligentsia, though in many cases they upheld their links with their tribes.

The only attempt of tribal heads to organize as a political power during the Anglo–Egyptian rule failed completely. The Socialist Republican party, established in 1951 to give back to the tribes some of their political influence, discovered very quickly that even amongst the tribes themselves the power of the popular Islamic leadership, and especially of the *Anṣār*, was greater than that of the tribal heads insofar as political representation of the tribes in the state was concerned. The repeated attempts since independence to arrive at a tribal-political organization only serve to strengthen this conclusion. Although groups of non-Arab tribes, such as the Beja and the Nuba, occasionally succeeded in winning representation in Parliament, this did not endanger the supremacy of the religious-political forces which reigned supreme in every parliamentary confrontation. What, therefore, is the uniqueness of popular Islam and from whence its political supremacy in Sudanese society, preserved despite the changes of time?

First of all, it is noteworthy that the importance of popular Islam in other Muslim countries, even in those near the Sudan, such as Egypt and Libya, is recognizable up to the present day – although its status is not identical to that in the Sudan. Popular Islam's source of strength in the Sudan derives from the manner by which Islam penetrated the area. It was further strengthened by its prolonged isolation from centers of institutionalized Islam, by the primitive social character of the Sudanese population, and the development of the *Anṣār* (after their military-political defeat in 1898) from a puritan *jihād* movement into a so-called legitimate branch of popular Islam. The rise of popular Islam in the Sudan to dominant political power in the twentieth century is also due to a number of causes. As in other Muslim countries under their rule, the British authorities in the Sudan sought to avoid active and visible interference in all matters concerning religion. Since institutionalized Islam of the al-Azhar type was viewed by the authorities as the arm of anti-British Egyptian nationalism, popular Islam, following an initial period of suspicion, became the natural ally of the British rulers. The same causes also motivated British suspicions of the young Sudanese intelligentsia, which, partly because of educational policies during the Condominium, remained too weak to combat the traditional power centers. The fact that the small Ṣūfī orders did not become involved independently in the political struggle, as well as the outstanding leadership qualities of the two Sayyids, permitted concentration of all forces in the competition between the Khatmiyya and the *Anṣār* and centralized the tribes and the young political parties around the popular Islamic leadership. This last point is especially important since it can explain the changes which occurred in the political disposition of the two traditional power centers – the tribes and popular Islam. When the tribe lost its political power, it sought the protection of the religious order to which it belonged. The tribal population had no need for modern political parties centered in the towns and headed by university graduates. The tribe as a social-economic frame and the popular Islamic order as a focus for religious and political loyalty fulfilled the needs of most of the Sudanese tribal population up to the present time. Herein lies the advantage in the political status of the *Anṣār* over that of the Khatmiyya, in that the *Anṣār's* main power was derived from the tribal population, while the Khatmiyya, though also enjoying tribal backing, had its main support from the urban population, forcing it to compete with new political factors, some of which were the products of secondary and higher education. The latter could not see any contradition between their traditional adherence to a Ṣūfī order and giving their political loyalties elsewhere – for example, to al-Azharī's National Unionist party, or even to the Communists.

Since the Sudan won its independence in January 1956, the supremacy of popular Islam in the field of politics has been even more noticeable than in preceding periods. The parliamentary election campaigns – both before the ʿAbbūd revolt in 1958 and after the return of parliamentary rule in 1964 – showed, again and again, that without far-reaching economic and social changes, there is no force in the Sudan capable of standing up against the centers of religious-political power. The military revolt of 1958 was carried out with the tacit agreement of the religious leadership and even won the support of the Khatmiyya. The ʿAbbūd regime's ban on political parties did little damage to the centers of popular Islam and hence the renewed supremacy of the *Anṣār* and Khatmiyya since the general elections of May 1965. The extent to which this supremacy has been undermined during Numayrī's regime is a matter of conjecture. There is no doubt that political neutralization of the leaders of popular Islam since the May 1969 coup and the massacre of the *Anṣār* in March 1970 have undermined the traditional political organizations considerably. However, no clear-cut stand can be taken since Numayrī's regime also affected other political forces such as the Communists, and the ultimate political map of the Sudan depends, inter alia, on the longevity of the present regime and on its policy in the future.

NOTES

1 H.A. MacMichael, *A History of the Arabs in the Soudan,* 2nd impression (London, 1967), lists more than fifty tribes who claim to be of Arab origin.

2 For a detailed description of the "holy families," see P.M. Holt, *Holy Families and Islam in the Sudan,* Princeton Near East Papers, no. 4 (1967); see also P.M. Holt, "The Sons of Jābir and their Kin: A Clan of Sudanese Religious Notables," *Bulletin of the School of Oriental and African Studies* 30 (1967): 142–57. Islam penetrated Dārfūr from three different directions: West Africa, the Nile Valley, and the Arabian Peninsula. The heads of the "holy families" played a central role in this process too. For details, see: R.S. O'Fahey, "Saints and Sultans: The Role of Muslim Holy Men in the Keira Sultanate of Dār Fūr (Paper presented to the A.S.A.U.K. Conference, School of Oriental and African Studies, University of London, September 1971).

3 R. Hill, *Egypt in the Sudan 1820–1881* (London, 1959), p. 96; P.M. Holt, *A Modern History of the Sudan* (London, 1961), pp. 49–52.

4 For examples relating to the tribes of Kordofan and Dārfūr, see S.M. Nur, "A Critical Edition of the Memoirs of Yūsuf Mikhā'īl" (Ph.D. diss., University of London, 1963); R.C. Slatin, *Fire and Sword in the Sudan* (London, 1896), p. 93.

5 Na'ūm Shuqayr, *Ta'rīkh al-Sūdān al-qadīm wa'l-hadīth wajughrafiyatuhu* (Cairo, n.d. [1903]) 3: 109–12.

6 See, for example, Talal Asad, *The Kababish Arabs* (London, 1970), pp. 158–60: see also Slatin, pp. 153–6, who tells about the split in the leadership of the Rizayqāt, one of the important Baqqāra tribes in Dārfūr.

7 *Fakī* – a corruption of *faqīh* (jurist); meaning in colloquial Sudanese Arabic both teacher, whether of religion or Sufism, as well as healer, holder of religious (usually Ṣūfī) office, and a variety of other functions.

8 Holt, *Holy Families,* pp. 4–5.

9 *Anṣār,* supporters, was the name originally given to the Prophet's supporters at Medina. In the Sudan, the Mahdi called his supporters *anṣār* when he fled from the Nile to the Nuba Mountains in September 1881. The name was revived by Sayyid 'Abd al-Raḥmān, the Mahdi's son, when he started to organize his religio-political movement during World War I.

10 Shuqayr, 3:112; 'Abd Allāh 'Alī Ibrāhīm, *al-Sirā' bayn al-mahdī wa'l-'ulamā'* (Khartoum, 1968), p. 8.

11 Lieutenant Colonel Stewart, *Report on the Soudan* (Khartoum, 9 February, 1883) C. 3670.

12 'Abd Allāh 'Alī Ibrāhīm, pp. 22–43.

13 *Manshūrāt al-imām al-mahdī* (Khartoum, 1964), 2; P.M. Holt, *The Mahdist State in the Sudan, 1881–1898* (London, 1958), pp. 41–2.

14 *Waqā'i' Uthmān Diqna* (Khartoum, 1964).

15 Shuqayr, 3: 354.

16 Holt, *The Mahdist State,* pp. 130–1.

17 Ibid., pp. 141–6.

18 Ibid., pp. 135–6.

19 Major F.R. Wingate, D.S.O., A.A.G., *General Military Report on the Egyptian Sudan, 1891* (War Office, London, 1892), compiled from statements made by Father Ohrwalder.
20 *General Report on the Egyptian Soudan, March 1895,* compiled from statements made by Slatin Pasha.
21 Memorandum presented to Lord Cromer, 4 April 1897, signed Sirdar, Sudan Archive Durham (hereafter cited as SAD) 266/1/1.
22 Memorandum to Mudirs, enclosure in no. 1, Cromer to Salisbury, 17 March 1899, FO/78/5022.
23 *Ma'mūr* was the title used by the Egyptian government for the official in charge of a *ma'mūriyya,* a subdivision of a province (also *markaz* or *qism*).
24 G. Warburg, *The Sudan under Wingate* (London, 1971), pp. 137–54; see also below.
25 *Sudan Government Memoranda:* a) *General Administrative Policy;* b) *The Powers of Village Sheikhs,* (Khartoum, n.d.).
26 Sir Harold MacMichael, *The Anglo–Egyptian Sudan* (London, 1934), pp. 243–57.
27 Lloyd to Chamberlain, 30 April, 1929; FO 371/13875; for details see below.
28 Maffey to Loraine, 18 July 1930, FO 371/14565.
29 Sir James Currie, "The Educational Experiment in the Anglo–Egyptian Sudan," *Journal of the African Society* 34 (1935): 49.
30 *Nāẓir 'umūm* – inspector general, administrative title given to the head *shaykh* of nomadic or seminomadic tribes who was charged with carrying out government policy within his tribe, mainly in the fields of taxation and justice.
31 See, for example, Talal Asad pp. 171–7; see also I. Cunnison, *Baggara Arabs, Power and Lineage in a Sudanese Arab Tribe* (London, 1966), pp. 134–6.
32 Sir Angus Gillan, "Note on the Future of the Mamur," 31 December, 1928 (private papers of Sir Angus Gillan).
33 See pp. 260-265.
34 Creed to Gillan (private), 1 April 1947, enclosing "Draft First Report by the Sudan Administration Conference" (private papers of Sir Angus Gillan); see also K.D.D. Henderson, *Sudan Republic* (London, 1965), pp. 89–90.
35 K.D.D. Henderson, "Nationalism in the Sudan," SAD 478/3.
36 For details see G. Warburg, "Religious Policy in the Northern Sudan: 'Ulamā' and Sūfism 1899–1918," *Asian and African Studies* 7 (1971): 89–119.
37 Enclosure in Wingate to Milner, 31 August, 1919, SAD 204/1.
38 Warburg, "Religious Policy . . .", pp. 114–19.
39 Stack to Wingate, 3 July 1919, SAD 237/11; see also Norman Daniel, "The Sudan," in *Islam in Africa,* (eds.). J. Kritzeck and W.H. Lewis (New York, 1969), pp. 202–13.
40 Report of Assistant Director of Intelligence, Khartoum, 14 March, 1919, (very secret) FO 371/3716.
41 L.O.F. Stack, "Note on the Growth of National Aspirations in the Sudan," enclosed in Wingate to Milner, 31 August, 1919, SAD 204/1.
42 *Egyptian Gazette,* 5 May, 1922.

43 Davies to More (private), 20 September, 1924, FO 141/669.
44 R. Davies, "Memorandum on the Policy of the Sudan Government towards the Mahdist Cult," *Secret Intelligence Report,* no. 7, Khartoum, 11 December, 1926, FO 371/11613.
45 Craig to More, 15 September 1924, FO 141/669.
46 N. Henderson, "Report on the Sudan," May 1925, FO 371/10905.
47 For details on the political development of the nationalist movement during this period, see Muddathir 'Abd al-Raḥīm, *Imperialism and Nationalism in the Sudan* (London, 1969), pp. 89–134.
48 Lloyd to Chamberlain (private), 26 February 1926, FO 800/259 "Memorandum on the Policy of the Sudan Government towards the Mahdist Cult," *Secret Intelligence Report,* no. 7, FO 371/11613.
49 *Secret Intelligence Report,* no. 9, FO 372/11614. This provides a partial explanation of the weakness of the *Anṣār* in the Sudanese army, especially among the officers, after independence.
50 Archer to Lloyd (secret), 2 April 1926, (including twelve enclosures), FO 371/11612.
51 "Note on Meeting at the Palace," ibid.
52 Appendix in *Secret Intelligence Report,* no. 9, FO 371/11614.
53 C.I.D. minutes of 220th meeting, 24 February 1927, FO 371/12374.
54 *Sudan Intelligence Report, 1926,* FO 371/11614.
55 *Secret Intelligence Report,* no. 3, May 1926, FO 371/11613. The organization was dissolved a month later when its leaders found that their activities were not favored by the authorities, *Secret Intelligence Report,* no. 4, June 1926, FO 371/11613.
56 Bābikr Badrī, *Ta'rīkh ḥayātī* (Omdurman, 1961), 3: 41. According to Badrī, the split between the Shawqiyyīn and the Fīliyyīn – the denominations of the two camps, derived from the names of their leaders – was the result of the differences between the two Sayyids, encouraged by the British Administration.
57 Ibid., p. 102.
58 "Note on Post-Treaty Egyptian Relations" (secret), Civil Secretary's Department, Khartoum, 27 May 1938 (private papers of Sir Angus Gillan).
59 Details of the political struggle are described by Muddathir 'Abd al-Raḥīm, pp. 125–32; an elaborate discussion of this topic will be found in my forthcoming study on Popular Islam, Nationalism and Communism in the Sudan.
60 *Report of the Governor General on the Administration, Finance and Conditions in the Sudan in 1945* (Sudan no. 1, 1948) CMD-7316.
61 Bābikr Badrī, 3:72.
62 Ibid., p. 67; see also Henderson, *Sudan Republic,* pp. 94–7.
63 *Report of the Governor General on the Administration, Finance and Conditions in the Sudan in 1947* (Sudan no. 1, 1949) CMD-7835.
64 Henderson, *Sudan Republic,* p. 97.
65 J.S.R. Duncan, *The Sudan: a Record of Achievement* (Edinburgh, 1952), pp. 248–51.
66 Henderson, *Sudan Republic,* pp. 101–2.

67 Henderson, "Nationalism in the Sudan," SAD 478/3.
68 Duncan, p. 175.
69 "Note on Political Parties in the Sudan," Civil Secretary's Office (Khartoum, 19 April 1953).
70 Henderson, *Sudan Republic,* pp. 104–7.
71 *Ahrām,* 2 January 1956.
72 Daniel, p. 206; on the relationships of the Communists and the Muslim Brothers with the Khatmiyya and the *Anṣār,* see Muddathir 'Abd al-Raḥīm, pp. 133–4.
73 *Weekly Review,* 17 May 1958.
74 Henderson, *Sudan Republic,* p. 225; see also H. Shaked, E. Souery, and G. Warburg, "The Communist Party in the Sudan" (Paper presented to the Conference on the Soviet Union and the Middle East, Tel Aviv University, 26–30 December 1971).
75 *Ahrām,* 27 June 1956.
76 *Al-Sūdān al-jadīd,* 16 January 1957; *al-Jumhūriyya,* 14 May 1957.
77 *Al-Sūdān al-jadīd,* 8–14 September 1957.
78 *Ahrām,* 2, 7, 9 June 1958; *Weekly Review,* 26 April 1958; *The Middle East and North Africa 1970–71* (London, 1971), p. 658.
79 First statement following coup d'etat, 17 November 1958, quoted from English translation in Hisham B. Sharabi, *Nationalism and Revolution in the Arab World* (Princeton, 1966), p. 169.
80 Henderson, *Sudan Republic,* p. 130.
81 *Sudan Weekly,* 4 April 1958; 9 May 1958; BBC (Arabic), 10 November 1959.
82 *Al-Ayām,* 18 May 1960, quoted in *Middle East Record 1960* (hereafter cited as *MER*), p. 415.
83 *Reuter,* 30 November 1960, in *MER, 1960* p. 417.
84 *Daily Telegraph,* 12 April 1961, in *MER, 1961*, p. 469.
85 *Al-Hayāt,* 12 July 1961, in *MER, 1961,* p. 473.
86 *Al-Hayāt,* 25 August 1961, in *MER, 1961,* p. 470.
87 *Al-Sūdān al-jadīd,* 18 April 1961; *MER, 1961,* pp. 408, 417.
88 *Middle East Mirror,* 21 October 1961; see also Yusuf Fadl Ḥasan, "The Sudanese Revolution of October 1964," *The Journal of Modern African Studies* 5, no. 4 (1967): 491–509.
89 S.R. Smirnov, ed., *A History of Africa 1918–1967* (Moscow, 1968), pp. 174–5; Henderson, *Sudan Republic,* pp. 213–16.
90 Ibid., p. 225.
91 For details on the confrontation between Numayrī's regime and the Communists in 1970–71, see H. Shaked, E. Souery, and G. Warburg, "The Communist Party in the Sudan."

MILITARY COUPS D'ETAT IN THE ARAB WORLD DURING THE SIXTIES

ELIEZER BE'ERI

The military coup is a common event in the Arab world of the twentieth century. This fact has been recognized by many historians, sociologists, and political commentators of various schools, who have described and analyzed it from various points of view. Although the Arab world is not the only region in which military coups are frequent and habitual, most Arab governments have come to power as a result of military coups, and their principal, or exclusive, support is derived from the army. All this has been sufficiently established and needs no further proof.

This paper seeks to provide an answer mainly to the following questions: whether the military coups in Arab countries during the sixties differ from, or resemble, previous military coups; what are the differences and the similarities; can a stabilizing tendency, a process of development, or, perhaps, a new historical course be discerned?

I shall define some concepts, summarize previous research in the field, and discuss the pattern of the military coup.

DEFINITIONS

"The sixties": This period has been arbitrarily defined as approximately the last ten years before the writing of this paper. The period covers the nine years following Syria's secession from the union with Egypt until 'Abd al-Nāṣir's death, from 28 September 1961 to 28 September 1970, and these two events can be regarded as delimiting the "sixties" in the Middle East.

In this context, the "fifties" will denote the 12½ years following Husnī Za'īm's coup in Syria (the first Arab military coup after World War II) until Syria's secession from the union with Egypt, i.e., the span between the events in Damascus from 30 March 1949 to 28 September 1961.

"The Arab World" defines all member states of the Arab League and all other countries in which Arabic is the official and spoken language, from Oman to Morocco.

"Coup d'état," "revolution," and "revolt" are common terms for the overthrow of an existing regime and the establishment of another by violence or threats of violence.[1] Furthermore, they may either succeed in toppling the regime or entail the defeat of the insurrectionists. The borderlines between these three forms of rebellion are vague: a revolt may turn into a revolution, and a coup may be the beginning of a revolution, or a stage in a revolution. Furthermore, opinions differ widely with regard to the definition and evaluation of such events. Nevertheless, we must discern clear distinctions between the three types of insurrection. This is not merely a matter of semantics, but is essential to understanding the social nature of the phenomenon and its place in history.

A revolution is a basic and all-embracing change of the socio-political regime; it is an expression and result of activity by the masses. A coup d'état is a surprising, sudden change of regime by the action of a small group of rebels. A revolt is an uprising of an ethnic, social, or political group aimed at changing its status, without aspiring to basic changes in the existing regime.

A recent and typical example of a revolt is the uprising of the National Liberation Front in Ceylon, which began on 5 April 1971. A fortnight after the outbreak, the commander in chief of the government troops estimated the number of active rebel fighters at approximately two thousand.[2] They were active in the central and southern parts of the island, and about one hundred kilometers from the capital, Colombo, and the regime's headquarters. In the Middle East, the 1925 insurrection of the Druze in Syria can be regarded as a typical revolt – though of no bearing upon the substance of this inquiry. None have claimed, or are likely to claim, that the events of 23 July 1952 in Cairo, 14 July 1958 in Baghdad, 8 March 1963 in Damascus, or any of the numerous similar occurrences in the present-day Arab world were revolts. The initiators of these events define them as "revolutions," their opponents consider them "coups d'état," and thus the opinions of political observers differ.

Essential to a revolution is the element of mass activity. The seizure of power is neither its beginning nor its essence, and even less its consummation.

The political leadership of a revolution presents itself at the head of the movement, defines its aims, organizes, and directs; but it does not create the movement. The leadership draws support from a wide public, or from the masses it activates, with whom it maintains close contact. Here lies the revolution's power and momentum, and this is its essence. The storming of the Bastille preceded reform of the French Constitution, just as strikes and land seizures by peasants in Russia preceded the overthrow of the Tsar.

In contrast, the principal element of a coup d'état, or a *putsch,* is the seizure of power; sometimes, it is the coup's sole purpose. A coup d'état is not a movement, but an operation; it is not a process, but an event; and the decisive factor in its success is not persistence, but surprise. This is achieved by secrecy in preparation, and this secrecy is maintained by strictly limiting the circle of conspirators, planners, and executors. The public takes no part and remains passive, like the audience of a show. Like an audience, too, the public is expected to applaud at the end of the performance.

A revolution or a revolt may start in a faraway province or a rural region; a coup d'état takes place in the capital. There have been coups in provincial cities, such as the *putsch* of ʻAbd al-Wahhāb Shawwāf – March 1959 in Mosul (no. 12 in the Appendix); that of Jāsim ʻAlwān – April 1962 at Aleppo (no. 19); that of ʻĀrif ʻAbd al-Razzāq – June 1966 in Mosul (no. 30); and of Salīm Ḥāṭūm and Ṭalāl Abū ʻAsalī, who arrested the Syrian president and chief of staff on the Israeli front in September 1966 (no. 31). Not only were these exceptional cases, but they all failed, and their initiators were either arrested, killed, or forced to escape. A coup d'état which does not immediately and directly hit the center of government is almost certainly going to fail. In this sense, a *putsch* is the very opposite of guerrilla warfare. The typical coup is the sudden, swift, crushing strike into the heart of the regime. Its primary aim is the overthrow of the titular head – king, prime minister, president, or army commander – by arrest, assassination, or dismissal and the seizure of central power centers, such as army headquarters, the central airport, the radio station, and the main post office.[3] Since a *putsch* is aimed at the regime's center, the most vulnerable regimes are those with the highest degree of centralization.

A military coup is carried out by military plotters using armed power. Sometimes the threat of the use of military power without its real activation is enough to carry out a successful coup. Due to the very essence of the *putsch* most of these operations in various parts of the world have been purely military coups, or in which civilians cooperated with army conspirators. In coup-stricken Latin America, some have been carried out by civilian political groups without military participation. In the Middle East, however, all coups, successful or not, were either purely, or mainly, military.

In the ideology and historiography of Arab regimes established by coup d'état of officer-politicians, the definition outlined above finds no recognition. The events and actions for the seizure of power are defined and termed "revolution," and the regimes pretend to regard themselves as "revolutionary." The most honored and prestigious title aspired to by public figures in the Arab world during the sixties was the adjective "revolutionary." In the most popular self-view of modern Arab history, the seizure of power in Egypt by the Free Officers on 23 July 1952 is regarded as a crucial event in the annals of the Middle East. The event is called a "revolution" by most Arabs and, as such, is seen as the model for the national and social liberation of Arab society – initiating a new era, like the French revolution in 1789 and the Russian revolution of 1917.

The stormers of the Bastille in 1789 and the Bolsheviks in 1917 regarded themselves in the very act as perpetrators of a revolution; but the Egyptian officers of 1952 did not regard themselves in this light. The term "revolution" (*thawra*) had not previously been in common usage with them. In the first announcement, "awakening" (*nahḍa*) and the "blessed movement of the army" were mentioned. The decree dissolving political parties on 18 January 1953 was issued by the commander in chief of the armed forces, who was the supreme authority in the state as "head of the army movement." Only in February 1953 was the concept "revolution" introduced, with the foundation of the Revolutionary Command Council.[4] Since then it is common – not only among Arabs – to consider these events revolutions.

We shall return to the question of *putsch* and revolution in the present-day Arab world. Though in defining the concept, agreement is easily reached, there still is widespread disagreement in assessing the concrete historical and political phenomena.

THE SIXTIES IN THE WORLD

The indirect influence – as a model and example – of military coups in the world on Arab military coups has been minor and barely recognizable. While there may be some similarity with coups in Latin America, the origins of the Arab ones are not based on conscious study, transfer of ideas, and methods of operation from there, nor on any tangible contacts between the personalities or groups involved. Rather, similar social conditions stimulate similar reactions – just as a certain type of soil and climate will produce similar vegetation in regions far apart.

Nevertheless, the influence of the world political atmosphere on trends and actions in the Middle East should not be disregarded. If, in the thirties of this century, armies had refrained from interfering with politics anywhere, it would have been highly unlikely that groups of officers would plan coups and seize power in our area, as actually happened in Iraq, the first independent Arab state. Consequently, the study of military coups in neighboring regions during the sixties is relevant to an understanding of events in the Arab world during the same period.

Nineteen sixty was the "African Year". Until 1953 there were only three sovereign African states south of the Sahara: Ethiopia, Liberia, and South Africa. In 1958 Guinea achieved independence and sovereignty, and between 1960 and 1970, thirty-one states followed. With independence, the military coups began. Between 1960 and 1969 there were twenty-four military coups in sixteen of the African states which had become independent during the sixties: 1960, Congo-Kinshasa (now Zaire); 1963, Togo and Dahomey; 1964, Uganda, Kenya, and Gabon; 1965, Congo-Kinshasa and Dahomey; 1966, Central African Republic, Upper Volta, Nigeria, Ghana, Congo-Brazzaville, Togo, and Burundi; in 1967, Togo, Sierra Leone, Ghana, and Dahomey; 1968, Congo-Brazzaville and Mali; 1969, Somalia and Mali. This list includes both successful and unsuccessful coups, but not revolts in one or the other military unit. Four of the African states appear twice: the two Congos, Mali and Ghana. Togo and Dahomey appear three times. They are the states which initiated this wave of frequent military coups in Africa subsequent to 1963. In mid-1967, a military man who ruled in cooperation with a few other officers and civilians was at the head of one out of every four former colonies. These included Sierra Leone, Upper Volta, Dahomey, Togo, Ghana, Nigeria, Congo-Kinshasa, the Central African Republic, and Burundi.

It is rather impossible to point out a common denominator for the nature of society, economy, or politics of these states. Graded by various developmental critera, these heterogeneous countries range from highest to lowest in Africa. Regimes overthrown by the military range from the Pan-Africanism of Ghana – militant, socialist, and with a revolutionary trend – to that of Yameogo's Upper Volta – with the orientation of a satellite state. These nine countries include the most populated (Congo-Kinshasa) and least populated states (such as Togo, Dahomey, and Burundi). At the time of the military regime's establishment, they included the biggest and most professional armies in tropical Africa, as well as the smallest, run by recently promoted noncommissioned officers.[5]

The similarity between events in different parts of the world and various regimes could stimulate comparison and generalization, which in turn might lead to the formulation of so-called "rules," the substance and real content of which would be very limited. Furthermore, the identification of common aspects often blurs the distinctive and specific characteristics of each event in every country.

It should thus be clear that, apart from the similarities, there are also great differences between military interference in the politics of Arab countries and that in the new states of tropical Africa. One example will illustrate our point: Togo.

Togo gained independence in April 1960. This country of one and a half million inhabitants always had a very small army, initially consisting of only two companies.[6] In the mid-sixties, the army had one infantry regiment and auxiliary units of 1,200 men, a navy with 250 men, and 1,300 policemen.[7] At the end of the sixties the strength of the army remained almost unchanged, at some 1,500.[8] The smallness of this force did not prevent the military coups of 1963 and 1967. Moreover, the army itself implemented the coup of 1963 and was also the principal ground and object of the struggle.

At the end of 1962, President Sylvanus Olympio, on financial grounds, decided to further reduce the tiny army. At the same time, some seven hundred Togoans, mercenaries (privates, corporals, and sergeants) in the French army of Algeria, were dismissed from the service, following that country's independence in July 1962, and returned to Togo. They hoped for, and insisted on, making their living as professional soldiers in their homeland, which in the meantime had also become independent. However, Olympio had not merely tried to reduce the army for allegedly financial reasons, but also had an aversion to these mercenaries who had served in the army of a European colonial power.[9] There could have been other motives of suspicion among various tribes. In any case, the ex-mercenaries, with part of the army, organized and executed a coup d'état on 13 January 1963. Olympio was assassinated, his brother-in-law Nicolas Grunitzky became president, and the soldiers discharged from the French army were admitted to that of Togo.[10] Grunitzky's presidency was dependent on army support, and on 13 January 1967 he was overthrown by a second military coup. In April 1967 the colonel who had been the actual initiator of the 1963 coup, Colonel Eyadema, became president – a position he still holds.

The example of Togo illustrates the differences in circumstances, purpose, and result of military coups in different countries, the extent of the deviation from similar events in the Arab world, and the caution to be applied in deducing rules and avoiding unfounded generalizations. It is a fact, however, that interference by the armed forces led by their commanders determined the course of history in various parts of the world during the sixties. The future of some states was not decided democratically, nor by revolution, but by a military coup d'état.

In non-Arab states of the eastern Mediterranean, Turkey and Greece, the army also intervened decisively in political life during this period. Turkey had a democratic regime, which, though not ideal, was based on elections and freedom of political association after the victory of the Democratic party in the May 1950 elections. In May 1960, however, Cemal Gürsel, at the head of a group of senior officers, launched a successful coup d'état. Since then, Turkey swings between rule by an officers' cadre and the reestablishment of parties and parliamentarianism, followed by renewed intervention of the army, and so on – up to the stage of military action, which forced Süleyman Demirel's government to retire in March 1971. In Greece there was a military coup on 21 April 1967. Since then a group of officers rules the country draconically.

There is no proof that the coups and other military interference in Turkey and Greece directly influenced similar events in Arab countries. The plotters and executioners of Arab military coups had no need of foreign inspiration, since they found more than enough precedents at home. It could, however, be assumed that the state of mind and patterns of operation elsewhere consciously encouraged similar trends and means. Furthermore, it could be expected that public opinion, both at home and abroad, would accept the facts thus established.

It is, therefore, legitimate to ask if it was indeed mere coincidence that the sixties, rich with military interventions in the political life of the adjacent regions, were also years of frequent and intensive army action in the political life of the Arab world.

ARAB MILITARY COUPS DURING THE SIXTIES

Frequency

The most remarkable aspect is the increased frequency of military coups.* [11] In the 12½ years of the fifties, there were 14 coups; in the 9 years of the sixties, this rose to 26. Between Zaʿīm's coup in Syria in

* See Appendix.

March 1949 (no. 1) and 'Alī Hāmid's coup in November 1959 (no. 14), the average rate was one coup every nine months. After Syria's secession from the United Arab Republic in September (no. 15), until the *putsch* in Libya in September 1969 (no. 40), the average rate was a coup every four months. Whereas it would be unwise to deduce generalized conclusions from such limited data, it can nevertheless be asserted that the phenomenon of army intervention in Arab politics, eminent during the fifties, increased greatly in the sixties.

Domains

Army interference was also geographically more widespread, and military coups were staged in more countries. Before World War II, a military coup occurred in only one Arab country – Iraq.[12] It was the first Arab state outside the Arabian Peninsula to gain independence and was also the first to have a military coup.

Between 1949 and 1951 military coups were restricted to Syria. Damascus takes pride in being the "heart of Arabism," and, indeed, with regard to the frequency of military coups, it occupies first place. Of the forty military coups which occurred during the fifties and sixties, fifteen were in Syria.

In 1952 Egypt entered the circle. Following the struggle in 1954, when Najīb was removed, Nasser's regime achieved a stability maintained throughout the sixties, and until his death. Whether the Egyptian regime of the sixties was still a military dictatorship will be discussed elsewhere.

In 1957 'Alī Abū Nuwār's abortive coup took place in Jordan (no. 9). Its failure excluded that country from the circle of states experiencing military coups for the entire fifties and sixties.

In 1958 another coup took place in Iraq. Nūrī Sa'īd's regime, which had put an end to military coups at the time of Hitler and the "golden square" in 1941, was ousted by Qāsim. Since then, there have been seven more military coups in Iraq.

In 1958, Sudan – as if to intimate coming events in Africa – joined the circle and has remained a country of repeated military coups.

Syria, Iraq, and Egypt may be regarded as central to the policy and ideology of Arab nationalism and as the leading staging points for military coups. The Sudanese coup in November 1958 heralded the spread of the phenomenon beyond its original confines, and in this sense the sixties were the years of extension: south to Yemen since 1962 and the Popular Republic of Southern Yemen in 1968; west to Algeria in 1965; Libya in 1969; and to other non-African Arab states.

NEW COUNTRIES

It is most significant that (as noted above) three more Arab countries, namely, Yemen, Algeria, and Libya, entered the coup circle in the sixties. All three, Yemen, Algeria, and Libya, lie outside the geographical center located between Iraq and Egypt. The characteristics of these coups and subsequent developments differed in each of these countries.

Much has been written about the coup d'état in Yemen on 26 September 1962.[13] This event can be regarded as a link in the chain of conspiracies and attempts on the ruler's life, coups, clashes between Zaydis and Shafi'is, rivalries among various tribes, and other violent struggles which characterize Yemeni history. This coup, however, was basically new in two ways: politically, since it established a republic; and socio-politically, since the generators and implementers were modern army officers.

The coup was not sufficiently effective to tip the scales of power, and a protracted civil war erupted in Yemen, which soon turned into a conflict between Yemenites and Egyptians. Egypt first dispatched an army to assist the republican forces – also faced with Saudi Arabian support of the royalists. However, Yemeni weakness, together with the Egyptian takeover, soon produced a situation in which Sallāl assisted the Egyptians, not vice versa.

Following the Six Day War and the Khartoum Conference (29 August – 1 September 1967), the Egyptians were forced to evacuate Yemen, and Sallāl became powerless. On 5 November 1967, when Sallāl was in Baghdad – on his way to the celebrations of the Bolshevik revolution's anniversary in Moscow – a military coup deposed him. Two colonels and a few lieutenant-colonels came to the presidential palace, the Ministry of Interior, and the radio station and announced Sallāl's removal from all offices and the establishment of a new regime.[14] The coup was carried out without a single shot being fired. It was nonetheless clear that the coup's success was a direct result of the military nature of the operation. As in many other cases of military coups, the threat of military force sufficed to paralyze the opponents.

Upon the Egyptian retreat and Sallāl's removal, the republican regime at once became stabilized. Though there were political upheavals, the Imam's regime was not to be renewed. In this respect Sallāl's coup, and that of the officers who deposed him, brought about basic change.[15]

In Algeria the circumstances of army intervention differed. Algeria became independent in July 1962. Until that time, French oppression greatly contributed to Algerian unity, though the country was rampant with intrigue. With the French withdrawal, the existing inner conflicts became further aggravated and almost led to civil war in the first three months of independence. Algeria, which had just provided every freedom lover in the world with a model war of liberation, suddenly turned into an arena of internecine conflict among groups of plotters, who attempted to camouflage their personal ambitions with the terminology of revolutionary ideas.

From this struggle, Ahmad Ben Bella emerged victorious, and on 27 September 1962 he became prime minister, and the new era began with a personality cult and dictatorship. Ben Bella's actual takeover was supported by the Algerian army and its commander, Col. Houari Boumedienne. During the Algerian revolt, two anti-French armies were formed: the interior army, or guerrilla forces, and the exterior army, or regular forces. The interior army comprised approximately ninety thousand men at the end of the war.[16] Its capacity was limited to irregular warfare; administratively and politically, it was divided into six practically independent units, and the discipline as a whole was weak. The exterior army comprised twenty-five thousand men in Tunisia and another fifteen thousand in Morocco. Since the French sealed off the borders this army was prevented from entering Algeria and participating in the fighting. Colonel Boumedienne, the army's organizer and commander, succeeded in training his troops into a regular force. When entering Algeria after the war, this army had no battle experience and was not covered with glory. It had, however, the capability to decide the internal situation, and Boumedienne, with his army, supported Ben Bella. In the latter's first cabinet, the colonel became minister of defense; and in two subsequent cabinets he rose to deputy prime minister, in addition to retaining the defense portfolio. Ben Bella turned the limelight upon himself, while his regime actually depended on Boumedienne and the army. While gradually occupying all major offices and positions – president of the republic, prime minister, secretary general of the party, and supreme commander of the armed forces – Ben Bella also removed all other national leaders, but failed to halt the purge before it reached Boumedienne. When the latter realized that his turn was near, he decided that, if one of the two leaders were to go, it would be the boastful Ben Bella, and not the taciturn soldier.

At half-past three in the morning on 19 June 1965 a small military unit with a few tanks occupied Ben Bella's residence and dispatched him to a remote desert place of confinement far from the capital. At 8 A.M. the radio station and at 8:15 the airport were taken over. At noon the "message of the Revolutionary Council" was broadcast to proclaim Algeria's new leader to his people and to the world.[17]

The coup resembled a similar operation by Husnī Za'īm in Damascus of March 1949. Minimal military force ensured secrecy and surprise; late at night a swift and powerful blow struck the heart of the regime without involving any part of the civilian population. The result was complete success, without bloodshed or resistance.

Ben Bella's fall astonished the world, especially 'Abd al-Nāṣir and the Egyptians, who were completely mistaken in their evaluation. The surprise was especially great since international attention had been focused on Algeria during that particular week: on 25 June 1965 the second Afro-Asian Conference was due to open in Algiers. Chaired by Ben Bella, it was to mark the decade since Bandung, with the participation of the then-United Nations secretary general, U Thant, and the heads of more than sixty states. It seems that Ben Bella had also prepared a meeting with de Gaulle and a visit to the United States. All these undertakings, including the conference, were not realized.

Circumstances were quite different in Libya in the summer of 1969 – where the decisive turning point in that country's modern history was also initiated by a military coup.

Libya, with its vast area and meager population, aroused the world's interest in the mid-sixties upon the discovery of large oil reserves. Not only was the quantity immense, but the oil was superior in quality, close to Europe, and not dependent upon the Suez Canal or pipelines through Syria. Moreover, counting on the tranquil and resolute monarchic regime, security against internal turbulence could be assumed. Who doubted that Libya would remain a stable base for Western air forces and navies in the Mediterranean for a long time to come?

All this was changed in the course of a few hours on the morning of 1 September 1969. The plotters had no difficulties and met no resistance, and the rifle shots heard in Tripoli and Benghazi that day were probably fired in the air by a soldier happy to have won without battle. The king was abroad; his heir was apprehended in his pajamas by a lieutenant and three soldiers; the presence in the country of fifteen thousand British troops was not felt.

The new and unprecedented element in the Libyan coup was the youth of all the officers involved. The ages of coup initiators in the Arab world had been between thirty-five and forty-five. Younger than average, Mundhir Windāwī of Iraq was twenty-eight at the time of his abortive coup in 1963, and Ḥāṭūm, the Syrian, was twenty-nine at the time of his equally abortive try in 1966. The initiators of the first two Syrian coups in 1949 were older than average: Za'īm was fifty-five at the time and Ḥinnāwī, fifty-one. These were actually coups of the army command against the existing regime. Ibrāhīm 'Abbūd, head of the Sudanese coup in 1958, was fifty-eight at the time and also belongs to this group. The typical Arab military coup is carried out against the supreme command by officers of medium rank, between captain and colonel, about forty years old, and in command of brigades or divisions. 'Abd al-Naṣir was thirty-four in 1952; Qāsim, forty-four in 1958; 'Ārif was thirty-seven in 1963; Sallāl, forty-five in 1962. The officers of the 1969 Libyan coup, however, were all under thirty. With the single exception of Adam al-Ḥawwāz, twenty-nine, the only captain and the oldest among them, they were all lieutenants and second lieutenants. Al-Ḥawwāz, promoted to colonel, was minister of defense in the cabinet established on 8 September 1969, but soon disappeared. He was not mentioned in the statement announcing the composition of the Revolutionary Command Council on 10 January 1970 and the establishment of a new cabinet on the sixteenth of January.[18] In the autumn of 1970 he appears again, accused of conspiracy, and is sentenced to death. In the weeks after the victory, but not at once, Mu'ammar al-Qaddaffi revealed himself as the strong man among the officers of the coup, at which time he was a lieutenant of twenty-seven.

The Ousting and Restoration of Officers' Regimes

In my book I described the ousting – by civilian uprising – of 'Abbūd's military dictatorship in the Sudan as a significant occurrence.[19] Though it is clear that "one should not assume that the dictatorship will eliminate itself," I did emphasize 'Abbūd's ousting as possibly signifying the beginning of a new development. The demonstrations and strikes of October 1964 in Khartoum were "a popular uprising with numerous and diverse supporters – workers and intellectuals, businessmen and office workers, northerners and southerners. It was hardly by chance that the most overt military dictatorship was the first to fall this way."[20]

Since then, more than six years have passed, and the elimination of Sudan's military dictatorship, not only remained the first in the Arab world, but also the only occurrence of this sort. Prediction is dangerous. But it is possible and even essential to understand historical trends. The present tendency in the Arab world is not toward reduction of military interference in political life and the elimination or self-dissolution of military dictatorships, but toward more intervention and the fostering of military regimes. The ideological pretensions are possibly more sophisticated, the propoganda slogans more high-flown in their progressive and revolutionary wording, which does not change the facts.

In the Sudan military dictatorship was renewed. The civilian regime, established upon 'Abbūd's fall, faced the same difficulties and failed on the same issues as the civilian regime of ten years earlier. It, too, was destroyed by a military coup – the officers of the 1969 revolt were, however, anti-imperialist, anti-Western, and at first pro-Soviet, and pro-Communist in orientation.

Most illustrative, not only of the situation and events in the Sudan, was a report in the *Neue Zürcher Zeitung* on the "reinforcing of Moscow's influence in Sudan."[21] The report was written in Khartoum and dispatched a few days before the coup of 25 May 1969; it reached the editorial board and was printed unchanged a few days after the coup. The full translation of its last paragraphs reads:

> As in many other developing countries, the army is the only power group not bound to particular interests. The officers' corps of the Sudanese army became significantly younger after 'Abbūd's ousting. These cadres politically reveal great wakefulness and criticism. The parties' efforts to introduce their own men into the officers' cadre – in order to divide the army and disable it politically – seem to have met with only partial success; however, this has further sharpened the officers' conception of the political problems.
>
> The attacks on the army and its leadership following the elimination of the military regime stopped long ago. Today one feels that the simple citizen and broad circles of the intelligentsia look up to the officers once again. The economic freeze, inflation, and flourishing corruption are obvious, with no visible countermeasures. And most people feel that only strong men – the army – might help. The army attentively records this turn in public opinion; its self-consciousness, damaged for a long time, is strengthened.
>
> The Sudanese Communist party has so far used the trade unions and a few professional organizations to exert its influence. Even in the union of railroad workers and the lawyers' organization, representatives of the bourgeoisie significantly reduced Communist influence. Many observers relate this less to a turn in political outlook than to the concentration of the Left on a single cause: the penetration of the officers' corps. If there is such a strategy, which, obviously no

one openly admits, the Soviet military, the weapons, and the first advisers who arrived in the meantime, will be regarded in a new light in a country in which a military coup is no longer considered an impossibility. In the officers' cadre of an army dependent on Soviet advisers and equipment, even a minority of Communists could achieve more than a majority of ministers in a civilian government of 1964–65.

With this background, it can be better understood what motivates a powerful group of politicians of all parties to improve relations with the United States and West Germany, and why Ismā'īl al-Azharī, the head of state, postponed his official visit to the USSR – ostensibly because of lack of time.[22]

The interval between the writing and publication of this report turned it from an appraisal of the situation into an historical description. It could be asked whether this report could have also been written in Damascus in April 1949, in Cairo in June 1952, in Baghdad in June 1958, and again in Khartoum in October 1958. Practically the only change is the position of the USSR in the region.

The circumstances, opportunities and methods of military intervention in the Arab world were basically the same in the sixties and fifties. The intensity increased; the results, however, did not change.

THE REVOLUTIONARY COMMAND COUNCIL

At the end of the sixties, supreme government institutions called "Revolutionary Command Councils" were established in four Arab states; at the time of writing, these councils still exist. The four states are Iraq, Algeria, Libya, and Sudan. These institutions are the expression of the establishment of a military dictatorship. Syria and Egypt preceded these countries in founding similar councils.

The first institution of this kind was the ten-member "Supreme War Council" established on the day of Sāmī Ḥinnāwī's ousting in December 1949.[23]

The first one bearing the name "Revolutionary Command Council" – and serving as a model for others – was that in Egypt, headed by Najīb and set up in January 1953. It had fourteen members and existed until a constitution was adopted ithe summer of 1956.[24]

Those councils were composed exclusively of army officers. They did not replace a government, nor did they side with it, but stood above it. The abolition of the Egyptian council in 1956 manifested the transition to formal democracy and parliamentarianism, which had then been declared in Egypt.

Between 1956 and 1963, Arab officers did not refrain from plotting, revolting, and otherwise interfering in political life. They abstained, however, from establishing similar councils, since they emanated too strong a stench of dictatorial arbitrariness. Later, these hesitations were overcome, and the Revolutionary Council became an accepted institution.

On 8 February 1963, together with 'Ārif's first coup which ended Qāsim's regime, a fourteen-member "National Council of the Revolutionary Command" was established; the number of members was later increased to twenty by the Ba'th Regional Command. The members' names were never published, and some were unknown even to higher ranks; they were mostly officers.[25] In the provisional Iraqi Constitution of May 1964, this council is mentioned in several paragraphs: the president takes an oath "before the National Council of the Revolutionary Command and the Council of Ministers in joint convention" (Par. 42); if the president resigns, "he will address his resignation to the National Council of the Revolutionary Command" (Par. 54).[26] The greatest significance probably lies in the constitution's omissions: it does not include even the vaguest intimation of the council's composition, who nominates or elects its members, on what grounds, and to whom it is responsible. Little is known about the council's activities; apparently, it discontinued itself or was formally abolished in 1965.[27] In April 1966, when a new president had to be elected upon the accidental death of President 'Abd al-Salām 'Ārif, it could not have been done constitutionally (Par. 55), since the "National Council of the Revolutionary Command" did not exist. 'Abd al-Raḥmān 'Ārif was thus elected president by the government and the defense council.

"The Revolutionary Command Council" appeared again in Iraq following the military coup of Aḥmad Ḥasan al-Bakr on 17 July 1968.[28] The changes in government at the end of July and in August 1968 were declared in the name of the Command Council and on its behalf. On 21 September a new temporary constitution was published, according to which almost all legislative and executive power was concentrated with the council.[29] In July 1970 another provisional Constitution was published in Iraq, which states that "the Revolutionary Command Council is the supreme institution in the state" (Par. 37).[30] Following in great detail are the council's powers, which were in fact limitless. Again, however, not one word is found regarding the council's composition and to whom it is responsible.

Until 17 July 1969 the Iraq "Revolutionary Command Council" consisted of five members, all army officers. On the same day, in an amendment of the new provisional constitution, their number was increased to ten.[31] Among the new members were also a few civilians, but the officers were in the majority. All the council's members were members of the Ba'th party.

The Syrian Council of Revolutionary Command reappeared, though it was short-lived. The Ba'th military coup of 8 March 1963 was carried out on behalf of "The National Council of the Revolutionary Command." The same afternoon its composition had been fixed. It is doubtful, however, whether a clear decision had been taken on who would be the council's members. Although it was meant to have seventeen members, only twelve names were published.[32] Moreover, in mid-April talks on the establishment of a federation were held between representatives of Egypt, Iraq, and Syria. Nāṣir did not conceal his doubts concerning the status of the Syrian delegation and the authority of the Syrian administration in general. He asked who actually ruled Syria. Rāshid Qutaynī answered that there was a twenty-member "Revolutionary Council," half officers and half civilians. Nāṣir insisted further and asked for their names. The Syrian spokesmen, Quṭaynī, Ziyād Ḥarīrī, and Fahd al-Shā'ir, evaded the question and mentioned only the officers' names.[33]

Nevertheless, two facts emerge: The council consisted of officers and civilians, the officers comprising half or more. The council's composition was not agreed upon, certain, or constant, and it is assumed that its composition was kept secret with a definite aim.[34] In the above-mentioned discussion with 'Abd al-Nāṣir, a hint of this can be discerned. It is possible, on the other hand, that no one was able to announce the council's composition, since it may not have been agreed upon in the tumult of inner struggles. A book on Syria, published by the United States Army, contains the best information available, and reads: "The size and composition of the Council were not known. The Provisional Constitution stated only that it should be composed of 'its present members,' meaning the members of the National Council of the Revolutionary Command. It was believed, however, to number about 50 members. Official pronouncements in late 1964 and early 1965 indicated that the Council would be enlarged to between 100 and 150 members chosen chiefly on an occupational basis, but this had not yet been done in mid-1965."[35] In the provisional Syrian constitution of April 1964, it was established that "The National Revolutionary Council will act as a legislative power and will supervise the activities of the executive" (Par. 31).[36] In fact, however, these regulations were not carried out. With Amīn al-Ḥāfiẓ's rise to power after the summer of 1964, the council ceased to exist, and the regimes established after February 1966 emphasized the Ba'th party administration pattern. The regime basically remained a military dictatorship, but did not need a "Revolutionary Council."

In Algeria, Boumedienne founded a "Revolutionary Council" immediately after the coup of June 1965. It included Boumedienne as president, fifteen officers, nine former officers, and two civilians – twenty-seven in all.[37] In 1970 it had only fifteen members.[38]

In Sudan a "Revolutionary Command Council" was established right after the coup of 25 May 1969. It had ten members: nine officers and one civilian, Abū Bakr 'Awaḍ Allāh, the new prime minister.[39] Ja'far Numayrī was president of the council since its establishment and nominated himself prime minister at the end of October. The "Revolutionary Command Council," still the supreme body in the state, is apparently composed exclusively of officers.

The same goes for Libya. The announcement of the coup on 1 September 1969 was made on behalf of the "Revolutionary Command Council." The new temporary Libyan Constitution was published on 11 December 1969 in the name of the council. It states that the "Revolutionary Command Council" is the supreme authority in the state; it nominates a government, declares war, signs contracts, etc.[40] The council consists of ten members, all officers.

Thus, at the end of the sixties, there were "Revolutionary Command Councils" at the head of four Arab states: Iraq, Algeria, Libya, and Sudan. The structure of these bodies was never officially published; the way their numbers were elected – and they were not responsible to any institution of the public – was never legally established. They were bodies which in their very nature abolished the separation of the functions of legislation and execution – that same principle which was recognized as the basis of democracy long ago. The "Revolutionary Command Council" is institutionalized arbitrariness.

SOME CONCLUDING REMARKS

Paragraph 8 of the Algerian Constitution of 1963 reads: "The National Army is a popular army. Faithful to the traditions of the struggle for national liberation, it serves the people under the orders of the government. It assures the defense of the territories of the Republic and participates in the political, economic, and social activities of the country within the framework of the party."[41]

This is the typical wording of a common and frequent attitude. The question remains what were the results of the activities of the army in the Arab states.

Without making an overall summary, some significant points can be recalled:

1. Regarding the army as a political or social factor, one actually means the officers' cadre only. The social and mentality gap between the soldiers and officers remained unchanged during the sixties. Actions and activities were only those of the officers.
2. Compared to the fifties, the circumstances, motives, and patterns of the Arab military coups hardly changed in the sixties. The intensity of the officers' interference with the political life of their countries even grew.
3. The status of army officers in all Arab states continuously improved. Their personal prestige and public influence grew, their salaries increased, and those who ended their military service occupied senior positions in the political, administrative, and economic systems of their countries. This rise in the status of the officers' cadre also influenced other countries, such as Jordan, where there have been no military coups or officers' regimes.
4. The officers' regimes, more than others, succeeded in relieving their countries of Western guardians. They did not succeed in advancing toward democracy and stability and sometimes even impeded progress. A military coup usually provoked a countercoup.
5. In a few basic aspects Nasser's Egypt also failed to reach its pretentious goals. We give the exact words of a scholar who cannot be suspect of negative prejudice: "The revolutionary regime, despite the wide popularity of President Nasser among the Egyptian masses, has never felt altogether secure and has never developed a full measure of legitimacy . . . . The bedrock of political support on which Nasser has been dependent is the Army officer corps. Their strong influence naturally strengthened the tendency to build up the military establishment."[42]
6. War has always been the supreme test of every regime, not merely for a military regime, but also for the army itself. During the sixties this test was the Six Day War. It would be wasting one's breath to explain why the regimes and armies of Egypt, Jordan, and Syria failed this test. If there was any difference between monarchical Jordan, and Egypt and Syria which have been "liberated" by revolutionary officers, it lay mainly in the fact that smaller Jordan demonstrated greater military ability, and in that its officers and soldiers showed more determination. Even if Egypt could excuse the defeat by telling the story of an alleged surprise, this does not hold for the Syrians. Ṣāliḥ Mahdī 'Ammāsh's account in his book *Men Without Command* may be true: namely, that Syria had a strategic reserve, not in support of the Syrian army at the front, but in Damascus as a protection for the rulers.[43]

During the fifties the officers' interference in politics excited many hopes among the Arabs and caused numerous disappointments. In the sixties, they roused much less hope, but no less disappointment.

NOTES

1 Eliezer Be'eri, *Ha-Qetzuna we-ha-shilton ba'olam ha'aravi* (Merhavia, 1966), p. 81. The English version is *Army Officers in Arab Politics and Society* (Jerusalem, 1969), p. 102.
2 *Neue Zürcher Zeitung,* 24 April 1971, p. 5.
3 Some books have been written on the subject of the coup d'état, describing some typical coups, defining its essence, and analyzing its method of operation. The first was written in 1931: Curzio Malaparte, *Technique du coup d'état.* The book was written in French and translated into German and English: *Der Staatsstreich* (Leipzig-Wein, 1932); *The Coup d'Etat* (New York, 1932). The book is quite brilliant, but deficient in its accuracy. More fundamental is Donald J. Goodspeed, *The Conspirators: A Study of the Coup d'Etat* (London and New York, 1962). Interesting, but overgeneralized, is Edward Luttwak, *Coup d'Etat: A Practical Handbook* (London, 1968).
4 Be'eri, *Ha-Qetzuna,* pp. 80–1; Be'eri, *Army Officers,* pp. 101–2.
5 Aristide R. Zolberg, "Military Rule and Political Development in Tropical Africa," in *Military Profession and Military Regimes,* ed. Jacques van Doorn (Paris, 1969), p. 175.
6 William F. Gutteridge, *The Military in African Politics* (London, 1969), p. 43.
7 David Wood, *The Armed Forces of African States,* Adelphi Papers, no. 27, (London, 1966).
8 *The Statesman's Yearbook 1969/70* (London, 1969), p. 953.
9 Gutteridge, p. 43.
10 Wood, p. 12.
11 The appended list of all coups – according to our definition – in the Arab world during the fifties and sixties includes both successful and abortive coups which reached a stage of real action toward the seizure of power.
12 Be'eri, *Ha-Qetzuna,* pp. 21–38; Be'eri, *Army Officers,* pp. 15–40.
13 Yael Vered, *Hafikha u-milhama be-Teyman* (Tel Aviv, 1967), pp. 254 ff; Be'eri, *Ha-Qetzuna,* pp. 157–9; Be'eri, *Army Officers,* pp. 223–8; Dana Adams Schmidt, *Yemen: The Unknown War* (London, 1968), pp. 315 ff.
14 *Middle East Record 1967* (Jerusalem, 1971), 3: 601–3.
15 Important to the understanding of the developments in Yemen is Haggai Erlich, "The Tribes in Yemen and their Role in the War 1962–1968," (in Hebrew) *Hamizrah Hehadash (The New East)* 20 (1970); 1–19, 129–68.
16 J.C. Hurewitz, *Middle East Politics: The Military Dimension* (New York, 1969), p. 189.
17 The clearest description of the events in Algeria between 1945 and 1966 is probably found in Arslan Humbaraci, *Algeria: A Revolution that Failed* (London, 1966), 308 pp.

18 *The Middle East Journal,* 24 (1970): 194.
19 Be'eri, *Ha-Qetzuna,* pp. 154–6, 326; Be'eri, *Army Officers,* pp. 221–2, 463.
20 Be'eri, *Ha-Qetzuna,* p. 341, Be'eri, *Army Officers,* pp. 479–80.
21 *Neue Zürcher Zeitung,* 1 June 1969, p. 6.
22 *Ibid.*
23 Be'eri, *Ha-Qetzuna,* p. 52; Be'eri, *Army Officers,* pp. 60–1.
24 Be'eri, *Ha-Qetzuna,* p. 86; Be'eri, *Army Officers,* p. 109.
25 Majid Khadduri, *Republican Iraq* (London, 1969), pp. 196–7.
26 *Hamizrah Hehadash,* 14 (1964) 379–86.
27 Khadduri, p. 264.
28 Meir Pa'il, "Patterns of the Revolutionary Officers' Regimes in Iraq and Syria," (in Hebrew) *Hamizrah Hehadash* 19 (1969), 198.
29 *Orient* (Paris), no. 47/48 (1968), pp. 325–36.
30 *Hamizrah Hehadash,* 30 (1970), 361–9.
31 *Al-Jarīda* (Beirut) 18 Nov. 1969.
32 Be'eri, *Ha-Qetzuna,* pp. 111–12; Be'eri, *Army Officers,* p. 152.
33 *Maḥādir jalasāt mubāḥathāt al-waḥda* (Cairo, 1963), pp. 43–51; Malcolm Kerr, *The Arab Cold War 1958–1967,* 2nd ed. (London, 1967), pp. 69–70.
34 Marcel Colombe, "Remarques sur le Ba'th et les institutions politiques de la Syrie d'aujord'hui," *Orient,* no. 37 (1966): 60.
35 U.S. Army, *Area Handbook for Syria* (1965), p. 177.
36 *Hamizrah Hehadash* 14 (1964), 197–204.
37 Humbaraci, pp. 230–2.
38 *The Middle East and North Africa 1970–71* (London, 1970), p. 169.
39 A.H., *Neue Zürcher Zeitung,* 28 May 1969.
40 *The Middle East Journal,* 24 (1970), 194, 203–7.
41 Quoted in Hurewitz, p. 196.
42 Malcolm H. Kerr, *The United Arab Republic: The Domestic and Economic Background of Foreign Policy,* The Rand Corporation (1969), pp. v-vi.
43 According to an article on the book *Rijāl bilā qiyāda* (Baghdad, 1971), in the daily newspaper *al-Quds* (Jerusalem), 2 April 1971.

APPENDIX

MILITARY COUPS D'ETAT IN THE ARAB WORLD, 1949–1969

	Date	Country	Head of Revolting Officers	Rival	Result
1.	30 March 1949	Syria	Za'īm	Constitutional republican regime	Success
2.	14 August 1949	Syria	Ḥinnāwī	Za'īm	Success
3.	19 December 1949	Syria	Shīshaklī	Ḥinnāwī	Success
4.	29 November 1951	Syria	Shīshaklī	Army-dependent president	Success
5.	23 July 1952	Egypt	'Abd al-Nāṣir and Free Officers	Monarchy	Success
6.	25 February 1954	Syria	Atāsī, 'Abū 'Assāf, Jadīd, Hamdūn	Shīshaklī	Success
7.	26 February 1954	Egypt	Khālid Muhī al-Dīn	'Abd al-Nāṣir	Success
8.	26 March 1954	Egypt	'Abd al-Nāṣir and 'Āmir	Najīb	Success
9.	13 April 1957	Jordan	'Alī Abū Nuwār	Monarchy	Failure
10.	14 July 1958	Iraq	Qāsim, 'Ārif	Monarchy	Success
11.	17 November 1958	Sudan	'Abbūd	Constitutional republican regime	Success

	Date	Country	Head of Revolting Officers	Rival	Result
12.	8 March 1959	Iraq	Shawwāf	Qāsim	Failure
13.	22 May 1959	Sudan	Shīnān	'Abbūd	Failure
14.	10 November 1959	Sudan	'Alī Ḥāmid	'Abbūd	Failure
15.	28 September 1961	Syria	Kuzbarī, Naḥlāwī, Dahmān	Nāṣir	Success
16.	31 December 1961	Lebanon	'Awad, Khayr-Allāh	Constitutional republican regime	Failure
17.	28 March 1962	Syria	Naḥlāwī	Army-dependent regime	Success
18.	31 March 1962	Syria	Badr A'sar at Homs	Military regime	Success
19.	1 April 1962	Syria	'Alwān at Aleppo		Failure
20.	26 September 1962	Yemen	Sallāl	Monarchy	Success
21.	13 January 1963	Syria	Nahlāwī	Zahr al-Dīn	Failure
22.	8 February 1963	Iraq	'Ārif	Qāsim	Success
23.	8 March 1963	Syria	Ḥarīrī	Military regime	Success
24.	18 July 1963	Syria	'Alwān	Military regime	Failure
25.	13 November 1963	Iraq	Windāwī	Military regime	Failure

	Date	Country	Head of Revolting Officers	Rival	Result
26.	18 November 1963	Iraq	ʻĀrif	Military regime	Success
27.	19 June 1965	Algeria	Boumedienne	Ben Bella	Success
28.	16 September 1965	Iraq	ʻẠbd al-Razzāk	ʻĀrif	Failure
29.	23 February 1966	Syria	Jadīd, Ḥāṭūm	Amīn al-Ḥāfiz	Success
30.	30 June 1966	Iraq	ʻAbd al-Razzāq	ʻĀrif	Failure
31.	8 September 1966	Syria	Ḥāṭūm	Baʻth military regime	Failure
32.	27 December 1966	Sudan	Khālid Husayn ʻUthmān	Constitutional republican regime	Failure
33.	5 November 1967	Yemen	al-Iryānī, al-ʻAynī	Sallāl	Success
34.	15 December 1967	Algeria	Zubayrī	Boumedienne	Failure
35.	20 March 1968	South Yemen		Kahtān al-Shaʻbī	Failure
36.	17 July 1968	Iraq	al-Bakr	ʻAbd al-Raḥman ʻĀrif	Success
37.	30 August 1968	Yemen	ʻAbd al-Wahhāb	al-ʻAmrī	Failure
38.	25 February 1969	Syria	Ḥāfiz al-Asad	Jadīd	Success
39.	25 May 1969	Sudan	Numayrī	Constitutional republican regime	Success
40.	1 September 1969	Libya	Qaddaffi	Monarchy	Success

THE ORGANIZATION OF NOMADIC GROUPS IN THE MIDDLE EAST

EMANUEL MARX

Only in recent years have the nomad tribes of the Middle East become the subject of intensive anthropological and sociological research. Today, with the help of this work, it is possible to obtain a clearer picture of the ecological conditions under which these societies exist, their social organization, and their relationships with the outside world.

I shall attempt to formulate some generalizations regarding the factors which influence the size of territorial and political units and the concentrations of power in them.[1] It will become clear that the commonly accepted sociological picture of the tribe as a segmentary political organization is incomplete and that these societies are, in fact, much more complex than was thought. Alongside the tribe – which fulfills important functions in society – other organizational forms exist which, although perhaps not as prominent, are, nevertheless, very important.

The travelers, missionaries, and administrators of the nineteenth and twentieth century wrote profusely about the Bedouin. Most of this literature is tinged with romanticism and enlarges on the personal qualities of the Bedouin male. He is described as an individualist; a lover of freedom who struggles heroically with nature's forces; a lover of adventure and war who behaves chivalrously to the defeated, keeps his word, and fulfills the obligations of hospitality even unto his last crust of bread. These characteristics are assumed to be found in the "true" Bedouin, the camel breeder belonging to strong aristocratic clans who, in his wanderings, penetrates the heart of the desert. Tribes which breed sheep and goats are regarded as morally and physically inferior, and those who cultivate the soil are even lower on the scale.[2] Such classics as the works of Niebuhr, Burckhardt, Palgrave, Doughty, Jaussen, Musil, and Lawrence[3] influenced generations of readers and left their mark on scholarly works dealing with the nomads of the Middle East.[4]

The portrait drawn in these descriptions is, of course, not entirely imaginary, but rather represents the Bedouin as he sees himself. Some of the authors did have long and continuous contact with the Bedouin, but did not examine the working of their society, and were content with reporting what the Bedouin told them. Others attempted to describe the Bedouin, but showed no interest in depicting gray everyday reality, since they generally preferred to present the more exotic aspects of nomad life in order to titillate their readers. Even the most acute observers largely emphasized those aspects of society which the Bedouin themselves regard as the most important, relying on Bedouin informants whose statements were often normative and culture-bound. The few scholars who lived with the Bedouin for longer periods also wrote about the other aspects of nomad life, but wherever actual behavior contradicted the norm, they regarded such behavior as exceptional.

This duality is apparent in the works of both Doughty and Musil – two travellers who knew the Bedouin better than others. For example, the picture painted in Musil's book, *The Manners and Customs of the Rwala Bedouins,* is very different from the one reflected in his journals, published in several volumes, among which *Arabia Deserta*[5] is probably the most interesting. Although both books deal with the same tribal group, the reader gets the impression that they concern two different peoples. The difference between them is that the former is based on ethnographic research and the second on observations of the reality. In one place in his travelogue, Musil describes how he collected the material for his book on Bedouin manners and customs:

> "From sunrise until four o'clock in the afternoon I sat in my round tent. In the morning Mḥammad usually brought me some informant, with whom I closeted myself. Often I found it impossible to question him, for he would not answer me until he had told me all that was in his mind . . . he would . . . gaze longingly at the exit of my tent. How gladly would he have disappeared through that exit to avoid the torment of my questions! Only when he was explaining something to his own liking would he show more animation."[6]

Musil was convinced that the personal concerns of the Bedouin are not a part of the basic system of customs and beliefs which, in his opinion, guide the Bedouin way of life.

There is no hint of such methods of research in *The Manners and Customs of the Rwala Bedouins;* there Bedouin ideology is presented as a living reality and a scientific truth. The result of such an approach can already be seen in the opening sentence of the book in which the author asserts that "the Rwala [Ruwālā] are recognized by all their neighbours as being the only true Bedouin tribe of northern Arabia."[7] Not many Bedouin would agree to such a partial statement and Kennett is right in saying that "although various tribes vie with one another in their claims to be the oldest, and so on, yet as a rule one tribe will recognise the just claims of another to be 'out of the top drawer'."[8]

The common belief that our knowledge about the Bedouin is extensive and that we understand their society better than other sectors of the population of the Middle East is unfounded.[9] We actually know less about Bedouin society than about the Arab rural population. The rich raw material to be found in the books of Epstein, Jaussen, Doughty, Musil, and others has still not been properly exploited.[10] I say this in spite of the efforts made by various writers to marshall the information available on Bedouin society in various fields: Oppenheim on the history of the tribes; Gräf and Chelhod on law; Henninger on the family; Sweet on ecology; Feilberg on the tent.[11] These authors give orderly accounts of the situation in the particular field which each of them chose to examine, but, to my mind, the information is not transformed into theory. Several attempts were also made to analyze the characteristic traits of Bedouin society, e.g., Bacon, Montagne, Patai, and Coon.[12] These are thorough and important works, and some of them show brilliant insights. However, they also hold a hidden danger: in some respects they continue, and even reinforce, the distorted traditional image of Bedouin society and thus prevent the researcher from taking new departures. I have myself experienced this. Before entering this field of research, I had fixed ideas about Bedouin society and once in it I found it hard to free myself of them. This is certainly true of other scholars as well. In all the works on Middle Eastern nomad societies, one will find that the scholar struggles with the traditional image of Bedouin society, and in most of them a remnant of the Bedouin's viewpoint still remains. But, in recent years, a more factual – if less impressive – picture of these nomad societies has begun to emerge. Several new monographs have appeared which, perhaps, do not yet permit us to redraw the picture of the Middle Eastern nomad, but at least enable us to attempt a tentative re-analysis.

How does this recent work differ from that of earlier writers? It can immediately be seen that most of it does not deal with the Bedouin in the narrow traditional sense of the word. Thus it does not examine a tribe of nomadic camel breeders. I presume that the scholars did not reach these tribes, both because of the physical difficulties involved in such an operation and because the number of such Bedouin has dropped considerably in the last generation. The new work also differs in that the authors are trained anthropologists, in that it is based on other types of data, and in that it pays attention to subjects not discussed extensively in previous work. The new type of researchers lived for a comparatively long period of time in the societies which they describe. They did not collect their material at random, but in a systematic and concentrated manner. For the most part they limited themselves to examining a well-defined region and a limited number of people. Unlike their predecessors, they relied less on information given by informants from the society under investigation and more on personal observation; they depended less on estimates and more on measured and verified data. I refer to the work of Asad, Barth, Cunnison, Marx, and Peters, all of which appeared in the decade between 1960 and 1970.[13]

The concern with a set of common problems is recognizable in all these monographs and papers, and, as a result, they give a new impetus to thinking on several subjects in anthropological theory.

I intend to discuss here two subjects to which the researchers have given a great deal of attention: ecological influences on the life of the nomads and the interrelationships between them and the settled population.

These two spheres are intimately related and cannot be separated even for the purpose of an analytical exercise. Any society is a whole whose parts are interlinked, and this fact is reflected in the analysis, where seemingly irrelevant subjects will intrude and the same ground be covered repeatedly. The subjects which I have chosen only constitute a starting point for a much wider discussion. We must approach the analysis of a society much as a man wishing to eat a cake. He will not swallow it all at once. Rather, he will cut a slice of it at any chosen point and then cut up the remainder and eat the pieces one by one. Even if we are aware that a society must be described as a closed system, we have no choice but to start the analysis at some point and shall never be able to present the society as a whole.

According to the *Encyclopaedia of Islam,* Bedouin are "pastoral nomads of Arabian blood, speech, and culture [who] are found in the Arabian Peninsula proper and in parts of Iran, Soviet Turkestan, North Africa and the Sudan."[14] Since our interest does not concern language or origin, but is focused on ecological problems, I shall depart from the customary definition and discuss Middle Eastern tribes who exploit arid regions for animal breeding. Thus, I shall not deal with Bedouin who do not specialize in breeding animals, as, for example, some of the tribes of southern Sinai, nor with Bedouin who have become sedentary, such as the Iraqi Shabāna.[15] The analysis does however relate to tribes who are not regarded as Bedouin according to the accepted meaning. I shall discuss not only Arabic-speaking tribes, but also the Persian-speaking Basseri of the Fars district in Iran; and not merely camel breeders or sheep and goat herders, but also the Sudanese Baggāra (the dialectal form of Baqqāra) who are Arabic-speaking cattle breeders. The analysis can also be applied to other nomad tribes which will not be explicitly discussed, such as the Nuer of South Sudan or the Turkana of Kenya.

To avoid misunderstanding, it should be noted that animal husbandry is not always the sole, or even main, occupation of the nomads. They themselves, however, take the raising of animals very seriously and regard it as the principal economic branch and as the mainstay of their culture. All these nomads are organized in tribes, but this trait is not unique to them: there are also sections of the settled population which maintain the tribal framework.

Throughout the discussion I shall touch upon the differences between various nomad societies. I see no point in giving a detailed catalogue of such differences, unless it be possible to understand the origin of the difference and from that learn about the factors which mold the life of the society. Although the anthropologist cannot create laboratory conditions, he has a tested method for isolating variables: he compares several descriptions or case studies of similar social phenomena. Since reality is infinitely varied, the anthropologist expects to find differences between similar cases and will then attempt to isolate the variable or variables which can account for the differences. If he arrives at the conclusion that the difference must be ascribed to a certain variable, he then tries to verify his assumption by arranging his series of cases in logical order. If he finds that there is continuity between the cases, he is able, from his series, to reconstruct a full picture of the behavior of that specific variable.

In this way he may sometimes study processes which extend over many years, although his field work usually only continues for a year or two. Thus a series of synchronic descriptions facilitate the understanding of continuing processes.

I shall illustrate this method by an example: An anthropologist wishing to understand the changes in relationship between parents and children as the children grow up and the parents age is not obliged to study the process for a quarter of a century. It is sufficient if he takes observations from a series of families with similar sociological traits, who differ from each other in age alone, and then arranges them in a sequence. If he obtains a regular and continuous picture, he is entitled to assume that in the conditions prevailing in the society under examination, the relationships between parents and children will develop in a certain manner, on condition that the environment remains unchanged. I intend to apply this method to the material of nomad societies.

THE TERRITORIAL ORGANIZATION

There is considerable ecological variety in the Bedouin areas. Some regions have fertile soil and an abundant supply of water and, if these resources were exploited more intensively than for grazing, they could adequately support a densely settled population. Other regions are blessed with fertile soil, but suffer from a serious limitation: a shortage of reliable water sources. Consequently, they can only support a small settled population. In the absence of sophisticated technology, the water supply cannot be increased, and part of the population is therefore forced to wander in small groups over the area in order to draw water when and where it is available. When the reserve of water is exhausted in one place, the camp moves to another, in a fairly regular annual cycle.

Most of the Bedouin areas do not lack pasture during ordinary years. As the Bedouin population grows and the herds increase – and sometimes this process is accompanied by an expansion of the settled population which in itself causes a further decrease in pasture areas – pasture also becomes a scarce commodity. Such changes are liable to end this way of life since the continuous coordination of two scarce factors of production – neither of which has a substitute – is beyond the capability of the nomad. Even in regions which usually supply all the Bedouin's needs, such situations may occasionally arise and cause a crisis. Musil describes such a situation: "Hmār avowed that he had no memory of any such egregiously unfavorable season in thirty years. Where pasturage was abundant, water was absent, and where there was water, there was no pasturage."[16]

Shortage of water is due to inadequate rainfall and the many fluctuations thereof. The Bedouin needs minimal precipitation even in areas of winter grazing and certainly in summer grazing grounds. The claim that the Bedouin lives in almost arid zones ignores the basic fact that the whole area of his wanderings – and not only the region considered to be his undisputed tribal territory – must be regarded as one unit of living space. The data assembled in Table 1, from various monographs on nomads, indicate that in the nomad areas the annual average rainfall does not drop below approximately 100 mm, and that nomad areas also include regions with an annual rainfall of 900 mm which are unquestionably suitable for agriculture.

TABLE 1

AVERAGE ANNUAL RAINFALL IN NOMAD REGIONS (in mm)[17]

Tribe/Region	Country	Rainfall in	
		Rainy Season Pastures	Dry Season Pastures
Cyrenaica	Libya	400	50–100
Kabābīsh	Sudan	200+	100
Ẓullām	Israel	200–400	100–200
Basseri	Iran	250	250
Baggāra	Sudan	900	450

Today it is generally accepted that an average annual rainfall in excess of 250–300 mm is an adequate precondition for growing grain on a regular basis. Regions where rainfall is low, but does not fall below 100 mm per year, can support farmers on condition that there are water resources which are not directly dependent on rain, or can give a living to men engaged in a combination of economic branches, e.g., agriculture, grazing, and hunting and who, by so doing, decrease the risk of becoming the victim of local droughts. In regions where rainfall is less than 100 mm per year, the spring vegetation lasts for a short period, sometimes only a few weeks. Therefore, they can be exploited economically only when they form part of a larger territory also comprising areas blessed with more abundant rain. These norms may be modified by additional ecological factors, such as the quality of the soil and the proximity to wells and roads, all of which influence the practical utilization of any particular region. Modern technology can, of course, overcome natural disadvantages and erect a permanent settlement on a site where rainfall is sparse.[18]

Even in arid regions it happens that a particular geological formation drains the rainfall of a considerable area to one locality. Thus oases are formed, which depend only to a very small extent on the frequency of rainfall and which can support permanent settlement. However, not all the oases in Bedouin areas are settled, there being those which never become more than wells at which the nomads water their herds. In order for an oasis to support permanent settlement, it must be large enough to support a population capable of defending itself against groups of nomads wishing to exploit its resources. This implies that the point at which an oasis will become a permanent settlement differs from place to place. Since the power concentrations of the nomads change from generation to generation, oases may be deserted even when the natural conditions remain unchanged.[19]

In the climatic conditions of the Middle East, a rainfall of 100–200 mm, not only moistens the soil in pastures and fills water holes and wells, but will also, in the "normally" dry years (those without severe drought), cover temporary water deficits that can result from an irregularity in the anticipated rainfall. This "irregularity" comprises annual fluctuations in quantity and variations in distribution of rains during the season, constant differences in quantities of rainfall in various parts of the region caused, for instance, by its topography, and also the varying geographic distribution of rain from season to season. For example, in the Ẓullām region of the eastern Beersheba plain, average annual rainfall fluctuates between 200 mm in the West and 120 mm in the Southeast, over a distance of only 35 km. Annual fluctuations in rainfall are striking: the maximum registered in Beersheba was 336 mm (in 1933–34) and the minimum 40 mm (in 1962–63). Even a year of normal rainfall can end in drought. This happened during 1960–61 in the Negev, when 185 mm were measured; after the first rains in November, there was a pause for six weeks during which none of the autumn sowing germinated. In January and February heavy rains fell, most of which ran off into the wadis and was not absorbed in the soil. Following these rains many Bedouin sowed their land a second time, but in March scorching east winds caused the second sowing to wither. Many Bedouin in that year harvested only straw and no grain.

Every year there are showers which cover areas of a few square kilometers and leave adjacent areas dry. One never knows where these rains will produce good pasture and where they will fill the water-holes.

In other regions too, rainfall poses severe problems to the Bedouin. Musil describes how the seasonal fluctuations and the geographic distribution of rain make the life of the Bedouin difficult[20] and force the Rwala tribe to operate an intelligence network to keep the *shaykh* informed on the state of pasture.[21] Doughty notes that a guest among the Bedouin is safe from the questions of those assembled in the tent until after he finishes the meal. "Yet after some little discoursing between them as of the rain this year and the pasture, they may each commonly come to guess the other's tribe."[22] It is apparent that these Bedouin have a keen interest in information on the distribution of rainfall.

The main method by which the Bedouin attempts to overcome the irregularity of rainfall is by wandering over a large territory sufficient to cancel out the influence of geographic distribution and annual and seasonal fluctuation of rainfall and which will include areas rich in water. In such a territory, he will find pasture and water for his herds throughout the seasons and will even reserve an area to which he can retreat in the last hard days of summer. The type of rainfall to a large extent determines the annual range of his wanderings. In the Negev, the Bedouin will range up to 60 km, in Libya up to 100 km and more, and the Rwala move up to 800 km. Among the Bedouin of the Negev, only a part of the region in which they wander is under the direct control of the tribes, since the better areas have been settled in recent generations. The tribes of Libya and the Rwala control practically the whole range of their pastures. In order to overcome fluctuations of rainfall, they were compelled to form big organizations which were strong enough to retain control over areas, parts of which were suitable for agricultural settlement. The big Bedouin tribes are territorial organizations which provide their members with pastures suitable for their needs throughout the seasons of the year. Covering such a territory often requires an organization comprising a large number of men. Bedouin tribes in Libya fluctuate in size between six thousand and thirty thousand; the Rwala tribe in the Syrian Desert number thirty-five thousand persons and some 350 thousand camels.[23] The fact that the Bedouin who desired to exploit the Wādī Sirḥān area for pasture were obliged to assure themselves of permanent access to pasture during all seasons of the year and to insure themselves, as far as possible, against fluctuations in rainfall was crucial in determining the size and organization of the Rwala. I do not wish to argue that the Rwala tribe did not exist before it moved to Wādī Sirḥān. It is known that they previously lived in northern Arabia together with other tribes of the 'Aneze confederation, and Doughty found, even in his day, tribesmen who remembered that they had in the past lived in the neighborhood of Khaibar.[24] It is probable that they moved to the new territory in the mid-eighteenth century, driving the Mawālī before them.[25] However, as sociologists, we are not so much concerned with this proven historical continuity. The Rwala in the neighborhood of Khaibar lived in ecological conditions different from those of the Wādī Sirḥān, and the new area required a different kind of social organization, which influenced every aspect of their culture. We know that even the historical traditions and genealogy of the tribe changed under the influence of their migration.[26] Climate and pasture, neighboring tribes, and governments were the factors that dictated to these men, who wished to find their livelihood in the Wādī Sirḥān, the form and scope of their political organization and the size of the territory which they were compelled to control. Membership in this organization gave each tribesman a formally equal right – that could not always be realized under equal conditions – to exploit the pasture and the water sources of the whole area. That this tribe is mainly a territorial-ecological organization becomes evident from the fact that the largest tribal units do not necessarily have a leader.

Sometimes the tribal group, or confederation, has a name or, in other words, an ancestor denoting its unity, but no territorial center or locality in which the leaders of the subunits would assemble. Such a tribe has no established leader, and there are no formal arrangements for coordination between its subunits. Unity exists primarily in the consciousness of its members, to whom it is self-evident that their livelihood depends on their gaining free access to the whole territory. Whenever necessary, a number of leaders of the autonomous political groups – but never all of them – meet to discuss arrangements for grazing and coordinated exploitation of water sources. They often succeed in reaching agreement, but occasionally they also argue over resources. Whichever be the case, the tribe, i.e., the formal right to exploit the territory, continues to exist.

The right to utilize resources in the territory is granted in normal times to tribes that are not members of the confederation. Jaussen, for example, relates that in the area of Kerak, during the summer, a number of tribes of different confederations gather and pasture their herds in common.[27] But the host tribe retains the privilege of first access in the event of shortage; whether it is capable of safeguarding this right is a different question, and, as Jaussen puts it, "the pastures are open to all the nomads, with a certain priority right to the tribe in whose territory they happen to be."[28] When observers of Bedouin society define the tribal confederation as a loose association of tribes,[29] they usually refer to a territorial unit such as described above. Such a unit may, under certain circumstances, develop political leadership and organs of government, and the history of the Arabian Peninsula provides numerous examples of ephemeral Bedouin states which crumble as rapidly as they appear. When leadership arises in the tribe, its scope may rapidly expand beyond the organization of pasture and water. Out of a desire to guarantee the tribe's livelihood, the leadership will attempt to gain control over other resources that are used by its members: supervision of transport routes and of the caravan traffic, and of the market towns in which the nomads exchange their animals and produce against the products of the settlers and trade goods. In due course, the leadership of the tribe moves to the occupied town, which then becomes the capital of a small kingdom.[30] The need for pasture and water alone never brought about the rise of a strong tribal leadership, and certainly not the formation of a Bedouin state. The economic advantage of permanent and guaranteed control over territory does not weigh in Bedouin eyes against the burdens imposed by a central authority in the form of compulsory military service[31] and payment of taxes. Doughty shows that, although the annual tax collected by Ibn Rashīd only amounted to "eight or nine shillings for every household: yet the free-born, forlorn and predatory Beduw grimly fret their hearts under these small burdens; the emir's custom is ever untimely, the exaction, they think, of a stronger, and plain tyranny." Doughty immediately goes on to explain why the Bedouin are nevertheless ready to accept the burden of the ruler: "Yet yielding this tribute they become of the prince's federation, and are sheltered from all hostility of the Arab in front."[32] So, under the pressure of hostile neighbors, the Bedouin are compelled to seek the patronage of a ruler or to create for themselves a political association that can match that of their enemies. The source of these pressures is not in the Bedouin tribes, but in the permanent settlement, since only it can maintain comparatively large, regular military forces. When the rulers or neighbors exerted constant military or administrative pressure on any group of tribes, they compelled it to organize within a large framework and brought about the development of aggressive leadership. This was necessary both for negotiation with the powers that be and for defense against attack. The tribesmen knew, of course, that it was beyond their power to match the government's military forces, but they could by these means prevent harassments and small punitive actions. The authorities had to realize that only serious military operations could take on the Bedouin. Whenever a Bedouin tribe instituted tribal government, this brought about a chain reaction, since it placed its neighbors in the position of having to make the awkward choice between creating another, perhaps even stronger, organization to combat the aggressive neighbor, joining other tribes or seeking the protection of the government authorities. Whichever it was to be, it merged in a bigger political framework.

This was the process undergone by the Rwala confederation in the nineteenth century due to pressure of the Ottoman authorities in

Damascus, on the one hand, and the kingdom of Ibn Rashīd in Ḥāil, on the other. The Rwala tribes range over the Wādī Sirḥān and, thus, at various times entered the sphere of influence of both rulers. Towards the end of the summer, they approached Damascus and were open to pressures from its ruler, while in the spring they reached the southern limits of their wanderings, Jauf and Taima, where they came under the influence of Ibn Rashīd. In order to protect their independent existence, the Rwala were compelled to join forces, thereby making the *shaykhs* of the Sha'alān family their leaders, even though the number of their slave warriors was not more than a few tens. Because of their dependence on the two rulers, the Rwala did not support either side, but kept up constant negotiation and intrigue with both. Even the two attempts of the Rwala to control the Jauf oasis, the one in 1870 and the second in 1909, were not carried out on the initiative of the Rwala, but, in the opinion of Philby, at the instigation of the Ottoman authorities.[33]

The same phenomenon recurs, on a more modest scale, in the Negev. Here the Israeli military government confined the tribesmen to a closed area for the greater part of the year, and all the inhabitants became dependent on the economic resources available in it. The Bedouin became subject to indirect rule by the tribal chiefs, and in this manner the tribe was strengthened and the *shaykh* became a very influential leader. The edge of this political organization was directed against the "peasants," landless Bedouin who earned a living as share-croppers. Every peasant depended for his livelihood on the Bedouin landowners and knew that if he established strong political groups, this could not improve his economic lot. Nevertheless, the peasants are organized in minimal political groups similar to those of the Bedouin, since by doing so they can prevent unnecessary annoyances and react to Bedouin provocations.[34]

Although, in one respect, there is a parallel between the Bedouin of the Negev and the tribes of North Arabia, they differ greatly in other matters. The ecological conditions of the Negev do not require such a large territorial organization as that of the Syrian Desert and North Arabia. Furthermore, the territorial organization of the Negev Bedouin extends only over part of the regions which supply them with pasture and water. It covers the spring pasture on the deserted hills east and southeast of Beersheba and the early summer pasture in the Beersheba plain. Thus, the Ẓullām tribal group secured access to all the pastures in the hills east of the Beersheba plain and down to the cliffs overlooking the Dead Sea. All the members of the tribal group and, in normal times, members of other tribes as well have equal rights to exploit these grazing grounds. At the beginning of summer, the flocks pass through the harvested fields of their owners and graze on the stubble left on them. Then they continue westwards to the stubble fields of villages. They graze on vacant state land or on areas belonging to the western Negev settlements and sometimes continue northwards up to the Ramleh area.

The Negev Bedouin thus belong to territorial organizations which control only part of their water and pasture requirements. In the literature these territorial organizations, such as the Ẓullām, the Qderāt and the Ḥkūk, are called tribal groups, but the Bedouin themselves have no special term for them and do not regard them as political groups in the sense of such active groups as the tribes. In other cases, such groups may be called confederations (*qabīla*), such as the Jahalīn or the Ta'āmrah of the Judean Desert. The tribal groups are just territorial units without a center of government or supreme leader. Tribes coordinate their activities by means of contacts between the *shaykhs* – whose marriage links create convenient channels of communication – and by means of individuals belonging to the various groups who have also woven marital relationships. The confederations are homologous to tribes, and, even if they have a central meeting place and a formal leader (*shaykh al-mashāyikh*), their tribal government is usually very limited. The territorial organization is not necessarily a large one; often a small territory will supply all the resources needed for the yearly cycle of wandering. The Jahalīn tribe numbers less than one thousand. But the 'Azāzmah, who, despite their being a confederation, had no central meeting place or supreme leadership, numbered twelve thousand up to 1948. The Ẓullām group of tribes numbers five thousand and also has no formal supreme leadership.

Territorial organization permits the Bedouin to cope with most of the ordinary annual and seasonal fluctuations in water and pasture, but does not protect them from the more serious fluctuations. Connections with neighboring units at the level of the tribal groups and above can help, up to a point. Genealogical connections between neighboring tribal groups reflect, among other things, the desire of the groups to extend their control over rainfall fluctuations even further, by opening up additional possibilities of movement. However, such "kin relationships" between the tribal groups do not always stand the test of the hard reality of a drought year and even less oblige the relatives to go to war together – as some scholars had assumed in the past.

The Bedouin conceptualize the territorial organization as a kind of political group whose membership is based on agnatic kinship. They usually relate how a named forefather acquired rights to the area of land which they occupy. Members of the tribe inherited these rights through their fathers who were the sons and grandsons of this ancestor. Since, according to Bedouin custom – which, incidentally, contradicts the Muslim law code (*Sharī'a*) – only sons can inherit the lands and flocks of their father, this therefore is unassailable evidence, in their eyes, of their territorial rights. Patrilineal descent and the ideological connection between the ancestor, whether male or female, and the ownership of land is common among all the Bedouin.

Thus, the four Ẓullām tribes have a genealogy which, although not identical in all its details, does support the claims of the tribesmen to the territory. Their belonging to a group of tribes serves as justification and a kind of charter for their ownership of the territory. The tribesmen explain that their forefather came some two hundred years ago from the north of the Arabian Peninsula to the Negev and settled in its eastern part, which was then uninhabited. This forefather was called Ẓālem, and the word Ẓullām was derived from this name and means "the men of Ẓālem." The sons of Ẓālem are the ancestors of the present day tribes. According to one interpretation of the genealogy, Abū Jwe'id was the primeval resident and owner of the region. Ẓālem married Abū Jwe'id's daughter, and through this marriage his descendants acquired their right of occupancy on the land.

TABLE 2

The origin of the Ẓullām tribes according to the version of the Abū Rbē'ah tribe

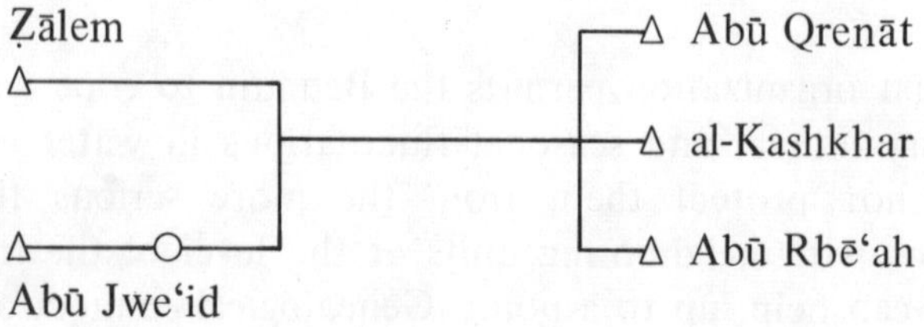

LEGEND

Woman ○
Man △
Relationship through marriage
Relationship through descent

NOTE: I have replaced the traditional names of the ancestors by the names of the tribes as used today. *E.M.*

That Ẓālem, in variance with Bedouin custom, acquired his right to the land through a woman, does not bother anybody. Ẓālem had the right of the firstcomer and was not yet subject to the rules intended to guarantee continuity of control in an area and the balance of power between the various groups. A member of the Abū Jwe'id tribe explained the matter by saying that in actual fact Ẓālem had not arrived in a completely deserted country: he found in it already the father of the Abū Jwe'id and he, Ẓālem, only acquired his right to the land by marrying his daughter. Thus, the Bedouin explained to his own satisfaction his tribe's right of ownership of the area, but he did not explain since when a woman inherits land.

The version of the origin of the Beni Ṣakhr (also called Dahamsheh) tribe east of the Jordan, reported by Jaussen, is similar in various points to the genealogy of the Ẓullām. A man named Dahamsh found an abandoned baby in the desert, brought him up, and gave him his daughter in marriage. Four sons were born from this union and these are regarded as the forefathers of the Beni Ṣakhr tribe.[35] Apparently, the forefathers of the Ṣkhūr (plural of Ṣakhr) also did not inherit their land from their primeval ancestor, and rights of ownership came to them only through their mother, the daughter of the landowner. The Ṣkhūr are divided into three groups of tribes, each headed by a *shaykh.* There is no supreme *shaykh* for the whole tribe, and the tribes even war with each other.[36] Only the territory of the confederation is considered to belong to all the tribes, and everyone has equal rights of access to it.

This type of genealogy also solves the contradition between the Bedouin contention that they are the descendants of ancient Arab tribes and their claims to ownership of land. If the land was owned by the ancient inhabitants of the territory, then the later immigrants from Arabia could not obtain rights to it. Both in the Ẓullām and the Beni Ṣakhr versions, the founding fathers acquired their right to the land through marriage with the owner's only daughter.

In Cyrenaica, all the "aristocratic" land-owning Bedouin claim to be descended from a common mother called Sa'ada. The nine large, aristocratic tribal confederations are her descendants and through her they acquired rights to the land.[37] Except for Sa'ada, mother of all the tribes, no women figure in the genealogy. Robertson Smith brings together examples of tribal ancestresses from early Arabia[38] and remarks that "there is no tribe with a female eponym in which the main groups have not male eponyms."[39] It would be possible to cite many examples of present day Bedouin tribes where women appear at the apex of the genealogy as owners or inheritors of the land,[40] thereby contradicting the rules of inheritance practiced today – while all the offspring of these mothers appearing in the genealogy are male, thereby confirming the validity of these rules of inheritance. It will shortly become clear that the female connection with the land in apparently patrilineal societies is not only meant to confirm ownership of the territory, but also refers to a specific type of political organization.

All Bedouin groups claim to be descended from the male or female eponym of the tribe. Bedouin are unable to give the names of the ancestors intervening between the eponym and the last few generations and therefore are never certain whether their origin from the forefather is direct and how many generations have passed since his time. In this manner, all the groups of landowning Bedouin in a tribe, whether they be large or small, and even those whose origin may be outside the group, may claim descent from the eponym and thus assert their right to the land.

In the Negev, groups which either own very little, or even no, agricultural land are considered by the land-owning Bedouin to be, paradoxically, peasants (fellahs). These peasants do not claim descent from a named ancestor who settled in the tribal area, although membership in the group is based on the common origin. For example, the Abū Ṣa'alūk group of peasants contends that Ṣa'alūk ("The Beggar") was the nickname of their ancestor whose real name had been forgotten and who dwelt in their country of origin, Morocco. The descendants of Ṣa'alūk wandered through Egypt to the Gaza Strip until they reached the Ẓullām around 1910. They add that "the first to come here were six men who were brothers and cousins to each other" and who bought a little land in the region.[41] The Abū Ṣa'alūk who live in the Ẓullām area have, therefore, no common ancestor through whom they could link up with the tribal ancestor and claim rights on the land.

The Bedouin genealogies are certainly inaccurate from a historical viewpoint. Even the small groups usually have difficulty in tracing the kinship ties between all their members. It is therefore even harder to rely on details of ancestors who lived, according to the Bedouin themselves, some seven or eight generations ago. However, the genealogy does represent reality of a kind: it is the Bedouin's conceptualization of their distribution on the land and gives some indication of their political structure. It thus says very little about the past, but a great deal about the present. Much as the inheritance is divided among all a man's sons, so Bedouin view the distribution of tribal land: each brother gets a portion of the property, and after the division the brothers are not obliged to manage the assets jointly. As the membership in agnatic groups is acquired at birth and is thus "permanent," and a person cannot belong to two groups at one and the same time, so is the arable land neatly divided between the groups and acquired chiefly by inheritance. The genealogical connections between the groups also represent their joint ownership of pasture that is accessible to all their members. Even while speaking of cooperation between "agnatic" groups such as these, the Bedouin stress the differences between them, such as in their often-quoted saying, "I am against my brother, my brother and I are against my cousin, my cousin and I are against the stranger."[42] Eliahu Epstein (Elath) describes the situation as follows: "Each and every tribe has its land in the desert and has the sole right of exploiting it and its springs, rights which over the course of time have become the accepted law of the desert. When two Bedouin tribes are on good and friendly terms, one may occasionally camp as a guest on the other's land – with its consent. But encroachment on another's land causes arguments and is one of the most common causes of desert wars."[43] It may be added that in some cases a tribe will collect a payment for the right to pasture on its lands.

So far the tribe and the clan have been viewed as organizations that secure and hold the territory necessary for the livelihood of the Bedouin. They protect it both against the invader from outside and against the tenants or clients from within who wish to gain control of the land. The tribe is structured much like a military organization: it comprises a large number of small close-knit groups capable in the time of need of coalescing in predetermined manner in order to act within larger units. At the head of each unit stands a leader. The members of the small groups live and wander at no great distance from each other and consider themselves to be agnates even if there is no clear relationship. Members of this group believe that they are the descendants of a common father whose name they bear. The genealogy also serves them as a rough guide to their amalgamations into larger groups – according to the (disputable) logic that two neighbors living in adjacent areas with similar ecological characteristics have common interests. The common interest is translated into the idiom of kinship. Agnation signifies the unity of the members of the small corporate groups, and the same is expected of the relations between groups linked up in a larger framework, and, accordingly, the ancestors of these groups are represented as agnates of each other.

When viewed as a series of fighting units, the Bedouin tribal organization is segmented, embodying many of the characteristics which appear in the classic description of Evans-Pritchard[44] – the most important being that the units amalgamate for common action only in times of emergency and in times of tranquillity break up into small segments. However – as opposed to the sociological model – in real life the units do not necessarily amalgamate according to the genealogical scheme; the amalgamation is always according to the governing interest of the particular moment. In normal times, when no external enemy threatens the groups, they are free to engage in disputes between themselves which occasionally lead to bloodshed.[45] A conversation held between Musil and one of the leaders of the Rwala shows how far matters can go. The *shaykh* told him, "The Fad'ān are unbelievers to us, hence we fight them." When Musil reminded him that the Fad'ān were of the same origin as the Rwala and that both of them were of the 'Aneze Bedouin, the *shaykh* replied: "I know that they are related to us through their blood and faith, but they have deceived us, hence they are worse than all the foreigners and Christians and we are in holy war against them."[46]

He who looks upon Bedouin society in a tranquil period will perceive barriers between the groups, territorial frontiers, acts of violence, and blood revenge. He will find it difficult to understand how Bedouin belonging to the various groups are capable of managing and exploiting jointly pasture and water sources. This is difficult enough even when there is political coordination. There is evidence that the Sha'alān, the well-known chiefly family of the Rwala confederation, could not prevent banditry even between the tribes under their supervision.[47] Such supreme *shaykhs* cannot overcome the discord since they do not have tools of control, apart from the agnatic units, and maintain only minute military forces of their own. The situation is even worse in tribal confederations which do not have a senior *shaykh*.

How can units which are constantly at odds, such as these, divide between them the pasture land and the water in an equal and fair manner and permit members of rival groups to live side by side? This is a problem with which most of the descriptions of Bedouin society have not dealt. Many of the authors were not even aware of the existence of such a problem. Only Sweet points out that "though it is logical to suppose that freedom of access to adequate pasturage is a condition of tribal life, how this is regulated within the tribal structure of north Arabian Bedouin society has not been fully understood."[48]

We lack detailed information on this subject for all but two Bedouin societies: the Ẓullām tribes in the Negev and the tribes of camel breeders in Libya. We know how the land is divided in these societies both in ordinary years and tranquil periods and in drought years when the area becomes insufficient for all the population and their flocks. Normally, pasture lands are not divided permanently between the various groups, but in practice the strong groups that are settled in proximity of these lands control them. Other Bedouin are entitled to use the pasture areas when there is sufficient grazing. When grazing is restricted, access is given to Bedouin from the outside only through marital relationships which were created especially for this purpose. These marriages create a close-knit network of contacts spread all over the tribal territory.

In both Bedouin societies, there is an "inferior" sector which bears most of the suffering caused by drought or increase in population and flocks. These are the "fellahs" in the Negev, or the "clients" in Libya, who do not have a share in the land and are not absorbed in the tribal-military organization and who can, therefore, be driven off when space becomes tight. The distinction between the owners of land and the landless is essential for the understanding of Bedouin society.

A detailed examination of these and other phenomena shows that the corporative organization based on quasi-agnation is only part of the structure of Bedouin society. It is just the showcase of this society, desiring to appear to the outside observer as a warrior society. The Bedouin, steeped all his life in this ideology, sincerely believes that this is the real essence of his society and that the other aspects are coincidental, atypical, or exceptional. While he is capable of interpreting various aspects of his society in an entirely objective fashion, the Bedouin possesses only one model, or conception, of his total society, namely, that of a segmentary political organization. Therefore, for him, all economic marriage contacts are private arrangements, and every agreement with a tenant or a client is made only in order to give him a personal economic benefit. It is even more surprising that until recent years scholars have fallen in with the same ideology and did not diagnose the part played by marriage links and of the clients in Bedouin society.

Amongst the Negev Bedouin, each marriage serves the interest of a small group of real agnates, including brothers and cousins, who together decide how to match their sons and daughters. Since the weight of whole groups stands behind these marriages, they are stable, and the number of divorces infinitesimal.[49] An intimate and constant contact is maintained, particularly between the two men closest to the woman – her husband and her brother (or her father), both of whom are responsible for her, though in different ways. The woman frequently visits her family of origin, sometimes for several weeks, and during such long visits the husband comes to visit her. The members of the family of origin on their part return these visits. The woman provides a link between the two groups and carries information and requests in both directions and cares for the continuing relationship. It has already been noted that the heads of the Ẓullām tribal group are connected through marriage. Even when the chiefs of the tribes quarrel over tribal interests, their wives keep up regular contacts with their families of origin and do not cease the exchange of visits. Occasionally, the husbands accompany their wives on these visits, and then it becomes clear that the heads of disputing tribes are in-laws who treat each other with respect and friendship.[50]

Even more impressive is the fact that practically all marriages of tribesmen are contracted inside the common territory. All the 130 marriages between the Bedouin of the tribe of Abu Jwe'id of which I possess details were effected in the Ẓullām region. Some of these marriages took place within the tribe, and others with other Ẓullām tribes. Only three women married Bedouin of a neighboring group of tribes, but the three husbands permanently resided amongst the Ẓullām. All the marriages took place between Bedouin, and I did not hear of any matches between Bedouin and peasant sharecroppers. Thus all the matches created links between landowners. All these marriages serve the various interests of the parties as individuals and groups. These close-knit links permit the Ẓullām to jointly exploit the pasture and water to be found in the territory under their control and also serve them in the pursuit of other interests. In tranquil times, these connections play an important part in daily life. However, the Bedouin attach considerable importance also to the interests of their groups. Therefore they do not exploit all the marriages in order to create economic contacts, but use a number of them for the maintenance of political connections within the corporate groups and between the groups. However, the overall result of these marriages was the creation of a network of kinship relationships which extends to all Bedouin groups of the tribes, and through this means there was created in practice the Ẓullām "group of tribes."

CAUSES OF CHANGE IN BEDOUIN SOCIETY

The lack of any marital connections between the Ẓullām Bedouin and their peasants underlines the united front which the owners of land have put up against their sharecroppers. The Bedouin know that kinship relationships with them would break down the fence separating the two economic classes. In any case, approximately half the population in the Bedouin areas is composed of peasants, some of whom have succeeded in acquiring a bit of land, although no peasant group has reached a point where it can do without additional land. Even the Abū 'Arār, the wealthiest of the fellah groups, still lease forty per cent of their land from the Bedouin. The head of every peasant family establishes a personal relationship with a Bedouin landowner. In order not to give the peasant rights of tenure, and in order to keep the right of grazing on stubble in summer, the Bedouin do not lease their lands for more than a season. The terms of lease are equal everywhere. Although the peasant is allowed to lease from a new landowner every year, he cannot expect to improve his terms of lease; at most he will receive slightly better land. Obviously, the uniform and short-term contracts are intended to leave the Bedouin with a free hand in the management of the land. The peasants were given a foothold as long as land was plentiful and for as long as the Bedouin themselves could not cultivate the agricultural lands of their regions. By leasing surplus land to tenants, the Bedouin received welcome additional income without investing any effort. Any change in the Bedouin population necessarily influenced the situation of the peasants. A small Bedouin population could absorb a large number of peasants; however, an increase in the number of Bedouin immediately caused some of them to be pushed out. The peasants thus served the Bedouin landowners as a tool for efficient exploitation of the economic resources in their region – notwithstanding changes in the demographic situation. It was therefore important for the Bedouin not to tie the fellahs either to themselves or to the soil.

It must be added that for several decades this unintended, but useful, arrangement operated well in the Negev, but from the forties of this century onwards, it was upset for various reasons. During the Second World War, the Allied forces offered employment in the erection of army camps and airfields in the Negev, and many youngsters – both Bedouin and fellahs – found work in the camps. As a result of the fact that the income from such work was much higher than the income of a sharecropper, a part of the fields in the Negev remained uncultivated. During the first years after the establishment of the State of Israel in 1948, the opposite situation was created. The military government restricted movement into and out of the Bedouin area and issued only a limited number of short-term movement permits. By this the authorities wished, amongst other things, to prevent cheap Bedouin labor from competing with new Jewish immigrants for the few jobs available at the time. The military government thus cut off the Bedouin from the national labor market. The authorities dealt with the Bedouin through the tribal chiefs, and anyone registered with one tribe generally remained attached to it. Accordingly, the fellahs of the Ẓullām tribes were forced – as before – to cultivate the Bedouin lands as sharecroppers, in spite of the fact that better paid work was available outside the area. These peasants remained attached to the Ẓullām tribes and to the traditional terms of lease and were unable to benefit from state land given to the landless Bedouin of other tribes at nominal rents. During all that time, the population grew rapidly, and with it the demand for land mounted. The Bedouin themselves needed larger areas for cultivation, while the fellahs, who were increasing at the same rate, were left with less land. As a result, the area of land under cultivation increased year by year, until all the 175,000 dunams considered as cultivable in the Ẓullām area were sown, and tenants were found even for the less fertile lands.[51]

Approximately in 1960 a change occurred which prevented a further deterioration. The employment situation in the country improved, and the granting of exit permits from the Bedouin area was liberalized. Thus the state, in its turn, used the Bedouin as a whole for absorbing fluctuations in the supply of manpower in the national economy – much as the Bedouin landowners had exploited the fellah tenants. As a result of this change, the young Bedouin and fellahs again went to work outside and the area under cultivation in the Ẓullām area was drastically reduced. Some fellahs even left the region for good.

Several parallels exist between the Bedouin of the Negev and the Bedouin of Libya. The nomadic population of Cyrenaica is divided into aristocractic landowning Bedouin and into clients with no right to land and water and who use these resources only with the permission of their owners. Only the aristocratic clans figure in a genealogy that encompasses all their confederations and tribes. Peters states: "Descent from Sa'ada . . . in theory gives [a man] rights to land in Cyrenaica, [but] his genealogical position in a particular group gives him rights in a particular strip of territory, but not in all."[52] Peters attaches significance to the choice of Sa'ada as ancestress of all the tribes: "Female names can be used to show a greater notion of cohesion than the mere use of male names, and the significance of a female name placed at the apex of the Cyrenaican genealogy is that it is a symbol of full brother unity at the highest political level."[53] If we were to place in this quotation the word "territorial" in place of "political," we could arrive at the same concept already described above. Sa'ada, the ancestress, represents the participation of all the aristocratic tribes at a level that encompasses the whole area exploited by the Bedouin. By rights of this participation, every Bedouin is entitled, in theory, to enjoy the natural resources of the whole territory. There is no political association of the tribes at this level, and if there were, it would become a serious rival to the state.

The Bedouin population in Libya was partially wiped out during twenty years of war against the Italian conqueror, and all the aristocratic Bedouin tribes needed reinforcements in order to exploit their territory. Each aristocratic Bedouin group therefore attempted to draw in clients, both in order to exploit the resources and to prevent encroachment by larger groups of aristocrats. Nevertheless, they did not want to grant the clients ownership rights on the resources and therefore abstained from accepting them into "agnatic" political association.

The landless clients formed sixteen percent of the Bedouin population[54] and the aristocratic Bedouin were therefore not afraid of the clients ever being able to create a united political front against themselves. They therefore did not prevent marriages with the clients. On the contrary, Bedouins gave their daughters to clients in order to bind them. By right of the kinship, they permitted clients the use of cultivable land and water, but, in the opinion of Peters, the kinship never became membership in the corporate organization that held the rights on the territory. Each and every year the clients were obliged to renew their agreement for the use of agricultural land and water (there was never shortage of pasture).[55]

The Bedouin of Cyrenaica – similarly to the Ẓullām tribes – spread a network of marital relationship over the whole territory. Agnatic groups systematically married into other groups. But they skipped over adjacent groups with resources similar to their own and preferred to marry into more distant groups.[56] These Bedouin also created marriage links with residents of the oases and they specifically stated that they were "marrying dates." The efforts of individuals and of sections of agnates to secure access to economic resources of various types here too produced the network of kinship relationships covering the width and breadth of the Bedouin territory and making for contacts between the members of all the political groups.

The Bedouin's intention to exploit the clients without granting them rights were frustrated here as well. The Italian authorities had already demanded equal access rights to the wells for all citizens and the order was carried out at wells close to permanent settlements.[57] Peters also tells of a case – certainly one of many – where a group of clients gained control over the territory and water of the aristocratic group to which it belonged. The small aristocratic group was forced to stand aside while the clients watered their flocks at its own well.[58] It may be supposed that the authorities justified such an action as the right of a Bedouin group to benefit from public property. It appears that in Libya no pressure of population on territory has as yet developed and following the discovery of oil wells during recent years, it may be assumed that the surplus population will be drawn to better paid work with the oil companies. Possibly even a considerable number of young Bedouin have already begun to leave the tribes in order to accept regular work at the oil installations or in the towns.

On the other hand, in the Basseri tribe of south Iran, a serious population surplus and over-grazing has developed. Here the authorities exercise full control over the tribe and even regulate its movements. At the same time the tribe has increased rapidly. According to one version it has tripled during the course of the last thirty to forty years.[59] At present, the Basseri do not have tenants or inferior groups who can be pushed out, since the tribe grazes its flocks on land belonging to the state, which will not permit discrimination between groups. They are, therefore, obliged to draw off the surplus population. Barth is of the opinion that there are two mechanisms which balance the relation between land and flocks. Such a balance is possible, he claims, when the flocks belong to an individual, and not to a large group. In such a case, various mishaps can strike the individual, force him out of the game, and make him settle on the soil[60] – the implicit, but probably correct, assumption being that sheep growing gives quite a good income as compared with agriculture.[61] A herdsman whose flocks have been so far reduced that he can no longer support his family leaves the clan and becomes a farmer. In the conditions of the Fars district, a man apparently has no choice but to work in one of these two primary occupations. However, owners of large flocks are also cast out for another reason: the social pressures on a wealthy man increase, and he becomes afraid of investing all his capital in animals liable to be afflicted by epidemics, acts of banditry, etc. Therefore, he invests part, or all, of his capital in the acquisition of land and in this manner either leaves the game or reduces his flocks.

Barth is of the opinion that these processes have prevented the uncontrolled growth of population and flocks. However, it can be safely assumed that the mechanisms are not so well adjusted as to maintain a perfect ecological balance. It may rather be assumed that, as with the Rwala tribe,[62] an impoverished man can get a new flock either as a gift or a loan. Since there is no central authority that supervises the size of flocks, every family head is liable to find it more difficult each year to find grazing, but will still try to increase his flock. That is what happened in the Negev. Only a very serious situation is likely to cause a reduction in the flocks.

Amongst the large Bedouin tribes of north Arabia, demographic pressures express themselves in a different form. For so long as they maintain effective control over their lands, and there are no outside forces interfering in their affairs, men and herds spread out relatively evenly over the face of the territory. The good pasture attracts larger herds than the bad pasture, and the distribution is done on the basis of thorough and continuing intelligence operations. When the population grows and the herds multiply in a specific region, they spread over a greater area. When the territory is large, small demographic fluctuations are absorbed without being noticed. However, fundamental demographic changes are not amenable to simple solutions and cause the tribes to spread out beyond their own territories. Changes such as these happened from time to time amongst the large tribes and caused intertribal warfare. We have, for example, detailed historical descriptions of the expansion and contraction of tribal territories in the Negev in the nineteenth century.[63]

CONCLUSIONS

It has been shown that Bedouin herds do sometimes exploit land that is not fit for cultivation and which, without this exploitation, would remain unused. But, the Bedouin prefer to pasture their herds on good rain-soaked land. Furthermore, part of the pasture must always be of this type and is needed in order to maintain the herds at the end of the dry season. Therefore, the Bedouin are interested in controlling agricultural land or at least in exploiting underpopulated agricultural areas. Periods of political turmoil – when settlements are abandoned and destroyed, and agricultural land is released for pasture – are convenient for the Bedouin. However, they are interested in destruction of agricultural settlements only up to a certain point; they need the settlements in order to sell their animals and produce and to purchase foodstuffs and industrial products. The method of exploitation of land by the Bedouin is extensive and becomes possible only when there are wide, unsettled spaces. In these conditions, the breeding of animals by the Bedouin method is profitable, as the labor force employed is relatively small: one herdsman can control a camel herd of 70 to 80 head,[64] or a flock of sheep of 150 head, and where conditions of production are primitive, his product will be of greater value than that of the farmer. But when land becomes scarce and thus an expensive economic factor, the breeding of animals loses its advantage.

The Bedouin confederation, or tribe, is a territorial unit, extending over areas of pasture and water sources sufficiently large to permit the Bedouin to cope with the ordinary environmental hazards. The size of the territory required and the outside political forces brought to play on the tribe are the factors which determine the number of its members. If the tribe's population is small, then it is unable to maintain full control over the territory, and its chances of overcoming the ecological difficulties decrease. Then, one of two processes takes place: either the whole, or a part, of the area is taken over by other and stronger groups, or the clan increases its strength by absorbing additional population. In either fashion land is redistributed.

The terms "confederation" and "tribe" are somewhat misleading, as they convey the impression that they are a part of Bedouin military organization and that this organization controls a territory. In practice, the military organization is based on small agnatic groups, capable in time of need of uniting with other groups, primarily for short military actions. However, there are long respites during which the Bedouin looks after his own business – which in any case is difficult enough – and has no time for joint political activity. He is unable to allocate much of his resources to a permanent administration that would coordinate the activities of various groups and protect the territory against encroachments. Sometimes there is no permanent political leadership at the level of the large territorial units. When that is the case, practical control over the area, and coordination between the groups moving about in it, is achieved by means of an extensive network of personal contacts at various levels: the leaders of large political groups maintain good contact between themselves, the small political groups cooperate with each other on various matters, and almost every Bedouin maintains economic contacts with other men in the territory. This network of personal relationships spreads over the whole territory and in effect promotes coordination and interdependence between all the members of the tribe. Insofar as these contacts are stable, they are institutionalized as kinship relationships, marriage links, brotherhood, and friendship.[65] In this context, these relationships must be viewed as channels of communication between the parties through which they both cooperate and carry on their disputes and arguments.

Since the Bedouin live on land which is, at least in part, suitable for cultivation, it is not surprising that some of them engage both in pastoralism and in agriculture. In this way, they guarantee to themselves a complementary livelihood and reduce the risk involved in failure of one branch of the economy. Besides, they can thus vary the foodbasket. They organize their cycle of movement in such a way that in the ploughing and harvesting seasons they pass close to their cultivated areas (Ẓullām and Baggāra). Only those tribes whose range and route of movement does not permit an arrangement whereby each family of herdsmen also engages in agriculture make use of one of the following solutions: either the tribal population is divided into shepherds, camel-nomads, and farmers (Libya), or a nontribal population cultivates the soil in tribal territory, and the nomads take a part of the produce (Rwala, and to a certain extent the Basseri).

Two factors, which often appear in concert, bring about the decline of the Bedouin: a strong central government and a growing population. Each government sees in the tribal organization an independent concentration of power attempting to enforce its own law and evade payment of taxes and other civil obligations, and causing harm to the settled population. Governments wish to settle farmers on the agricultural lands held by the Bedouin, on the one hand, and, on the other, to secure control of water sources. By means of settling the land and opening access to water for all, it restricts the Bedouin's movements and may also be taking from his essential pasture lands. Reduction of pasture land turns the breeding of animals into a less worthwhile business, fraught with greater risk, and, in order to balance their economy, the Bedouin themselves may turn to agricultural cultivation. Under the protection of the government, agricultural land becomes the property of the individual, and by this means the Bedouin close off to themselves additional areas which are required for efficient grazing. The owners of extensive areas of land do not suffer from this situation. But Bedouin whose agricultural land is limited, or who do not own land, are unable to find the summer pastures that they need. By this means, central governments weaken the Bedouin economy even without taking any direct action against the breeding of animals.

Parallel with the rise of central government, there often occurs a rapid growth of population, both of the Bedouin and of the settlers. The pressure of population on the land, therefore, increases quickly, and while the cultivated lands at the disposal of the Bedouin become more and more limited, the number of Bedouin and their herds increases in the remaining area. If, at the same time, the economy develops and access opens to new forms of livelihood, it is assumed that many Bedouin will give up the breeding of animals. These are the main causes of the decline of the Bedouin way of life. The explanation often heard that the decreasing value of the camel as a beast of burden and for riding is the chief cause is mistaken.[66] Meat prices are high, and, if the Bedouin had at his disposal the area required for breeding cattle, then the business would still be worthwhile today. Only the reduced size of the Bedouin territory, the growing pressure on the land, and the existence of new types of employment yielding higher income brings about the decline of breeding of animals by the Bedouin method.

NOTES

1 I am grateful to Dr. Eliahu Elath, Dr. Shlomo Deshen, Dr. Itzhak Eilam and Dr. Moshe Sharon for their remarks on an earlier version of this paper.

2 H.R.P. Dickson, *The Arab of the Desert* (London, 1951), pp. 108–13, naively describes this system of ranking.

3 C. Niebuhr, *Travels Through Arabia* (Perth, 1799); J.L. Burckhardt, *Notes on the Bedouins and Wahábys* (London, 1830); W.G. Palgrave, *Personal Narrative of a Year's Journey Through Central and Eastern Arabia* (London, 1868); C.M. Doughty, *Travels in Arabia Deserta* (New York, 1937); A. Jaussen, *Coutumes des Arabes au pays de Moab* (Paris, 1908); A. Musil, *The Manners and Customs of the Rwala Bedouins* (New York, 1928); T.E. Lawrence, *Seven Pillars of Wisdom* (London, 1935).

4 For example, the account of the Bedouin in C.D. Forde, *Habitat, Economy and Society* (London, 1934), ch. 15, is based mainly on Musil's material.

5 Musil, *The Rwala Bedouins;* A. Musil, *Arabia Deserta* (New York, 1927).

6 Musil, *Arabia Deserta,* p. 17.

7 Musil, *The Rwala Bedouins,* p. xiii.

8 A. Kennett, *Bedouin Justice* (Cambridge, 1925), p. 23.

9 This opinion is also expressed by J. Gulick, "The Anthropology of the Middle East," *Middle East Studies Association Bulletin* 3, no. 1 (1969): 3.

10 An exception is a paper by H. Rosenfeld, "The Social Composition of the Military in the Process of State Formation in the Arabian Desert," *Journal of the Royal Anthropological Institute* 95 (1965): 75–86, 174–94, which is based to a great extent on Musil's material. It must be pointed out that Rosenfeld uses Musil's travelogue extensively, but refers only rarely to the book on manners and customs.

11 M. von Oppenheim, *Die Beduinen* (Leipzig, 1939); E. Gräf, *Das Rechtswesen der heutigen Beduinen* (Walldorf-Hessen, 1952); J. Chelhod, *Le droit dans la société bédouine* (Paris, 1971); J. Henninger, "Die Familie bei den heutigen

Beduinen Arabiens und seiner Randgebiete," *International Archives of Ethnography* (1943); L. Sweet, "Camel Pastoralism in North Arabia and the Minimal Camping Unit," in *Man, Culture and Animals: The Role of Animals in Human Ecological Adjustment,* ed. A. Leeds and A.P. Vayda (Washington, 1965); C.G. Feilberg, *La tente noire* (Copenhagen, 1944).

12 E.E. Bacon, *Obok: A Study of Social Structure in Eurasia* (New York, 1958); R. Montagne, *La civilisation du désert* (Paris, 1947); R. Patai, *Golden River to Golden Road,* 3rd ed. (Philadelphia, 1969); C.S. Coon, *Caravan: The Story of the Middle East* (New York, 1951).

13 T. Asad, *The Kabābīsh Arabs* (London, 1970): F. Barth, *Nomads of South Persia* (Oslo, 1961); I. Cunnison, *Baggāra Arabs: Power and the Lineage in a Sudanese Nomad Tribe* (Oxford, 1966); E. Marx, *Bedouin of the Negev* (Manchester, 1967); E.L. Peters, "The Proliferation of Segments in the Lineage of the Bedouin in Cyrenaica," *Journal of the Royal Anthropological Institute* 90 (1960): 29–53; E.L. Peters, "The Tied and the Free: An Account of Patron-Client Relationships among the Bedouin of Cyrenaica," in *Contributions to Mediterranean Sociology,* ed. J. Peristiany (Mouton, 1968); E.L. Peters, "Some Structural Aspects of the Feud Among the Camel-Herding Bedouin of Cyrenaica," *Africa* 37 (1967): 261–82.

14 C.S. Coon, "Badw," in *Encyclopaedia of Islam,* 2nd ed. (Leiden, 1960).

15 R.A. Fernea, *Shaykh and Effendi* (Cambridge, Mass., 1970).

16 Musil, *Arabia Deserta,* p. 110. A romanticized account of such a crisis can be found in C.R. Raswan, *The Black Tents of Arabia* (London, 1936), pp. 85 ff.

17 Sources: Cyrenaica: E.E. Evans-Pritchard, *The Sanusi of Cyrenaica* (Oxford, 1949), pp. 30–32; Kabābīsh: T. Asad, *The Kabābīsh Arabs*, p. 13; Ẓullām: E. Marx, *Bedouin of the Negev*, pp. 20–1; Basseri: F. Barth, *Nomads of South Persia,* p. 3; Baggāra: I. Cunnison, *Baggāra Arabs,* pp. 30–2.

18 D.W. Lockard, in a book review in the *American Anthropologist* 72 (1970): 400, describes the process of settlement of Saudi-Arabian Bedouin around pumping stations of the Tapline Co. A regular supply of water brings about a significant change in the way of life of the Bedouin.

19 In the Negev, there are numerous examples of well-centers which sometimes supported a settled population and at others only served as watering-places, like Beersheba, Tall al-Milḥ, and ʻArʻarah.

20 Musil, *The Rwala Bedouins,* pp. 8–16.

21 For example, Musil, *Arabia Deserta,* p. 110.

22 Doughty, *Travels in Arabia Deserta,* p. 624; in vol. 2, p. 662. Doughty illustrates the many fluctuations and irregularities of the rains. See also Asad, *The Kabābīsh Arabs,* p. 13.

23 Raswan, *Black Tents of Arabia,* p. 20, refers to seven thousand tents; Oppenheim, *Die Beduinen,* 1: 120–2, mentions, 4,630 tents. If we accept Oppenheim's estimate, that an average of seven persons live in each tent (p. 12), we shall arrive at a population of 32,410.

24 Doughty, *Travels in Arabia Deserta,* pp. 376–7.

25 Oppenheim, *Die Beduinen,* 1: 68–70; M. Ma'oz, *Ottoman Reform in Syria and Palestine 1840–1861* (Oxford, 1968), p. 137.
26 Bacon, *Obok: A Study of Social Structure in Eurasia,* p. 125, details the changes in the genealogy of the Rwala over the course of a hundred years, by comparing the lists of Burckhardt, Doughty, and Ashkenazi.
27 Jaussen, *Coutumes des Arabes,* p. 117.
28 Ibid., p. 240.
29 See, for example, Y. Shim'oni, *'Arvei Eretz-Israel* (Tel Aviv, 1947), p. 137; V. Müller, *En Syrie avec les Bédouins* (Paris, 1931), pp. 200–2, gives his own interpretation of this phenomenon. In his opinion, the whole political organization of the Bedouin is based on kinship relations. As these become more distant, so the contact between tribesmen gets weaker. Only at the level of the tribe does this process cease "and only due to the personal authority of the sheikh at its head." Müller does not touch at all on the fact that the tribe is for the most part the largest political unit, while the confederation is no more than a territorial unit. On the other hand, Bacon (p. 127) clearly perceived that "the genealogical segments larger than the tribe do not operate as political units."
30 H. Rosenfeld, "The Social Composition of the Military in the Process of State Formation in the Arabian Desert," pp. 79–85, illustrates the beginnings of this process among the Rwala and its more advanced stages in the Shammar kingdom of Ḥāil.
31 Rosenfeld (pp. 176, 182) cites sources showing that the Bedouin cooperated – sometimes involuntarily – in the military ventures of Ibn Rashīd; some of them served in lieu of payment of tax.
32 Doughty, *Travels in Arabia Deserta,* p. 394.
33 H. St. J. Philby, *Sa'udi Arabia* (London, 1955), pp. 228, 251. We possess a detailed description of the first abortive attempt of the Rwala to take control in J. Euting, *Tagbuch einer Reise in Inner-Arabien* (Leiden, 1896), 1: 131–4; and of the second attempt which gave the Rwala control of Jauf for a few years up to 1922, in Musil, *Arabia Deserta,* pp. 162 ff. According to Musil, in this case some of the leaders of the divided House of Rashīd invited the Rwala to take Jauf. Even then the Rwala *shaykh* opposed his son's occupation of the settlement.
34 Marx, *Bedouin of the Negev,* pp. 77–80, 206–9.
35 Jaussen, *Coutumes des Arabes,* p. 107.
36 Ibid., p. 114.
37 E.L. Peters, "The Proliferation of Segments in the Lineage of the Bedouin in Cyrenaica," pp. 29–30.
38 W. Robertson Smith, *Kinship and Marriage in Early Arabia,* ed. S.A. Cook (London, 1903), pp. 29–30.
39 Ibid., p. 37
40 G.W. Murray, *Sons of Ishmael* (London, 1935), pp. 245–6, 307.
41 Marx, *Bedouin of the Negev,* p. 114.
42 Y. Yehuda, *Mishlei 'Arav* (Jerusalem, 1932), 1: 75.
43 E. Epstein, *Ha-beduim* (Tel Aviv, 1933), p. 14.
44 E.E. Evans-Pritchard, *The Nuer* (Oxford, 1940), pp. 142–4. This is the

simplest and clearest exposition of the theory of segmentary organization. Evans-Pritchard emphasizes that each segment is a territorial unit, that the small segments are the elements in a larger organization, and that the large units are activated only for war.

45 Musil, *Arabia Deserta,* p. 22; Jaussen, *Coutumes des Arabes,* p. 110.

46 Musil, *Arabia Deserta,* p. 426.

47 Ibid., pp. 24–5. Musil tells how he was robbed by members of a clan "attached" to the Sha'alān. When he complained that he was a member of the household of the *shaykhs,* the robbers were not at all impressed, even though they did believe him.

48 L. Sweet, "Camel Pastoralism in North Arabia and the Minimal Camping Unit," p. 136.

49 Even though in the Negev – as elsewhere in Islam – the argument can be heard that there is nothing easier than divorce since it is enough for the husband to pronounce the formula of divorce in order to cast off his wife. This contention contributed to the mistaken view – still maintained by some scholars – that the rate of divorce in Arab society is high, as in R. Patai, *Golden River to Golden Road*, pp. 105–6.

50 Musil, *Arabia Deserta,* p. 22, records the *shaykh* of the Rwala tribe as saying to the heads of the 'Amarāt, another tribe of 'Aneze Bedouin, "We as the chiefs of our tribes are enemies but as men we are the best of friends." I suggest (though I cannot find documentation for this in the literature) that marital connections existed between the two families of *shaykhs,* as is common among the great *shaykhs.* Thus, for example, there has been a connection for generations between the heads of Rwala and the heads of the Fad'ān confederation. See Oppenheim, *Die Beduinen,* 1: 103; Raswan, *The Black Tents of Arabia,* p. 88.

51 The continuing cultivation did not cause a great decrease in crops, in spite of the fact that the Bedouin do not improve their soil nor rotate crops. Because of the frequent droughts, good harvests are attained on the average only once in every four years, and thus the fertility of the soil is preserved.

52 E.L. Peters, "The Tied and the Free," p. 175.

53 E.L. Peters, "The Proliferation of Segments in the Lineage of the Bedouin in Cyrenaica," p. 29.

54 E.L. Peters, "The Tied and the Free," p. 169.

55 Ibid., p. 186.

56 E.L. Peters, "Some Structural Aspects of the Feud among the Camel-Herding Bedouin of Cyrenaica," p. 274.

57 E.L. Peters, "The Tied and the Free," p. 177.

58 Ibid., p. 173.

59 F. Barth, *Nomads of South Persia,* p. 115.

60 Ibid., p. 24.

61 U.Mor, "Ha-beduim ba-negev – seqirah klalit" [The Bedouin of the Negev – General Survey], *Ha-beduim* (Prime Minister's Office: Jerusalem, 1971), p. 17, claims that this is true also in the Negev.

62 A Bedouin reports that fifty camels were demanded of him as blood money.

The head of the tribe gave him twenty-five camels as a gift, and the remainder were given him by other tribesmen [Musil, *Arabia Deserta,* p. 463].

63 ʻĀrif al-ʻĀrif, *Taʻarīkh bir al-sabʻ wa-qabāʼilaha* (Jerusalem, 1934). A large section of the book is devoted to a description of the tribal wars in the Negev. The accounts were taken from the Bedouin, and, according to good Bedouin tradition, the wars were explained as personal arguments between leaders over wives and horses or as a result of insults to elders. Since there are no full figures on the size of the tribes and their herds, it is almost impossible to reconstruct the ecological and demographic factors in these wars.

64 Musil, *The Rwala Bedouins,* p. 366.

65 R.N. Pehrson, *The Social Organization of the Marri Baluch* (New York, 1966), p. 16. In this society, marriages are not stable, and permanent economic and political contacts become established as "friendships." The friends address each other as "bradir" (brother).

66 This is the explanation advanced by ʻĀrif al-ʻĀrif, *Al-qaḍāʼ bayn al-badw* (Jerusalem, 1933), p. 224.

NOTES ON THE CONTRIBUTORS

GABRIEL BAER is Professor of History of the Muslim Countries at the Hebrew University of Jerusalem. He is editor of *Asian and African Studies,* the English journal of the Israel Oriental Society, and author of *A History of Land Ownership in Modern Egypt 1800-1950* (London, 1962) and *Population and Society in the Arab World* (London, 1964). He has also written various articles dealing with the social history of the Middle East, some of which appear in his most recent book, *Studies in the Social History of Modern Egypt* (Chicago, 1969).

ELIEZER BE'ERI a member of Kibbutz Ha-Zore'a, has been engaged for many years in the study of Arab society. He is the author of *Army Officers in Arab Politics and Society* (Jerusalem, 1969), and various articles in Hebrew and English on the role of the military in the contemporary Middle East.

L. CARL BROWN is Garrett Professor in Foreign Affairs and Director of the Program in Near Eastern Studies of Princeton University. Brown is the author of various studies on North Africa, among them an annotated translation of a political treatise by Khayr al-Dīn al-Tūnisī, *The Surest Path* (Cambridge, Mass., 1967). He is the editor of *State and Society in Independent North Africa* (Washington, 1966) and *From Madina to Metropolis; Heritage and Change in the Near Eastern City* (Princeton, N.J., 1973).

URIEL DANN is Associate Professor in the Department of the History of the Middle East and Africa at Tel Aviv University. He is the author of *Iraq under Qassem; a Political History 1958-1963* (Jerusalem, 1969) and several articles in the field of modern Middle Eastern history.

MOSHE MA'OZ is Associate Professor of History of the Muslim Countries at the Hebrew University of Jerusalem. He is the author of *Ottoman Reform in Syria and Palestine 1840-1861* (Oxford, 1968) and various articles on the history of Syria and Palestine during the Ottoman period.

EMANUEL MARX is Associate Professor in the Department of Sociology and Anthropology at Tel Aviv University. He is the author of *Bedouin of the Negev* (Manchester and New York, 1967) and several articles on Bedouin society.

YEHOSHUA PORATH is Senior Lecturer of History of the Muslim Countries at the Hebrew University of Jerusalem. He is the author of *Emergence of the Palestinian Arab National Movement 1919-1929* (in Hebrew, Jerusalem, 1971). Porath is editor of *Hamizrah Hehadash,* the Hebrew journal of the Israel Oriental Society.

GABRIEL WARBURG is Senior Lecturer in Middle East History at Haifa University. He is author of *The Sudan Under Wingate* (London, 1971) and several studies on modern Sudanese and Egyptian history.

MENAHEM MILSON who edited this volume, is Senior Lecturer in Arabic Literature at the Hebrew University of Jerusalem. He is author of various studies on Arab intellectual tradition and Modern Arabic Literature. His study and translation of Suhrawardī's *Ādāb al-Murīdīn, A Sufi Rule for Novices* is forthcoming (Cambridge, Mass.).